P9-AFY-823

ALL THOSE MORNINGS . . . AT THE *POST*

All Those Mornings...
At the *Post*

THE TWENTIETH CENTURY IN SPORTS
FROM FAMED *WASHINGTON POST* COLUMNIST
SHIRLEY POVICH

EDITED BY LYNN, MAURY, AND DAVID POVICH
AND GEORGE SOLOMON

PublicAffairs
New York

Published in the United States by PublicAffairs™,
a member of the Perseus Books Group.

Book design by Mark McGarry
Set in Electra

Povich, Shirley.
All those morning. . . at the Post: the twentieth century in sports
from famed Washington Post columnist Shirley Povich.
p. cm.
Includes index.
ISBN 1–58648–315–3
1. Sports—History—20th century—Sources. I. Washington Post. II. Title.
GV576.P68 2005
796'.09'0904—dc22
2005042565

FIRST EDITION
10 9 8 7 6 5 4 3 2 1

For Shirley and Ethyl and all the Poviches,
who always rooted for each other.

For Hazel, Aaron, Mark and Greg Solomon.

For the Graham family and Shirley's Washington Post *colleagues.*

CONTENTS

A Man for the Ages

Tony Kornheiser

Nobody ever covered sports longer, or better, for a great newspaper than Shirley Povich did for *The Washington Post*. For 75 years Shirley wrote elegantly for *The Washington Post*, and for generations of Washingtonians, Shirley *was The Washington Post*. He was there in the morning, like the sun, lighting your way. To give you some idea of the length of Shirley's career, when he started writing about sports in the 1920s there was no NFL yet, no NBA yet, no NHL yet; there was major league baseball, but there were no teams south of Washington, D.C., no teams west of the Mississippi River, and no night games because baseball stadiums didn't have lights!

I have been blessed in my career to have typed alongside Shirley Povich and Red Smith, the greatest newspaper sportswriters of them all. I worked with Red at *The New York Times*, and with Shirley at the *Post*. They were sophisticated thinkers and graceful writers. They were gentlemen and scholars, witty and urbane, impeccably dressed and unfailingly polite. When they took you apart in print they did it so skillfully, you never felt the blade, you just watched your blood run down the page.

I adored them both and did everything I could to be like them, including wearing a fedora to games. The people who read my work said I couldn't even carry their typewriters (does anybody remember typewriters?). But in fact, I did. I carried Red's typewriter up to the press boxes at Yankee Stadium and Shea Stadium. And I carried

Shirley's typewriter out to his car from RFK Stadium and the Preakness. I always felt honored to do so.

One week in the early 1990s *Sports Illustrated* attempted to sell some extra magazines by naming its all-time baseball team. The team spanned over 80 years, and while I suspected nobody on *Sports Illustrated* had actually seen all these players in action, I was quite sure Shirley had. So I asked him about the wisdom of their choices. Shirley agreed with all the position players, but when I told him that Christy Mathewson had been picked as the right-handed starting pitcher, he was outraged.

"Walter Johnson crushed Christy Mathewson," Shirley declared.

I told Shirley I wasn't certain SI had gotten the left-handed starter right either. They picked Warren Spahn. I leaned towards Sandy Koufax.

Shirley shook his head disapprovingly. His choice was Lefty Grove, and he started to explain.

"I was talking to Walter Johnson once . . ." he said.

Whoa! Time out! He was talking to Walter Johnson? Walter Johnson was born in 1887. His first year in the majors was 1907. Presumably they called him Big Train because planes weren't invented yet.

"You talked to Walter Johnson?" I stammered. And I began grinning.

Shirley continued: ". . . And Walter said to me, 'Shirley, that Feller kid is fast, but not as fast as Lefty Grove.'"

That Feller kid?

Bob Feller was going to be 80 that year.

Almost everyone was a kid to Shirley. Undoubtedly you've heard of the famous Jack Dempsey–Gene Tunney "long count" heavyweight fight in 1927. Shirley covered it. He covered Sammy Baugh, college and pro. He covered Connie Mack. He covered Babe Ruth. One time in the 1930s when the Yankees weren't in the World Series, Shirley sat one seat over from Ruth in the press box; Ruth was being paid to provide commentary for a New York newspaper. I have this fantasy that the Babe would lean over and say, "Shirley, do I go with a transitive verb or an intransitive verb here?"

But Shirley's career spanned such a long time that he also covered Derek Jeter, Evander Holyfield, and Tiger Woods and found qualities to admire in each of them. (Shirley was Old School before anybody knew there was Old School.) He kept one eye on the past for the sake of perspective, but he always had both feet in the present. He could tell you about Calvin Coolidge, who was president of the United States when Shirley began writing at *The Washington Post*, and he could tell about Calvin Ripken, who was at shortstop when Shirley celebrated his 75th year there.

The night in 1995 that Ripken broke Lou Gehrig's record for consecutive games played Shirley rode up to Camden Yards to cover the game. He was one of two people in the stands that night who had also been to Gehrig's farewell game in 1939—the other was Gehrig's teammate at that time, Joe DiMaggio.

Lots of thrilling things happened that night, including Cal hitting a homer and then, pushed out there by his teammates, Cal taking that victory lap around the outfield, shaking hands with as many fans as he could reach. The spontaneity of that moment, the waterfall of joy pouring out from everybody in that stadium gives me chills still as I recall it. But the greatest thrill for me that night was to be sitting next to Shirley in the press box. I was on his right, and my colleague and friend Michael Wilbon was on Shirley's left. It was like we'd won the lottery and became Shirley's honor guard. Usually we are big yakkers, Wilbon and I. But on this night we were spellbound in silence, listening to Shirley tell stories about Gehrig, Ruth, and DiMaggio. It was an oral history of the golden age of baseball.

Late in the game somebody fouled a pitch back sharply to the press box. I saw the ball heading straight at Shirley, and I reached for it to protect him. Fortunately, it missed Shirley and landed harmlessly in Wilbon's ample stomach. Wilbon held it aloft, to the cheers of the other sportswriters, and was stuffing it into his bag when our sports editor George Solomon suggested to him that Shirley might want the baseball as a souvenir, considering Shirley was at Gehrig's last game. Wilbon happily agreed and handed Shirley the ball, which was part of a special batch of balls with orange stitching and the imprint "Streak Week" in honor of Cal's accomplishment.

Shirley put the ball in his suitcoat pocket, and watched the rest of the game and much of the postgame ceremony. Around midnight he and George Solomon left Camden Yards to drive back down to Washington. I was finished writing by then, and I walked with them out to the parking lot. There, Shirley took the ball out of his pocket, and with a motion practiced over almost 90 years, he began flipping it casually up and down with his left hand. And in that clear late summer night, with that special baseball in his hand and a spring in his step, Shirley Povich was forever young.

TONY KORNHEISER joined *The Washington Post* in 1979 as a general assignment reporter. He became a sports columnist in 1984 and a Style columnist in 1989. Before joining *The Post*, he had been a sports reporter for *Newsday* from 1970 to 1976 and with *The New York Times* from 1976 to 1979. Kornheiser co-hosts ESPN's "Pardon the Interruption," with fellow *Post* columnist Michael Wilbon.

Words to Live By

Michael Wilbon

I was a rookie reporter in 1980 when I met Shirley Povich for the first time. I didn't have a car and caught a ride with Shirley to Capital Centre in Landover, Maryland, for a closed-circuit telecast of a fight. I had been assigned to write a local reaction story and I was scared to death. Shirley told me, "It's natural to be nervous. Don't worry about it. I remember one of the first fights I covered..." Shirley paused and I thought he'd say Joe Louis–Max Schmeling, 1938. But he said, "It was Dempsey–Tunney in 1927, the long-count fight."

I was stunned. My awe of him overwhelmed my anxiety. Like everyone else I ever knew who wanted to be a sportswriter, I idolized Shirley Povich. I loved him, treasured him, pinched myself that he knew my name and that I got to sit next to him at games, genuflected at every single encounter with him. He wanted young writers to treat him as an equal, but I couldn't. Every year we worked together it became more difficult.

In one of the most transient cities in America, there was one clear voice that influenced Washington from Prohibition to the Great Depression to World War II to Vietnam to Watergate to Iraq: the voice of Shirley Povich. In particular, Shirley and another recently deceased sportswriting vet—Sam Lacy of the African-American newspapers—were the clearest and sharpest voices in their demands for racial justice on and off the field.

It wasn't so much specific advice from Shirley that I most remember. It was just the way he lived and carried himself every day. He and Lacy never had to dispense wisdom; they oozed it. They wrote their convictions, no matter how unpopular those might have been. They were able to view the world critically, but never turned into cynics. That's why they've been held in such high esteem by the people they covered and those of us who could only hope to be their equal some day.

We would be stunned when Shirley would talk about a conversation he had with Babe Ruth or Walter Johnson or Sammy Baugh. One day I asked him if he had any idea how much that freaked us out and he replied, "It's only time. In 50 years, some young fellow is going to point at you and say, 'See that old guy over there? He knew Michael Jordan.' And you're going to think, 'What's the big deal?'"

MICHAEL WILBON joined *The Washington Post* in 1980 after spending two summers as an intern in the sports department. He became a sports columnist on the paper in 1990. He has won numerous awards and three times has been named among the top three sports columnists in the country by the Associated Press Sports Editors. Wilbon co-hosts ESPN's "Pardon the Interruption" with fellow *Post* columnist Tony Kornheiser.

In the Beginning

*In the Words of Shirley Povich
as Remembered by his son Maury Povich*

There I was in 1920, a small-town boy from Bar Harbor, Maine, standing next to this huge man — huge at least by our standards — in the second fairway of the Kebo Valley Golf Course. He was six feet tall and 230 pounds and about to hit a shot that would be meaningful to both of us. For him that swing would produce a caddie for the next three summers. For me, a 15-year-old boy, that inaccurate but explosive shot would produce a career that would end 78 years later.

I didn't even want to be there. Twenty minutes before, Russ Richardson and I had been running down the fifth fairway, trying to outdistance the pursuing assistant caddie master, on our way to the swimming hole. Our badge numbers hadn't been called all morning, and it was almost 80 degrees, unbearable for Maine.

I could outrun just about any caddie master, but by chance he was a college fellow and in between breaths came the threat: "You'll lose your badges if you don't get back to the caddie yard."

That did it for me. Summer was earning 80 cents a loop caddying for the summer people — "aristocrats" we called them. The Rockefellers and the Vanderbilts, the Pulitzers and the Schiffs. And this 230-pounder.

I didn't know his name then, only after my mother asked me that evening who I had worked for that day. After I described him, I said, "He had EBM on his bag."

She said, "Well, that must be Edward B. McLean." She knew all of the summer people, and so did my father.

Mr. McLean, in spite of his girth, was a handsome man, about 50, small mustache, but quite friendly. Even during the first hole he asked about me, wondering how a 15-year-old held up in the off-seasons of Maine.

Then came the shot from the second fairway, from his spade mashie, about 170 yards.

It was beyond my world. Beyond the green. Beyond the road. Nearly beyond the woods, which were beyond what I just mentioned.

While I followed the ball, he paused and said, "Son, give me another ball. No one can find that one."

Well, fine, except, gee, what a challenge. I knew every tree trunk and root and leaf in those woods, and I thought—he said no one could find that ball—maybe I could find it. I wasn't sure, but I really thought I could. So I went into those woods and within a minute I found the ball. He exclaimed, "I've never seen anything like this."

What he didn't know was I knew those woods like I knew my house. Shucks, no caddie ever lost a ball in those woods, not if you wanted to make your 80 cents. Who knows, if you found a couple balls, maybe you'd make a dollar. And besides, we combed those woods for the old gutta percha balls because in Bar Harbor, the shoe-maker would vulcanize those gutta percha balls to cover the holes in our football bladder. Back then the inside of a football looked like a rubber tube. There was no other way a leak could be fixed, not in Bar Harbor.

The rest of the round went routinely and when we had finished Edward B. McLean said, "What's your name?"

"Shirley."

"Well, Shirley. Will you caddy for me tomorrow? I'll tell you where I live and you meet me there and we'll ride out together."

And then he shook my hand and pressed $2 into it. My Lord, $2. Who ever heard of such a thing? That's enough for 45 holes. And so the bond was sealed. Edward B. McLean, multi-millionaire, friend of the president of the United States, and owner of *The Washington Post* newspaper, and Shirley Povich, the seventh of nine children of Lithuanian immigrants, Nathan and Rosa, who at 15 looked forward mostly toward summer.

My father, Nathan Povich, had arrived in America in 1878 at age 12, with his father, Simon. Like so many Jewish immigrants from Russia or the countries controlled by that abusive monarchy, they had fled the cruelty and discrimination and buried their wounds with the prospect of living in freedom, especially religious freedom. It was somewhat difficult for Simon to forget the wounds, since he, like other eligible young men in the Jewish *shtetls*, had an eye put out, willingly, to avoid conscription in the Czar's armed service.

Arriving in Boston they began their new lives as peddlers, walking northeast, with packs on their backs. And what would they peddle, you might ask—needles, threads, small pots and pans and notions.

Rosa and Nathan Povich in Maine (1930)

Later, they graduated to horses, so they were no longer poor peddlers; they had transportation. With horses they could travel 20 miles a day, staying in the homes of their customers.

After several years making as much as they could while sending money home to their loved ones in Europe, they settled in Bar Harbor and began to bring their family to their beloved new country. And with the later Povich crowd came a young distant cousin named Rosa. I'm somewhat foggy as to whether the relationship between Rosa and Nathan was prearranged or love at first sight, but so be it. They created our American clan, ten children in all—the first born drowned as an infant in Frenchman's Bay, which surrounded Bar Harbor.

By the turn of the century my father had prospered, in our eyes, but by today's standards, I guess you could call it modest. We lived on Main Street in a frame house that my father had actually had moved from the shoreline after their infant son drowned. No more peddling on horses. He owned his own store on the first floor, a furniture store, which catered mostly to those "aristocrats" who summered on Mount Desert Island. My mother took in boarders, and the rest of the rooms were taken by the nine of us children. That's why my parents knew of Edward B. McLean, because his people bought furniture from my father for his 40-room "cottage."

So when my mother identified my rich golfer as Mr. McLean, she did so with some sureness. She knew the home, she knew the furniture, and she knew of his 40 horses. She also knew most of what happened in our town—she wasn't nosey, but curious. My mother wanted to know everything about America, and that's why she knew of both the rich and the rest of Bar Harbor.

She fell in love with her new country. Both she and my father went to school to learn English and both became citizens. They were so proud to be Americans, free of their totalitarian past and, most important, free to practice their Jewish faith, which was handed to us in the strictest sense, Orthodox. That meant keeping kosher and every week gathering for the Sabbath service. But you needed ten men, a *minyan,* to conduct a service, and you had to be Bar Mitzvah age for that, and that's why I found myself at the wharf every week when the boat from Boston came in, trying to pick out who I thought might be Jewish so we could fill the *minyan*. I'm not saying I could always bring a Jew home, but a hot meal was enough bait for most men.

My parents took the American way of life seriously, especially the political system, and the right of the vote. So it was appropriate for the local politicians to call on my parents, looking for their support come election time, in this small enclave. My mother used to tell us about her first visit from the selectman, which was as close as Bar Harbor came to having a mayor back then. My mother welcomed this very Waspish gentleman, who was going to explain to her how politics worked in Bar Harbor.

"Mrs. Povich, my name is Samuel Stafford, and I'd like to give you some background on what goes on here."

"Why, Mr. Stafford, won't you have a chair."

"Mrs. Povich, I'd like to welcome you as a member of the voting public. I am the first selectman of Bar Harbor. My family has been here for three generations. My father was first selectman before me, and our family owns the bank, and the boathouse."

"Why, Mr. Staffford, that's nice. Why don't you have two chairs."

When I think back on those occasions when I have written of the high and the haughty, and what approach I took to lighten their self-importance, I think of my mother's offer of two chairs to Mr. Samuel Stafford and I clap.

Growing up in Bar Harbor in the 20th century's second decade was a joy to us kids. We never understood our elders' complaints about the weather. We didn't care whether it rained or snowed. For in Maine, we had five seasons, not four—spring, summer, fall, winter, and thaw, when the snow came down off the mountains in rivulets and you walked to school in calf-high boots through the slush.

My favorite spot in Bar Harbor was the wharf, because as I grew into my teens I fell in love—with baseball. And what did the wharf have to do with the greatest American game? I'll tell you what. That's where I got the news about yesterday's game. The boat from Boston would arrive at dusk with all the boxscores of the previous afternoon and, like today, we and all of Maine and New England would root for one team—the Red Sox. But you had to make decisions as to which newspaper you should read—the *Herald, Globe, Post,* or *Transcript.* At two cents apiece, who could afford more than one? I picked the *Post* and followed my favorite sport from spring to fall. What a pair, baseball and newspapers. I didn't have a clue that the two would be so dear to me the rest of my life.

At this tender age, I was naïve about so much. Such innocence was displayed in high school about of all things, my own name—Shirley. It is Jewish tradition that newborns are named after an ancestor, and so my parents named me after my late grandmother, Sarah. Since they couldn't name me Sarah, they looked around for English names starting with "S" and up came Shirley. My gosh, there were four other boys named Shirley in my school—and the golf professional at Kebo Valley, too. It's an old Yankee name carried from England, no different than Marion or Evelyn, all boys. There was no thought about a girl named Shirley until up popped a new girl in school, Shirley Johnson. To me, that was ungodly. It was the last time I ever witnessed the teasing of a girl named Shirley.

The day after my introduction to Mr. McLean, I arrived at his house, promptly at the appointed hour. Greeting me with a big hello, he pointed me to his car and we stepped into the luxurious interior of a new Rolls Royce. It was incomprehensible to me, the way these people lived and traveled. And I must say, we townie kids were not envious or jealous of their money and their toys, just in awe. I never talked much to the big man, because of my New England upbringing— polite but taciturn. But he took a liking to me, I could tell, because from that day forward, that Rolls Royce would stop on Main Street to drop me off before Mr. McLean went home to his "cottage."

Two summers later, I waited through June and most of July for Mr. McLean to arrive in his private railroad car. He didn't come. I caddied for many of the other summer people, longing for Mr. McLean and that $2 tip. Apparently, another gentleman had taken a liking to me. He asked for my help quite a bit. You may have heard of him, Joseph Pulitzer. I didn't know it at the time, but he was another newspaper mogul, owner of the *New York World*, among other papers. He was a better golfer than Mr. McLean, but he was older, and by that time his eyesight was poor. Good caddies to him were a necessity.

So one day he said to me, "Shirley, what are you going to do after the summer?"

"I don't know, Mr. Pulitzer. I just graduated from high school. I'll probably go to college, Bowdoin or Maine." In 1922, if you wanted to go to college, all you needed was the money, no entrance exams, not even for Harvard. And like today, in-state schools didn't cost that much.

"Well, why don't you join me in New York? I could get you a job at the *World*." I thanked him and told him I'd think about it.

A week later, in August, Mr. McLean showed up and we picked up where we left off the summers before. One day he said, "Shirley, I know you graduated school this year. What are you going to do this fall?"

"I don't know Mr. McLean. There don't seem to be any jobs around, so I'll probably go to college, Bowdoin or Maine."

"Well, sonny boy, why don't you come with me to Washington? I'll send you to my alma mater, Georgetown. You'll caddie for me at my own course, which I built at my home, and I'll find you a job at *The Washington Post*."

Well, how about that? Within a week, two job offers at big city newspapers. I had never even been in a newspaper office. Being a good caddie has its rewards. Right then, I decided to accept Mr. McLean's offer. I liked him better than Mr. Pulitzer. I felt we had a relationship, and those tips helped, too. But of course, there were my parents and their consent, although two of my brothers and one of my sisters were already living in Washington, working for the government and going to school. That might swing the day.

That evening, as usual, Mr. McLean dropped me off at the house on Main Street. He told his chauffeur to wait and up he went to the second floor to call on my parents. He told them what he would like to do, assured them I would be in good hands, and won their consent. Sometime in September, he asked me to come to Washington with him in his private railroad car and begin my big city life, but that offer never was realized. When I told my parents Mr. McLean's plans, there was a quick, stern rejection.

"There will be no traveling on the High Holy Days," my father said. With thoughts of my new dreamy world, I had completely forgotten about the Jewish Holidays. So Mr. McLean traveled to Washington in the comfort of his private railroad car, and I followed later, in steerage, because of my modest circumstances.

The trip to Washington included bumming a ride to Boston with friends, a boat ride to New York, and a train to the nation's capital. At the age of 17, I was stepping outside the state of Maine for the first time in my life. Arriving in Boston, I bowed to embarrassment rather than nerve. I slept on the Boston Common because I was afraid to go to a hotel. I had no idea how to register. But don't count me out yet. I had enough sense to take my belt and strap the handle of my straw suitcase to my body. I had been warned about snatchers. So I spent my first day outside my past, strapped to my suitcase reading the baseball stories in the Boston newspapers. What I discovered was that the World Series was being played in New York. Could it be that my first major league baseball game might be the 1922 World Series?

I arrived at the Battery in New York the next day and inquired about World Series tickets. Bleacher seats to the Series were $2 apiece, the money saved by not taking that hotel room in Boston. So I lugged my suitcase all the way to the Polo Grounds, not knowing I could have stored it at the station. When I got to the game, all the seats were gone, so a kid pointed me to this huge hill beyond the stadium known as Coogan's Bluff. Up I went, with bag, to sit on the hill and watch my first major league game. I didn't really see the game. I saw half a game. From that perch you could see the left fielder, the third baseman, the shortstop, and the centerfielder occasionally, if he drifted towards left field. I never saw Babe Ruth, Frankie Frisch, or Casey Stengel. They played, but not on my side of the field.

That night I took the train to my new home, Washington, D.C. I raced up five flights of stairs, never knowing about this contraption called an elevator. My brothers welcomed me warmly after the laughter subsided over the missed elevator. The next morning I took the streetcar up Wisconsin Avenue to the in-town estate of the owner and publisher of *The Washington Post*, Edward B. McLean, my patron. I knocked on the door, and the butler opened it and showed me to the back terrace and there it was in front of me, the most beautiful golf course I had ever seen, next to one of the busiest streets in the city. And there was Mr. McLean on the first tee, with some other gentlemen, laughing and drinking whiskey in glasses. He spotted me, gave me a warm handshake and said, "Shirley, I'm so glad you're here. Just in time too. I want to introduce you to the man whom you'll be caddying for." He moved me towards a tall handsome man. "Shirley, I want you to meet the president of the United States, Warren G. Harding. Mr. President, I want you to meet Shirley Povich, of Bar Harbor, Maine, the best caddie in the United States."

How much fortune could a 17-year-old from Bar Harbor expect on his first day in the most important city in the world? Even more. After the round Mr. McLean whispered, "Shirley, wait from me inside. I'll see you after I tend to my guests."

I watched them from inside. Another round of drinks. This being prohibition, the strictest sense of the law was being violated by none other than Warren G. Harding. But as I was to find out quickly, in Washington there was great liberty taken about this and it didn't take me long to indulge moderately in the hard-drinking world of newspapermen.

About an hour later, Mr. McLean came inside, sat me down, and gave me these instructions. I was to go to *The Washington Post* and find the business manager, Arthur D. Marks. I was to tell him that I was sent by the owner and was to be given a job. Then I was to go to

Povich as an eager young reporter at The Post *(1923)*

the Dean of Georgetown University and enroll in law school and tell him to send the bill to Mr. McLean. You might ask about a high school graduate enrolling in law school. In 1922, it was perfectly acceptable. No need for an undergraduate degree. I thanked him and left, clueless as to the whereabouts of *The Washington Post* and Georgetown University. The visit to the school would wait for the next day. The visit to the *Post* could not come fast enough.

Village boy that I was, those street cars in the big city were too great a challenge. I ran and walked the five miles to *The Washington Post* thanking several pedestrians for their directions. And the unexplainable fortune beginning with the matching of me and Mr. McLean on the fairways of Kebo Valley would continue as I knocked on the office door of Arthur D. Marks, business manager of *The Washington Post*, and announced myself.

"My name is Shirley Povich. Mr. McLean told me to tell you to give me a job." The words tumbled out with little confidence.

"How do I know you're not lying?" Mr. Marks said with a look of high suspicion. Then the questions came and my answers, sprinkled with a tone of evident innocence, convinced him I was incapable of deceit, like inventing a conversation with the owner.

And here is where this extraordinary chance continued. He could have sent me anywhere — to the circulation department, to the composing room, to the press room, or to the stereotypers. Looking back, I believe there were two reasons why my life was destined. All those departments were under his supervision. He didn't need nor care for me to be in his life. Also, this was mid-afternoon, and all those areas were unoccupied since the newspaper itself wasn't printed until well after midnight.

"Go up to the city room and tell Mr. Fitzgerald you're the new copyboy he's been asking for," he said as he brushed me away.

I went upstairs and there was Mr. Fitzgerald in the middle of this huge room full of activity. Why it was the same Mr. Fitz I had caddied for several times in Bar Harbor when he was the guest of Mr. McLean! And I had found a lot of his lost balls, too. I told him my story and he smiled. "That's great, Shirley. You're going to work for me." The way he said it was protective — something I needed dearly in this new world. Little did I know what a copyboy did, but I was soon to find out this lowly position held low pay, too — $12 a week. My big bonus came on Sundays when Mr. McLean slipped me a $20 bill for my weekend caddie duties. He did it with a wink, as if he knew all too well the miserly pay scale at the newspaper.

I found out quickly about the life of a copyboy. You did anything anyone told you to do — running for coffee, separating the copy as it came in over the ticker, making sure the desk editors had everything they needed. They called. You answered. All of that led little by little to rewriting copy sent in late at night from reporters who were somewhat strangers to the English language, and that's where the thirst for my native language took hold. In those first two years at the *Post* I fell in love with the newspaper. It wasn't long before I was on the streets late at night, covering vice and other police activities. In the beginning I went with the reporters. By 1923, I was doing my own reporting, but I had to give up covering the Vice Squad when the police department found out I was underage. My name never appeared with a byline—too precious to entrust to an 18-year-old.

That changed in the summer of 1924, the year the Washington Senators won the first of their three American League baseball pennants and their only World Series. I came to the sports department with the blessing of the sports editor, Norman Baxter, who had seen me hanging around his area, reading stories from the wires because of my love for baseball. And besides, he offered me a five dollar raise.

THE TWENTIES

It was the "Golden Age" of sports, cherished even more so as the distance between then and now lengthens. Giants like Babe Ruth and Jack Dempsey, Bobby Jones and Walter Johnson, Bill Tilden, Jim Thorpe, and Red Grange became gods to a newspaper-reading public starved for heroes after World War I. The 1920s began without radio. It ended with a country enraptured with this wondrous invention, as well as movie newsreels, touting these grand figures. Their vivid nicknames—"Murderer's Row" and "The Four Horsemen of Notre Dame"—turned these sportsmen into myth. That was the Golden Age.

It was in that climate that Shirley Povich joined the sports department of *The Washington Post*, a newspaper that in the 1920s was ranked fourth in a five newspaper city. His early duties included rewriting wire stories, writing headlines. And those were the good jobs. He also ran for coffee and answered telephones. And then finally in the spring of that year came the inevitable assignment for a rookie sports reporter—covering the high schools.

But in 1924, Washington became fascinated with its beloved Senators, a baseball team that would win in that year its only World Series. It was those Senators that would provide Povich with his first significant byline. In 1926, Povich was called to the office of his patron, Edward B. McLean.

"Shirley, how do you like your new job?"

"Fine, Sir. What new job?"

"You're the new sports editor. They didn't tell you yet? Act surprised."

Shirley Povich became the sports editor of *The Washington Post* at the age of 21, the youngest sports editor of any major metropolitan newspaper in the country, and the youngest man on his own staff. His department, counting himself, totaled seven. (Today the *Post* has more than 65 staffers in the sports department.) Because of his new duties, he dropped out of Georgetown University Law School. He also decided to write his own daily column. First called "Following Through," the title was changed later to "This Morning." It graced the breakfast tables of Washington for the next 72 years.

Povich was in high company for a kid in his twenties, competing against the likes of Grantland Rice, Westbrook Pegler, Damon Runyon, and Heywood Broun. And for the financially strapped *Post*, he found it near impossible to enlarge the scope of sports coverage. It took him one year to convince the bosses to allow him to cover a big non-Washington event—the rematch between Jack Dempsey and Gene Tunney in Chicago. The most famous fight in history ended in the "long count" controversy, but marked the launch of Shirley Povich as a 132-pound heavyweight sports writer.

Povich's first major byline. Detail at right.

My Name in Type, Upside Down and Backwards

It was 1924 and I could not have been plunged into sports writing in a more exciting year, or era. The Senators were about to win two American League pennants in a row, and in August of that year I saw my first important by-line on a story. By-lines were not given freely in those years and mine was a reward, Mr. Baxter said, for the story I did on the Senators' return from New York after mopping up the Yankees in a three-day series and taking over the American League lead.

The article was about the Senators and their reception by the crowd of more than 5,000 fans who waited at Union Station until midnight to greet the new league leaders. I handed the story in to Mr. Baxter who, on reading it, said simply, "It's a nice story, Shirley. I'm going to put your name on this." From him, no compliment could have been higher.

I could scarcely wait for the morning paper to see my name in print. In fact, I did not wait. I snuck downstairs into the composing room and stole a galley proof of my article off the proof press, feasting my eyes on "By Shirley L. Povich." Even this did not suffice me. I sidled over to the make-up banks where the sports pages were being prepared for the press and searched until I found my story in type and my name at the head of it, backward and upside down, as it appeared to me. Not till I ran my fingers across the metal and actually fondled my name in type was I certain of this dream come true.

—Shirley Povich, from his memoir, *All These Mornings* (1969)

Happy and Tough,
Is Harris' Picture Of Nats' Sentiments

"We're happy and we're tough to beat," so spoke Manager Stanley (Bucky) Harris, youngest manager in baseball, as he stepped from the train last night at Union station, with his victorious crew of Washington Nationals, fresh from a triumphant tour of the West, climaxed by a successful invasion of Yankee Stadium, where they dropped the world's champion New Yorkers in four straight games, to come home at the top of the American League standings.

"We had the breaks, but we made 'em," declared Bucky. "There was no stopping us once we were in reach of the top. Our pitchers came through, our sluggers slugged and the spirit of the team never once ebbed. We have got a real ball club and fear no team in the league. Here's hoping that September 25 will find us in a like position. And we hear that pennant flapping."

Bucky was taken aback with the size of the crowd and the reception given the homecoming team.

"It sure does make us feel like going out and knocking every team for a loop," was his comment.

Johnson and Martina Ready

"Johnson and Martina are ready to do their stuff in today's games. We are going after these games from the first ball pitched, and with the smoke ball king at his best, and Martina in shape, we will be satisfied only with a double victory.

"Those games in New York certainly brought a show of spirit. Pandemonium reigned on our bench in the third game of the series when Wid Matthews brought Russell home with the winning run in the ninth inning. Our boys literally carried the spitball twirler from the plate to the bench. He later performed nobly when he retired the Yanks in the last half of the ninth.

"How those boys played ball. Sparky Matthews, Peck, Rice, Judge, Bluege, Ruel, Goslin, Mogridge, Zachary, Zahniser, Russell"—he named them all—"performed like ones possessed. It isn't easy to pick out an individual star. Sparky's presence sure was a tonic. And how he hit and fielded. Peck, performing against his old mates, bobbed up at every turn with a needed hit or a marvelous stop to send a run across or nip a budding Yankee rally. Little Muddy Ruel played the game of his life."

Bucky Waives Credit

Bucky, radiant, waived all credit for himself. But Washington fans cannot forget that he was a member of the National infield that accepted all chances without an error in the final three games of the series and had only one misplay throughout the whole four games.

Mogridge, Zachary, Russell, Marberry and Zahniser came in for plenty of praise.

"Those two left-handers just south pawed the champs to death," was the way the happy manager put it. "Marberry certainly showed he had the goods yesterday. In the second, third, fourth, fifth and sixth innings not a semblance of a hit was made off the tall Texan. Zahnizer was not knocked out. Russell relieved him in the third game when I tried for another run by using a pinch hitter for Paul.

"We have no lost ground to make up. We are at the top and mean to stay there. We are figuring on copping both games today, and then watch us step. Of course we realize that the clubs are closely bunched and that anything may happen. No team will be underrated. As long as we win our games we are not worrying, and we're out to take every one from now on."

JUNE 26, 1924

Senators Win Their Only World Series

No sporting event in Povich's lifetime could equal the thrill of the Washington Senators winning their only World Series, four games to two, over the New York Giants in 1924. Hall of Fame pitcher Walter Johnson won the clinching game in relief. Povich was a kid sports writer, assigned to write the play-by-play boxes as well as the color stories. In 1994, 70 years after being on the scene, he looked back on Washington's greatest baseball triumph.

1924: When Senators Were Kings;
Seventy Years Ago, It Was Washington's World Series

The likes of it had never been known before. This was baseball history. The Washington Senators in a World Series. This is not fiction. It happened in 1924. I was there. The Washington Senators vs. the New York Giants of John McGraw, in the seven games of the Fall Classic.

In America's mind-set, it ranked as one of the great improbables, to be considered with such other unlikelihoods:

That we would put a man on the moon.

That Lou Gehrig's streak of 2,130 consecutive games would be excelled.

That a chimpanzee's co-star in an old Hollywood film would be elected president of the United States—twice.

It was never thought that the Washington Senators, long scoffed at as the American League's patsies, would ever win a pennant, much less a World Series. You remember the World Series, the annual event that would have started tonight, if it hadn't been canceled because of a players' strike.

For most of the years of the century Washington's baseball teams had been the butt of the constant vaudeville joke—"Washington, first in war, first in peace, and last in the American League." But there they were, that October day 70 years ago, winners of the American League pennant and squaring off against the Giants in the first game of the World Series before 35,760 at Griffith Stadium.

I was in the press box, along with 150 other reporters whose desks were a plank in the upper deck behind home plate. As a kid sportswriter for *The Washington Post* I could be trusted only with doing the play-by-play—a no-fail job.

My neighbor in the press box, according to the seating plan, was to be, of all people, Babe Ruth. He had signed on to cover the World Series for the Christy Walsh Syndicate. That sort of thing was commonplace for the game's big stars. They would be provided a press box seat, along with a ghostwriter and telegraph operator, and never set their pen to paper.

But minutes before the game, the word had come over the wires that Ruth had suffered an appendicitis and had been rushed to Emergency Hospital. Thus, his ghostwriter also dismissed himself for the day.

When Christy Walsh arrived and was told about Ruth's absence, and why, he bellowed quickly, "Get me an operator!" Walsh took Ruth's seat and began to dictate: "Washington, D.C., October 1, by Babe Ruth, paragraph, quote. As I lie here, in Washington's Emergency Hospital, as a native New Yorker my heart is with the Giants, but as an American Leaguer, it is my duty to root for the Senators." And so it went.

Anyway, it is most proper to relate how the Senators got there, into that World Series.

They got there by looking the vaunted New York Yankees in the eye in the last month of the race and knocking them out of the pennant, won by the Senators by a two-game margin. Remember, these were the Yankees who'd won the last three AL pennants—the Yankees of Ruth, Bob Meusel, Joe Dugan, Wally Pipp, Wally Schang, and Everett Scott, plus the pitchers Herb Pennock, Waite Hoyt, Bob Shawkey, and Bullet Joe Bush.

They got there under the surprising leadership of the youngest manager in AL history. "Griffith's Folly," it was called, when owner Clark Griffith selected his 26-year-old second baseman, Stanley "Bucky" Harris, as his new manager.

It was in the final days of the pennant race that the upstart, astonishing Senators took it to the Yankees, wiping out their league lead by winning 16 of their last 21 games. It was Walter Johnson, who, above all others, was seizing the moment. The Legend kept the Senators alive by throwing a 13-game winning streak at the Damn Yankees and their hopes of a fourth straight pennant.

The shine was off Johnson's fastball, but not all of it, and he was also relying on a sweeping curve. Ask who, at the age of 36, in his 18th season with the Senators, was the leading pitcher in the American League and the answer is Johnson. He posted a 23–7 record and of course he led the league in strikeouts and ERA, and lent his own .283 batting average to the proceedings.

Unquestionably those 1924 Senators were the class of the league. Teaming with Johnson to give them superb pitching were the veteran left-handers George Mogridge and Tom Zachary. Striving for more depth late in the season Harris divined something about Curly Ogden and claimed him on waivers from the Athletics. Ogden gave Harris eight wins in a row.

That was the year too when the relief pitcher was invented by Harris. For that job he selected the big Texan, right-handed Firpo Marberry, whose delivery included sticking a huge (size 13) shoe into the batter's face, and then letting loose his steaming fastball. Marberry set an AL record by appearing in 50 games.

Walter Johnson warming up a few days before the 1924 World Series, the only World Series the Washington Senators ever won

And those Senators could hit. Four .300-plus swatters—the out-fielders, Goose Goslin (.344), Sam Rice (.334), Earl McNeely (.334), and on first base the slick Joe Judge (.324). The weakest hitter on the team was Manager Harris himself (.268), but he was not an easy out.

Besides Judge and Harris in the infield were the ex-Yankee short-stop Roger Peckinpaugh and a young grab-everything Ossie Bluege on third. The Senators' catcher, a clever one, was little Muddy Ruel, a .283 hitter and the only big league ballplayer ever known to be admitted to practice law before the Supreme Court of the United States.

A series of challenges came October 1924, with the Senators a World Series team, and now the nation's capital exploded emotionally. Inured to the excitement of presidential inaugurations, calm in the midst of history-making legislation, and callous to the fetes for visiting princes and potentates, the population went wild at the approach of the Series. For the pennant winners, a Pennsylvania Avenue parade led to the White House, where both President and Mrs. Coolidge promised to attend the Series opener. They would attend all four home games.

The sentiment for the Senators against the Giants was nationwide, with Walter Johnson's coast-to-coast admirers having lusted for that day when he would finally be on the World Series stage. Unfortunately, it would support the aphorism that hope deferred is often bittersweet. Johnson made two starts, lost them both, though they were tough, hard-bitten defeats.

In that Series opener, Johnson pitched seven consecutive shutout innings over one stretch and fanned 12, but was beaten in 12 innings, 4–3. He was the victim of cheap home runs by Bill Terry and George Kelly into the temporary bleacher seats that fronted the left field wall, installed to accommodate more fans.

Zachary held the Giants to one run in the second game until the ninth, when Kelly and Hack Wilson singled home runs to make it 3–3. But the Senators got to Jack Bentley in their half of the ninth to win it on Peckinpaugh's double.

The games moved to the Polo Grounds and the Giants took the

Series lead, two games to one, by beating Marberry, 6–4. And now it was Mogridge starting the fourth game. For the Giants it was Virgil Barnes and he had trouble with Goslin.

If Johnson was number one in the hearts of Senators' fans, Goslin was number two. He swung the biggest bat on the Senators. He cared not whether the pitching was left- or right-handed. He hit home runs from his exaggerated, left-handed stance, crowding the plate so often that the umpires commanded him to stand back. He once jested of his prominent beak, "With my pull stance I was a one-eyed hitter. Couldn't see past my nose. If I coulda seen that pitch with both eyes I'da hit .600 in this league."

In the third inning of Game 4, Goslin got the Senators a 3–0 lead with a three-run homer off Barnes. By the fifth, the Senators were in front 5–1 with Goslin driving in four. The Senators won, 7–4. Goslin's contribution: 4-for-4.

In Game 5 Johnson gave back the Series lead to the Giants when he weakened in the eighth, also mishandling a bunt, and was a 6–2 loser. Evidence that he wasn't well-rested was seen in his mere three strikeouts. Across the nation Walter Johnson fans were saddened.

For Game 6, with the Series back in Washington, Harris not only made the choice of a winning pitcher, Zachary, but personally saved the Series from ending in six games in favor of the Giants. With McGraw's team holding a 1–0 lead, Manager Harris singled to right to get both runs home in a 2–1 victory that extended the Series into a seventh game.

A Fitting Finale

For the vital last game in Griffith Stadium, the President and Mrs. Coolidge were present again, along with 31,677 fans. They had no inkling of the high intrigue that had taken place before a ball was pitched.

Manager Harris had hatched a plot. He would start right-hander Ogden to trick McGraw into starting the Giants' left-handed batting order. Meanwhile he would have his own left-hander, Mogridge, warming up secretly under the stands. After Ogden faced one hitter, Mogridge would go in, keeping such feared left-handed hitters as Terry at a disadvantage.

Ogden struck out Freddie Lindstrom on three pitches, then walked Frankie Frisch and Mogridge came in. But the game would take a dreary turn for the Senators with the Giants going into the eighth inning with a 3–1 lead.

Then, the Senators rebelled. Nemo Liebold, pinch-hitting for rookie third baseman Tommy Taylor, doubled down the left field line. Ruel, hitless until then in the Series, singled. Bennie Tate, batting for Marberry, walked to fill the bases. But their hopes sagged when McNeely flied to Irish Meusel in short left.

This left it up to Harris, who met the issue, and the ball. He singled to left to get two runs home for a 3–3 game.

Now Harris needed a new pitcher going into the ninth and the crowd was clamoring, "We Want Johnson!" When Johnson strode to the mound the stadium was in an uproar. He could yet win a World Series game and so much of America would be pleased.

However, when Frisch tripled with one out in the top of the ninth, it was ominous. Here Harris ordered an intentional walk to Ross Youngs. Now, with Johnson facing Kelly, a long fly could beat him. He disposed of Kelly on three wicked fastball strikes, got Meusel on an inning-ending groundball, and it was extra innings.

Trouble for Johnson too in the 11th. Pinch hitter Heinie Groh led off with a single, and Lindstrom sacrificed. Now it was Frisch, the triple-sacker of two innings before. Johnson dealt with him by striking him out. Facing Youngs and Kelly again, Johnson repeated his heroics of the ninth inning—walked Youngs intentionally and fanned Kelly for the last out.

A bit more trouble for Johnson in the 12th. Meusel led off with single. But Johnson fanned rookie Hack Wilson, got a force out and a fly out and had pitched his fourth consecutive shutout inning in relief.

In their own 12th the Senators would emerge as World Series champions. Lady Luck had beamed on them. Against the Giants' fourth pitcher, Bentley, Ruel with one out lifted a pop fly to catcher

Hank Gowdy behind home plate, an easy out, except that Gowdy stepped on his mask and the ball spilled out of his mitt, a World Series boo-boo that would be long remembered. Whereupon, the reprieved Ruel doubled down the left field line to put the winning run on base.

Johnson, a strong hitter, batted for himself and grounded to short-stop Travis Jackson, who fumbled—a big break for the Senators, with Ruel holding second. Now it was McNeely who would be remembered for all time for his "pebble hit."

Third baseman Lindstrom was poised for a routine play on McNeely's sharp grounder, maybe an inning-ending double play. And then for the Giants—horrors. For the Senators—glee. Whatever McNeely's ground ball hit, a pebble or a divot or a minefield, it took a freak high hop over Lindstrom's head into the outfield for a single and Ruel flew home from second with the run that won everything for the Senators.

In Griffith Stadium the crowd catapulted out of the stands to thrash onto the field and to dance on the dugout roofs, refusing to leave the park until long after nightfall.

The next day, of course, it was up Pennsylvania Avenue toward the White House for the World Series champions, the streets lined by tens of thousands. The city's joy was best expressed, perhaps, by the enthusiasm of the men on the hook-and-ladder float of the Cherrydale, Va., Fire Department, which flaunted a huge banner that read: "Let Cherrydale Burn."

It doesn't seem like 70 years ago.

OCTOBER 22, 1994

First Columns

Four years after arriving in Washington, Shirley Povich, 21, was writing his first column for The Washington Post. *Under the heading "Follow-*

ing Through"—which he later changed to "This Morning"—Povich
took on some of the same issues baseball is facing today: Commissioner
Kenesaw Mountain Landis and his relationship with club owners, and
the owners' determination to stop paying high salaries to the players as
well as their concern over the New York teams' payrolls inflating the
market. Sound familiar?

Judge Kenesaw Mountain Landis

There is a man of mystery. Mysterious in the manner that he so completely dominates his associates, who, in his present undertaking, are
his employers. He not only tells them what to do, but how to do it and
when. And he makes them like it. Sixteen major league magnates,
supposed to be business men and drivers of hard bargains, are so completely under the thumb of the man with the funny name and the
well-deserved title that it is strange if not mysterious or weird.

Judge Landis is either the possessor of some spark of personality
indescribable that puts him far ahead of his time or he is a grand hoax,
who has sixteen major league magnates so grandly hoaxed that it is
pitiful. Howsomever it may be, Judge Landis so commands the respect
of the magnates that they appear ready to do his every bidding—nay,
fawn upon him.

There is something in the presence of Judge Landis that makes the
self-will of strong men melt before him. There have been times when
matters have looked dark for the Judge. Dire things have been forecast
for his lot. Baseball has been ready to cast him out bodily; to strip him
of his power; to leave him high commissioner of baseball in name
only and roundly rebuke him for his audacity in attempting to lay
down the law to the magnates.

But Judge Landis has always emerged from his trials in major
league baseball triumphant. And then comes the reaction. The magnates appear to be at his very feet in their desire to display their faith in
the old man. They are ready to concede much. And the Judge has
accepted much.

Why the sixteen major league magnates fear the displeasure of the man whom they elected to arbitrate in their own cause is strange. The judge has declared repeatedly that he did not want the job. Even with the approach of 1927 and the termination of his seven-year contract at a yearly salary of $50,000, the judge gave the magnates reason to believe that he was not anxious to be reelected.

When the turnstiles stop clicking, 'tis said, the magnates start thinking. From the end of the season in late September until the annual meeting last Thursday the magnates have had time to reflect. Thoughts of the $50,000 yearly salary aroused the malcontents and there was a cry for Judge Landis' head. The feeling gained momentum, according to the tenor of press dispatches, and quite some time before the meeting organized opposition to Judge Landis was anticipated.

As the meeting drew nearer this concerted opposition to the judge seemed to melt. There was a break in the ranks somewhere. The meeting was held and Judge Landis tendered the portfolio of high commissioner again. Each league endorsed him virtually without qualifications. Judge Landis accepted another seven-year term and another increase in salary.

What sort of a man is he who, by his mere presence and demeanor and the dignity that goes with age, turns such an adverse situation into a rout of his enemies? Surely he is no ordinary personage. It may be the very audacity of his methods in flaunting the authority of his employers that gains him their respect. But whatever it may be, he is a master tactician in the handling of men.

Nobody has ever accused major league magnates of self-consciousness or of possessing an inferiority complex, but these facts when applied to their relations with Judge Landis were brought out in unmistakable terms at the National League meeting at New York the first of the week. The magnates took cognizance of the fact that Landis was dominating their affairs with consideration of their welfare, but evidently without consideration of their rights.

Something must be done to show the judge that they were not to be treated as serfs. Forthwith there was drawn up a resolution that Judge Landis be informed that the National League would tolerate no more of his despotism. But they didn't call it despotism. They were not yet ready for an open break. They clothed it in a meaningless combine of words and called it "benevolent despotism." In that act they protested the judge's alleged despotism and at the same time admitted they liked it by calling it benevolent.

The National and American League magnates also devised the brilliant idea of curbing the judge's authority by reviving the advisory board, which had ceased to exist in the judge's mind since two years before, when, at his insistence, the American League owners removed President Ban Johnson from the council.

So armed with that fine idea and the "benevolent despotism" resolution, the magnates made their way into the joint meeting, at which the commissioner presided.

At the meeting the magnates soon learned that it was one thing to plan the "benevolent despotism" and advisory council ideas in the sanctum of their own meetings and quite another proposition to present them to Judge Landis in the latter's presence. Somebody hit upon the happy idea of first tendering the judge the commissionship first and the resolutions afterward. They did, showing great courage.

With Landis wondering whether or not he was going to be returned to his high-salaried commissionership and virtually a lame duck at the meeting, the magnates had their one chance to make plain any grievances. But the courage was not there. The "benevolent despotism" and advisory board resolutions were lost sight of in the rush to climb aboard the commissioner's band wagon.

They clothed him with the full power of his office for another seven years, raised his salary to $65,000 yearly, endorsed wholeheartedly the policies of his administration and then mentioned incidentally their "benevolent despotism" and advisory board proposition.

Judge Landis, some man.

DECEMBER 18, 1926

Rising Payrolls

Rogers Hornsby has departed from St. Louis, and with him has departed the period of plenty for big league ball players. The Hornsby case is but another of the succession of moves by major league club owners to retrench themselves in the business of conducting high-grade baseball on an economic basis.

The transformation has been gradual and subtle, but pronounced. The ball players once again have been reduced to their former status as the employees of baseball, mere chattels to be sold or traded at the will of the magnates, to be directed and paid like the humblest clerks at the discretion of the club owners.

Since the close of the 1926 season, the magnates, by wholesale discharges of managers and the release of stars, have sounded the demise of the reign of the ball players and the retrogression toward the days when five-figured salaries were a rarity and long-term contracts unknown.

Baseball, huffing along in the self-same easy manner that marked the game since the organization of the American League in 1900 received its first injection of frenzied finance in 1920 when New York's two colonels, Ruppert and Houston, of the Yankees, proceeded to buy the league pennant by purchasing outright at fancy figures the stars of the Boston Red Sox.

Babe Ruth, Sam Jones, Walter Hoyt, Joe Bush, Herb Pennock, Everett Scott and Wally Schang were involved in the deals that transferred a pennant-winning team in Boston to Father Knickerbocker's children in the Bronx.

Rupert and Houston were the first to pay the high salaries to their ball players. The one objective of a big leaguer was to play for a New York team. Other magnates were forced to meet the competition of the Yankees or the Giants and high salaries soon became general. With them the demands of the ballplayer increased.

Efforts of the club owners to build or buy pennant-winning teams contributed to the frenzy of the finance of the game. Soon the ballplayers were dictating their own terms virtually and usually carried their points. For a span of years New York clubs with their prodigious check books held the upper hand and witnessed three intercity world's series.

First hint of the concerted move of the magnates to put an end to the high salaries of ballplayers came with the resignation of Tris Speaker as manager of the Cleveland Indians. Previously Ty Cobb had resigned as pilot of the Tigers for reasons considered personal and Eddie Collins had been released outright by President Comiskey of the White Sox. Speaker's departure from the game so close upon the heels of Cobb and Collins carried much significance. Three high salaries were topped off major league rosters.

Hornsby's case, engineered by President Breadon of the Cardinals, was the most apparent and open display of the new attitude of the club owners since the close of the 1926 season. Hornsby was made a flat proposition of signing up at $50,000 or be traded. He refused and was traded and the deal proved the most sensational in recent years.

Even the man, who led his team to a league pennant and then to the world's series championship was not to flaunt the power of the club owners—not in their present attitude toward high salaries and long-term contracts. Hornsby, firm in the belief that he was too valuable a player to be disposed of, was rudely disillusioned. Breadon merely went a step farther than was the case of other club owners and made good his threat.

Hornsby's case is certain to live long in the memories of the ball players. If a star like the former manager of the Cardinals could not demand his price and receive it, then there is small chance that the rank and file of the ball players can continue to make their petty demands and see them fulfilled.

The club owners after a period of docile obeisance are again in control of the situation. They have undermined the belief of the invincibility of the stars of the game by the simple method of relieving them from duty and by mutual agreement of the magnates seeing these stars with their heavy salaries slip out of the pastime.

Only by working in agreement could the magnates affect the transformation and that they have worked in perfect accord is attested by the fact that Cobb, of Detroit; Speaker, of Cleveland; Sisler, of St. Louis, and McKechnie, of the Pirates, have either been released outright or relegated to the ranks minus the huge salaries and with their demands stifled by the firm action of the club owners.

DECEMBER 22, 1926

Walter Johnson

The greatest Washington Senator of them all, Walter Johnson, compiled a record of 417–279–12 from 1907 to 1927. His ERA was 2.17 and he struck out 3,508 batters. A member of Baseball's Hall of Fame, Johnson also managed the Washington Senators from 1929 to 1932, posting three winning seasons. In a foreword to Henry W. Thomas's 1995 biography of Johnson, Povich wrote that he was captivated not only by Johnson's pitching skills, but also by "the manner of the man, his modesty, humility, and humanity while surrounded by a game that in his era was the playing field of roughnecks."

Johnson Honored By 20,000 At Park, But Detroit Wins

Walter Johnson pitched, and he didn't win, but who cares if he didn't win?

Win or lose, Walter Johnson was the hero to the 20,000 persons who assembled in homage to the greatest of all pitchers, and no mere ball game could rob him of the esteem in which admiring fandom of a generation has learned to regard him.

There at American League Park yesterday, Walter Johnson, the man, had his day. It doesn't matter that he was relieved in the ninth inning and that Detroit won, 7 to 6. It doesn't matter that he didn't pitch a good game, for there, amid the plaudits of a fandom that had learned to regard the man as ideal, epitomizing all that a man and a ballplayer should be, Walter Johnson cleft the portals leading to the completion of his twenty years of service as a pitcher for the Washington Baseball Team.

There a span of twenty years of toil was marked and there were reenacted the scenes of that day in August, 1907, when Walter Johnson, a gangling youth from Weiser, Idaho, 19 years old, pitched his first game in the big league and introduced a speed ball that was to carry him to fame and fortune through a glorious career with the same ball team.

Thanks Fans Over Radio

Walter Johnson, the pitcher, and Walter Johnson, the man, heard the praises of the 20,000 and the big pitcher, who likes to be called "Barney," was quite overcome. He responded to the entreaties of the 20,000 to say something and into the same radio microphone that had carried word of the pregame ceremonies throughout the land, Walter Johnson stammered, simply, "Folks, this is wonderful, and I appreciate it."

And the 20,000 folk believed him. For twenty years Walter Johnson gave his all and asked little and yesterday when admiring fandom singled him out as its hero the big pitcher appreciated it.

The gifts of the fans were material as well as ornate. Walter Johnson, sober and steady, giving his all and asking little, was made independent for life. Proceeds of the game were presented to the big pitcher in the form of a check to the amount of $14,746.05. The array of other individual presentations literally overwhelmed Johnson.

Cited by American League

It was Johnson the man more than Johnson the pitcher whom the 20,000 chose for their tribute. His pitching deeds, written indelibly in the record books, were open evidence of his physical achievements but written even more indelibly in the minds of fandom throughout the nation was his worth as a man, a family man, and a citizen and the sterling qualities that have endeared him to the people of a generation.

Walter Johnson was cited by the American League for his twenty years of service. Although illness prevented Ban Johnson, president of the American League, from making the presentation personally, the big pitcher received the first "distinguished service medal" ever bestowed by the league upon any ball player. The medal, in the shape of a Maltese cross, was studded with 20 diamonds, one for each year of Johnson's service, and bore a picture of the pitcher in the center. Actual cost of the medal was $1,000.

The medal denoting 20 years of service is insufficient to commemorate the deeds of Walter Johnson during that time. As Johnson stood out there in the pitcher's box yesterday he was the only ball player still in active service, with the exception of Ty Cobb, who participated in that memorable game against the Detroit Tigers, August 2, 1907.

August 2, 1907, and August 2, 1927, differed widely, the 500 "first timers" at the game yesterday will tell you. They will tell you how on that August 2, 20 years ago, Walter Johnson, the big country boy from Weiser, Idaho, pitched his first big league ball game in the ramshackle park on the same site and introduced the blinding speed ball that was to make him the sensation of the game. They will tell you how the Detroit Tigers, baffled by his speed, were forced to resort to a bunting game and by that method scored three runs, enough to defeat Johnson and Washington, 3–2.

Out there in the pitcher's box yesterday it was a vastly different and very much the same Johnson who faced the Tigers on that day 20 years ago. Johnson yesterday was the same good-natured, easy-going country boy, his head unturned by his success and playing the game to win, but the blinding speed was gone.

The terror of batters for more than a decade was no more. The fast ball that had opposing batsmen cringing at its very velocity had melted with years.

Walter Johnson yesterday was "mixing them up." Ten years ago it would have been a strange sight to see Walter Johnson pitching a curve and alternating it with a slow ball but the man who has served longer with the same club than any pitcher in baseball had tempered his failing speed with an effective change of pace. He was throwing curve balls but he isn't a curve ball pitcher and he was beaten.

But the day that the fans wanted to please Walter Johnson, Johnson tried to please the crowd. So he threw his speed balls with all the speed he could muster for four innings then he weakened in the fifth inning because he wanted to please the crowd with his speed balls. Then the Detroit Tigers, no longer baffled by the veteran, won the game when he did weaken...

Oh yes, they played nine innings and Walter Johnson didn't win, but who cares if he didn't win? ...

AUGUST 3, 1927

Covering The "Long Count"

Our publisher Ned McLean's touch was not consistently Midas-like, and the Post *was developing a balance of payments problem. This slowed just enough in 1927 for me to make my first long trip as a sportswriter. It was Dempsey–Tunney the second time around, in Chicago at Soldier Field.*

My high spirits on arrival at ringside were drenched when I saw my seat fifty rows back, forty-eight rows from the Western Union operator who would be telegraphing my account over the wires back to the Post. *That's when I realized that being the youngest sports editor of any big daily in America carried no guarantees of acceptance. The fight officials took one look at me—in my early twenties, looking even younger, with the name of Shirley—and decided I was putting them on. Only the intervention of one of the class guys of our profession, Sid Mercer of the* New York Journal, *brought me close to ringside.*

*I almost wished Mercer hadn't talked to the promoter, Tex Richard,
because now I found myself literally rubbing elbows with the likes of
Grantland Rice, Damon Runyon, Heywood Broun and Westbrook
Pegler before he went off the deep end and saw Communists behind
every tree.*

*Not only was I in their company, I was expected to compete with
them. I bled from every vein and perspired from every pore in an attempt
to put a coherent story together, certain that I never could contest with
any of them in the quality of the descriptive powers of their prose. I felt
like some of those kid fighters from the four-round prelims who were now
watching Dempsey and Tunney with exactly the same kind of awe
which gripped me.*

—**Shirley Povich, from his memoir, *All These Mornings* (1969)**

Willard, Ohio, Sept. 23—Out of the maze of doubt of the cross-fire
that has questioned his supremacy, the shadows that would becloud his
claim, Gene Tunney today stands against the pugilistic horizon in bold
relief, the heavyweight champion of the world, and worthy of the
crown that has been worn by past masters. By right of might Gene Tunney proved his claim last night at Soldier Field. Against Jack Dempsey
he proved himself a champion in every sense that the word implies,
proved it conclusively, convincingly, and the scoffers were shown.

They made capital of the "long count" in the seventh round of
Thursday night's battle, did the scoffers and the doubters, the die
hards and that element that could not conceive of defeat for Jack
Dempsey. They pounced upon that "long count" as their alibi in a last
vain effort to discount the victory of a champion and the defeat of
their favorite.

The count was long, no doubt of that, but in what manner the
"long count" benefited the champion and handicapped the challenger is not clear in view of the circumstances.

Gene Tunney could have arisen from the canvas at the count of five had he so elected. By the time the referee had tolled to three on the second count, he had recovered sufficiently to regain his composure.

Lying there on the resin-covered floor of the ring, Gene Tunney played the game like a champion, taking full advantage of the rules that protected him, waiting until the count of nine had been reached before he went back to the battle. And his conduct after that knockdown was worthy of any champion whoever fought a fight.

Getting up, Gene Tunney ran. The champion ran, but it was no disgrace to run. It was the sensible thing to do under the circumstances, and in running Tunney acted the part of a champion who knew what to do when there was no logical alternative.

Then it was that Gene Tunney showed that he was a fighting man. His conduct in the ring against Dempsey following that knockdown in the seventh round was letter perfect and won him the fight, won him the renewed confidence of his supporters and won him the faith of those who had doubted. Gene Tunney, bringing into play the science that he studies, boxed himself out of a trying situation in the seventh round and fought himself into the hearts of the fans in the eighth, ninth and tenth.

He was a true fighting machine when he came up for the eighth round and, drawing on the stamina he had stored by a life-time of clean living, he actually outslugged Jack Dempsey in the last three rounds of that fight, beating Dempsey to the punches, carrying more steam in his blows and trying for the knockout that he said he would attempt.

The 150,000 in the stadium that night knew that Gene Tunney could box. Now they know that he can also fight, that he has courage and gameness to match and is the fit ruler of the boxers of the world. For Jack Dempsey, than who there has been no gamer fighter, it can be said for him that last Thursday night he was in error. He overlooked his one possible opportunity. He forgot when he knocked Gene Tunney down in that seventh round with those awful short hooks to the jaw that he must repair to a neutral corner.

He extended Tunney precious seconds when he waited for Referee Dave Barry to motion him to the far side of the ring, where Dempsey should have gone himself without being ordered.

Then and there Jack Dempsey dismissed his one opportunity to finish Tunney if he could. Tunney benefited to the extent of those three or four seconds that elapsed between counts, but he was not in distress and a true count would surely have found him on his feet to resume the battle. And when he did arise to his feet, Dempsey showed no desire to finish his man.

In the final analysis, Jack Dempsey, with the desire or with it not, was unable to finish his man. Dempsey faced in Tunney a master boxer, who capitalized every advantage and found the courage to rally from impending defeat.

Gene Tunney faced in Dempsey a ring-weary slugger with a heart of iron and fists of thunder whose stamina was unequal to the effort and who succumbed to the exactment of time's penalty.

SEPTEMBER 24, 1927

Unlike many observers at the Dempsey–Tunney fight, Povich always believed "the long count" was fair. More than forty years after the fight, he explained why.

Tunney was winning the fight with his masterful footwork and textbook jabs over the aging "Manassa Mauler," who kept stalking after him. Then it happened, in the seventh round.

Dempsey trapped Tunney in Tunney's corner employing his crouched style and hidden so much that all you could see was his close-cropped black hair and hairy chest and arms mounted atop legs with bulging calves. Tunney, the stand-up scientific boxer, was trying to fight off the thrashing, brawling jungle fighter with his jabs. He owned only one real punch, a right over the heart, but you won't land a punch like that against a crouching fighter.

Suddenly Dempsey scores with a left hook lashing out of his crouch and finding Tunney's chin. Tunney sags to the floor and Dempsey is hastening the trip by pounding him to the canvas with a ferocious hail of rights and lefts to the top of the head. The timekeeper began a count, but the referee, Dave Barry, didn't pick it up. He has spotted Dempsey standing there, instead of retiring to a neutral corner, a rule seldom enforced. The rule was ignored flagrantly in an earlier fight when Dempsey actually stepped across a fallen Luis Firpo and stood menacingly at his side, right hand cocked in case Firpo got up before the 10-count. . . .

The lingering opinion to this day is that it was a tragic defeat for Jack Dempsey, a victim of injustice who lost all to a referee's incompetence. But to set the record straight, Dempsey was not a popular fighter at that time. Strong resentment against him smouldered from the World War—we didn't have to number our wars then—because he did not serve in the armed forces. . .

Dempsey profited immensely from the long count. He became an instant national favorite, a man wronged, an underdog with whom the guy in shirtsleeves could identify. The sentiment endures. From it Dempsey has won the respect and affection previously denied him. In the four decades since, it remains my conviction, and I know he agrees, that the long count was not without its blessings for Jack Dempsey.

For the record, Tunney never would have stopped Dempsey in his prime. At his peak, Dempsey would have licked anybody of that day or any other day. Louis, Marciano, Clay—you name them. Dempsey was better.

—Shirley Povich, from his memoir, *All These Mornings* (1969)

Greatest Team Ever?

The 1927 New York Yankees, led by Babe Ruth and Lou Gehrig, are considered by many baseball historians and fans to be the greatest baseball team ever assembled. Their World Series sweep of the Pitts-

burgh Pirates reinforced that belief as Povich's front-page story cap-
tured the drama of the last game and the Pirates' stunning defeat.

Yanks Win Title, 4–3, On Wild Pitch And Ruth's Homer

New York, Oct. 8—Truth is stranger than fiction. They like to tell in story books of how, in the last half of the ninth inning, with the bases full, our hero knocked a home run and won the game. Or how, in the last half of the ninth inning, with the bases full, the chosen hero struck out the next three batters and saved the game.

But they have not told of how, with the bases full in the ninth inning and none out, the potential hero struck out the next two batters and then, on the threshold of success and fame, he loosened a wild pitch and lost the game.

And thus ends the story of how, today, the New York Yankees defeated the Pittsburgh Pirates in the fourth game of the world's series by a score of 4 to 3 to win the championship in four consecutive games, rivaling the victory of the Boston Braves over the Philadelphia Athletics in the series of 1914 and the triumph of the Chicago White Sox over the Chicago Cubs in the series of 1906.

John Miljus, World War veteran, and a tall, right-handed pitcher, who has graduated to the major leagues and been shunted to the minors, later to be taken on by the Pirates and developed into a mainstay of their pitching staff, was the potential hero, but also the actual "goat" of today's game, a sad figure after that unhappy wild pitch in the ninth inning, with the bases full and two out as a result of his striking out Lou Gehrig and Bob Meusel just a few minutes before.

Bucs in First Threat

Baseball has witnessed no more melodramatic ninth inning and its fateful ending than was presented in today's game. It was a lucky and unlucky climax, a happy and unhappy ending, a glad and sad turn of events for the Yankees of New York and the Pirates of Pittsburgh.

Doubly disappointing to the Pirates was the wild pitch of Miljus. The Pirates, carrying the standard of the National League into the world's series as foes of the Yankees, hailed as the greatest team of all time, had played miserable baseball until today, when the true Pirate team threatened finally to stay the power in the Yankee bats and themselves carry on to victory.

In the background, unmistakably, and silhouetted in bold relief against the procession of events which marked the contest, was the one and only Babe Ruth, the Bambino, who had almost won the game for the Yankees single-handed by hitting another of his terrific home runs, with Mark Koenig on base, in the sixth inning of the contest, with the score tied. It was Babe Ruth's second home run of the series and broke his own record of nine in world's series competition which he set yesterday.

Moore Goes Route

The last pitching hope of the Pirates, the bespectacled Carmen Hill, and another pitching mainstay of the Yankees, Wilcey Moore, started to pitch today's fourth game and innocently set the stage for the fateful ninth, aided by an error by Lazzeri in the seventh inning which had helped the Pirates to tie the score with a two-run rally and send the game into the last half of the ninth.

A pinch hitter forced Hill out of the game in the seventh inning, and Miljus assumed the pitching burden for the Yankees. Moore twirled the entire game for the Yankees, and it was the pitching of this 30-year old veteran, rescued from the South Atlantic League last spring by Miller Huggins, which aided mightily in the Yankees victory.

Miljus survived the eighth inning safely, but at the start of the ninth he gave first evidence of what was to follow by walking Earl Combs, first to face him, on four straight balls. Koenig's bunt down the third base line was safe and Combs went to second. Confronted with this ominous situation, Manager Bush ordered Miljus to walk Babe Ruth, the next batter, filling the bases.

Not Quite a Hero

Here was something for Miljus to conjure with, the bases full, the score tied, and a New York sort of a hit, error or outfield fly ready to be converted into the winning run. But he faced Lou Gehrig calmly. He gave Gehrig a low ball and Gehrig swung futilely. His next offering was another ball. Then Gehrig struck at a wide curve. A ball followed. Miljus struck Gehrig out with a low inside curve.

Bob Meusel was next up. The same situation obtained. Any sort of a hit, error or outfield fly could account for the winning run. Miljus faced Meusel as calmly as he had faced Gehrig and he slipped over a strike on the first pitch. A low ball was not offered to Meusel. Meusel swung viciously at a slow curve and missed. He fouled the next pitch down the third base line. Miljus struck Meusel out on a slow curve.

Yankee Stadium was in a frenzy. New York fans or not, the 52,000 persons in the stands accorded the veteran a tremendous ovation. Here was being executed a baseball rarity. A veteran pitcher was matching his physical skill and his pitching acumen against three batters renowned for their slugging and on the result hung the championship and thousands of dollars in gold for the players of the teams.

The 52,000 persons in the three-tiered stands and the bleacher seats of Yankee Stadium, transformed again into a human arena by the masses that had gathered there, breathlessly awaited every pitch. And Miljus was unruffled. Three runners were tugging at the bases, ready for any break.

Tony Lazzeri was the next batter. The same Lazzeri that faced something of the same situation in the decisive game of the world's series between the Yankees and the St. Louis Cardinals last year. The same Lazzeri that faced Grover Cleveland Alexander, Cardinal pitching veteran, with the bases full, and struck out.

Miljus faced Lazzeri as he had faced Gehrig and Meusel, calm, unruffled and unperturbed. His first pitch to Lazzeri was over the plate and baseball history was repeated when Lazzeri fouled the ball far into the right field stands as he had fouled a ball into the right field stands against Alexander in that memorable game of the 1926 world's series. It was a potential home run, but it was foul, and Lazzeri, the 52,000 people in the stadium and the millions who were listening in awaited the next pitch of Miljus.

Then a strange thing happened. The ball that Miljus threw was a wild pitch. It was a side arm curve and it left the beaten path to the plate 10 feet in front of Catcher Gooch, it developed into a sweeping curve that "broke" with an eccentric dart far to the outside of the plate. Gooch made a gallant effort to catch the ball. He did manage to get his big mitt in front of it but it bounded away. It bounded from his mitt in the general direction of the Pittsburgh bench and Earl Combs was already speeding to the plate from third base. Before Gooch could recover the ball, Combs, with a last joyful leap, had touched the plate. The game was over.

The last game of the 1927 world's series shamed every other in point of interest, action and good baseball. There was even the "master minding," which until this contest had played a very minor role. Manager Huggins, of the Yankees, and Manager Bush, of the Pirates, were called upon to display the baseball tact and judgment that had carried the two teams to league pennants.

Bush, on the defensive, bore the most difficult task, and, only for Miljus' wild pitch, he might have scored a decisive personal triumph. It was he who delegated Miljus to stay the Yankee attack after Hill had been relieved by a pinch hitter in the seventh inning and it was he who ordered that Babe Ruth be passed in order that Miljus might have a chance to strike out Gehrig and Meusel in the ninth inning.

Bush's tactics were sound, for Gehrig and Meusel and Lazzeri are known to be frequent strike-out victims. Each had fanned once before in the game, and Lazzeri had struck out twice. Huggins played the game wisely. Twice he refused to take Moore from the game when a successful pinch hitter might have decided matters with little more ado. He discounted Moore's battling prowess in banking upon him as the team's pitcher and again his judgment was proven right.

Again Babe Ruth came to the aid in time of need. Carmen Hill had been an enigma from the second inning until the sixth.

Then Babe Ruth hit another of his home runs. Koenig was on base, and it was a terrific clout. It was nearer center field than right field, and it settled in the bleachers, far up among the tiers of seats. The home run broke the 1-to-1 tie in which the teams had been locked since the first inning. It gave the Yankees a commanding lead and was the decisive hit of the contest.

Carmen Hill justified every confidence that Manager Bush had placed in him as his starting pitcher. He allowed the Yankees one run in the six innings he pitched. He walked just one batter, and in the first inning, after the Yankees had knocked three consecutive singles, he struck out Lou Gehrig, Bob Meusel and Tony Lazzeri, the same trio that faced Miljus in the ninth, and he slipped a third strike over on each.

Opposing Hill was Wilcey Moore, winner of more than 20 games in his first season as a major leaguer, after spending more than ten years as a pitcher in the minor leagues. Moore's sinker ball was not an absolute puzzle, and he was in difficulties on very few occasions. He allowed a run on two hits in the first inning, and he allowed two runs on one hit, his own error and Tony Lazzeri's error in the seventh inning, which enabled the Pirates to tie the score and revive their hopes when it seemed that four straight defeats was their inevitable fate at the hands of the Yankees.

The Pirates went down fighting. For the first time in the series they played like the team which won the National League pennant by a brilliant spurt at the finish. Wright and Traynor and Grantham provided Hill and Miljus with sensational support. Only Lloyd Warner's unimportant error marred their performance in the field, overlooking, of course, the ill-fated wild pitch of Miljus, with the bases full and two out in the ninth inning, and the score tied.

OCTOBER 9, 1927

THE THIRTIES

IF THE 1920S WERE THE GOLDEN AGE OF SPORTS, THE 1930S could be called the Beginning of the Modern Era. Newspapers introduced coverage of events far beyond their city limits to compete with national radio coverage.

It was also the Depression era with economic forces overwhelming Shirley Povich's patron, Edward McLean. The owner was absent from the newspaper too often. He had been tainted by the infamous Teapot Dome scandal that led to the downfall of his friend, Warren Harding. The stock market crash dried up his money. His lifestyle sent him into a downward spiral ending in his being institutionalized. His newspaper was failing, and finally, in 1933, it was auctioned off on the steps of the *Post* for $825,000 dollars. Two days later the new owner was revealed, Eugene Meyer, a financial wizard from Wall Street. He was also the father of Katharine Graham, who became publisher of the *Post*, and grandfather of Donald Graham, the paper's current CEO and Chairman of the Board.

Of Mr. McLean, Shirley Povich said, "What can I tell you? He was the reason for my being at the paper. I will never speak ill of him although his indiscretions were obvious." It said much of the famous Povich loyalty and kindness, which extended to the dozens of reporters who worked with him, his competitors at other newspapers, and the players whose names rest in the Baseball Hall of Fame, many of whom wouldn't be there without his efforts.

Now at the age of 28, Povich was to witness the final World Series to be played by the Senators. Other papers were guilty of trying to hype circulation by loading up their sports pages with columns ghost-written by Babe Ruth, Ty Cobb, John McGraw, and others. Even though the new owner, Eugene Meyer, brought resources to the paper, Povich still penned this promotional house ad for the money-starved Post:

THE POST TAKES PLEASURE IN ANNOUNCING MAHATMA GANDHI,
AIMEE SEMPLE MCPHERSON, COL. LINDBERGH,
THE KING OF ENGLAND, AND 'MACHINE GUN' KELLEY WILL
NOT COVER THE WORLD SERIES FOR THE POST....

NO GHOST WRITERS WILL HAUNT THE PAGES OF THE POST. THE
SPOOKS WILL BE MISSING, BUT THE FACTS WILL BE THERE.

REACH FOR A POST INSTEAD OF A GHOST.

The 1930s also provided an introduction that would last a lifetime. Povich met Ethyl Friedman on a blind date in 1930. The coupling would last the next 68 years. After they married in 1932, Ethyl traveled often with Shirley—their honeymoon was to the Senators' spring training camp in Biloxi, Miss.—but soon she would be staying at home with their three children. Their first son, David, was born in 1935, Maury came along in 1939, and daughter Lynn in 1943.

It was family life that steered Povich to a different approach with his writing. He admitted that youth and hero worship had prevented him from taking a step back and looking at his work and those he covered with some dispassion. "After I got married and had children, I realized the squeeze play, the bunt, and friendship with the ball players were not quite the end of the world. I didn't have to playmake. As I began detaching myself from the ball players, I gained the independence and the exhilarating confidence that no matter who they were, or what happened on the ball field, I would be able to write it as it happens. The skillful writer awaits the event—then reports it. You say to yourself, 'They're the ball players. Let them play the game. I'm a reporter.' It's a necessary separation."

That "maturity," as he called it, was evident in Povich's writing style as well. Before, he said, "I was constantly overwriting. I was considerably less critical than I should have been. I never asserted any

Shirley and Ethyl in 1932, beginning a
marriage that would last 66 years

individuality in those days." Where his sentences had been wordy and
rambling, his writing got crisper and more economical, the sentence
structure less complex. "I'm not a rewriter. I like lucidity and I am a
firm believer in getting the key—the musical key, if you will," he once
said. "I must have the key in the first 50 or 100 words. And once I hear
it, it will flow."

Povich gave up running the sports department in 1935, but still set
the direction of the section and supervised the hiring for the next
three decades. By now, he was becoming a must-read in a town that
welcomed its new National Football League team in 1937, the Sammy
Baugh–led Redskins, which won their first championship in their first
year on the field. As he expanded his horizons, Povich wrote about
Hitler's Olympics, chiding U.S. Olympic officials for yielding to Nazi
efforts to keep their track free of Jewish athletes and Hitler for ignoring

the triumphs of African Americans. In April 1939, he wrote a column about how many capable and extraordinary black baseball players were being kept out of the major leagues by unwritten rules of segregation.

Three months later, Povich was at Yankee Stadium on July 4, the day the great Yankee first baseman, Lou Gehrig, bade farewell to baseball, his life soon to be cut short by amyotrophic lateral sclerosis (the disease that was eventually to be named after Gehrig). He also was in Chicago the day Babe Ruth supposedly pointed to the center field fence before homering against the Cubs in the World Series. Povich always doubted the Babe's "called shot."

The other major topics of the decade—Bobby Jones retiring from golf in 1931, the banning of Shoeless Joe Jackson from baseball in 1934, and the victory of Seabiscuit over War Admiral in 1938—overshadowed a little noticed event that took place on August 29, 1939. A baseball game between the Reds and Dodgers in Brooklyn became the first sports event ever televised. Indeed the modern era of sports was underway.

Golf Classics

Nearly 75 years after this column appeared, golf is consumed with the same argument: Will the game be ruined by technology? Then and now it's about the ball. Golf companies came out with a new ball in 1931. It was the year Bobby Jones retired from competitive play, only a season after he won the Grand Slam. In this piece, Povich speculated that the game would never be the same because of both events.

Bobby Jones' voluntary retirement from competitive golf coincident with the birth of Big Boy, the bigger and lighter ball, may amount to what historians dote on referring to as a new era—in the royal and ancient sport of pounding the gutta-percha pellet around the pasture lands.

Nineteen hundred and thirty-one in our present highly respected Gregorian calendar well may come to be known as the year 1 A.J.— After Jones—in golf, if the present discontent and unrest over the U.S.G.A. ukase that decreed Big Boy as the only lawful ball for tournament play subsides under the sheer weight of time and realization of the helplessness of the man who plays the game.

The line of demarcation in the new golf calendar is formed of equal parts of Jones' decision to retire and the legalization of Big Boy.

New Order is Here

Jones' retirement alone might well have signaled the close of an era in golf in the light of his conquests here and abroad unapproached by any other golfer in the history of the sport that reaches back into the fourteenth century. But the arrival of Big Boy has hailed beyond question a new order in the game what with complaints by even our best pros of Big Boy's antics in the wind and the wails of the garden variety golfer at Big Boy's penchant for rimming the cup on his putts.

Unless Jones recants and decides to enter the open tournaments, for which he still is eligible, every important golf event of the next few years will be open to the suspicion that the outcome might have been far different with Jones competing. To the millions who recognize Jones as the peer of them all, every tournament carrying a national or international title will bear the taint of Jones' absence from the competition.

Just how far-reaching the Atlantan's withdrawal from the competitive phase of the game will be, time alone will tell.

Many Belittle Jones

Conversely, there is the possibility that Big Boy, if sustained in time by the golfing public and the U.S.G.A., as is indicated, will have the effect of detracting from Jones' achievements.

If the best of the golfers of the present crop and of future generations fail to equal the records set by Jones, there will always be those who can belittle the Atlantan's feats with the observation that Jones' triumphs were the result of the smaller ball, more controllable in the wind and more effective on the greens.

The new generation of golfers can consign Jones to a former era of golf that can not be justifiably compared with the game of their day as a result of the disparity in the behavior of the ball which Jones had at his command and the bigger and lighter ball that has been decreed. Jones may still be a hero of golf legend, the best of his time, but his greatness can always be regarded with the suspicion that he might not have been able to do so well with Big Boy.

Remember Cravath

This column can go back into sports history to substantiate its theory of fallen idols. Baseball offers the most pertinent example. With the introduction of the lively baseball, the greatest batters of the dead ball era were supplanted by the Ruths, the Wilsons, the Gehrigs and the Kleins.

There is no claim that Babe Ruth can not hit a baseball farther than any ball player past or present, but the introduction of the lively ball had the effect of obscuring a really great hitter like Gavvy Cravath, of the Phillies, who was able to lead the major leagues one season with a mere twelve home runs and gain recognition as the greatest home-run hitter of his time.

Ask the baseball fan to name the best hitters of baseball. Cravath's twelve home runs with the dead ball gain him little consideration in the light of Ruth's record-breaking 60. There was chap named Buck Freeman who held the American League record of 19 before Ruth came along. He wouldn't be mentioned either in a modern list of the truly great. But he was the best of his time. But conditions are different. There ought to be a moral in that for those who swear by Bobby Jones.

JUNE 22, 1931

Did the Babe Call the Shot?

*One of the legendary moments in the history of American sports
occurred in the 1932 World Series when Babe Ruth supposedly pointed
to centerfield before hitting a home run to that very spot against the
Chicago Cubs. But did it happen?*

*The year 1932 produced another historic sight before my still apprecia-
tive eyes. It was Babe Ruth's "called shot" home run in the '32 World
Series. I was in Chicago's Wrigley Field on that day when Ruth
brought everybody out of their seats with the damnedest demonstration
you ever saw.*

*Everybody knows the story—Charlie Root was pitching for the
Cubs, the Yanks and the Cubs had been jockeying each other fiercely
all through the Series, stemming from the Yankees' resentment because
the Cubs cut their old Yankee teammate, Mark Koenig, in for less than
a full share of the World Series pie. Root throws a called strike against
Ruth, then throws what Ruth considers a quick pitch, a pitch delivered
before Ruth had sufficient time to get set. Ruth, whose temper matched
his appetite, flared up. He pointed, apparently toward centerfield, and
hit the next pitch to that exact spot where he appeared to be pointing,
the most satisfying home run probably of the seven hundred and four-
teen of his life.*

*But did he really call his shot? Baseball tradition says so, and tradi-
tion extended over a sufficient period of time tends to become regarded
as fact. The real fact is that Babe Ruth's "called shot" home run was no
called shot at all. He never did say anything like that to Charlie Root,
or to anybody else. Bill Dickey, the great Yankee catcher of those years,
was in that game. He confessed to me in later years that it didn't really
happen that way. What did happen?*

*"Ruth just got mad about that quick pitch," Dickey explained. He
was pointing at Root, not at the centerfield stands. He called him a
couple of names and said, "Don't do that to me anymore, you _____."*

"How do you know?" I asked.

"Because Ruth told us when he came back to the bench."

"How come you never told anybody?"

"All of us players could see it was a helluva good story. So we just made an agreement not to bother straightening out the facts."

They were right. It was a helluva good story. It has endured over the years, and nobody has been hurt. On the contrary, it has provided base-ball with one of its classic folk tales. It just never happened, that's all.

—Shirley Povich, from his memoir, *All These Mornings* (1969)

Senators Lose to Giants in World Series

The Washington Senators lost the 1933 World Series to the New York Giants, four games to one, in what would be the team's last appearance in the fall classic. For the next 40 years, Povich covered a losing team. But as Red Smith once said of Povich's years with the second division, "You learn baseball by covering the last place team, not the first. You learn through their mistakes and young players talk to you about them." Povich put it simply, "You learn to detach yourself—after all it's only a game. Thus, you can have some fun."

Well, now, that was a world series for you. Go back to the days of the Hitless Wonder White Sox of the 1906, the prewar triumphs of the Phillies, Braves and Red Sox, finger through the postbellum records of the Yankees, Cardinals and Athletics and you will find no series more pleasing to the eye than the world series of 1933.

Thrills, indeed, were a dime a dozen at the Polo Grounds and Griffith Stadium. And at $3.90, $5.50 and $6.00, the fans were saturated with sensations. Recall to mind those scores of the 1933 world series—4 to 2, 6 to 1, 4 to 3, in 10 innings. Thus did victory and defeat hang by a slender thread. One pitched ball, one batted ball separated the winner from the loser in four of those five games.

Giants Had What it Takes

Those Giants had what it takes, no doubt of that. And there is a measure of consolation for the Nats in the fact that they were beaten by a great ball club, making its own breaks and capitalizing on them to the fullest extent.

To Manager Bill Terry, of the Giants, no credit can be denied. To Manager Joe Cronin, only sympathy. It was a case of Terry's ball team making Terry's strategy and master-minding letter perfect by its execution. Cronin's ball team, in the language of the press box, made Cronin look bad by its futility.

The Nats, pride of the American League, the team that won the pennant by one-run victories, were met, in the world series, by a foe using the same steel. The Giants, too, were a one-run ball club, getting the breaks by making them, and they made more breaks than the Nats.

Povich admired Clark Griffith, owner of the Washington Senators (1930s)

Hubbell in Hero Role

And when, in years to come, they search the records for the hero of the 1933 world series, there will be no dispute as to his identity. Carl Hubbell will leap out at them from the pages of baseball history—the hero by popular acclaim and by the might of his deeds. No doubt, there.

No single ball player ever entered upon a world series assignment with quite the responsibility that confronted Hubbell. And no ball player ever fulfilled Terry's. There you have it—the difference between the Nats and the Giants of 1933. Washington had no Hubble.

Washington came to learn that the aura of invincibility erected about Hubbell was no myth. Behind him, he had a supposedly weak team, virtually dependent on superpitching that Hubbell could give it. And Hubbell did give the Giants of the fullest of his screwball and fast curve to inspire his mates with a sensational pitching feat in that first game, to win in 11 innings that fourth game that was the turning point of the series.

Took It on Chin

Personally, I took it on the chin. After those first two defeats of the Nats I came back for more, in my own stubborn way—and got it. Oh well, my opinions never sold for more than three cents at any corner news stand, or by carrier boy. So don't be too harsh with me.

Before the series, I was wondering what the Giants were going to use for base hits. Now I know. They used Washington's pitching for base hits. What became of Washington's great pitching? New York base hits, that's what it became. And what became of Washington's great hitting? Strikeouts, pop-ups and double plays, that's what.

So, I'm tucking my chin behind my shoulder the next time. I can take it—but it hurts.

OCTOBER 9, 1933

Jesse Owens

It was a year ago at this time that Washington Negroes couldn't see Jesse Owens in their own midst for craning their necks at Joe Louis. They were both supposed to be honored guests of the colored Elks convention here, but in the idolatry of Louis, Owens was the forgotten man of the honored-guest list.

Owens had broken three world track records in a single afternoon not so long before. Comparatively, Joe Louis' feat of knocking out Primo Carnera paled, but the trim-built Owens was content to play a distinct second fiddle to the prize fighter's popularity. Good naturedly he demurred as the crowd demanded a glimpse of Louis, beseeched the fighter for autographs, shouted his name and never thought to inquire who the well-groomed fellow in the background might be.

It struck this department at the time that the colored folks of the Capital were shamefully neglecting a man of their race who was destined for even greater fame than Louis. Here on the one hand was an illiterate young pug who had knocked out a former champion. On the other was—well, Jesse Owens.

Jesse Owens then was a young man who had not only demonstrated that he could run faster and jump farther than any other mortal, but already was a distinct credit to the race. He won you over with his neat personal appearance in striking contrast to Louis' gaudy ensembles. To talk with him was refreshing after a session with the prize fighter and his monosyllables.

If either were ever to figure in the uplift of the race, then Owens would be that man. Louis might capture the imagination of the folks who laid great store by physical prowess and the dynamite concentrated in a left hook, but Owens, an honor student at Ohio State University, seemingly fitted the time-worn description—a gentleman and a scholar.

He had the good sense, too, on that particular day of which I speak, to remain discreetly in the background. He was well aware of the fact that Louis' climb in the prize ring had been more spectacular than his own feats on the cinder path. Negroes, after all, were no great followers of track and Owens' achievements had taken place in a field not calculated to appeal to the bulk of his people who could, contrastingly, easily exult over a string of knockouts by Joe Louis.

But a year later finds their positions reversed. Jesse Owens, making Olympic history, with two titles already won with record performances and another looming today, is quite the undisputed idol of his race, or should be. Joe Louis has found fame to be both fleeting and fragile.

One well-directed right hand flung by Max Schmeling which landed on the point of Louis' jaw could and did tear down the high esteem in which his brethren held Louis, the symbol of their physical prowess. Joe Louis on the floor taking the full count was no longer an idol—just another fighter, and his people had been, perhaps, a bit too hasty in their acclaim for him.

But Jesse Owens' fame will endure. Defeat may come today, next year or in the next Olympics, but the feats that he inscribed in the record books will stand until the greatest track athlete in the history of the world, indeed, another super man, comes along to better them. But still defying parallel will probably be Owens' performance of shattering three world records on a single afternoon.

Joe Louis may yet win the heavyweight championship of the world. I think he will, sure as shootin'. And again his people will tumble over themselves in frenzied adulation. But that element which prefers to sit back and take a circumspect survey of individual contributions to the uplift of the race will be constrained to cast a mighty vote for Jesse Owens in any comparison with Joe Louis.

AUGUST 5, 1936

The Evil Olympics

The Modern Olympics began in 1896. Forty years later, they became subject to political drama and controversy. In 1936 in Berlin, U.S. runner Jesse Owens, an African-American, won four gold medals and deflated Adolf Hitler's doctrine of Aryan superiority. Although Povich was not on the scene because the Post *did not have the money to send him, his perceptions of the event and what the world would face were prescient.*

What Price Olympics Glory—America's Sports Public Demands

Nazi Prejudice Seen As Marring Events

As America's triumphant track athletes head homeward from Berlin, olive-crowned and basking in a slew of new records, a diffident voice that is beginning to boom in a rising crescendo is asking:

What price Olympic glory?

And the little group that for two years strenuously opposed American participation in the games at Berlin is beginning to find vindication.

They are the folks who refused to believe that the leopard would or could change his spots; who distrusted the Nazis when the Nazis said—as the American threat to withdraw from the games began to develop—that there would be no discrimination against non-Aryans in the Berlin Olympics.

To which echo is now flinging back a rasping "Oh yeah?"

Why, then, did Herr Hitler find it convenient to leave the royal reviewing stand when the distinctly non-Aryan Jesse Owens emerged as the winner of the 200-meter title and was being led back in the direction of Hitler's box by non-German officials?

Throughout the Olympiad, Hitler was busily receiving German winners in the weight events, Italian and Finnish champions, and saluting the Nordic Americans who happened to win. But there is no record that Herr Hitler even once took official recognition of the six championship efforts of American Negroes.

American Athletes Snubbed

America was thus collecting a daily insult in company with its daily titles. At least that was what we are constrained to believe from the dispatches from Berlin, which vied with the accounts of the competition in the telling of the snubbing of American athletes and the sour-grapes manner in which their victories were received.

The last full measure of insult to America was dealt in the Nazi press of August 5, the day following the United States team's greatest performance of the Olympiad, when four gold medals fell to the Americans.

The rap at America was as officially Nazi as a Hitler suggestion. It appeared in the newspaper owned by Dr. Paul Joseph Goebbels, Hitler's minister of public enlightenment and propaganda. And it was certainly enlightening as far as the Nazis' promise to behave is concerned.

When Jesse Owens, center, won four gold medals at the 1936 Berlin Olympics and was snubbed by Hitler, Povich posed the question, "What price glory?"

The August 5 article in *Der Angriff*, as relayed to America by the Associated Press, read:

"If America didn't have her black auxiliaries, where would she be in the Olympic games?

"If the Americans hadn't enlisted their black auxiliary forces, it would have been a poor lookout for them. For then the German, Lutz, would have won the broad jump; the Italian, Mario Lanzi the 800-meter run, and the Hollander, Martin Osendarp, the 100 meters. The world would then have described the Yankees a great Olympic disappointment.

"It must be plainly stated," the newspaper continued, "that the Americans aren't the athletic marvels we thought they were, despite Owens, Metcalfe, Woodruff and Johnson."

Thus it was that the Nazis officially greeted the greatest display of athletic ability ever to mark an Olympiad, and if it weren't for the pathetic betrayal of their pre-Olympic pledges by the Nazis their reaction would be no less than downright laughable.

Der Angriff Nazi Paper

At that there is a laugh for Americans in the very name of Dr. Goebbels' official organ—*Der Angriff*. Especially for those Americans who know the vernacular of the turf, where owners strive to name their horses for both the sire and the dam, thus seeking a combination of the names of both.

And to them, *Der Angriff* sounds very much as if it were something by Angry out of Mastiff—in other words, a mad-dog newspaper.

But the Nazi press, which sought to deify Herr Hitler throughout the Olympic games even to a greater extent than it ordinarily salaams to the No. 1 Nazi, reached even greater heights on August 8, when, according to the Associated Press:

"Gloom pervaded the German morning papers today over the event in the stadium yesterday when, in the presence of Chancellor Hitler, Germany's soccer team lost to Norway, 2–0.

"'How could it ever happen?' the sports press cries, bewildered. Germany's hopes centered on winning the gold medal in this event. With the crack Uruguay team out of competition, they figured themselves the Olympics' best bet. Norway, on the other hand, was figured as a minor contender.

"So sure was Germany of victory on the soccer field that Hitler for the first time failed to appear in the Olympic stadium proper. All German victors until now have told the German press in interviews that they think only of Der Fuehrer while competing, and outdo themselves when he's there to watch them."

The Nazi press' indignant "How could it happen?" now apparently takes rank with the equally indignant American expression: "They can't put you in jail."

It was over the protests of a strident minority that the Old Guard of the American Olympic Committee steered the United States into the Olympics and refused to heed the plea that Germany sought to use its assignment as Olympic host to further Nazi propaganda.

Opposition Was Choked Off!

But the cat was let out of the bag almost immediately after the Old Guard railroaded through the national convention of the Amateur Athletic Union the vote to participate in Berlin after a parliamentary maneuver that choked off American opposition.

Evidence that Germany was already discriminating against Jewish and Catholic candidates for the Nazi Olympic teams and that Germany was already planning to convert the Olympiad into far-flung Nazi propaganda never found its way into that A.A.U. meeting as a result of the double-dealing of the Old Guard, who had promised an hour's debate before the question of American participation was put to a vote.

Without debate, then, the decision to compete at Berlin was imposed upon the objectors and the latter soon were to have their chance to shout "foul!"

Because immediately upon American acceptance of the Germany invitation to compete, there appeared throughout Europe huge posters portraying Herr Hitler in full Nazi regalia and full Nazi stature proclaiming:

"I summon the youth of the world to the Olympics."

That, despite the fact that the Olympics are supposed to be an invitation affair with a natural anathema to the word "summons." Thus the Nazis were not long in prostituting their role as Olympic hosts.

Was it a Neutral Meeting Ground?

And there were times during the progress of the Olympics when apparently there was great doubt whether the Olympiad was a neutral meeting ground for the athletic talent of the world in fair competition or a legal holiday in celebration of the ascendancy of National Socialism.

The machine-gun practice of Hitler storm troopers in a field nearby rattled over the Olympic scene almost continually, according to the dispatches. And "Deutschland Uber Alles" took a distinct second place among the airs rendered in the Olympic Stadium as the strains of the "Horst Wessel Song," the Nazis' tribute to the No. 1 Nazi martyr, was proclaimed as the hit of the week.

With the notable exception of the American, English and French teams, the competition of most other nations violated the spirit of the Olympics by taking on a fierce political aspect. Germany's teams were competing not for the honor of the sport as much as for Nazism. Italy's forces appeared to be carrying not the banner of fair play and may the best man win, but the flag of Fascism. If there were Communists among the competitors, then it's a safe bet that they were running, jumping and lifting weights for the glory of Karl Marx.

More and more, the Olympics appear to be essentially a political undertaking as far as many nations are concerned, thus defeating the ideals in which the Olympiad was conceived. The Germans and Italians now lean heavily to the theory that sports is a patriotic duty to show off the superiority of their political systems above all others.

Olympic Ideals Lost

The Peruvian team so far lost sight of the Olympic ideals that it with-drew from the games after losing a protested soccer game to the Aus-trian team. And the people of Peru that night dignified the new political theory of the games by smashing windows in the German consulate at Lima, shouting angrily in downtown streets and tearing down an Olympic flag that was flying atop the building of a German company whose proprietor represented the German Olympic com-mittee in Peru.

But neither has America come out of the Olympics with clean hands. Participation in the games by the United States had no relation to the broad scheme of American politics, but in the lesser vale of per-sonal and petty politics the United States stands as an offender.

After enacting the promise from the Nazis that there would be no discrimination against Jewish athletes who sought to compete on Ger-man teams, the United States Olympic officials stand accused at least of practicing the same discrimination which they decried among the Nazis.

With an excellent opportunity to illustrate to the Nazis the com-plete lack of discrimination against non-Aryans on the United States team, the American track coach deliberately withheld from competi-tion the only two Jewish lads who had been taken to Berlin on the United States squad.

Marty Glickman and Sam Stoller had been appointed during the workouts in Berlin as members of the United States' 400-meter relay team. But on the appointed day of the race both were told they would not be able to compete.

American Coach Dismissed Two

Lawson Robertson, the American coach, declared that he was in great fear that the Germans or the Dutch would beat the American relay quartet in the 400. He needed his strongest team on the day. Thus, he dismissed the Jewish lads, Glickman and Stoller, and replaced them with one Foy Draper and Owens, who had already won three gold medals.

The American team won—easily, by 15 meters. Robertson's fears had been unfounded. Yet the Jewish lads, with a chance to bring home a medal, were denied the chance to run.

There may have been a reason for Robertson's decision to bench the Jewish boys. It was his duty to place his best team in competition. But Robertson's reasoning didn't jell after the 1,600-meter relay. The United States team was beaten by 12 yards in that race and his two outstanding men for that—Archie Williams and Jimmy LuValle—weren't entered in the race by Robertson.

It was only another sour note in an Olympics that had a lot of curdling aspects.

AUGUST 16, 1936

A Kid Named Feller

If there is any secret to the amazing speed with which Bob Feller turns a baseball loose, then young Feller doesn't know it.

Baseball's new pitching sensation who arrived in Washington yesterday with the Cleveland Indians to find himself something of a curio, broke down and confessed that he couldn't explain his 15 strikeouts against the Browns last Sunday.

"I just reared back and let it go," said the 17-year-old Feller after obliging newsreel men and still cameramen in a half hour demonstration of his pitching form.

The beardless youth who in his first start in the big leagues struck out as many batters as Walter Johnson was ever able to strike out in the prime of his 29-year pitching career, is just a bit bewildered by his sudden fame.

And well he might be. Six weeks ago he was a candy butcher in the grandstands of the Cleveland park, daring not to hope that some day he'd wear a big league uniform. He had pitched a little, had been pitching for three years, in fact, with various sandlot teams in Iowa and Cleveland, but organized baseball was another world to him.

Out in Meter, Iowa, he used to play pitch and catch with his dad, a former semipro player, and when he got a chance to play with a kid team he started as a shortstop. But first basemen used to complain about the way he hammered the ball across the diamond into their mitts and to keep peace on the team he turned pitcher.

He was a pretty good pitcher, too, good enough to pitch his team into the national semipro tournament last season at Dayton, Ohio, where he struck out 18 in a night game and gained the attention of C.C. Slapnicka, Cleveland Scout. Cleveland signed him to one of their New Orleans farm contracts, brought him to the Cleveland lots, and gave him a job selling peanuts and candy during this summer.

As part of the show during an exhibition game with the Cardinals last July 7, they called him out of the stands, gave him a uniform and let him pitch for three innings. You know what happened—how he struck out eight Cardinals in those three innings and found his name in screaming headlines.

Even then Cleveland club officials did not permit themselves to elate too much. In fact, Feller wasn't even invited to take the Eastern trip with the team the next day. Then changing his mind a week later, Manager Steve O'Neill sent for the lad.

He found his way into his first regular ball game at Griffith Stadium a few days later when he went in with the bases full, hit one batter to force a run across and then escaped with only one-run damage by striking out Buddy Lewis and making Joe Kuhel pop up.

He had pitched a couple of other relief shifts before O'Neill consented to start him at Cleveland against the Browns last Sunday. But there was no intimation that he would even win his game, to say nothing of bettering the season's strikeout mark of 12, held by Buck Newsom, by three strikeouts.

But things began to happen immediately. St. Louis hitters moved up and away from the plate with great regularity, swinging and missing

third strikes. He struck out at least one hitter in every inning but t̄
eighth. Twice he retired the side on strikeouts. By the end of the sev̄
enth inning he had struck out 14, an average of two per inning.

They weren't standing there taking called strikes, either. Umpire
Harry Geisel, who worked the game behind the plate, reported here
yesterday that only two of Feller's 15 strikeouts were called third-
strikes.

And Feller was working, too, with a rookie catcher as his battery-
mate. Behind the bat was young Charley George who was catching
the second game of his life in the big leagues.

The consistency with which young Feller was striking 'em out
finally began to wear on the nerves of the Browns. Anyway, in the
ninth, when Ed Coleman was sent in to pinch hit for St. Louis, he
approached the plate warily.

"I s-ss-say, H-h-harry," Coleman stammered to Geisel, "is-ss he r-re-
al-l-ly f-f-fast?"

Geisel agreed the young Feller was fast and after the game he
ended all dispute about the lively ball.

"I saw the lively ball that day," said Geisel. "I never saw a ball come
up to the plate any more lively than those balls that kid was chucking
up there."

He's got control, too, apparently. Last month at Cleveland when
the Yankees and Indians staged a pre-game field day, they set up a
small hoop at which pitchers of both teams aimed in an exhibition of
control. In five throws young Feller threw five bull's-eyes. The nearest
any other pitcher came to that record was three bull's-eyes by Mel
Harder.

AUGUST 26, 1936

The Washington Redskins

*The arrival of George Preston Marshall's Redskins from Boston in 1937
began an ongoing obsession Washington still has for its National Foot-*

ball League team. From Sammy Baugh to Sonny Jurgensen, Bobby Mitchell to Art Monk, the team has had its share of stars—and its Hall of Fame coaches, including Ray Flaherty, Vince Lombardi, George Allen, and Joe Gibbs. The Redskins also won the National Football League title their first season, which Povich describes here.

Baugh Stars As Redskins Annex Title

Wrigley Field, Chicago, Dec. 12—In a wild, frenzied battle for points on the frozen turf of Wrigley Field, the deft arm of Slingin' Sammy Baugh prevailed today and Washington's Redskins emerged as the champions of the National Football League.

From the stabbing efforts of Baugh's rapier-like heaves, the big bruising Chicago Bears, champions of the west, reeled and stumbled and finally yielded to the Redskins 28 to 21. It was a triumph of Baugh over brawn, of East over West.

Huddled in the stands Spartan like, in the sub-freezing temperature that hovered around 20 degrees, were 15,878 football fans who had heard tell of Baugh and the Redskins and saw for themselves today. It was a disappointingly small crowd, but it was a lot of football that they witnessed.

At the end of the half, the game belonged to the Bears by a score of 14 to 7, with the Redskins seemingly in rout as Nagurski and Manders and Nolting and Masterson poured through the Washington line and bulled their way into the lead.

And then, in the third quarter, Sammy Baugh began to strike. Once, twice, three times he uncoiled the deadliest of all throwing arms and each time he found a receiver for touchdown passes. Into that third period Baugh and the Redskins packed a 21-point up-rising, dashing away with the ball game as a gang of bewildered Bears had no reply.

It was a mob of infuriated Bears that gave ground before Baugh and late in the fourth quarter, when tempers were short and the title was slipping from the paws of the Bears, fighting broke out.

In a wild melee of fist slinging that look place beyond the sidelines near the Washington bench, Baugh was the central figure off the field even as he was on the field, for it was a punch aimed at Baugh by 210-pound 6-foot–3 Dick Plasman, big bad Bear end, who played his college football at Vanderbilt, that set off the flare-up of open fist slinging that had been taking place surreptitiously in the scrimmages throughout the game.

Baugh had run Plasman out of bounds after the latter had caught a pass, and it was within 5 feet of the Redskins bench that the Bear end lashed out at Baugh. Then Baugh punched back and Redskins reserves leaped to their feet rushing to Baugh's aid.

From across the field came both Redskins and Bears and for a half minute it was a free-for-all, but game officials restored order. No penalties were given but Plasman, when he went back to the playing field, was dripping blood from the nose and limping noticeably.

It was a rough bruising ball game from the outset with both teams slipping and skidding on the hard ridged, frost-coated turf despite the fact they were shod with rubber-soled basketball shoes.

Baugh Passes to Tie

As late as the third period, after the Redskins had tied the score at 14–14, the Bears were in command with a 21–14 lead. Then it was with a pass to Wayne Millner, Sammy Baugh fetched the tying touchdown and 5 minutes later won the ball game with a pass to Ed Justice.

Thus Washington, which had waited 24 years for its first baseball pennant, won its first big league football championship in its maiden year in the National League. For Redskins heroes aside from Baugh were plentiful today.

There was Cliff Battles, who drove to that first Redskin touchdown and there was Ed Justice who caught the pass and dashed across the goal for the winning score. There was Riley Smith, the public accountant from Alabama, who gave a public accounting of his place-kicking skill by sending a placement through the post after each Redskin touchdown. And there was also bushy-handed Wayne Millner.

If Baugh had even a close rival for honors, it was Millner, over shadowed all season by his colleague at the other end Charlie Malone, but today Miller was transcendent—a sure-handed, light-footed messenger of grief for the Bears.

Millner Sprints Over the Line

When the Redskins needed a touchdown to wipe out that 14–7 lead of the Bears in the third quarter, it was Millner who plucked a Baugh pass out of the nippy air and galloped 35 yards in a breath-taking sprint to a touchdown on a play that, over all, ate up 55 yards.

And when a few minutes later the Redskins needed another touchdown to tie the Bears, it was Millner again who leaped into the air at midfield snatched another pass from Baugh and legged it 50 yards to that important touchdown.

It was quite a going over that the Redskins gave the Bears statistically. Fifteen first downs they amassed to the Bears 11, and 464 yards they gained to the Bears' 348. Despite the ground-eating charges of Nagurski and Manders and Nolting, it was Cliff Battles who led both teams in yards gained from rushing with a total of 77.

It was a cool 500 that Sammy Baugh batted with his passes today, completing 17 of 34 he heaved for a total of 352 yards, more yardage than the Bears could make either running or passing. Amid the ohs and ahs of the 15,878 in the stands he was flipping long ones and short ones and shovel passes and flat ones and finding a receiver for half of his efforts.

Eight minutes after the opening kick-off, Washington had a touchdown—the fruits of a 53-yard uninterrupted march, Baugh completing three passes en route with the ball on the Bears 7-yard line. Baugh handed the center's snap to Battles on a reverse play and Battles dashed around the short side of the line untouched. He literally dove across the goal. It was the much-publicized "short-side" play of the Redskins that had shaken Battles loose for 76 yards against the Giants the week before.

Three minutes later the Bears had tied the score. Striking back with all the fury that their big backs and beefy line could muster, the Bears stomped 80 yards to a touchdown. A 60-yard pass play from Masterson to Manske put the ball on the Redskins 19 and the Bears required only two plays to put it over. Nagurski charged 9 yards around left end and Manders literally waded through a hole at center for 10 yards and the touchdown.

Irwin Makes First Down

Now the Bears were rampant. Getting possession of the ball again at midfield, they produced a touchdown in four plays. Manders taking a pass from Masterson and racing 25 yards across the goal with the help of Wilson's block of Battles who claimed he was clipped from behind on the play. With the Bears' reserves back in the game the second quarter produced no score.

But almost immediately after the start of the second half, with the Bears regulars in action, Sammy Baugh touched off the Redskins counter-charge.

After Don Irwin had made a first down on the Bears 45, Millner dropped a pass from Baugh, but on the next play he cut sharply across from the opposite end of the field, took a pass that Baugh virtually hung on a peg, and in a race with Masterson, scored on a 35-yard run. Reliable Riley Smith added the extra point to tie the game at 14 to 14.

It seemed for naught however, when the Bears climaxed a 77-yard drive down the field with a touchdown scored on a pass from Masterson to Manske across the goal line that sent Chicago into a 21-to–14 lead.

But the Redskins had an almost immediate reply. Fading back from his own 22-yard line, Baugh fired a 40-yard pass to Millner, who took the ball on the dead run exactly in midfield, found himself virtually free and led Nagurski and Manders a 50-yard chase across the goal line once more. Riley Smith tied the score with a place kick for the extra point.

But that wild third quarter, which had already produced 21 points, was to produce 7 more, and it was the Redskins who authored that final and decisive touchdown. After stopping a Bear drive that ended with a punt to a touchback, the Redskins charged back. The touchdown play like their first scoring play of the afternoon was a repetition of a play that had scored against the Giants.

Ed Justice, who until that point had taken no part in the pass catching, drifted down field while Baugh faked a short pass to Malone and then heaved a long spiral that Justice gathered in on the 11-yard line. From that point it was a romp for justice.

And that is the story of the Redskins and what they did today.

DECEMBER 13, 1937

Louis–Schmeling

Povich could not cover the second Joe Louis–Max Schmeling fight in New York in 1938 because he was on the road with the Senators. But he wrote about the fight beforehand, believing Louis would win. Louis did, too, in the first round.

Five dollars will get you eight if you think Max Schmeling will reclaim the heavyweight championship of the world on the evening of June 22 when he climbs into the Yankee Stadium battle pit against Joe Louis.

Those are the most recent odds on the title battle posted by Broadway betting commissioners and if they are proved to be false odds, they are at least interesting. They are interesting because the fellow who was beaten into a sorry-looking pulp and knocked out in the twelfth round is now the favorite to beat his conqueror.

If you're asking why, we don't know. We don't know what particular elements could effect the odds to the extent that Louis is a pronounced favorite. But it's simple to guess why Schmeling is not a heavy favorite in the betting, and you've probably beaten us to the conclusion. It's Schmeling's age, of course.

Joe 9 Years Younger

Schmeling is 33 now, fighting a fellow who is 9 years younger. There was the same disparity in their ages two years ago this month when they last battled for the title, but two years added to a fighter of 31 are far more significant than the same space of time added to the age of a lad of 22. Guys in their thirties don't wear their age as easily or as becomingly.

The odds against Schmeling rocketed for that very reason after the Barney Ross–Henry Armstrong affair. There was no doubt that advancing years as much as Armstrong's busy fists beat Ross. That fact brought Schmeling supporters up sharply. After all, the fellow is no longer a young man. He's 33. Ross, you remember, was only 29, yet he had slowed up amazingly.

The 8-to-5 odds on Louis are still startling, however, despite Schmeling's advancing years. There was certainly nothing flukey about the manner in which the German cut Louis down in 1936. It was a well-planned, methodical fight in which he found the Negro's weakness, played on it, stunned him, cut him up, then knocked him out.

After that fight, there was no doubt that the better man had won. To those fight folks who had long been shouting that the first good man who would stand up to Louis and fight him would win, Schmeling was complete vindication. He exposed the lad as a young fellow who had been brought along too fast, perhaps, who hadn't learned how to protect himself from the most elemental punch in the game—the right to the chin.

It's Instinctive

"The fellow who doesn't know how to keep from getting hit with a right to the jaw rarely learns. It's instinctive." That was the jubilant shout of the Joe Louis detractors after the Schmeling affair.

And the Schmeling supporters are disposed to shout down also the possibility that the German may have slowed up appreciably during the two intervening years since he last fought the Negro. He has taken care of himself, they say. And they may have something there, for Schmeling's training and conditioning has been something of a religion with him. If any fighter can beat off the challenge of advancing years, it appears to be the German.

In his two tune-up fights for the Louis affair, Schmeling has shown the same superb conditioning he brought into the ring last June. He knocked out Harry Thomas in nine rounds and Steve Dudas in five. In both of those battles he was the same mechanical annihilator, biding his time until he chose to throw his right and watch 'em drop.

Has Schmeling Rusted?

But after the first flush of surprise and disappointment following Louis' debacle against the German, the Negro's followers were able to find a deal of solace in Louis' exhibition.

He was an easy mark for a right hand, that was true enough, but he was facing the sharpest shooting right hand in the business. To what degree that right hand has rusted none can tell. But for those who still like the Negro's chances of beating Schmeling there is this in his favor: There is no longer any doubt of Louis' ability to take it. He was knocked out, it was true, but for nine rounds after he was dazed by Schmeling's first crushing right he stayed upright, absorbing one of the worst fusillades of punches since Dempsey cannonaded Willard into defeat at Toledo in 1919.

That's what the betting folks like about Louis. That and his youth.

JUNE 11, 1938

Match Race of the Century

No horse race in the history of thoroughbred racing has ever captured the imagination of the country like the 1938 match between Seabiscuit and War Admiral at Baltimore's Pimlico Race Track. The race, described so eloquently by Laura Hillenbrand in her best-selling book, Seabiscuit: An American Legend—*later turned into a movie—was won by the Biscuit. Hillenbrand quotes from Povich's scene-setter in her book. On the day of the race, Povich left the writing of the lead story to the* Post's *racing writer, Walter Haight. He would never upstage one of his own reporters.*

40,000 Jam Pimlico for "Big Race"

Baltimore, Nov. 1—Horsedom's Mecca for the day, Old Pimlico, fairly creaked and bulged with 40,000 devotees in deep salaam to the race of the year. It was War Admiral vs. Seabiscuit, the prospect of 90-odd seconds of head-to-head racing by the most esteemed horseflesh in the land that produced the record event.

Judy O'Grady and the Governor's Lad—thousands of 'em—were there among the throngs that jam-packed the grandstands and the clubhouse, over-ran the lawns, snuggled against the rails and flooded into the infield.

Dripping with swank was the clubhouse where the Brahmins of the turf held forth in sables and silks, in tweeds and hard hats, lifting lorgnettes and sporting field glasses. And Milady who was ahead of the vogue actually blossomed in purple lipstick. Honest.

"Citadel of High Society"

Beyond the high fences that separated clubhouse from grandstand were the bulk of the milling thousands, the folks who could produce cash, perhaps, but no pedigrees. For the Pimlico clubhouse long has been the Citadel of High Society and woe in the wistful who cannot show a clubhouse badge.

The weather man, a kindly soul today, played ball with young Alfred Gwynn Vanderbilt, whose magic name had produced, finally, the War Admiral vs. Seabiscuit affair. The cool autumn air, sunlit and minus a chill, was the perfect recipe for a racing day. Vanderbilt, who had brought all the pressure of his social and financial prestige to bear in arranging for Pimlico the thrice-postponed meeting of the Admiral and the Biscuit, looked out on a scene that was epochal in racing.

Across the rich brown loam of the track, curried and manicured for days in preparation for this race, special betting booths had been set up in the infield to accommodate the overflow thousands. Long before post time the record for Pimlico crowds had fallen.

Who Do You Like?

As early as 11 o'clock the assault on the gates began as incoming trains dumped their cargoes into Baltimore's rickety stations and choked roads finally disgorged the motorists hard by the track gates. Five races were to precede the feature, but the babble was only of War Admiral and Seabiscuit and "Who do you like?"

It was a gay throng as post time neared for the big race. Gay, perhaps, because four of the five favorites in the early races had galloped home and rewarded the great bulk of the bettors. But actually it was the gayety of immense anticipations — the anticipation of seeing, finally, if War Admiral could run away from Seabiscuit.

This time, there was no possibility that the race would not eventuate. At 8:30 o'clock in the morning, Spencer Jarvis, chairman of the Maryland Racing Commission, had examined the track and said, simply, "The race is on." He was the final judge, by agreement of owners Riddle and Howard.

Admiral Appears First

At 3:35 P.M., a concerted shout was heard among the customers who had found standing room at the stretch turn and it rolled on toward the grandstands and clubhouse in a succession of outbreaks of applause. It was War Admiral making his way down the middle of the track from the Riddle stables, en route to the paddock, for the saddling.

Like something out of "The Birth of the Nation" and looking for all the world like a Ku Kluxer horse, War Admiral was attired in a white blanket and white hood as he stepped jauntily along behind his lead pony. The oh's and ah's reached a voluminous crescendo as the little son of Man o' War passed the closely-packed stands. The folks were standing in tribute. Two minutes later, the sentries at the stretch turn unloosed another roar. It was Seabiscuit heading paddock-ward from the Howard barn. And this time the applause was greater. There was no doubt that the hard-used Seabiscuit, a self-made horse as it were, was the sentimental if not the betting favorite.

The Biscuit was blanketed like something out of a circus, gaily caparisoned in the flaming red of the Howard stable, with the triangular CHS monogram in bold relief in its whiteness against the red. Continuous were the cheers as the Biscuit headed down track and finally disappeared into the paddock gate.

Admiral Heavy Favorite

And then the odds board, flashing the trend of the early betting, showed the first figures: "War Admiral, 1–2; Seabiscuit, 7 to 5." But there was a gasp, three minutes later, when War Admiral was flashed at 1 to 5 and Seabiscuit zoomed to 5 to 2.

As if the result were a foregone conclusion, the bettors had flocked to War Admiral, the "smart money" as well as the two-dollar driblets of the not-so-well heeled customers. But to some, Seabiscuit at 5 to 2 appeared attractive, and the next odds showed War Admiral only 1 to 4 while the Biscuit dropped to 2–1.

Povich set the scene of the epochal race between Seabiscuit (in the lead) and War Admiral at Pimlico. Seabiscuit won by three lengths. (1938)

A hush fell over the scene as Happy Gordon, perennial lead rider of Maryland's tracks, nosed out of the paddock gate in the van of a young parade. It was, finally, Seabiscuit and the Admiral on the track. Nose to tail and tail to nose, they proceeded postward.

Betting windows were glutted and the indecisive who had delayed too long could not get down a wager at the new odds of 1 to 4 on the Admiral and 2 to 1 on the Biscuit. Friendly wagering swept the stands as neighbor bet with neighbor according to his choice and inclination. Thousands of dollars in wagers never reached the mutuel machines.

Jaunty of step, regal of bearing, War Admiral moved friskily behind the lead rider, the picture of prize horseflesh. And in striking contrast was the parade of Seabiscuit. The Biscuit, head hung, lazy of motion, was showing complete, overwhelming and colossal indifference. The scene that met the eye then was not reassuring to the backers of the Biscuit.

But suddenly, in a terrific upset of the dope, Seabiscuit, the calm, well-mannered, bolted into a run a sixteenth from the starting point at the head of the stretch and carried Jockey George Woolf a full half mile in a canter around the track. It was a strange development, because War Admiral was supposed to be the bad actor in this two-horse race. But the Admiral was moving along as nicely as you please while his suddenly temperamental opposition was making a display.

One False Start

From his starter's platform, George Cassidy waited for Woolf to bring the Biscuit into line for a walk-up start, a throw-back to the olden days of racing. But with the pair seemingly in alignment, Seabiscuit reared suddenly and they were off to a false start, galloping 20 lengths before the red flag fell and sent them back to Cassidy.

But the second time there was no false start. They were off as one, War Admiral and Seabiscuit. The Biscuit and the Admiral were under way, finally, in the race that racing fans had demanded.

Would they give the fans a race that would be a supercharged scene? They would, that was soon apparent as both jocks hauled out whips in an effort to gain an early advantage. They would provide a race entirely fitting for this day of days in turfdom. That was apparent, too, when on the back stretch they presented an unforgettable picture as if horse had been superimposed on horse, swinging into unison and straining for precious inches.

NOVEMBER 2, 1938

The Negro Leagues

It was 1939, eight years before Jackie Robinson would play for the Brooklyn Dodgers and integrate Major League Baseball. One spring evening, Povich and his friend, former Senators' pitcher Walter Johnson, took in

a Negro League game between the Homestead Grays and Newark
Eagles at the Senators' training field in Orlando. Povich reported how
well they played and shared his belief that these ball players were not
being treated fairly. He would share these opinions with Post *readers for*
the next 60 years.

Orlando, April 6—There's a couple of million dollars worth of baseball talent on the loose, ready for the big leagues yet unsigned by any
major league clubs. There are pitchers who would win 20 games this
season for any big league club that offered them contracts, and there
are outfielders who could hit .350, infielders who could win quick
recognition as stars, and there is at least one catcher who at this writing is probably superior to Bill Dickey.

Only one thing is keeping them out of the big leagues—the pigmentation of their skin. They happen to be colored. That's their crime
in the eyes of big league club owners.

Their talents are being wasted in the rickety parks in the Negro
sections of Pittsburgh, Philadelphia, New York, Chicago and four
other cities that comprise the major league of Negro baseball. They
haven't got a chance to get into the big leagues of the white folks. It's a
tight little boycott that the majors have set up against colored players.

It's a sort of gentlemen's agreement among the club owners that is
keeping Negroes out of big league baseball. There's nothing in the
rules that forbids a club from signing a colored player. It's not down in
black and white, so to speak. But it's definitely understood that no
team will attempt to sign a colored player. And, in fact, no club could
do that, because the elasticity of Judge Landis' authority would forbid
it. And the judge can rule out of baseball any character whose presence he may deem "detrimental" to the game.

Just how a colored player would be detrimental to the game has
never been fully explained, but that seems to be the light in which they
are regarded by the baseball brass hats. Perhaps it is because there is
such an overwhelming majority of Southern boys in big league baseball who would not take kindly to the presence of colored athletes and
would flash a menacing spike, or so. Perhaps it's because baseball has

done well enough without colored players. It's a smug, conservative business not given to very great enterprise and the introduction of new and novel features.

There have been campaigns aimed at smashing the boycott. One New York newspaper openly advocated the signing of Negro players, and Heywood Broun has often berated the baseball magnates for drawing the color line. But despite the presence of thousands of colored customers in the stands, the club owners have blithely hewed to the color line. They are content, seemingly, to leave well enough alone and make no concerted play for Negro patronage.

A $200,000 Catcher

But in its restricted localities, Negro baseball has flowered. There are Negro teams which now might do very well in big league competition even if they played as a Negro entity. The Homesteads of Pittsburgh are probably the best colored team. They train in Florida each spring, even as do the American and National League teams. The other evening at Tinker Field, the Homesteads met the Newark Eagles of the same colored league. Curious Washington players flocked to the game and went away with deep respect for colored baseball.

Walter Johnson sat in a box at the game, profoundly impressed with the talents of the colored players. "There," he said, "is a catcher that any big league club would like to buy for $200,000. His name is Gibson. They call him 'Hoot' Gibson, and he can do everything. He hits that ball a mile. And he catches so easy he might just as well be in a rocking chair. Throws like a rifle. Bill Dickey isn't as good a catcher. Too bad this Gibson is a colored fellow."

That was the general impression among the Nats who saw the game. They liked the Homestead catcher, and they liked the big, lanky Negro pitcher for the Homesteads who struck out 12 Newark players in five innings. They liked the centerfielder who can go a country mile for the ball, and they liked the shortstop, who came up with fancy, one-handed plays all night. They had to like 'em. They were swell ball players.

Until last season there was a colored pitcher around named "Satchel" Paige. The colored folks have a penchant for picturesque names for their idols and "Satchel Paige" was so-called because of the size of his feet. He was 6 feet 3, a left hander and a whale of a pitcher. "He retired last year at the age of 44," said Jimmy Wasdell, "and he was still a great pitcher. I've been on clubs that barnstormed against Negro teams and in a dozen games against this Paige we never beat him. He beat Paul and Dizzy Dean one night, 1–0, and we only got one hit off him. I was the only minor leaguer on our club."

Johnson Was Mistaken

Negro baseball is now a flourishing game, but as long as 30 years ago, the colored folks had their swell ball teams. Walter Johnson on a barnstroming trip in 1909 went to Harlem to pitch for a colored team against the Lincoln Giants.

"I didn't know it was to be a colored team," Johnson was saying, "but they were paying me $600 for the day's work and that was big money. I went up there with my catcher, Gabby Street. Gabby was from Huntsville, Ala., and he didn't like the idea of playing colored baseball, but that $300 he got was too much to overlook.

"It was the only time in my life that I was 2-to-1 to lose. Those were the odds they were offering against me. I'll never forget the first hitter I faced. He was an outfielder they called Home Run Johnson. Up at the plate he says to me, 'Come on, Mr. Johnson, throw that fast one in here and I'll knock it over the fence.' That's what he did, too. But that was the only run they got off me and I won the game, 2–1.

"I didn't like the way this Home Run Johnson was crowing about his hit, so the next few times up there I buzzed a couple close to his head just to scare him. He was hitting the dirt all day. Then in the last inning he didn't even wait for me to cut loose. He ducked before I let the ball go. Then he got up off the ground to see what had hap-

pened and struck his head in the way of a slow curve I had just cut
loose."

APRIL 7, 1939

Gehrig's Farewell

*Few moments in the history of sport can match the 1939 tribute the Yan-
kees gave their star first baseman Lou Gehrig, who was suffering from
amyotrophic lateral sclerosis (the disease that would later be named for
him). Sitting in the press box, Povich tapped out one of his most powerful and poignant leads.*

Iron Horse "Breaks" As Athletic
Greats Meet in His Honor

New York, July 4—I saw strong men weep this afternoon, expression-
less umpires swallow hard, and emotion pump the hearts and glaze
the eyes of 61,000 baseball fans in Yankee Stadium. Yes, and hard-
boiled news photographers clicked their shutters with fingers that
trembled a bit.

It was Lou Gehrig Day at the stadium, and the first 100 years of
baseball saw nothing quite like it. It was Lou Gehrig, tributes, honors,
gifts heaped upon him, getting an overabundance of the thing he
wanted least—sympathy. But it wasn't maudlin. His friends were just
letting their hair down in their earnestness to pay him honor. And they
stopped just short of a good, mass cry.

They had Lou out there at home plate between games of the
double-header, with the 60,000 massed in the triple tiers that

rimmed the field, microphones and cameras trained on him, and he couldn't take it that way. Tears streamed down his face, circuiting the most famous pair of dimples in baseball, and he looked chiefly at the ground.

Seventy-year-old Ed Barrow, president of the Yankees, who had said to newspapermen, "Boys, I have bad news for you," when Gehrig's ailment was diagnosed as infantile paralysis two weeks ago, stepped out of the background halfway through the presentation ceremonies, draped his arm across Gehrig's shoulder. But he was doing more than that. He was holding Gehrig up, for big Lou needed support.

Ruth, Meusel, Hoyt, Pennock

As he leaned on Barrow, Gehrig said: "Thanks, Ed." He bit his lip hard, was grateful for the supporting arm, as the Yankees of 1927 stepped to the microphone after being introduced. Babe Ruth, Bob Meusel, Waite Hoyt, Herb Pennock, Benny Bengough, Bob Shawkey, Mark Koenig, Tony Lazzeri, all of the class of '27 were there. And Gehrig had been one of them, too. He had been the only one among them to bestride both eras.

Still leaning on Barrow, Gehrig acknowledged gifts from his Yankee mates, from the Yankee Stadium ground crew, and the hot dog butchers, from fans as far as Denver, and from his New York rivals, the Giants. There was a smile through his tears, but he wasn't up to words. He could only shake the hands of the small army of officials who made the presentations.

He stood there twisting his doffed baseball cap into a braid in his fingers as Manager Joe McCarthy followed Mayor La Guardia and Postmaster General Farley in tribute to "the finest example of ball player, sportsman and citizen that baseball has ever known," but Joe McCarthy couldn't take it that way, either. The man who has driven the highest-salaried prima donnas of baseball into action, who has baited a thousand umpires, broke down.

"I saw strong men weep," wrote Povich when Lou Gehrig, stricken with the disease that later would be named for him, was honored by the Yankees. (July 4, 1939)

"You Were Never a Hindrance"

McCarthy openly sobbed as he stood in front of the microphone and said, "Lou, what else can I say except that it was a sad day in the life of everybody who knew you when you came to my hotel room that day in Detroit and told me you were quitting as a ball player because you felt yourself a hindrance to the team. My God, man, you were never that."

And as if to emphasize the esteem in which he held Gehrig though his usefulness to the Yankees as a player was ended, McCarthy, too, stepped out of the fringe full into the circle where Gehrig and Barrow stood and half embraced the big fellow.

Now it was Gehrig's turn to talk into the microphone, to acknowledge his gifts. The 60,000 at intervals had set up the shout, "We want Lou!" even as they used to shout, "We want Ruth"—yells that they reserved for the only two men at Yankee Stadium for which the crowd ever organized a cheering section.

But Master of Ceremonies Sid Mercer was anticipating Gehrig. He saw the big fellow choked up. Infinitesimally Gehrig shook his head, and Mercer announced: "I shall not ask Lou Gehrig to make a speech. I do not believe that I should."

Then Lou Made a Speech

They started to haul away the microphones. Gehrig half turned toward the dugout, with the ceremonies apparently at an end. And then he wheeled suddenly, strode back to the loud-speaking apparatus, held up his hand for attention, gulped, managed a smile and then spoke.

"For weeks," said Gehrig, "I have been reading in the newspapers that I am a fellow who got a tough break. I don't believe it. I have been a lucky guy. For 16 years, into every ball park in which I have ever walked, I received nothing but kindness and encouragement. Mine has been a full life."

He went on, fidgeting with his cap, pawing the ground with his spikes as he spoke, choking back emotions that threatened to silence him, summoning courage from somewhere. He thanked everybody. He didn't forget the ball park help; he told of his gratitude to newspapermen who had publicized him. He didn't forget the late Miller Huggins, or his six years with him; or Manager Joe McCarthy, or the late Col. Ruppert, or Babe Ruth, or "my roommate, Bill Dickey."

And he thanked the Giants—"The fellows from across the river, who we would give our right arm to beat"—he was more at ease in front of the mike now, and he had a word for Mrs. Gehrig and for the immigrant father and mother who had made his education, his career, possible. And he denied again that he had been the victim of a bad break in life. He said, "I've lots to live for, honest."

And thousands cheered.

JULY 5, 1939

THE FORTIES

THE DECADE BEGAN WITH CLOUDS OF WAR IN EUROPE AND sunshine in America. In 1941, baseball fans were transfixed on two treats: Joe DiMaggio setting the record-breaking 56-game hitting streak and Ted Williams hitting over .400, the last Major League player to do so. It all changed on December 7, 1941. That day, in Griffith Stadium, the public address announcer at the Redskins–Eagles game began urgently summoning military and government officials to report to work. Povich's column captured the eerie sense of dread that dawned on the 27,102 fans. The sun had retreated.

During the war, most of the top professional athletes, including Williams, DiMaggio, Joe Louis, and Hank Greenberg went into service. While President Roosevelt declared baseball an acceptable wartime function—and encouraged more night games so that defense workers could attend—more players from the major and minor leagues were drafted or enlisted than throughout World War I. Povich wanted to cover the war but the *Post* editors would not let him go. So he conceived and promoted a charity game with the Washington Senators that raised $2,125,375, the second largest athletic gate in history after the Dempsey–Tunney fight.

Povich, married with three children, was nearly 40 in November of 1945 when he finally got his long-awaited wish to become a war correspondent for the *Post*. He was sent to the Pacific where he filed a number of front-page stories before a painful back injury, resulting from bumpy airplane rides and an overturned half-track, prompted his return home that summer. In Okinawa, he ran into Ernie Pyle, an old newspaper pal, and shared some of Pyle's last hours with him. Pyle had invited Povich to go with him to Ie Shima, one of the unknown islands involved in the campaign. Povich was about to accept when the ship's doctor told him he had two fractured vertebrae and couldn't go. It was there, on Ie Shima, on April 18, 1945, that Ernie Pyle was killed by a Japanese sniper.

When the war ended in August 1945, the country was ready to resume its love affair with sports. DiMaggio, Williams, Greenberg, and all the others came back to the playing fields; Joe Louis climbed back into the ring, not quite the fighter he once was; Ben Hogan, Sam Snead, and Nelson Byron made headlines on the golf courses; and horse racing boomed. But the biggest sports story of the decade took place in 1947, when Jackie Robinson of the Brooklyn Dodgers became the first African-American to play baseball in the major leagues in the modern era.

And Povich was out front. One of the few white sportswriters who had been campaigning for baseball integration since the 1930s, his heart and his typewriter warmed to the moment.

Veteran black sportswriter Sam Lacy, who spent most of his career at the Baltimore Afro-American, talked about Povich before he died in 2003 at the age of 100. "In the thirties and forties," he recalled, "when the push was on to integrate Major League Baseball, Shirley Povich was one of those who supported me when Jackie Robinson was trying to get into the game." He also remembered that, "In 1942, at a fight at Griffith Stadium, I had a press ticket but no seat. Shirley had a seat down in about the third row of the press section. He said, 'What are you doing standing here, Sam?' I said, 'They don't have a seat for me.' He said, 'Come on down here, I have one next to me.' That was the beginning of press seat integration. When somebody like Shirley would support you, all of them started to accept you."

The Redskins' Longest Day

The famous 73–0 rout of the Redskins in 1940 underscored Povich's compassion as a sportswriter. Never piling on in defeat nor gloating over victory, he was always generous to the players.

If you're wanting to know what happened to the Redskins yesterday, maybe this will explain it: The Bears happened to 'em.

The Redskins' 73–0 defeat by a team that they had licked a month ago doesn't add up. But there it was. It reminds us of our first breathless visit to the Grand Canyon. All we could say is: "There she is, and ain't she a beaut." When they hung up that final score at Griffith Stadium yesterday, all we could utter was: "There it is and wasn't it awful."

We're going to win one title right here—the championship for understatement—by saying that the Redskins didn't play good football yesterday. But somehow, we can't get mad at the Redskins. It was an agonizing experience for those poor fellows who probably are more angry at themselves than you or us could ever be toward them.

We saw Redskins in tears after the ball game. Some of these elder players weren't sorry for themselves. They were ashamed of the way they let their Washington fans down. They were the fellows who lived through those lean days at Boston where they were playing under sufferance and who couldn't quite get over the friendliness and the warmth of Washington fans who tried to make big heroes of them.

We can't put in with the folks who say that the Redskins loafed and took it on the lam. They played a lot of bad football, and they were a picture of complete demoralization, but they were trying to play football, if blindly. The Bears, incidentally, are no gentle playmates.

That 73–0 score, of course, is no true comparison of the two teams. The Bears on their great day caught the Redskins on a horrible one. The Redskins, forced to gamble after they were two touchdowns behind in the first five minutes, profaned their game, and the avalanche of Bear touchdowns that followed came easy. The Bears were pouring it on a team that didn't need one or two touchdowns. The Redskins needed four by the end of the first half.

We're paying no attention to the latest telephone query from some gagster who remembers those eight passes the Bears intercepted and wants to know how far behind the line a Redskin back must stand this year before he can throw a pass to a Bear. This is no time for cracks, men, those poor fellows were suffering.

We'll never think that the Redskins could have won that ball game in the light of what happened, because the Bears—well, no team living, or deceased for that matter, could have beaten 'em yesterday. But the Redskins might have made a battle of it if the receiver had held onto that pass on the Bear's 4-yard line. When the Redskins muffed that touchdown, the Bears were relieved of pressure and went townward.

Those Bears were wonderful, weren't they? That "T" formation is really dread stuff and Coach George Halas comes pretty close to being the No. 1 offensive genius in the land. The Bears' ball carriers were under way at full speed before they had their hands on the ball and at the rate they were galloping when they hit something, it didn't make a difference whether there was a hole in the Redskins' line or not.

Halas' man-in-motion play was shaking his ball carriers loose through the middle, at the tackles and around the ends. The Redskins scarcely knew where the Bears would strike; and if they did know it didn't make much difference. The Bears' power plays were ghastly concentrations of blockers in front of ball carriers. The Redskins were first confused then so weakened physically by the pounding they were taking that they were helpless.

Halas turned back the clock to beat the Redskins. The Bears were getting their wondrous effects with the old "T" formation that was popular early in the century when the boys were playing the game in turtle-necks. Halas embellished it with some variations, but its form was basically the same with the quarterback taking the ball from center and handing it gently to a big back who was already in motion. The Redskins could never get set for that kind of an attack.

All of which brings up that game of a month ago when the Bears with the same sort of system couldn't score a touchdown against the Redskins. The Redskins knew how to meet the Bears' running game that day, obviously. How come, then, they were such foils for the same attack yesterday? Pardon us, please, if we sidestep that one, beyond noting that the Redskins yesterday simply played bad football.

The first 55 seconds of play were a shock to folks who knew the

Redskins. We mean when Bill Osmanski scored that 68-yard touch-down on the Bears' second play from scrimmage. On Osmanski's heels were Ed Justice and Jimmy Johnston, who finished noses apart in a race earlier in the season to decide the fastest Redskin. When nei-ther Justice nor Johnston could catch Osmanski, the Redskins were obviously in for a sorry afternoon.

DECEMBER 9, 1940

Shoeless Joe

In 1941, Povich went to Greensboro, N.C., to interview Shoeless Joe Jackson, who was banned from baseball for conspiring to fix the 1919 World Series despite being acquitted by a jury. Povich had heard much about Jackson from various players. Walter Johnson told him, "He was the only man who could whip that bat around fast enough to hit my fast ball on my best days," and Ted Williams said, "I want to hit like Jackson. Ty Cobb told me—'There was the greatest, son, and there's been nothing like him since, or before.'" Povich stayed in touch with Jackson until his death in 1951.

'Say It Ain't So, Joe'

Greensboro, N.C., April 10—I met a poor old rich man yesterday. In his garage he has a Packard and a Buick, and he owns the finest man-sion in Greenville, S.C., but he's busted, broke—broken-hearted. He's sick, and he's afraid he's going to die in what for 20 years has been his disgrace.

I sat with Shoeless Joe Jackson in the rickety grandstand as the Nats played the Tigers in Greenville. In disguised curiosity, players of the Detroit and Washington teams sauntered past to glimpse the man when his presence in the park was whispered about. They wanted a gander at the fellow their fathers had told them about. They stared at the man who, their dads had told them, could do more things better on a baseball field than any player who ever lived.

They saw a stout, florid-faced, powerful-looking man of 53. I found him sitting with his doctor. Without his physician, he could not go to the ball game. The latest of his heart attacks occurred only two weeks ago. "It was only a little joint," he said, "but it's got me scared." He smiled when he said it, and he didn't look scared. Neither was there a scare only resignation, to his tone when he continued, "I don't think I'll last long, now."

How to begin, how to ask a man like that about the tragedy in his life—the fixed World Series of 1919 that brought his banishment from baseball.

He saved me the trouble. He was anticipating me. He said, "I know what you're going to ask me. It's what they all ask me when they get their nerve up. Well, Sonny, I'm as innocent as you are. I had no part in that fix in 1919."

How now to draw him out? Was he bitter toward baseball, I asked. Did he have any resentment toward the game that had thrown him out?

"No," he said, curtly. "Not bitter toward baseball. I don't care for Judge Landis."

He didn't like Judge Landis?

"No, he didn't keep his bargain with me. He said if the courts declared me not guilty, he'd stand by me. That word wasn't kept when the court acquitted me in the Black Sox trial. How can I like Judge Landis?"

Now he was talking more freely about the Black Sox scandal. "The evidence in court showed that Buck Weaver and I were innocent. Even the fellows who were in on the fix testified that we had no part in it. My God, Sonny, did you ever look up the records of that World Series?"

What about the records, Joe, I asked.

"I can take you home and show them to you," he said. "The only three games the White Sox won in the series, Buck Weaver and I won for 'em. Did you know that I made more hits — twelve — than anybody in that series. And that it stood as a World Series record for total hits until 1930 when Pepper Martin got 13. Does that sound like I was laying down? My God, Sonny, all you have to do is look at the records."

Hoped Name Would Be Cleared

Some day, perhaps, they'd reinstate him, I said.

"I've lost hope, Sonny. That would be a happy day, but it won't come. It's hard to take, but what can a fellow do, 'specially when he's not going to be around much longer. They cut me off at my prime, I was only 32. But I don't mind that so much as the black mark I'll be taking along with me. I used to hope that they'd clear my name, but I guess they never will. My God, Sonny, that's the hard part."

He was born and raised in these parts, we remembered.

"That's right, Sonny, and they're fine people down here. They've always believed that Shoeless Joe Jackson never did anything wrong. They were so proud of me that this thing is hard on them, too. A few years ago the mayor of Greenville and 5,000 citizens signed a petition asking Judge Landis to clear my name, they wanted to show me they believed in me and that was wonderful. I only felt sadder when Landis turned them down."

One of the shoddy tricks against him he says, was the story about his "confession" of guilt in throwing the World Series to the Reds.

"There never was any confession by me. That was trumped up by the court lawyers. They couldn't produce it in court. They said it was stolen from the vaults. Does that sound right?"

I looked at him again and tried to visualize the superb athlete who could run and throw and field and hit so well that he was pressing Ty Cobb for ancient American League batting championships. I asked him how much he weighed in those days.

"In 1908 when I broke in, I weighed 175. When I got out in '20 it was 185. Today it's 235, and the doctor says some of it has to come off. I feel it when I'm in my garden.

What sort of a garden did he have?

"Hundreds of tulips, and white Scuppernong vines—I guess you call them white grapes. My wife and I have put in peach and cherry trees, that's where I spend most of my time. I only go to my business—I'm in the liquor business—for about an hour a day."

Scarcely true I thought could be those stories about the illiterate Joe Jackson who came out of the Carolina back country as a barefoot boy, hardly able to sign his name, I asked him about the shoeless business.

"I guess I was quite a dunce when I broke into baseball. I was playing barefoot in the old South Atlantic Association when the Athletics bought me. I guess a lot of people thought I was quite a fool when I was in the big leagues, but I saved my money. And now I read about a lot of those smart fellows of my time in baseball working on the WPA. I guess I wasn't so foolish, because I'm well fixed with those two big cars in my garage and a big new house and a pretty nice liquor business."

But he wasn't enthusiastic as he spoke. He sounded as if he'd trade it all for word from Chicago that baseball's ban on Shoeless Joe Jackson had been lifted.

Down in Greenville, they like to tell the story about Shoeless Joe playing the outfield barefoot in the old South Atlantic Association. The like to tell about the day, they say, when Shoeless Joe came in from the outfield and complained to his manager:

"You better clean up some of that old broken glass that's out in centerfield, or all of your balls are going to get cut up."

Joe Shows Same Keenness

Out there yesterday, watching the Nats and Tigers, seeing a big league team for the first time in years, he demonstrated the keenness that had helped to make him a great ball player. As Charley Gehringer followed Barney McCosky to bat, Jackson remarked: "Am I seeing double, or are those two hitters twins?"

Watching McCosky and Gehringer at the plate for the first time in his life, he had noted that in every detail their stance and batting strokes were identical. He had noted something that had probably escaped folks who saw the two players in action every day.

There used to be a story that Walter Johnson eased up on Jackson in those days when Jackson and Ty Cobb were fighting for the batting title.

"That may be true," said Jackson. "I know Johnson never liked Cobb. But if Walter was easing up against me, I never knew it. Some days I couldn't see his fast ball at all. I only heard it. The only way I could ever get a hit off him was to choke my bat and slap at the ball."

We don't like to bear down on the tremulo stuff, but when he talked of those old days, Shoeless Joe seemed real enthused . . . and he seemed very happy, too, when he recalled that his was the batting style that Babe Ruth had picked out among all other to copy . . . But when there was a lull in the old time baseball talks, he seemed real sad.

April 11, 1941

Gehrig Dies

When Lou Gehrig died in 1941, it was a sorrow for all of us writers. I was in St. Louis with the Senators, and I sat in my room at the Chase Hotel, chain-smoking, sweltering in those days before air conditioning, stripped to my shorts, pondering what to say about Lou Gehrig that hadn't already been said. It then occurred to me that Gehrig was always finishing second. He spent a career lifetime in Ruth's shadow. When he hit four home runs in one game, one of the few ever to do it, John McGraw retired that day and he got top billing. Now comes the sad day when Gehrig dies. But Kaiser Wilhelm dies the same day, and Lou

Gehrig is second once more. This became the theme of my story, and I poured out 4,000 words of tribute to that fine man.

—Shirley Povich, from his memoir, *All These Mornings* (1969)

Lou Gehrig: Baseball's Modest 'Iron Horse'

The death of Lou Gehrig was meaty subject matter for the obituary writers. They faithfully recounted and dramatized the 20-odd major league records he set, they rhapsodized on his durability as the Iron Horse of baseball, and muffed little of the valor with which he met the tragic turn that ended his life at 38.

The Lou Gehrig I knew was a big, friendly fellow with the deepest dimples ever worn by a masculine face. Typical of his self-negation was his custom of parking his automobile inconspicuously three blocks from Yankee Stadium and entering the park by a side entrance. Babe Ruth traditionally drove to a screeching stop at the main gates to make a gusty entrance for the fans assembled there. Even when his own feats surpassed the fading Ruth's, Gehrig would not horn into the Babe's party.

Somehow, Gehrig always seemed to miss out on top billing until he was stricken down by the dread germ that took him out of baseball, but more at that later. Of the millions who thrilled to his feats in baseball, only a few could know of the great depths of this man.

Last Christmas Eve, Lou Gehrig knew he was not long for this world. Ravaged by a disease known to medicine as amyotrophic lateral sclerosis, but recognizable to the layman as a form of poliomyelitis that was inducing a hardening of the spine, Gehrig was bed-ridden. The once-massive 220-pounder was reduced to an emaciated 150 pounds. Already he had been forced to abandon his desk at the office of the New York Parole Board.

Gehrig had scant control of his facial muscles and his once-grim jaw was slackened. On Parole Board papers that required his signature, he could make only a feeble mark. Newsmen shrank at reporting the pathos of his physical condition. But they were aware of it, and in newspaper offices throughout the land, Gehrig obituaries were already in type against the day, not far removed, when death would come to Lou Gehrig.

Yet last Christmas Eve, Gehrig's friends received the following greetings: "These are the times when all of us have much to be thankful for and much to be thoughtful about, times when it is particularly good to feel the warm, strong clasp of a friend's hand and so, this Christmas more than ever, we say Merry Christmas. Eleanor and Lou Gehrig."

Stricken in 1939

Baseball was not prepared, in 1939, for the shocking succession of events that projected Lou Gehrig among the front-page news. The headline that was expected some day, of course, read: "Lou Gehrig Benched." That would mean that the most amazing consecutive-game performance in baseball's history had ended. With thunderbolt effect came the flash three weeks later: "Lou Gehrig Paralyzed."

Here was the epitome of physical hardihood stricken down by a dread germ. The man who had broken all records for baseball durability with his play in 2,130 consecutive big league games over a stretch of 15 seasons now walked with a halting, fumbling gait at the age of 37.

The sickening flash that Gehrig was a paralysis victim marked the first time, actually, that the man whose heroics had been a bright chapter of baseball history had the headline all to himself.

Gehrig and his feats on the diamond were always in the shadow of his more spectacular teammate, Babe Ruth, and Lou was seemingly content that it should be so. But the consistency with which Gehrig missed the headlines for himself was aptly described by New York Columnist Franklin P. Adams who once referred to Gehrig as "the man who hit all those home runs the year that Babe Ruth broke the record for home runs."

Never Hero No. 1

For a few brief years, after Ruth's retirement in 1934, it seemed that Gehrig would finally come into his own as top man of the Yankees. He was the league's leading home run hitter. There no longer was a Babe Ruth to overshadow him. Possessor of none of Ruth's flamboyant color, Gehrig was about to step into the No. 1 role by a sort of default. He was getting nicely squared away for a plunge into this new acceptance in the Yankees scheme when along came the sensational Joe DiMaggio to surpass him as Yankee Hero No. 1.

On June 2, 1932, Gehrig hit four home runs in a game at Shibe Park, the first player in modern baseball history to accomplish that staggering feat. Surely there could be no denying Lou a place on the front page this time. But again his timing was bad. He hit his four homers on the same afternoon when John McGraw announced his retirement as manager of the Giants after fifty years in the majors, and top billing of the day went not to Gehrig but to McGraw.

When he was benched that day in May 1939, and when, three weeks later it was revealed that he was a paralysis victim, Gehrig in his sadness did command the headlines. He made the front pages, too, when he died this week, but even then his was not the top obituary of the week. The Woodchopper of Doorn, Kaiser Wilhelm, got top billing over Gehrig. Lou was always in somebody's shadow.

Tough Luck Pursued Him

Things could happen to Gehrig. I remember the year when Ruth was no longer the home run champion. Lou was in a race with Jimmy Foxx for the league's home run honors. That was in 1931. Gehrig missed tying Foxx for the championship by one home run, hitting 47. Actually he had hit 48 that season, but he could not be credited with that figure. The home run that didn't count was hit by Gehrig at Griffith Stadium in May.

It was another demonstration of Gehrig making news in a tragic sort of way. The home run that didn't count was a tremendous swat into

Griffith Stadium's centerfield bleachers. Lyn Lary was on base at the time. That was Gehrig's tough luck. The ball landed high into the concrete bleacher seats, and Lary, who was running with the pitch, looked up in time to see Center Fielder Sammy West make a catch. Lary did not know that West was catching the ball after it had bounced high out of the concrete seats back onto the playing field. He assumed that West was making a putout, and at third base Lary continued to the Yankees' dugout. Gehrig, thinking Lary had scored, jogged around to the plate only to learn that he was out for passing a runner on the bases.

Tough luck pursued Gehrig with a sort of relentlessness. A few years ago he was the guest on a national radio network as an endorser of the breakfast cereal "Huskies." When the point in the interview arrived where Gehrig was to say one word, coast to coast, he muffed it. The announcer asked him what breakfast food he ate to help him hit all those home runs. Said Gehrig: "Wheaties." Thus unwittingly he publicized the product of a rival firm.

Gehrig refused at first to accept the $1,000 check that was given him for his radio appearance, until the manufacturer of Huskies convinced him that his error had actually resulted in many times the normal publicity their product would have received.

Gehrig was up from the city streets and he had a pride in that fact. He liked to tell interviewers of the tough going in those early days and how lucky he considered himself. On a day when the Yankees played an exhibition game in Sing Sing, Lou was seen chatting familiarly with two convicts. Later he explained, "They used to be kids who lived in my block in East Harlem. They didn't get the breaks I did."

Strangely, Lou Gehrig, the perfect physical specimen, was the only one of four children of Henry and Christina Gehrig who survived childhood illness. Lou was born a few years after his parents emigrated from Germany. His father was an art metal worker at $9 a week, and his mother hired herself out as cook among the fraternity houses at Columbia University, where her pig knuckles and sauerkraut were campus favorites. The lad known as Lou was a tyke in Public School 132.

Started With Giants

His baseball background is well known; how he first gained notice by hitting a home run with the bases full, as a high school boy in a game against Lane Tech, of Chicago, at Wrigley Field in 1920 when his team was playing for the national championship; how he was signed later by the Yankees after his hard-hitting for Columbia University, and how he was farmed out to Hartford for two years before being recalled by the Yankees.

But not generally known is the fact that actually Gehrig should have been a National Leaguer. Andy Coakley, the old big league pitcher who was Gehrig's baseball coach at Columbia, recommended him to the Giants. Gehrig was paid scant attention by Manager John McGraw on a visit in the Polo Grounds. Half-heartedly the Giants sent him to Hartford where he played for most of a season under the name of Henry Lewis. Lou, chagrined at his cold reception by McGraw, quit the Hartford team to go back to college.

When the Yankees signed him at the end of his sophomore year at Columbia, he still belonged technically to the Giants, but McGraw was not sufficiently interested to pursue his claim, and gave Gehrig up to the Yankees.

Walter Johnson relates the first time he ever saw Gehrig. Lou was sent in as a pinch hitter for the Yankees in 1923. "He looked like a young blacksmith, with those big arms," Johnson recalls. "Anybody could tell he had power."

Long before he so gallantly met the test of those last doomed days, Gehrig's physical courage had many times manifested itself. The little finger of his right hand was broken on four occasions, but he insisted on playing every day to continue his consecutive-game streak. He had to be helped out of bed on a day in Detroit after a severe attack of lumbago, but he was in the lineup that afternoon. Earl Whitehill beaned him with a fast ball, but he did not miss the next day's game.

En route to Washington a few years ago, Gehrig played in an exhibition game at Norfolk with the Yankees and was a hospital case after being struck in the head by a bush league pitcher's high hard one. He reached Washington in time for the next day's game, and if he was plate-shy it was not evident. That afternoon he hit three-baggers before rain stopped the game.

Not Spectacular

I knew him as a fellow who had harmless superstitions. In a week when he was in a baffling batting slump, I saw him unload his pockets of various luck pieces. "I am Episcopalian," he said, "but look at these things I'm carrying." He displayed a Catholic medal that had been blessed in Rome and a Hebrew mazzuzah that contained a miniature scroll. "I carry these," he said, "because people who want me to do well sent them to me. If they are that interested in me, I appreciate it."

Aside from his feats with the bat, Gehrig did not know how to be spectacular. He had none of the color and flamboyancy of Ruth, which is one of the reasons that his top salary with the Yankees was only $34,000 compared to one $80,000 annual wage commanded by the Babe.

Tributes of His Friends

It was in Washington, in the spring of 1939, that Gehrig first hinted that his consecutive-game streak was about to end. He had fumbled a ball hit by Buddy Myer and was forced to throw to the pitcher to make the put-out at first. In the dressing room after the game, he said: "If I can't field that kind of a hit without the pitcher's help, I'm not doing this team any good."

His friends knew that something was pathetically wrong with Gehrig long before it was learned that he was in the throngs of paralysis. I saw him at dinner at O'Donnell's Restaurant in April 1939. He seemed gay. He wasn't though. After leaving their car at the restaurant parking lot, Gehrig's party made a run for it through the rain. Gehrig took a few steps and fell. They had to help him up. They walked, not ran, the remaining distance.

Lou had retired from baseball in the summer of 1939 when he accompanied the Yankees to Washington on an off-day and accepted an invitation to go marine fishing at Ocean City, Md., with the late Paul Townsend, Bucky Harris and Bill Dickey. He was a sick man, but fishing was one of his loves. When a 60-pound marlin struck Gehrig's line, Lou worked to reel him in. Townsend proffered the harness that would make the task easier, but Gehrig refused it. "This may be the last marlin I'll ever catch," said Lou. "I want to beat this one without any help." He did.

When Quentin Reynolds, former sports writer and now an ace on the staff of Collier's, was asked if he had ever witnessed such courage as was displayed by the people of London during the heaviest bomb attacks, Reynolds had an answer. The author of the vivid "The Wounded Don't Cry" said he had seen the courage of Londoners equaled—"by a professional ball player, Lou Gehrig, who is my champion."

JUNE 8, 1941

Summer of '41

It was the summer of 1941 and for baseball fans, it would never be better. Joe DiMaggio of the New York Yankees set the record for hitting in 56 consecutive games and Ted Williams of the Boston Red Sox set his mind on batting .400. Povich was one of the few, if not the only, sportswriter to hold the confidence of both DiMaggio and Williams, who rarely trusted the press. It was a testament to how these two oversensitive superstars viewed Povich's fairness.

The fellow who will probably end up as the batting champion of the American League is Ted Williams, gangling, turkey-necked outfielder of the Red Sox. Williams is rapping the ball at a .407 rate and he seems to be amazing nobody. It has long been known that the guy could hit.

During the past week Williams was paid an unsolicited compliment that was extreme, indeed. The Detroit Tigers gave a young University of Michigan outfielder named Dick Wakefield $50,000 to sign a Tiger contract, for one paramount reason: Wakefield bears a remarkable physical presence and facial resemblance to Williams, swings the bat in much the same manner, and the Tigers are willing to gamble $50,000 on the possibility that a young man of the Williams mold has a bright big league future, even before they've seen him swing a bat against good pitching.

Williams, with his high temper and sour-puss tactics when he is in a batting slump, will never be hailed as any model for American youth, but in one respect at least he has been a very estimable character. He is no good hitter by accident. He was probably the most indus-

In 1941, Ted Williams of the Boston Red Sox batted .406, the last major league player to hit .400.

trious young rookie ever to break into the big leagues. He worked at the art of hitting.

While other ball players were engaging in horse-play on the bench or rummy in the dressing rooms, Williams would peer ceaselessly at the pitching he saw in practice. He asked questions, chiefly about pitchers. He demanded to know what certain pitchers were throwing, and when. He asked for batting tips from Manager Joe Cronin and every old ball player he encountered. Hitting has been a passion with him.

In his early days with the Red Sox, Williams was in the ball park at 10 A.M., swinging a bat. The mere 30 minutes of pregame batting practice irked him. He wanted more, so he brought to the park all the semipro pitchers he could corral, and they pitched to him for hours while he perfected his timing. He was honing his batting eye for the afternoon's ball game.

As a hitter, Williams' chief charm seems to be his loose swing, the envy of all batters aside from those naturally gifted few who can get power otherwise. If the fellow has a weakness, the league's pitchers haven't found it yet. He has defied the old maxim about the low outside ball that is supposed to be the toughest pitch to hit. He murders pitching that is low and away.

Washington pitchers stopped him in one series last year with a new and thoroughly desperate trick. "Pitch to his strength," Bucky Harris commanded them, "and let him hit the ball. Throw inside, and take a chance." Harris was banking on the distance of the right field fences in the Boston park to defeat Williams. It did. The Washington right and center fielders, playing far back, hauled down a half dozen 400-foot drives by Williams.

He can be the problem child of the outfielders, however. In one afternoon at Fenway Park, he hit home runs over the left, center and right field walls and bounced another hit off the center field fence. He has cured his old weakness of swinging at bad balls and lately has been content to take a walk.

Williams is a very objective young man. He wants to lead the league in batting because it will bring him more money on his next year's contract. He lays great store by money, which of course is not an uncommon trait. But when Manager Joe Cronin last year shuffled the batting order and took Williams out of the clean-up spot, moving him ahead of Jimmy Foxx, he was mad. "There goes my chance to lead the league in runs-batted-in," he wailed, not caring whether Cronin heard him.

He was bitter against everything Boston last summer and told interviewers they could quote him. He said he didn't like Boston, the fans, the baseball writers or anything about the town, and that he wanted to be traded to Detroit. A temporary batting slump was vexing him, but he was not losing sight of the fact that the Red Sox were doomed to no better than fourth place and the Tigers might win the pennant with the resultant World Series split.

But Williams is happy now. Everything must be lovely in Boston with him these days. He is getting his basehits, and if there is anything a ball player likes better than a basehit it is three or four of the same. They will add up to pretty figures on his 1942 contract, especially if he winds up as the league batting champion, which he probably will.

JUNE 24, 1941

1941 World Series

Few World Series games ever produced the heartbreak that occurred in Game 4 of the 1941 World Series. The Brooklyn Dodgers had a 4–3 lead over the New York Yankees in the ninth inning, one strike away from tying the World Series at two games each, when Dodger relief pitcher Hugh Casey got the Yankees Tommy Henrich to swing at the third strike in what should have ended the game. What happened next produced a piece that was Povich at his best.

As Ken Burns described it: "The first thing you notice about Shirley are the words. The style so full of humor and moment, so exquisitely conscious of baseball's nearly unbearable drama. In a seemingly simple story about a World Series game, he seems to sense and know its historical importance; its principal players, bound by the merciless facts of

failure and loss; its purely abstract grace freed from time's constraints,
filled with mythic collisions of memory, home and family."

Brooklyn, Oct. 5 — The cruelest martyrdom of the 40 years of World
Series history was inherited today by big Hugh Casey, massive relief
pitcher of the Brooklyn Dodgers.

Casey pitched the dream pitch of today's fourth series game only to
see it back-fire and beat him in the strangest circumstance that ever
marked a series game.

Get this picture, please, of Ebbets Field, in the ninth inning: The
Dodgers leading, 4–3, nobody on base, two Yankees already out, two
strikes on Tommy Henrich. Big Casey on the mound, hearing 33,813
Brooklyn fans entreating him to strike out Henrich and even the series
for the Dodgers.

Casey winding up for the pitch he hoped would strike out Henrich
and clinch the game for Brooklyn. Casey feeling for the proper grip on
the curve ball he prayed would be the best pitch he ever threw in his
life. Casey letting that pitch go with just the proper snap. Casey watching it fool Henrich as it suddenly dipped from its course and twisted
low and inside. Casey watching Henrich swing and miss. Casey, the
losing pitcher of the day before, apparently having won his ball game.

Then Came the Yankee Deluge

You know what happened: how Catcher Mickey Owen muffed the
ball, how Henrich, a strikeout victim, reached base: how the Yankees,
capitalizing the break, rushed four runs across the plate. How the
strikeout that didn't retire the batter paved the way for Casey's defeat.
No pitcher ever had victory snatched from him in a manner quite as
brutal.

Down in the Dodger dressing room after the game, Casey called it
"The best pitch I ever threw." He said he wasn't trying to get it over
the plate. He wanted merely to lure Henrich into swinging at a bad
ball. He did. His catcher, Owen, took the full blame for the incident.

"The ball had so much stuff on it I couldn't hold it," said Owen.

We do not mean to play fast and loose with World Series history when we call Casey's defeat the most brutal of all. Other pitchers in other series have suffered cruel defeat, but somehow Casey's tragic beating this afternoon seems to merit special emphasis in the tragedy department.

We are mindful of what happened to Wild Bill Donovan, pitching for the Tigers against the Cubs in the opening game of the series of 1907. That was the day when Donovan went into the ninth inning leading the Cubs, 3–2. He had two strikes on Del Howard, a Cub pinch hitter, two were out, none were on base, when Donovan called his catcher, Germany Schaefer, to the box. "Just hold your mitt and bit outside and I'll hit for the third strike," Donovan said. He did hit Schaefer's glove for the third strike and Howard missed the swing, but Schaefer dropped the ball and Howard reached first. After that, Detroit infielders made three errors in the inning and the Cubs scored the tying run.

But Donovan didn't lose the ball game. It ended in a 12-inning, 3–3 tie.

The Case of John Miljus Revived

We remember Big John Miljus in the fourth game of the 1927 World Series in which the Pirates played the Yankees. Miljus was pitching for the Pirates in the ninth with the score tied at 3–3 when the Yanks filled the bases with none out. In this crisis Big Miljus struck out Lou Gehrig, and then he struck out Bob Meusel. Tony Lazzer missed two strikes by the margin of a foot when it happened. A wild pitch. Miljus' next pitch, a bit on the outside, bounded away from Catcher Johnny Gooch's mitt and the winning run scored from third.

But that wild pitch was Miljus' own undoing.

There was Jack Bentley pitching for the Giants in the twelfth inning of the World Series against Washington in 1924, with the score tied at 3–3 and two out in the ninth. With Ruel on second base, Earl

McNeely hit a soft grounder toward Third Baseman Freddie Linstrom. It was the famed pebble hit that took a weird bounce over Lindstrom's head for the winning run. It was a sad break in the luck for Bentley.

But for downright tough luck in a World Series we still like Casey's bitter experience today as the tops. He had been the losing pitcher the day before: He had come into the game as a relief pitcher with the bases filled with Yanks in the fifth inning and gotten the Dodgers out of the predicament. For three innings thereafter he was making his one-run lead stand up magnificently. He got rid of the first two Yankees in the ninth without trouble. He needed to retire only one more batter to even the series for the Dodgers and put an end to all fear of a rout by the Yankees.

And when the occasion demanded it, he threw the best pitch of his life. It's a heluva note when you lose because your best is too good.

OCTOBER 6, 1941

Ted Williams' Unspoken Query is Answered

Ted Williams, who hit .406 for the Red Sox, may be asking what a guy has to do to win the American League's most valuable player award, and the answer is simple enough: Get out of Joe DiMaggio's league.

In the season when Williams was the first American Leaguer since 1922 to hit .400, and in the same year when he outhit DiMaggio by 49 points, he is not the league's most valuable player. That honor went to DiMaggio by the vote of 24 baseball writers representing the league's eight cities. And it was a clear-cut margin for DiMaggio in the voting.

How come DiMaggio was rated over Williams? Well, the Yankee Clipper wasn't exactly idle in the season that Williams was having his greatest year. DiMag broke a record which, as a feat, surpassed even Williams' .406 batting average. Williams chose an untimely season for his heroics. He chose the season when DiMaggio was breaking a 50-year-old record for hitting in consecutive games.

The evidence is that the grand jury of press box inmates weighed Williams' .406 average against DiMaggio's 56-game consecutive hitting streak and found that DiMaggio's was pounding a neat .357 average for himself during the season, which ranked him as the league's third leading hitter.

There was another phase of the Williams–DiMaggio rivalry that probably came in for profound consideration and that was that DiMaggio's performance was highly instrumental in winning the pennant for the Yankees. Williams' .406 won no pennant for the Red Sox.

It Doesn't Take a Bat to Tell

It all adds up to an amazing sort of tribute to DiMaggio, this business of being outhit by 49 points and still being rated the most valuable

Yankee Joe DiMaggio lines a single to left field in a 1941 game in Washington. That season he established a record 56-game hitting streak.

player in the league. The guy must be quite a ball player even when
he doesn't have a bat in his hand. That, of course, is the nub of matters, in any comparison of Williams and DiMaggio. DiMag can do
everything better than Williams except hit and even that latter concession to Williams can be debated in DiMag's favor and with some plau-
sibility.

Clark Griffith, who has seen them come and go in the big leagues
for 55 years, is in complete agreement with the award to DiMaggio
over Williams. "That DiMaggio does more things a lot better than
Williams," the 71-year-old owner of the Nats commented. "I doubt if a
better ball player ever lived."

Tris Speaker, a name that has been accepted down through the
years as the last two words in outfielding skill, had no talents that
DiMaggio can't match, says Griffith. "That DiMag can go as far for a
ball as Speaker ever did and he has as good a throwing arm. Maybe he
plays ground balls a little better than Spoke. Sure, Speaker used to
play closer to the infield, but he didn't have the lively ball to contend
with. When you consider DiMaggio is a better hitter than Speaker,
you'd have to call him a better player."

Griffith declared that DiMaggio was the only center fielder in
baseball history who could make the play he did make in the first
World Series game against the Dodgers last month. "It was that
blooper into centerfield by Reese in the seventh inning. How DiMaggio got to that ball for a one-hand pickup I will never figure out," said
Griffith. "And then he made a throw to the plate that would have kept
a run from scoring if Dickey had held onto the ball. That was the best
fielding play of the series."

Griff Settles the "Clutch" Issue

With all due respect to Williams' .406 average, the Red Sox slugger is
not as dangerous a hitter in the clutch as DiMaggio, as the Nats'
owner sees them. "I don't want to take it away from Williams, because
if he improves much more the pitchers in this league won't be able to

get him out, but he can be pitched to easier than DiMaggio by good pitchers. They can bait him on curve balls that DiMaggio will hit. I'd say that both DiMaggio and Taft Wright are harder for a pitcher to fool than Williams, despite the averages."

No man in baseball swings a bat in the same manner as DiMaggio unless it's his little brother Dominic, of the Red Sox, Griffith observes. "DiMaggio brought the flat-footed batting stance into the big leagues," said Griffith. "Watch his left foot. It moves only a couple of inches. He takes no stride at all. By gum, Lou Gehrig ended up hitting with that same stance after DiMaggio joined the Yankees. He was smart enough to copy it after being a great hitter all his life with his own stance."

Williams' chief trouble, it seems, is, as we were saying, being in the same league with a guy like DiMag.

November 13, 1941

Japan Kicks Off!

War's Outbreak is Deep Secret to 27,102 Redskin Game Fans

"Keep it short."

That innocent-sounding order flashed to its football reporter at the Redskins–Eagles game by the Associated Press headquarters downtown prefaced the jolt that was to follow later in the afternoon for 27,102 exiting fans at Griffith Stadium yesterday.

If the reporter was wondering at the sudden insignificance of his football "lead," he understood fully a few minutes later in the first quarter when his office flashed this intimate message: "The Japanese have kicked off. War now!"

Unaware of the bombing of Hawaii and war in the Pacific, the bulk of the 27,102 in Griffith Stadium sat through the 2 1/2–hour plus game, thrilling to the three touchdown passes of Sammy Baugh.

But to the jabbering press box workers and eaves-dropping fans in the vicinity, the action on the field below was a blur in the light of events in the Pacific. Somehow, with America at war and lives already lost, a football game had lost its importance.

For the crowd, though, there was a hint of something of importance in the air. As early as the first eight minutes of the opening quarter, the public address system began a field day of its own. Important persons were being paged, too many important persons to make it a coincidence.

Intermittently the public address announcer interrupted his football spiel to summon big-shot fans from their seats.

"Admiral W. H. P. Bland is asked to report to his office at once!" The big horns blared midway of the first quarter. To the knowing, that meant the chief of the Bureau of Ordnance of the United States Navy.

"The Resident Commissioner of the Philippines, Mr. Joaquim Eilzalde, is urged to report to his office immediately!" came another announcement a few minutes later.

By the end of the half, there was a buzzing in the grandstands, but Redskins officials, appraised of the news, refused to permit a public address announcement of the outbreak of war.

"We don't want to contribute to any hysteria," said General Manager Jack Espey in forbidding the announcement.

Grid Fans to the End

The reports that did reach the customers were set down as the most part as incredible rumor and gossip. There was no lessening of volume in their cheers for the Redskins. At the game's end there was a rush for the goal posts by hundreds of exuberant fans.

But by the end of the first half, a lone photographer was working the ball game. All other camera men had been hastily summoned by their offices to speed to the Japanese Embassy and other points of interest.

The paging of notables continued throughout the second half.

"Jospeh Umglumph of the Federal Bureau of Investigation is requested to report to the FBI office at once," came an undistinct announcement during the between-half ceremonies.

"Capt. R. X. Fenn of the United States Army is asked to report to his offices at once," was announced preceding the second-half kickoff.

Papers Call Reporters

Newspaper offices loaded the public address system with frantic calls for star reporters who were at the game. The names of circulation managers were blared through the big horns, commanding them to return downtown immediately, as the news offices prepared to hurry extra editions on the streets.

Before the end of the first quarter, the radio-listening wife of one newspaper editor demonstrated her own news sense and took no chances that her football fan husband might not know of the war. She telegraphed this message to Griffith Stadium: "Deliver in section P, Top Row, Box 37. Opposite 35-yard line, west side. Griffith Stadium: War with Japan. Get to office."

In a box on the 50-yard line, Cabinet Member Jesse Jones was handed a message and departed from the game.

And for the 27,102 customers the only thing in progress was the football game they were watching. They were on their feet in high glee when big Joe Aguirre took Baugh's third touchdown pass for the winning points.

At the exits of the stadium at the end, though, news of war broke like a thunderclap as departing football fans encountered cab drivers and park employees who had been listening to radio reports of Japan's attack on Hawaii.

"That settles it," cracked one indignant football fan. "I'm going right home and tear down those Japanese lanterns."

December 8, 1941

Family Time

Povich rarely wrote about his children or himself. But this piece, which he wrote while covering spring training, focuses on his family, while showcasing his self-deprecating humor.

Orlando, Fla., Feb. 22—Among the folks I've met socially these last three vacation weeks are the three reasons I'm in 3-A. I have been playing Daddy to two little lads and their mother, and you can add, also, to Florida hotel men and real estate agents. It has been reunion all around. I rejoin my family, and the Florida real estate people make anschluss again with my dough.

I am no less fond of the two lads who have been holding their own very nicely with the Internal Revenue Department and who still represent $400 deductions in the income tax scramble. But I probably will be forgiven for delivering a slight fish-eye to their mother who, I learned, was devalued from a $2500 item to a mere $2000 exemption by the tax people. In fact, she said she was sorry.

In fact, you can't ever be mad with a girl like her. Who, but she, would say it so nicely on the card that came with the gift she bought me the other day because it was our tenth wedding anniversary. I liked it when she said, summing up pretty well, I thought, with the words, "Just Married, Ten Years Ago." The poets can't tie that one, huh?

I don't want to bore you with the bright sayings of little children, but my six-year-old, he's David, unloaded one on the first day of my vacation that was worthy of a lad at least three weeks older. Not in months had I bestirred myself at this breakfasting hour at 8 A.M. and so when I made the grade, finally, and took my place at the head of the table, he studied the strange man with a long look. Then he spoke. "You're Daddy. I presume."

Little Maury, he's "free years old," ain't hep to so many things yet. But we think he's got a nice inquisitive mind. There was, for example, that little incident the other day when he became three and his mother greeted him in the morning with a big hug and a kiss and then set him down and proudly wished him a very, very happy birthday. Maury looked her straight in the eye and blandly asked, "Why, Mummy?" He's going to learn a lot in this world if he keeps asking questions.

It was here in Florida last winter that I almost perfected a new technique for getting the nightly nose-drops in a squirming two-year-old who didn't like the idea at all. The basic maneuver was to grab a little windmilling hand with one of your own and clamp a scissors hold on his legs with one of your own big feet. That left your other leg free to deal with anything that might come up from the struggling little wild Indian. Then you called to his mother to take the bottle of nose drops from your teeth and apply same. This year I've simplified it. I don't have to call his mother at all. I have her standing by, ready to act on a mutually agreed signal from me at the proper moment when I have the patient semi-subdued.

In my time I have bit the dust a thousand times from toy pistols aimed at me by those two kids. I have been shot and killed as an Indian, an outlaw, a cattle rustler and just plain burglar or some equally sinister character who wasn't wanted around the house. And it doesn't count, if I don't go down. But lately, I'm a Jap or a nasty old German and I get plunked with bombs and anti-aircraft guns and everything else those two kids hear about in the art of modern warfare. Yesterday I was a submarine that had to lie on the floor like a docked fish and get myself rammed by a big toy fire-engine that served 'em as a cruiser.

Oh, yeah, and they've discovered the Lone Ranger, too. They've now gotten me to send away the bread wrappers and box tops and I find myself hoist by my own petard. The mails come in and with them the Secret Code. I get shot now by the Lone Ranger Club's own type pistol, I get ridden down by Silver, I get scared to death by the Lone Rangers Club Members mask and wounded by the Lone Rangers Silver Bullet. Then they get me retreaded and trot me out all over again, for the full treatment once more.

But I started out to tell you about the Florida Real Estate men.

They're wonderful. They look you straight in the eye and tell you about the wonderful bungalow they're going to rent you. We got one. They said it was some kind of circulating heat that we'd have. The only place that heat they were talking about circulates is inside the furnace. We could pick oranges off the trees in the yard. It sounded great, until you tasted the oranges. We didn't have to pick 'em; the trees let them fall like they were disowning 'em. And the hot water. Again they said I'd have all the hot water I needed. Do I look like a Russian peasant?

FEBRUARY 23, 1942

Sam Snead

Sam Snead was always a Povich favorite. Maybe it was his upbringing, growing up barefoot in the West Virginia hills. Maybe it was his three decade duel with Ben Hogan. This piece on Snead was written when Slammin' Sammy went to war.

Sam Snead dropped into a Washington recruiting station and joined the Navy the other day, and when he did a sizable hunk of color went out of professional golf. In a profession populated for the most part by grim, poker-panned young business men whose golf shots represent their only sparkle, Hillbilly Snead was a refreshing character.

When Snead came out of the West Virginia hills and down the pike in 1937, P.G.A Tournament Manager Freddy Corcoran all but embraced him. Here was a chap the galleries would like, even if he didn't win tournament. Snead had taken himself out of the West Virginia hills, but mixing with pro golf's station-wagon society couldn't take the West Virginia out of Snead and Corcoran welcomed the slightly bumptious boy from the uplands.

Pro golf was in something of a bad way when Snead happened

along to make Corcoran's job of humanizing the pros more easy. Walter Hagan and his surefire showmanship had already been lost to the
tournament circuit, Gene Sarazen wasn't taking the tours any more.
Bobby Jones had gone into retirement save for his once-a-year appearance in the Masters tournament, and Johnny Farrell and his sartorial
splendor were back numbers in big-time pro golf. The game needed a
shot in the arm, and that's where Snead came in.

Quit Job as $45-a-Month Pro

Corcoran was talking about Snead yesterday while in town to
arrange a Bob Hope–Bing Crosby war relief match. "That big fellow
had never seen a photographer's flash bulb until they exploded
around him after he won the Oakland Open with a 271," said Corcoran. "He was out in California for that tournament virtually
unknown. The papers were spelling his name 'Sneed.' He had been
making only $45 a month as a pro in West Virginia when he decided
to have a go at the winter circuit. He won the second big tournament he played in."

Corcoran vows that when Snead competed in the 1937 open tournament he didn't know who was the defending champion. "That
Snead just never took the trouble to check up on things like that. He
just went ahead and played his game, and it usually was a great one.
He didn't give anybody any trouble. You could start him at 7 o'clock in
the morning, when the prima donnas of the tournament were still in
bed, and pair him with the caddymaster, and it didn't make any difference to Snead. He never squawked. He was a tournament manager's
delight."

Snead's color was hard to define. There was nothing explosive
about the fellow, but he wasn't dull. He liked to banter with his galleries, and maybe that's why they liked him, that and the fact he could
hit those booming tee shots. "I've seen Snead in a good foursome,"
says Corcoran, "and Sammy looked as if he were the only player in

the lot who was having a good time. Maybe that's why the galleries like him."

Snead did all right after he came out of his West Virginia mountains. In the last five years he has earned probably close to $200,000 including $78,000 in P.G.A. purses and the rest in exhibitions, endorsements and honorariums. With all his wealth he retained his delightful naiveté.

"I remember the time I was with Snead in Boston," related Corcoran. "I took him in to see Jack Sharkey, who owns the town's biggest bar. Sammy was flabbergasted at meeting a fellow who had actually fought Jack Dempsey and Joe Louis. He asked Sharkey if they could hit hard. All the while Sharkey is hero-worshipping Snead, but when we left Sammy asked me if I thought I could arrange to get Snarkey's autograph for him."

Fancied Self as Ball Player

Baseball, not golf, was Snead's first love. He was a five-sport star in high school at Hot Springs, W. Va., and fancied himself as a catcher. At Sarasota one day when the Red Sox were training, Snead asked for a chance to hit in batting practice. Corcoran arranged it, and afterward Snead asked him, "What did Joe Cronin think of my batting form?" When Corcoran told him frankly that "Cronin doesn't like the way you hit a baseball," Snead for the first time in his life was miffed. "Tell that guy Cronin," he said to Corcoran, "that I don't like the way he hits a golf ball either."

They staged a driving tournament that year in Sarasota after Corcoran had bet that Snead could give any ball player 50 yards and outdrive him. The Red Sox nominated Jimmy Foxx and Jack Wilson, their two best and biggest golfers, to take Snead on. "Sammy gave 'em those 50 yards and then outdrove 'em by 50 yards," says Corcoran.

They never made any claims that Snead, for all his power off the tee, was golf's longest driver. That honor belonged to Jimmy Thomson, unquestionably, says Corcoran. "Sammy was a long hitter, but he didn't have Thomson's distance. A Snead drive and a Thomson drive was the difference between a Gehrig home run and a Ruth home run. They were both pretty, but Ruth's was usually the longest."

The story about Snead that we liked best is the latest one, which isn't a story at all, but simple truth. When he joined up with the Navy the other day, newspapermen asked Snead why he was joining up. "Me?" said Snead. "To help win the war," he added simply.

MAY 1, 1942

Povich's Nemesis

George Preston Marshall, founder of the Washington Redskins, gave Povich more reason for copy than any other individual in sports. Marshall thought of himself as a bigger than life impresario. What fodder for a columnist who loved to tweak the haughty. It was fun and at times very serious for Povich. The victim was forever outraged by the Post's most popular writer.

The dust-up began in 1938, when Marshall burst into Povich's Pullman room after a Redskins–Bears game, holding a check in the air, and boasted that it was the biggest check any visiting team had taken out of Chicago. The next day, as Povich moved through the cars, he noticed that Marshall had moved his players from the Pullman cars back to coaches, and some of the injured were lying in the baggage cars. Povich wrote about such penny-pinching in light of Marshall's boast. Marshall barred him from the locker room.

That incident is small stuff next to what happened in 1942. Povich reported that Marshall pocketed $13,000 from an Army Relief exhibition game on the West Coast, claiming the money as training expenses. Marshall sued Povich and the Post for $100,000 each. To Povich, that kind of money looked like $10 million.

What follows is the column that prompted the suit and the one after the verdict, in the Post's and Povich's favor, in which he repeated the charges all over again.

Secretary of War Stimson
c/o The White House Cabinet,
Washington D.C.

My Dear Mr. Secretary:

So you were "shocked," huh, by what you have learned of the tricky financial arrangements of the Joe Louis–Billy Conn fight in which your Army Emergency Relief Society was being played for a chump by Promoter Micke Jacobs and the managers of the fighters.

We merely want to observe that this is what usually happens when an amateur outfit like your Army Relief Society starts messing around with professional sports promoters. You traffic with them at your own risk. Sweet charity has been their dish for years. Only the naive or the otherwise preoccupied, like yourself, could be flabbergasted by the news that $135,000 would be taken out of the gate receipts to pay off the fighters and promoters before Army Relief got a dime.

While you are about it, Mr. Secretary, you could investigate, too, that football business in which your Army Relief Society was mixed up with pro football teams. In at least one instance, that stinks, too. We mean the game which the Redskins so kindly consented to play with your All-Western Army team at Los Angeles a few weeks ago for sweet charity's sake.

Like the Louis–Conn fight, that game was supposed to be played for the widows and orphans and families of our missing and maimed soldiers. Sure enough, when they split up the gate receipts, the widows and orphans came first—after the proprietors of the Redskins got their share.

By what right the Redskins' owners took $13,000 out of that gate before the Army Relief Society was paid off, we don't know. The game wasn't advertised as for the Redskins' benefit, if we remember rightly. But the owners of the Redskins skimmed more dough off the top of that one than they ever got for any other exhibition game on the Coast.

A couple of weeks later, the Green Bay Packers showed the Redskins owners up as money grubbing business men when they played that same All-Army team in Milwaukee. The Packers didn't hold out a dime "for training expenses." They gave everything to Army Relief, including free use of the stadium. The Packers had training expenses, too.

That's how the Redskins justified their $13,000 take—on the basis of training expenses for the game. But that was strictly malarkey, and it still smells. Army Relief was being used to pay expenses the Redskins would incur in any event. A week before, an intra-squad game had netted the Redskins $6,000 toward expenses.

When the Nats and Yankees played their Army Relief baseball games last summer, it would have been as sensible for Clark Griffith and Ed Barrow to take $15,000 out of the gates on the excuse that it had cost them that much for their spring training trips in Florida. But baseball, unlike the Redskins, was able to rise above the temptation to make a grab for at least some of the dough that was in the house.

Baseball's contributions to Army and Navy Relief is very refreshing in contrast to the smelly prize fight that was being cooked up and the hard-fisted deal the Redskins gave charity. The 16 big-league ball games played for service relief funds found the clubowners not only taking nothing, but actually paying their own way into the parks, as did the ball players and umpires.

It's too bad, Mr. Secretary, that the Louis–Conn fight arrangements had to turn out like they did, because the man on the street was saying "to hell with it," after the revelations that Louis would be paid $100,000 which was to go immediately to Promoter Mike Jacobs in payment of an old debt, and that Conn was to get $34,500 for the fight so he, too, can pay his debts.

It's too bad, because the fight was certain to develop a wad of dough, as much as a million, perhaps, for Army Relief, even after the fighters were paid. But the stench it developed at a time when we are being told we are losing this war because of lack of all-out effort wasn't helping matters any. It was best to forget the fight.

It's hard, though, to criticize Louis or Conn. Louis, particularly, squared himself with everybody during the past year when he laid his title on the line twice and risked a million-dollar chattel for Army and Navy Relief without asking—or getting—a dime. Conn is in the hands of his managers, with no voice in his own financial affairs. What happened was that fast-talking characters like those who infest the prizefight business painted a very pretty picture for your neophyte Army sports promoters, who fell for it and had a helluva mess on their hands until you straightened 'em out by calling the whole thing off. Nice going, Mr. Secretary.

S.P.

SEPTEMBER 26, 1942

I won't be needing that $100,000 I have been trying to scrape together for the past 12 months.

Pro-Football Inc., owners of the Washington Redskins (George Preston Marshall, president) seemed to think I owned that much scratch and wanted in, as we say in our set.

Pro-Football Inc. (George P. Marshall, president) sued me. They sued the publishers of *The Washington Post*, too, for $100,000. That may be a trifling sum to some people, but I did not want to be separated from my last $100,000 even if I did not have $100,000.

It was nice to think, however that Pro-Football Inc. (George Marshall, president) assumed that I possessed or could dig up $100,000 for Pro-Football Inc. (Geo. Marshall, president). And this the year of the withholding tax, too.

Pro-Football Inc. (G.P. Marshall, president) sued me and the publishers of *The Washington Post* because they didn't like what I said about their football game for Army Emergency Relief, played at Los Angeles on August 30, 1942. They didn't like it $100,000 worth.

That was the article that appeared in this space on September 26, 1942. I must have been feeling very blunt that day. I was commenting on the fact that Redskins took $13,000 out of the gate of the Army

Relief game in Los Angeles and I was asking the Secretary of War to investigate it.

Mr. Stimson had just called off the Louis–Conn fight for Army Relief because he didn't like the way the gate was being split, and he said he was "shocked." I said he should look into that football business, too, and being very blunt that day, I said, "In at least one instance, that stinks, too. We mean the game which the Redskins so kindly consented to play with your All-Western Army team at Los Angeles for sweet charity's sake."

I said some other things, too. I said, "Like the Louis-Conn fight, that game was supposed to be played for the widows and orphans and families of our missing and maimed soldiers. Sure enough when they split up the gate receipts, the widows and orphans came first—after the proprietors of the Redskins got their share."

I said, "By what right the Redskins' owners took $13,000 out of that gate before the Army Relief Society was paid off, we don't know. The game wasn't advertised as for the Redskins' benefit, if we remember rightly. But the owners of the Redskins skimmed more dough off the top of that one than they ever got for any other exhibition game on the Coast."

I said, "That's how the Redskins justified their $13,000 take—on the basis of training expenses for the game. But that was strictly malarkey, and it still smells." That's what I said.

And so the owners of the Redskins sued me and the publishers of the *Post*, and the *Post* retained Mr. Spencer Gordon as counsel for the defendants, and on Wednesday of this week we went into court before a jury and His Honor Justice James M. Morris of the District Court of the United States for the District of Columbia.

Mr. Marshall took the stand as a witness and put in evidence a letter from the War Department which he said was the contract and which stated that the owners of the Redskins were to be allowed 20 per cent of the receipts, to be limited to $20,000. The 20 per cent turned out to be $13,608.76.

On the witness stand I was asked by Mr. Milton King, counsel for

Pro-Football Inc., if I knew at the time of writing the article that the Redskins had a contract with the War Department, and the terms of it.

I quote now from the cross-examination of myself by Mr. King:

Q: "Let me ask you, you said you were proud of this article, you didn't take back anything, and you said you would write it again."

A: "That is true."

Q: "Would you write an article like that about the Redskins taking this money from orphans and widows without knowing the terms of the contract, again?"

A: "When the Redskins, or any other organization, sports organization, takes that much money from any such charity fund, I will be pleased to write the same kind of an article."

Q: "Whether you know whether they were taking it justifiably or not, you still think it is wrong?"

A: "I can see no justice in taking that much money out of a charity affair."

Here is paragraph 4 of the complaint filed by Pro-Football Inc. (G. Marshall, president) in the suit for libel:

"By reason of the publication of the aforesaid false, malicious, scandalous and defamatory article, and the statements therein contained, the plaintiff has been and is greatly injured in its good name, business and credit, and has been brought into great public scandal, scorn, shame and disgrace, and held up to public hatred, ill will, contempt, disrepute and ridicule, of residents of the United States, the District of Columbia and elsewhere, to the extent that many persons do suspect and believe that the plaintiff, in its conduct and practices in connection with its management and control as owner and proprietor of the aforesaid 'Redskins,' has been reprehensible, unscrupulous, fraudulent and unpatriotic, and has perpetrated a fraud at the expense of and to the detriment of a certain charitable organization, operating for the benefit of the armed forces of the United States, in time of war, and known as the Army Relief Society, and to the detriment of the widows and orphans of members of the armed forces of the Untied States."

The defendants pleaded (1) that the article did not libel Pro-Football Inc.; (2) that it was fair comment; and (3) that it was true.

The jury, in fewer than 20 minutes, brought in a verdict for the defendants who, we are happy to note, were the owners of *The Washington Post* and Povich.

This column rests—but only until there is occasion for further fair comment.

OCTOBER 30, 1943

Covering the War

After asking for years to be sprung from the sports beat for combat duty, Povich, 39, finally got assigned to the Navy as a Post *war correspondent in November 1944. He was sent to Guam to cover the next island-hopping invasion. It turned out to be Iwo Jima.*

Post Newsman First to Land On Iwo by Transport Plane

Iwo Jima, March 2 (Delayed)—This correspondent got mixed up in a Guinea-pig operation today that proved American Navy transport planes could land on Iwo's short, southern air strip in the midst of Japanese mortar fire.

I was the first American correspondent to fly into Iwo in anything bigger than a spindly wheeled Taylor craft or Piper Cub observation plane.

I went in on a twin-motored DC–3, at the end of a 700-mile flight from the Marianas. It was an airline type outfitted as a litter plane to evacuate 20 of the most seriously wounded.

We got no wounded. We did land and we did take off again.

Twelve times our 25-year-old pilot, Lieut. James Dungan of Exeter, Calif., circled the pear-shaped Iwo and thought it over before he took the chance and set down. His maneuvering gave me a front-row seat to the show on Iwo.

There it was, and this is what I saw as we were going in: What looked like American ships by the hundreds standing off shore. Big battleships and cruisers in sporadic bombardment of the Jap-held northern end of the island. They had to be careful now. (U.S. Marines were all over the place almost.)

I saw American planes letting the Japs have it unopposed by Nip airpower, strafing and dive-bombing the dwindling Jap area. I saw the

Povich was a war correspondent with the Navy. (1945)

bombs drop and then erupt in flashes that gave way to smoky shapes. On the southern tip atop Mount Suribachi, Old Glory was planted proudly, but now the battling had moved nearly 4 miles north.

It was a mélange of modern war with only the aerial dogfights missing, and there were tanks moving forward and low-flying planes dropping parachute packs of whole blood and weapons to the Marines.

The plane I was on was, in fact—it suddenly occurred to me—a flying ammunition dump. We were going in to take out the wounded, but we were taking in ammunition. Case upon case of mortar shells for the Marines. The stuff was laying peaceful-like on the floor of the ship.

There is no radio tower on Iwo. Pilot Dungan was in communication with a jeep that served as plane radio control.

"Hold off, it's too hot," he was told as we circled the island for the umpteenth time.

We could see Jap mortars hitting the air strip, lobbed from their positions to the north.

Pilot Dungan, however, was of no mind to return to the Marianas with his load of mortar ammo.

"I think I'll come in," he radioed.

Came the answer: "Think it over."

"I'm coming in," said Dungan.

He tilted his transport around Mount Suribachi to give that lump of rock a wide berth and then swooped low.

He didn't set her down, though. He was merely looking over the condition of the runway to find the holes he'd have to duck. He gave her the gun and lifted her up again. That was the last preliminary. The next time, he circled the mountain and moved in for a landing. To escape flying low over the Japs' heads—they still have artillery— Dungan took his ship in with the wind, not against it. That was a feat. He was taking the chance that he could put her down before he overran the field and landed in the Japs' laps.

He made it and the big door of the plane swung open. We were an object of curiosity—a heavy plane coming in. Ground crews met us with "Bring any beer?"

They unloaded the mortar shells eagerly but where were the wounded? There was some hitch. We were going to take back no wounded. They wouldn't expose the casualties to the danger of the Japs' mortar fire on the strip. While we waited, I talked to some Marines, still dug in nearby foxholes. They were raving at one Jap sniper entrenched beyond a ridge.

Lieut. Eicoff, a doctor with the Third Marine Division, was pointed out as a man with a steam-heated foxhole. The sulphur deposits had warmed the ash where he was dug in. I saw that Iwo ash, and sank to my boot tops in it. I saw the two little Rock Islands (Iwo Jima translated means rock island) a hundred yards off shore that the United States gunners cleaned out by day, only to find the Japs swimming back by night to use the rocks as observation posts. The inevitable jeep was everywhere on the harder surfaces.

There were cranes and derricks and supplies piled high. We had taken nearly three fourths of Iwo.

There was a new explosion near the runway. Jap mortar fire. Pilot Dungan ran for his plane and motioned me with him. The crew was aboard, and we climbed in.

"This is enough of this," said Lieutenant Dungan. "We're pulling out." We did. For a transport plane there is still too much woe on Iwo.

MARCH 4, 1945

Baseball in the Marianas

(Shirley Povich is in the Pacific theater as a *Washington Post* War Correspondent. When his duties permit he will write his "This Morning" column for the sports fans. These columns will appear from time to time as received—Editor's note.)

In the Marianas, March 3 (Delayed)—Last July, the Japs were

playing baseball on these islands when the word went out: Game called on account of Americans. That was the month the Marines landed on the beaches, chased the Nips into the hills and proceeded to take over generally.

Today I saw two teams of big leaguers play a ball game on the same diamond the Japs had carved out of the jungle. It was the Navy's idea of entertaining the servicemen in these parts, and it was popular. Six-thousand sailors rimmed the field and whooped it up for the boys they used to see in big league uniforms.

This was no USO troupe of baseball entertainers. The men on the field were former big leaguers who are in the Navy now. They don't have any soft berths. When they're not playing ball they have all the duties of Joe Blow in the Navy. They're sticking their necks out on long over-water flights in land planes to get to the island fields. And the outfielders could, conceivably, have their backs to Jap snipers in the woods.

Mace Brown, the old Red Sox pitcher, who is a lieutenant and the only officer with the outfit, manages the Fifth Fleet team that played the Third Fleet team skippered by George Dickey. The players are off 12 of the 16 big league clubs. They like the whole business of this baseball tour. They get taken around. The other day they went for a joyride with a B–29 crew that had seven missions over Tokyo to its credit.

On its next Tokyo flight, incidentally, that crew is going to let the Japs know what it feels like to get conked with a baseball from 35,000 feet. The boys left a dozen autographed balls, "To Tojo with love—" with the crew who said they'd heave 'em through the bomb bay doors on the target run.

There are baseball fields all over the islands, thanks mostly to the Seabees. What was an impossible gulch replete with a creek last week is a nicely graded diamond this week. Johnny Rigney, the White Sox pitcher, says there's only one complaint.

"There weren't any pitchers with those Seabees when they laid out the fields," says Rigney. "They must all have been hitters. The outfield distances are too short. What the Navy needs is some pitchers in their

Seabee battalions to think of these things when they go to work on a ball field."

Mace Brown is having a wonderful time, he says. As an officer and manager of the Fifth Fleet team, he nominates himself as a starting pitcher. "For 10 years in the majors I was a relief pitcher," he says. "I always wanted to know what it felt like to start a game. Now I know, and I'm satisfied. I'll take relief pitching."

There's not much doubt that the two teams out here could pool their talent and win the pennant in either big league. Besides Rigney and Brown, there are Johnny Vander Meer, Hal White, Virgil Trucks and Tom Ferrick to do the pitching. They have three pretty fair first baseman in Mickey Vernon, Johnny Mize and Elbie Fletcher. Billy Herman is playing second base, and Pewee Reese, third. Merrill May is a third baseman. There's a slew of outfielders, including Barney McCosky.

Mickey Vernon of Washington is the slugging star of the troupe at this point. They're using him as an outfielder and he has hit eight home runs in the first seven games on the islands. He rather likes the idea of playing in the outfield and is ready to kiss off his first basing career.

When Mr. Magellan ran across these islands 420 years ago and was so disgusted with the thievery of the natives who swiped the supplies off his ship, he didn't even bother to claim them for Spain. His name for Guam was "The Island of the Thieves." But baseball is not exactly a virgin sport on Guam. The native Chamorro kids are playing it every day. They learned it after the American occupation in 1898.

Along with the ball teams, the Navy is putting on a varied show for the guys in these islands. Traveling with the clubs are big-shot tennis players now in the Navy, headed by Bobby Riggs. He doubles as a ping-pong exhibitionist in matches with Bud Blattner, former Giant's shortstop who is one of the nationally-ranked table tennis players.

Also with the outfit are Fred Apostoli, the lightheavyweight champ, and Georgie Abrams, the Washington lad who is ranked the No. 2 middleweight. They stage boxing exhibitions every night. I saw their first bout, at Honolulu. It was a stinkeroo. They were both too clever. But now they've learned each other's styles and they make it look like the McCoy. Every night, mind you.

MARCH 9, 1945

D.C. Man Tells How He Made That Iwo Flag-Raising 'Shot'

Advance Pacific Headquarters, March 12—You've seen it, as who hasn't—the thrill-picture of the war thus far; that camera shot with all the beauty of a sculpture piece showing seven U.S. Marines silhouetted against the Pacific sky as they plant the American Flag on Mount Suribachi's crest.

At headquarters here they're calling it the greatest flag picture since Washington crossing the Delaware. They say you'll see it on the Nation's calendars for generations to come, and you probably will.

The photographer who got it is the most back-slapped man in this ocean area. His fame is at the stage where people point him out. All of a sudden he's a celebrity—"the camera man who got the shot of the flag on Iowa Jima."

He's Joe Rosenthal, Associated Press photographer from Washington D.C, a graduate of McKinley Tech High School in 1929. He says his greatest claim to fame of any kind heretofore was the Circle T he won as a pole vaulter on the Tech High track team.

Here's his story of the trek up the summit of Suribachi, already labeled Mount Plasma by the Fourth Marines on D-Day plus four:

"We were landing when the bos'n pointed out a red spot moving halfway up the volcano and said 'Gee, that must be the flag.' It looked like a picture to me, if I could make it, and I was the first man off the boat. That didn't take any courage: we were carrying explosives.

"I was unarmed, but I was lucky enough to pick up four Marines who were, and we started up the hill. The 550-foot climb took us a half hour. We had to sidestep Jap mines and circle the pillboxes the Marines were still cleaning out.

"The Marines on top were still looking for the best place to plant the flag when I got there, with my Speed Graphic. I'm too short to get the full picture, so they waited until I piled up rocks and sandbags from a Jap pillbox and shot from the top of the pile. Then they stuck her in, in the face of a breeze. That's all there was."

Rosenthal might have added that's all there was except the job of getting back to a ship that would get his picture out. He descended the volcano alone and boarded an amphtrack on the beach where the Japs were still pouring mortars.

It took him 19 hours to get to a ship less than a half mile off shore. The amphtrack had wounded aboard, and it was wallowing in heavy surf that pitched it back on the shore innumerable times. There was also the item of the Jap mortar firing.

Rosenthal went in originally on D-Day. He was chosen to represent the still photo pool, with his products available to all picture services. He shot sixty films. He figures the Suribachi picture as about his fortieth.

On D-Day his plans were fouled up a bit. He didn't go in on H-hour. He didn't land until three hours after the first wave made it. That was a bit disappointing. He wanted to make Iwo Jima his third straight H-hour landing. At Peleliu and Angaur he had gone in with the Marines in the first waves. In fact, he made both those H-hour landings within three hours of each other.

A year before he was in on the Hollandia business, so Iwo was his fourth campaign.

He got a late start in this war. You see, the Marines and Navy rejected him back in December 1941, on account of poor vision.

MARCH 13, 1945

11 Washington Soldiers Aid Final Mop-up on Saipan

Saipan, March 16—They've turned the mopping-up job on this island over to one of the Army's most respected infantry regiments—composed entirely of Negro troops officered by whites. And those white officers will match their men against any in the Army.

The mission of the colored boys is to kill 300 Japs, more or less, who still infest the caves and boondocks of Saipan, and day by day the Nips are being nipped by the sharp-shooting bully boys of the Twenty-fourth Regiment.

I found 11 fellows from Washington, D.C., among the troops doing the job, and retaining a boundless enthusiasm for it despite the fact some of them have been in this Pacific war for as long as 35 months.

There was Sergt. Raymond Knox of 237 12th pl. nw., for example, and I asked him how he liked the idea of Jap-hunting. Knox, who used to work for a venetian blind company, was quite blunt enough about it. He said, "We're trying to kill enough Japs so we can get home."

The Japs are tough to find and hard to kill sometimes, said Sergt. Charles Mays of 1911 R st. nw., who admitted the Japs had a certain kind of bravery. But he also observed, "They don't mind dying, and we don't mind killing 'em."

Other men from the Nation's Capital who are engaged in the job of eliminating the Nips are these:

Pfc. William Winston of 137 R st. ne; Pfc Samuel Compton of Arlington, Va.; Pfc Wilton Minor of 2313 H st. nw; Corpl. Bowman George of 635 L st. se.; Pfc. Harry E. Brady of 4829 4th st. nw; Pfc. Milton Douglas of 1831 Wiltberger st. nw.; Pfc. Edward Avery of 109 Q st. nw.; Corpl. Bunett Odell of 1633 B st. ne.; and Pfc. Dallas D. Mashore of 1810 H st. nw.

They're proud guys. Their regiment is Regular Army. It's been fighting America's wars since 1869, when it was organized in Texas, and fought Indian wars. They were the outfit that helped make the Battle of San Juan Hill a victory for the late Col. Teddy Roosevelt's

Rough Riders. They were with General Pershing in the Mexican border scrap. A lot of 'em were volunteers as human guinea pigs in the yellow fever experiments in the Spanish-American War, and some of them died for it.

Since January 1 this unit of colored troops has killed 185 Japs, captured the same number on Saipan. They go in and blast the Nips out of the jungle with rifle and mortar barrages. They know how to fight in the jungle. They haven't lost a man to the Japs. Only two of them have been wounded.

When the Marines left on January 1 it was estimated that there were no more than 300 Japs left on the island for the colored boys to eliminate. As we were saying, they've already killed or captured 370, and as many more may be left.

The Japs here lie low in the daytime, move mostly at night. They are concentrated chiefly in the dense undergrowth of a high cliff.

Povich, writing in a Japanese sugar mill, wrote about Negro troops in the war (1945)

Paradoxically, they are within rifle fire of important installations on Saipan. There are well-authenticated stories that on the night movies are shown on the island as many as 150 Japs sit on the cliffs and watch the show in the Army theaters.

The places where the Japs are hiding are the most inaccessible, but the colored troops rout them out with mortar fire, then move in in company sweeps and mop them up with rifle fire. The mortar barrages into the jungles average 35 dead Japs, with as many wounded.

Most of the Japs are armed. There's even a semblance of organization among them. At least one Jap officer is holding the whip over the Nips. There are arms and ammunition scattered all over the island, and the Japs even have American grenades. The grenades are their favorite suicide weapon.

The greatest results occur after the mortar barrages into the Japs' camps. That scatters the Japs and, free from their officers, they filter in to surrender. All is not harmony with the Japs, incidentally. Evidently they quarreled over many things, including the women they took into the jungles with them.

Persuasion as well as force brings the Japs in. Two sound truck units operating after a mortar barrage persuaded 14 Japs to surrender the first day. Three days later 53 walked in, 24 of them soldiers, 29 civilians. Apparently they were free of their officers. But after five days of rather wholesale surrender it suddenly stopped and they walked in in driblets. Apparently the officers had regained control.

These colored lads are avid souvenir hunters. They go for Jap flags and trophies of all kinds. One of the proudest Jap-hunters came back off a patrol one day with a live goose. He had killed a Jap who had the goose tied to his belt with a strong cord. "I kinda figured I could get that Jap without killing the goose," he said.

MARCH 17, 1945

Support the Troops

Please read this and buy another war bond in the Seventh War Loan
Drive because a lot of brave guys are wanting to come back from the
Pacific if their luck holds out.

They're having rough going. Thirteen men who were members of
the Fourth Marine Football team last fall won't be back in the line-up
next season. They got it on Iwo Jima, four killed, one missing and
eight wounded.

There's nothing glamorous about that Pacific war. The headlines
the other day said "Americans Smash Into Outskirts of Naha" on Okinawa. They didn't smash or crash or march or anything. They crawled
and hunched and bayoneted their way in, just like they were doing a
month ago.

The Okinawa casualties have already exceeded Iwo. At night on
Okinawa, you don't move. You lay on your blanket or in your hole and
you lie very still, because our sentries shoot anything that moves.
That's up front, of course, but the trouble is on Okinawa, with the Japs
infiltrating, you never know the front from the rear.

They knocked off one of our sentries one night. He was found in
the morning, bayoneted. The whole company of that 383d Regiment
of the Ninety-sixth Division pleaded with the captain to let 'em go
after the Japs. Buddyism is very real out there. That's the way they felt
about President Roosevelt and Ernie Pyle, buddies of theirs.

The Marines get a whopping lot of credit for the job they do, and
they are wonderful. But the Army troops in the Pacific do the same
work, though they take a bit longer. The Japs on Okinawa have everything to fight back with, and they're willing to die. Sometimes, killing
Japs is just like shooting rabbits, only those rabbits shoot back.

They had a whole battalion of our 382d Regiment pinned down for
two days below one ridge. Our fellows were catching it from Jap mortar fire. They couldn't locate the camouflaged Jap gun. The Japs use
smokeless powder in their mortars. This mortar was firing from
behind a trap door in the side of a hill. A flame-throwing patrol dug it

out. The Japs had camouflaged the gun with a swinging door made from the same sod as the hill. It had killed a lot of our guys.

There wasn't anything the Navy guys wouldn't do for our troops on the way to Okinawa. The Navy figured the Marines and Army guys were in for the dirty job of getting on shore and battling it out with the Japs. The Navy was comparatively safe, our sailors figured. They were almost motherly in the way they plied the troops with the after-chow snacks and dainties the troops couldn't get for themselves on shipboard.

But the Navy had it rough, too. The fact is that there were more casualties among the Navy men on ships at Okinawa in the first two weeks of the invasion than there were among the men on shore. The tough fighting was in the harbor in those early days of the campaign. Jap suicide dive bombers were knocking off our ships and our sailors in big numbers.

On shore, the Marines and Army had to deal with infiltrating Japs, many of them dressed in American uniforms. But on the ships, the Navy men had to deal with suicide Jap swimmers as well as the kamikaze bombers. It wasn't at all peaceful. The Navy had an off-shore war on its hands despite encountering no Jap fleet.

In the fighting lines, the fellows have a wonderful appreciation of what the home front is doing. In fact, the home front may under-estimate the magnitude of its own efforts. A citizen may be aware of the war plants in his home town. He may forget about the thousands of plants in thousands of towns. The troops don't!

The troops see the finished product! They see it all came out of the big end of the horn—planes and tanks and trucks and guns and shells and rations and derricks and cranes and jeeps and ships, big and little. They see it piled high on the beaches, in a quantity that is breath-taking, and they say, "Those people at home are really turning it out for us." They think you work awful hard.

So it would be nice to have them think so some more, because it helps them a whole lot, honest. So please buy another war bond, what I mean!

MAY 23, 1945

Farewell to The Big Train

Povich never liked writing obituaries because he didn't want to be the chronicler of the dead. But he also loved the players he knew. His 1946 column on the death of his friend, Hall of Fame pitcher Walter Johnson, was particularly painful for him to write.

Big league baseball was a hard game, basically unsuited to the gentle fellow. Ty Cobb was typifying the high success of a ball player in 1907 with his tough guy tactics, his unbridled ferocity on the baselines, his jabbering contempt for umpires and his readiness to fight for his rights, real or fancied.

Socially the ball players of thirty years ago rated only one cut above the plug-uglies of the professional prize ring. The stuffier hotels scorned the patronage of the ball teams. The average player could cuss like two troopers. A chaw of tobacco was a badge of the big leaguer. The corner saloon was their hang-out.

Into the brawling business of baseball in that era walked Walter Perry Johnson, the gangling farm boy from Idaho with long arms that dangled and a gait that smacked of the plow field. To the players on the Washington team of August 1907, here was a rube sure enough. They played poker, he played casino and checkers and went to church.

Refinement came to baseball later and the game became more of an honorable profession, attracting the college-breds and dropping pugnacity as a requisite. But Walter Johnson, the gentleman, hadn't changed. He was simply years ahead of his time.

The admiration that Walter Johnson won was something apart from the kind of acclaim lavished on sports heroes of his time. The noisy cheers for Ruth and Cobb were the product of the high excitement they produced, Ruth with his home runs, Cobb with his feats on the bases. The Nation's fans held Johnson in a special kind of esteem, something that came from the profound, reserved for the man of quiet deeds.

Walter Johnson, more than any other ball player, probably more than any other athlete, professional or amateur, became the symbol of gentlemanly conduct in the battle heat. Here was the man who never argued with an umpire, never cast a frowning look at an error-making teammate, never seemed to presume that it was his right to win, was as unperturbed in defeat.

Such was the fame and legend of Johnson, whose fast ball shattered pitching records wholesale, that it became a mark of distinction for the fan who could say, "I was there when Walter Johnson pitched his first big league game in 1907." Twenty years later when the Washington club staged a Walter Johnson day with special badges and a special section for those 700 fans who had seen Walter's big league debut, nearly 10,000 self-labeled eyewitnesses showed up to claim the privileges.

As late as 1920, Johnson was still throwing the fastest pitch known to baseball. Batters were in dread of stepping to the plate against him. Even in the Washington training camp of that year, it was the custom of his teammates when at bat to ask Johnson to lay off his fast ball, throw them his curve. He obliged willingly enough. In fact, his own speed disturbed him. Great was his fear that some day he would kill a batter.

On the occasion he did hit a batter with his fast pitch, he would be unsettled to the point of easing up thereafter. When he hit Eddie Collins, of the White Sox, on the leg in a Griffith Stadium game in 1924, and Collins went down, Johnson raced to the plate, the first to reach him. For five minutes Collins writhed in pain, with Johnson the most solicitous man in the park. When Collins indicated he could stay in the game, Johnson patted him on the back fondly, went back to his pitching.

Collins hobbled down to first base as the game resumed. It appeared as if he could barely make it. Little did the naive Johnson presume that Collins was putting on an act. Collins stole second on the next pitch. Johnson was not at all angered. Asked about it later, he said, "It was nice to know Eddie wasn't hurt."

Johnson was a five-year veteran with the Washington Club when

Clark Griffith moved in from Cincinnati to take over as manager. With the Yankees, in 1907–8–9, Griffith had watched the pitching feats of Johnson in admiration. "But I never really knew the man until the second time he pitched for me in 1912. That was the day up in Boston when it was 0–0 in the ninth and the Red Sox had a man on first with none out."

Griffith's story related how the next Boston batter hit what should have been a mere single to center, but the ball rolled through the legs of Center Fielder Clyde Milan and the winning run scored.

Johnson's only comment as he walked off the field the loser was: "Milan doesn't do that very often. Anyway, I should have struck that hitter out."

Among Washington's native adult population rare is the person who cannot recount a thrill at the pitching of Walter Johnson. Men grown up like to tell "of the time when—." There's one in our office who as a boy haunted the players' exit at the ball park to glimpse or perhaps brush against the Big Train.

He's Edward T. Folliard, feature writer, war correspondent, White House reporter and travel-mate of kings and potentates. And still a baseball fan. He wrote the story when Walter Johnson threw a silver dollar across the Rappahannock River several years ago. A few hours ago, Folliard telephoned me.

"That was the day I got my greatest thrill," he said, "when Walter Johnson took off his coat and made the throw across the Rappahannock. I was the fellow who was holding his coat."

DECEMBER 12, 1946

Integrating Baseball

The year 1947 marked Branch Rickey bringing Jackie Robinson to the Brooklyn Dodgers and Bill Veeck signing Larry Doby for the Cleveland Indians. Major League Baseball and the country would never be the same. Povich believed Veeck was more sensitive to Negro League owners than Rickey, who signed sixteen additional players the following year and essentially destroyed the Negro Leagues.

New York, July 4—Bill Veeck, the Cleveland owner who broke American League precedent by signing a colored ball player, did it at least the correct way in contrast to Brooklyn's grab of Jackie Robinson from the Kansas City Monarchs of the Negro National League.

The Kansas City squad squawked, and justifiably, a couple years ago when Branch Rickey whisked Robinson out of their lineup and put him in Brooklyn's Montreal farm without so much as an if-you-please.

Not a shilling passed between Rickey and the Monarch owners. When Veeck signed Larry Doby of the Newark National League club the other day, it was all very business-like with $15,000 being paid over to Mrs. Effie Manley, owner of the Newark franchise.

This Doby fellow is a considerable ball player, as I hear it, even with his .400 batting average in the Negro National League dismissed as an unsafe standard.

Mickey Vernon, who played with him on Navy teams at Great Lakes, says, "He's a good ball player." The Yankees, who saw a lot of him in Puerto Rico where he was playing on all-star teams last spring, are of the same opinion.

In fact Vernon, who saw much of Jackie Robinson during his tour with the Feller all-stars last year, asserts that Doby is a better ball player than the Brooklyn first baseman. "I don't know where Doby will end up with the Indians," Vernon said, "because when I saw him trying to play first base, he was no first baseman. He can play second or short, though."

That's where it may be rough for Doby. Of all the things the Indians don't need, a shortstop and second baseman head the list. He'll have to be a triple-distilled wonder to break in at short with Lou Boudreau, the league's leading hitter and the best shortstop in the majors, still around. And at second base the Indians have Joe Gordon, who rates as the finest in the league.

At first base, though, the colored boy from Newark might well make it with the Indians, even though he is something less than a good first baseman. If he can hit as the Cleveland scouts believe he will, well, the Indians will welcome him at first base inasmuch as their present first-sackers, Les Fleming and Eddie Robinson, are no balls of fire.

The Negro race is batting 1.000 thus far in the big leagues, with Robinson something of a sensational success with Brooklyn. Going into today's game he had a 20-game hitting streak going and was hitting more than .300. He's the fastest man on the club, leads the league in stolen bases, is tremendously popular with the Brooklyn fans, and is one of the chief reasons why Brooklyn is leading the league.

Robinson isn't a good first baseman, or even an adequate one, but his other talents counteract his defensive weakness. The complaints against him can be easily answered anyway. Natively, he's a second baseman or shortstop, and for a guy who is playing out of position, he is doing an immense job. At second base, he might well be the league's best, and certainly he would be the best-hitting second baseman.

It makes a lousy prophet of Bob Feller, incidentally. After pitching to Robinson on his all-star tour, Feller delivered the opinion, "That guy won't hit big league pitching." That's the thing Robinson has been doing best.

In fact, if the Brooklyn club's great need this year was not for a first baseman, Robinson probably would be playing second and as a second baseman he would doubtless be on the National League All-Star team. But at first base, he is a gone pigeon what with Johnny Mize and his 22 home runs overshadowing every other first sacker in the league.

Robinson doesn't scare easily, either. He's been hit by pitched balls seven times this year, more than any other player in the league, but you'd never know it the way he persists in his crowd-the-plate stance. He used to sit on the corner of the Dodgers' bench by himself, but now his teammates cotton to him and he's one of the boys.

If Doby is a good ballplayer, he will have fewer worries than Robinson did at the outset. The National is a rougher league than the American, which is not as sharp-tongued. And for the Negro with baseball talent, the significant item was that Cleveland had to outbid a couple of other big league clubs in signing a colored player.

JULY 5, 1947

The Babe Says Goodbye

It was a cold, raw day in 1948 when Babe Ruth—his once enormous body now savaged with cancer—said farewell to nearly 60,000 fans at Yankee Stadium in the Bronx. I was seven years old, sitting in the third deck at Yankee Stadium. "That's Babe Ruth," my father said. "He was the greatest ball player ever." In the press box below, unbeknownst to me, Povich was covering the day. How was I to know I was in the stadium with two of the most important men in my life?
—George Solomon,
sports editor of *The Washington Post*, 1975–2003

New York, April 27—They helped the Babe up the three steps of the Yankee Stadium dugout, a friend at each arm gently applying the lift the sick man seemed to need. But as he neared the microphones at home plate, he shrugged them off and seemed to square the shoulders that had powered 714 American League home runs.

It was Babe Ruth Day at Yankee Stadium, and the House That Ruth Built was tenanted now by 58,339 come to pay him honor. Now there were the cheers as the Babe made his way onto the field, but five minutes before a church quiet had reigned over the outdoor pews as Francis Cardinal Spellman delivered the invocation from home plate.

In his camel's-hair coat and camel's-hair cap that has been his favorite attire, The Babe stood by for the introduction, but it was taking too long. Now his shoulders were hunched and drooping again,

Babe Ruth at Yankee Stadium when his number 3 was retired. (June 13, 1948)

and he was coughing into his closed fist, and you could see he was not a well man if you had never been aware that the state of his health had been of national concern for weeks.

And then The Babe spoke into the microphones, and he mustered a broad smile beneath his broad nose, and what you heard was a husky croaking that bordered on a whisper, and he was saying, "Thank you very much . . . ," and his voice trailed off into a nothingness, and you knew it was an effort for him to speak.

But the Babe was battling it out. Now he was virtually snuggling his face against the mike as if it were something to be taken into his confidence and he was saying, "I thank heaven we have had baseball in this world . . . the kids . . . our national pastime."

Your thinking flipped back to July 4, 1939, when The Babe stood on the same ground, a well man then, and wound an affectionate arm around the shoulder of his pal, Lou Gehrig, who was a sick man. The gusty, booming-voiced Ruth of that day was going down the line for a friend, smiling through his own concern for the ailing Gehrig, and now he was standing there hurting from the ravages of his own illness, and the people were moved, and in prayerful mood.

You remembered that at the Gehrig Day it was that way, too, and your eyes were moist then and you had noted that even the photographers, those single-purpose guys with scarcely a thought for other than a picture, were wet eyed, too. And you thought, "Oh brother. When you see a photographer cry, it's real."

The Babe had said, "thank you very much, ladies and gentlemen . . . you know how bad my voice sounds. Well, it feels just as bad . . ." But he was smiling when he said it, though he wasn't fooling anybody.

And when he was finished, he stood erect again and waved a salute from his head. They didn't try to help him off the field. He seemed to need none, and it made you feel better.

Today baseball was pulling out all the stops for The Babe, now 53, and the Symbol of the game. There is doubt that a prelate of the church ever before went into a ball field in tribute to a baseball figure, but today Francis Cardinal Spellman . . . archbishop of the Diocese of New York, eagerly officiated at the invocation, and he said: ". . . We honor a hero in the world of sport, a champion of fair play and a manly leader of the youth of America. We beseech thee to bless him and his apostulate among every youth of the land that he may continue to encourage and inspire the young to live chaste, sober and heroic lives, disciplined by the highest ideals of sportsmanship for the glory of our beloved country, for the glory of thy beloved Self . . . Bless Thou with especial love him whom we honor this today."

Baseball Commissioner A.B. Chandler, American League President Will Harridge and National League President Ford Frick were there, too, to pay honor to The Babe, and perhaps it was Frick who stated it best when, addressing himself to Ruth, he said: "To Babe

Ruth, whose batting average through the years is exceeded only by the size of his heart, and whose capacity to hit home runs is surpassed only by his capacity to make and hold friends. That you ruined our National League hopes in many a World Series and too often batted our brains out and made us like it does not diminish our pride in your accomplishments." The 58,000 liked that speech.

APRIL 28, 1948

THE FIFTIES

THE DATE WAS OCTOBER 9, 1956 AND SHIRLEY POVICH WAS IN the press box at New York's Yankee Stadium after the Yankees' Don Larsen had pitched the only perfect game in World Series history, winning 2–0, over the Brooklyn Dodgers.

The minutes were ticking down to *The Washington Post's* 7 P.M. first edition deadline. Povich sat there a long time—long after the deadline writers had departed the stadium—before he came up with his lead. And then he began typing on his venerable Olivetti portable:

> The million-to-one shot came in. Hell froze over. A month of Sundays hit the calendar. Don Larsen pitched a no-hit, no-run, no-man-reach-first game in a World Series.

Published in various textbooks, the Page One piece became a model for journalism students and won several journalism awards as an example of inspired game coverage that still sets a standard to this day.

Indeed, Povich's success and reputation grew during this decade. He carved relationships with many of the famous athletes of the time, including Joe DiMaggio, Ted Williams, Mickey Mantle, Willie Mays, Sammy Baugh, Joe Louis, Rocky Marciano, Eddie Arcaro, Ben Hogan, and Sam Snead. These stars not only admired Povich for his work, but for the dignity and grace that he displayed on the job.

His status also was enhanced by the growth of the newspaper, spurred by the purchase of the *Washington Times-Herald* in 1954 that doubled circulation to about 400,000 and made the *Post* the only morning newspaper in Washington. According to Don Graham, now the company's CEO, Povich was rated the most popular writer on the newspaper and the reason many readers bought it each day. "Shirley had the gift of sincerity," says Graham. "It showed in his writing. He always wrote for the reader, not for the people who were running the teams. He was writing for the kid—as was the case for me—or the fan reading the newspaper in the morning."

"One of the most important things a newspaper does is to create a sense of community among its readers," the late Katharine Graham, former publisher of the *Post*, once said of Povich. "In a real sense all Washington gathered around Shirley's kitchen table to share the pleasure—or more likely, the pain—of the last game. I think Shirley alone was responsible for about a third of our readership. He's one of the cornerstones on which today's *Post* was built."

In a decade of stars, Povich covered DiMaggio, Louis, and Baugh as they closed out their careers and Marciano, Mantle, Hogan, and Snead in their heyday. But in Washington, he would be stuck with the

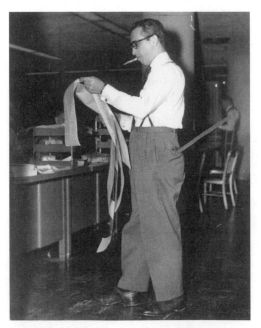

For many decades, Povich was rated the most popular columnist at the Post *and the most read columnist of all in Washington. (1951)*

lagging Senators and the Redskins, who had only two winning seasons all decade. Povich's hilarious parody of basketball—a piece he wrote for *Sports Illustrated* in 1958, in which he observed it was a game for lads with "runaway pituitary glands"—forever pinned him in the anti-basketball camp. It was a category he rejected, saying he rarely wrote about the sport because he did not understand the game, even though he played it as a kid. But he later applauded the exploits of Julius (Dr. J) Erving, Michael Jordan, and Wes Unseld, after his son, David, took him to Capital Centre in Landover, Md., to see them play.

He also covered many of the great sports events of the decade, including Bobby Thomson's three-run game-winning home run in the ninth inning that brought the New York Giants the 1951 pennant against the Brooklyn Dodgers, and the 1958 overtime NFL championship game won by the Baltimore Colts over the New York Giants in Yankee Stadium that catapulted pro football into the modern era. But it was his ground-breaking 13-part series on the integration of major league baseball, "No More Shutouts," written in 1953, that opened the eyes of many Washingtonians to the social significance sports was playing in race relations

Despite his writing success and the reputation he had gained among his colleagues from Grantland Rice to Red Smith, Povich's talent lay largely unnoticed by the sports reading public outside of Washington. That changed with an AP story on January 13, 1959. The story reported that Shirley Povich had been included in the first edition of *Who's Who of American Women*. There he was, listed between Louise Pound and Hortense Powdermaker, even though his entry included the fact that he was married to Ethyl Friedman and had three children. That was news even for the *New York Times*. Later, Povich appeared on the national quiz show "I've Got a Secret" and stumped the panel. The man named Shirley had a nationwide following now.

Hogan and Snead

The two most dominant golfers of the 1950s were Ben Hogan and Sam Snead. Povich knew them well, covered them and contrasted their abilities. He often played golf with Snead and loved to tell how if a member of their foursome would tee up the ball slightly in front of the tee box, Snead would say, "Let's play the whole course today, okay?"

The year 1950 has already witnessed its No. 1 comeback story, you'd have to say. Unless the Nats win the pennant. Ben Hogan's gallant bid for the Los Angeles Open golf title will probably stand as the peak display of resurgence by any athlete or group of them.

In the hats-off department Hogan must be rated tops. Less than a year ago, he was bedridden in a Texas hospital, his arms, legs and back in traction and his life in doubt after a head-on crash between his car and a hefty cross-country bus. If he lived, there was the high doubt that he'd ever swing a golf club in competition again.

Only a couple of weeks ago, he was still deemed far out of any contention for such an important tournament as the Los Angeles event with a field that rivaled the PGA in caliber. He was back on the golf course, true enough, but he was getting around on a motorized scooter between his long shots, so weak were the legs.

He didn't exactly win the L.A Open with its $15,000 prize money, but he came as close as he could without winning. He wound up in a tie for first place with Sammy Snead, after averaging 1 under par for the four 18-hole rounds.

The sensation was that little Hogan, after freely confessing that he expected to tire after the first round, actually shot better golf in his final rounds. He posted a 73 on the first day and then threw three consecutive 69s at the field. And when rain forced the postponement of his play-off against Snead for a week, there was general satisfaction among golf fans for the greater rest it would provide Hogan.

The medics, too, are grateful for Hogan. He was an example, they say, of the kind of spirit and attitude that aids recovery. His eagerness to return to action speeded Hogan's recapture of his health. He never wavered in his determination to get well and catch up with the fellows who were taking down the purse money in the tournaments he used to win. He's won the L.A. Open three times before.

Even when he was in the Army, Hogan's pride in his golf was unabated. Joe Novak, president of the PGA, tells how little Ben chafed at the constants references to Byron Nelson as "the world's greatest golfer." Hogan kept saying, "Wait until I get out of the Army. I'm the world's greatest golfer, not Nelson." He'd recall, too, how he used to beat Nelson when both of then were caddies on the same Texas course.

In his comeback, Hogan has captured some of the popularity that wasn't his before he was hurt. Despite his No. One rating at the top of the pros, little Ben was not a big favorite of the galleries. Golf fans admired his classic swing and his sensational shot-making, but he

The rivalry between Sam Snead (left) and Ben Hogan dominated golf for most of the 1940s and 1950s. (1955)

looked neither to right nor left and was the mechanical man of the links.

For such as the more personable and smiling Nelson, the carefree Jimmy Demaret and the hilly-billy antics of Sammy Snead, the galleries reserved most of their applause. There was always the tacit acknowledgement that Hogan was probably the best golfer of the lot, but he lacked the oomph and gallery-appeal of his colleagues, and Snead replaced him as the best box office draw.

Thus at Los Angeles last week, Hogan for the first time in his life was the sentimental favorite over the popular Snead. Even as Jack Dempsey gained wider popularity after his tough break in losing to Tunney on the long count at Chicago, Hogan came into his own after adversity struck him down. Almost unanimously the crowd was pulling for the game little figure of Hogan to take it all at Los Angeles.

Hogan's display of fortitude against the physical pain he must have been enduring during the four-day grind had something of a parallel, however, in Snead's own exhibition. Snead's gameness was of a different type, involving the mental hazards, not the physical. A supposedly weak putter, Snead had to sink 10-and 15-foot putts for birdies on the last two greens to get his tie.

Earlier in the tournament, Snead had been missing putts all over the premises and appeared to be out of it until he fired that final 5-under-par 66 onto the scoreboard. But when the chips were down, so were Snead's putts. It recalled Gene Sarazen's definition of Snead as a putter.

"Snead's reputation as a poor putter is one of the worst deserved," declared Sarazen. "Sammy isn't one of the good putters among the pros, but he isn't one of the weak ones, either. And what is generally overlooked is that he's probably the best long putter in the whole business."

JANUARY 13, 1950

Dempsey and Louis: Who Was Better?

In 1950, the Associated Press polled sports writers and broadcasters as to who was the greatest fighter of the first half of the century. Povich covered both Jack Dempsey and Joe Louis and remembered each fondly.

That great news gathering organization, the Associated Press, reports that Jack Dempsey was the greatest fighter of the half century. If that fact does not quite qualify as news, it is nevertheless interesting. A national poll of sports writers and broadcasters elevates Dempsey to the No. 1 spot over Joe Louis.

The temptation is to take it from there and speculate what might have happened had Louis and Dempsey been cast into the same era instead of attaining their peaks 20 years apart. Only one thing is certain—their fight would have been a beaut. Less certain, but quite probable, is the belief that Dempsey would have walked out the winner.

In Louis' corner you'd have seen the deadliest puncher in the history of the heavyweight ranks—the man who could numb you with one knuckle-packed bomb—but against Dempsey he'd have been in there with the fighter who could take a punch better than any other.

And only a Louis could have out-punched Dempsey, who could also tear a fellow's head off, but not with quite the same dispatch as Louis. It is significant that they were both exponents of the most destructive kind of punch in the fight business—the left hook.

Unlike Dempsey's iron-tough chin, there was a chink in Louis' armor, though, and it was doubtless the biggest factor in the poll's reluctance to rank him No. 1 despite the fact that he won more fights. Louis was on the seat of his own pants too many times and there must be the suspicion that he couldn't take a punch to the chin with any of the aplomb of the old Mauler.

Aging Jimmy Braddock, never known as a hefty hitter, had Louis down from an uppercut before yielding his title to Joe. And before that, Max Schmeling floored him five times before knocking him out.

Even as a champion, though never beaten, Louis was dumped on the floor once by such as Buddy Baer and Tony Galento, and three times the venerable Joe Walcott had him down in their two fights.

And one night in New York, Tami Mauriello tagged Louis in the first round and it appeared as if a new champion was in the making. Panic was all over Joe's face, and only his recuperative powers brought him back to the battle. Squared away once more, Louis knocked Mauriello out in the same round with a punch that ranked as one of the most explosive of all time, second only perhaps to the straight right hand with which he once knocked Lou Nova out.

Dempsey's record shows only two knockdowns, and one of those was in 1917 when he was stopped by Fireman Jim Flynn in the days when he was an unknown. In 1923, Luis Firpo knocked Dempsey through the ropes at the Polo Grounds, but it wasn't by a ponderous push. Dempsey was also down on one knee in the eighth round of the second Tunney fight but Tunney just grazed him with a right. Dempsey missed a wild right and then slipped to the canvas but was up without a count.

When Dempsey did yield the title to Gene Tunney in the Philadelphia upset in 1926, the Dempsey chin was no factor. Tunney simply outpointed an aging, supine Dempsey who was clearly through. In his training camp before that fight, it was obvious that he was old and rusty, what with Tommy Loughran, a light-heavyweight, exposing him as slow with the old tiger spring gone from all of his limbs.

If the A.P. erred in its poll, it was in referring to Dempsey's fight with Jack Sharkey, between the two Tunney fights, as a "warm-up." Dempsey won that one, but it was anything but a warm-up. He took an unconscionable beating from Sharkey for six rounds and was hit by everything save the ringposts, and it was a pathetic spectacle. He wasn't in distress, he simply was losing every round. And then in the seventh he stopped Sharkey with the only punch he aimed at the sailor's chin all night—a crushing left hook.

Gene Tunney was rated third among the heavyweights of the last 50 years, and there could be some quarrel with that ranking. Save for his two victories over the back-slid Dempsey, Tunney had the least impressive record of any champion in those years. He defended his title only twice, and the last time was against a hand-picked trial horse, Tom Heeney.

But in one respect, Tunney qualified for a superlative. He was the most sharp-shooting puncher of them all. He punched to spots and could achieve more blood-letting at the first sign of an opponent's cut than any other. He was no numbing puncher, but he specialized nicely in a solid right hand to the heart that could hurt more than was visible.

Tunney could take it, too, and he might have beaten such as Louis by his ability to maneuver a man in and out of position. But the most reasonable belief is that Louis would have caught up with Tunney somewhere within 10 rounds and hurt him with that streaking left hook, probably knockout. That's just an idea. Suppose you take it from here.

January 30, 1950

Booing Fans

Hank Greenberg has reintroduced the interesting subject of rabbit ears among ball players. The new general manager of the Cleveland Indians is now threatening to oust from his park any loudly booing fans who might get on the nerves of his athletes.

"Ball players have rabbit ears," Greenberg explains. "Try as hard as they might they can't shut out the boos. No matter how faint, one boo can give a player the false feeling that most fans are against him."

He isn't concerned with the mere second-guessers among the customers, only the "abusive pop-offs, those two or three obnoxious fans in every park who boo a player so much he develops the feeling he'd rather play on the road than at home."

Greenberg may be cutting out a larger order for himself than get-

ting back that pennant the Indians blew last season. Where the privileges of the fan who pays his buck–20 stop is apt to be a Solomon-like
decision. And the line between abusiveness and loudness isn't easily
defined, either.

Rabbit ears are no exclusive appendage of the ball players, however. Certain umpires have suffered from the same sensitive hearing,
and many a ball player has been thumbed out of a game for remarks
that he didn't calculate might be within the umpire's hearing.

Years ago, Umpire Brick Owens suddenly wrenched off his mask
from behind the plate and pointed vigorously at the Washington
bench. "I heard that," he yelled at Outfielder Heinie Manush, "and
you are out of the game."

When Manush protested he hadn't said anything loud enough to
be overheard, Owen came back, "I got rabbit ears."

With nothing more to lose, Manush let the umpire have it with, "I
always did think you could hear better than you could see."

But Greenberg is correct about the players' sensitivity to boos, and
no less than Ted Williams has borne him out. "If there are 10,000 fans
cheering and one booing, I hear the boo," Williams has often said.

General Manager Billy Evans of the Detroit Tigers just a couple of
months ago brought up the subject of the home-town fans booing certain ball players. He admitted it was one of the reasons Detroit traded
Dick Wakefield to the Yankees.

"Our Detroit fans were down on Wakefield so much that I felt
sorry for the boy all last year," said Evans. "We liked Wakefield, but we
wanted to trade him away from Detroit before they broke his heart."

The ball player who achieved the greatest triumph over the home-
grown boos is probably the Nats' Sherry Robertson. For years, he got it
good at every fumble or failure with the bat. As Clark Griffith's
nephew, he was particularly vulnerable. His chief crime was that he
couldn't pick his relations.

But Young Robertson never registered any dismay, even though he
felt it. He stayed in the lineup, kept taking that beautiful cut with his

bat and won the Washington fans to him with his gutty display. The fan who now boos Sherry draws black looks from his neighbors.

Not all the boos directed at ball players are especially meaningful. Babe Ruth was invariably hooted on the road when he walked up to the plate, but he'd greet it with smiles. The Babe knew they were polite boos, a tribute to him, and that booing was the thing to do for the same fans who were eager to applaud when he pleased them with a home run.

It's significant that the game's bigger figures get the louder boos. Williams, DiMaggio and Feller get them now. They know that when the time comes that they are not booed, they're no longer important.

It's significant, too, that Bill Veeck never concerned himself with the fans' booing, even the abusive ones, while he was running the Cleveland ball club for four years more successfully than any team was ever operated. Greenberg is moving in on delicate ground. Maybe the fans won't like what he is saying. Maybe they got rabbit ears, too.

FEBRUARY 23, 1950

Shot Heard 'round the World

Millions of fans claim to have been there. Novels have been built around the moment. Play-by-play tapes still sell. It was a memorable fall afternoon in the Polo Grounds when Bobby Thomson hit a three-run home run off Brooklyn's Ralph Branca in the ninth inning to give the New York Giants a 5–4 victory in the deciding game of the 1951 National League playoffs. Povich wrote the game story for the Post *and this eloquent column.*

New York, Oct. 3—And so it came down to the absolute last pitch of the 157-game season before it was decided that the Giants, not the Dodgers, would be in the World Series against the Yankees.

Hollywood's most imaginative writers on an opium jag could not
have scripted a more improbable windup of the season that started in
April and had its finish today in the triumph of Bobby Thomson and
the Giants.

Into that last blur of white that came plateward out of the pitching
fist of Brooklyn's Ralph Branca was compressed the destiny of the two
clubs that had battled for six months to get to today's decision. Before
Thomson swung, it was the Dodgers winning the pennant. A split-sec-
ond later the Dodgers were dead, and the Giants had it.

Branca was pitching to the goat of the final play-off game. Early in
the contest, Thomson messed up a promising rally for the Giants with
a stupid bit of heads-down base running that perhaps cost the Giants a
vital run, maybe more, in the game that was a 1–1 stalemate going into
the eighth.

But at the finish it was Thomson the hero who struck the blow that
got the Giants into the World Series. At a time when his pals were
praying for a single that would tie the score at 3–3, Tommy wound it
up with a home run that brought the Giants all the marbles.

The World Series that opens tomorrow has to be anti-climactic to
today's struggle. It's probably the only World Series ever to get second
billing on World Series eve to a mere pennant-clinching game. This
one today had too many situations and folks too tensed-up. All day the
Dodgers were looking like the team of destiny in their battle to beat
Sal Maglie, who had licked 'em five times this season.

But today they had Maglie licked with that three-run outburst in
the eighth that gave them a 4–1 lead, and back of big Don Newcombe
the Dodgers were a sensational fielding lot. Billy Cox and Peewee
Reese and Gil Hodges were denying the Giants the baseline with
their fancy stuff in the infield, and Newcombe was breezing to the big
win that would get the Dodgers into the Series.

The dark day was making Newcombe's fastball look faster, and he
had a four-hitter going into the ninth, and who would speculate that
he wouldn't last the inning out? But these Giants who wouldn't take
No for an answer when then were 13 1/2 games behind in August, were
not surrendering merely for the need of three runs in the ninth. Alvin

Dark's single, Johnny Mueller's single, Whitey Lockman's double, and Newcombe no longer was in there.

When they called for Branca to come out of the bullpen in distant right field, he had no suspicion he was walking into what was to be the sorriest mess of his career. Two pitches later, Branca was the losing pitcher. Next week he marries the boss's daughter, whose pappy is half owner of the Brooklyn club. The echo of that blast of Thomson's is apt to accompany the honeymooners.

All day Leo Durocher and his hated opposite number, Charley Dressen, were glaring at each other from the dugouts and the coaching lines, and it was Durocher who achieved the first advantage with a neat bit of strategy in the sixth inning. That was when the score was tied at 1–1 with Snider on first, one out, and the dangerous Jackie Robinson up. With the count two balls and no strikes on Robinson, Durocher dared to signal a pitch out by Maglie and he was guessing right. Dressen was sending Snider down, and he was out at second by 20 feet.

The Yankees, all of them were sitting in the stands today, waiting to learn whom they would have to play in the World Series beginning tomorrow, and they have to like the Giants better after this one. They were watching a team that could muster a Yankee-type finish just when their blazing stretch rush threatened to fall short of the ultimate goal of the pennant.

The Yanks could see that only super-fielding of Cox and Reese and Hodges were keeping the Giants off base in those early and middle innings and that here was a club that would require a lot of beating. It was a team, too, that was bouncing back after the previous day's humiliating 10–0 defeat and was unpanicked even by that three-run lead Newcombe held going into the ninth.

Before the game, Manager Casey Stengel cozily refused to declare which club he would rather battle in the World Series, but he did hint that he wouldn't mind playing the Dodgers. "I'd rather play a team with a one-legged catcher," he said, referring to Roy Campanella's serious injury. He isn't going to get his wish, which could be worse luck.

OCTOBER 4, 1951

Marciano–Walcott

Philadelphia, Sept. 24—Before the fight, it had been mostly a high current of Walcott talk because he was the more romantic of the two figures: a 38-year-old pappy of six who would be taking on two challengers in the same ring, Rocky Marciano and Father Time.

The smart money had installed Marciano as the 9-to–5 favorite; and that was understandable, but for those who were betting with their hearts instead of their heads, Pappy Joe was the man they took. The old gaffer had emotional box-office.

And even as the fight ended, the typists at the ringside found themselves bearing down heavily on the Walcott story after the perfunctory notice that there was a new heavyweight champion of the world, and that Marciano was it. The flash right hand that wiped out Walcott's early lead, like a home run with the bases full in the thirteenth, had come too suddenly to negate completely what had been the story line of the fight.

It had been sheer magnificence by Walcott, his defiance of the book that was supposed to remand 38-year-old fighters into discard, and his bossing of the young man who was trying to knock his head off. There he was out there, practicing all the fine arts of prize fighting that Marciano had never bothered to learn, and beating this young whipper-snapper who was supposed to lick him.

But that was yesterday, and last night. Time now, perhaps, to concede Walcott his hour of glory and bring the new champion, Rocky, into proper focus. The ultimate glory was his, the winner's, and none can be withheld from him. He answered a lot of things last night. Not only with that climactic right hand that won the fight for him. Before that happened, he had displayed championship stuff.

In a losing fight up to that thirteenth round, Marciano was a better fighter than he'd ever been in any of those 42 straight victories previously. He was crude, but crude compared only to Walcott the master stylist. Rocky had come out of his training camp as a fighter with more class.

That latter was evident in the first minute of the fight when he found himself on the seat of his pants, floored by something he hadn't bargained for; a sneak left hook that wily Walcott had thrown after feinting with his right shoulder. It was a murderous thing and Rocky dropped like the target of a pole-axe, but his head was clear and he had the gumption if not the wisdom to get up at the count of three from the first knockdown he ever suffered.

Rocky has more than Walcott could contend with. He was a half-blind fighter from the sixth round on, trying to bring Jersey Joe into view through eyes that were smarting and blurred from oil and saffron applied to Walcott's cut brow to stop the blood. The stuff had come off Walcott's gloves as he mopped the wound, and now it was on Rocky's face. He was blinking and cursing his luck.

But he wasn't missing by as much as in the Matthews and Savold fights, and except for that first-round sneak, Jersey Joe wasn't finding him wide open. What he was confronted with was an untamed gladiator who marched forward relentlessly to try to join the battle, unmindful of the way Walcott, too, could hit. Plain to see was Rocky's driving urge to win that title and his willingness to wade through fire.

Walcott fetched him some solid clouts but after that first round there was no distress for Rocky except for the stuff that got in his eyes. He had to be aware that he was losing the fight, but he was still carrying that right hand cocked, watchful of the chance to lay it against Walcott's chin and rid himself of the tormenting thing in there with him.

No disputing now that Rocky can hit. Harder than Dempsey. Louis, too, I'd say. At least faster if not harder, and with both hands, and able to generate more horsepower in a shorter arc. The right that ended it, traveled about 6 inches, no more than 8, and it wasn't a weary old man that Rock was knocking out. Walcott had caught a miraculous second wind back in the eighth and was still bossing the fight when the last punch came out of the night air.

Joe Louis had knocked out Walcott, too, but with a combination of four punches that would put the old man down. Rocky needed only one. He did hook a left at Pappy Joe after the right landed, but it was unnecessary. And remember, too, that when Rocky put Matthews down, it was from the other side, with two left hooks, back to back, thrown very fast, like the book says.

If Marciano's high popularity isn't immediate, it will come later. He's the home-run hitter of the heavyweights, best fitting the popular conception of what a world champion should be. Nobody has licked him since he came out of the Army to turn professional. You've got to go along with a 1.000 hitter.

SEPTEMBER 25, 1952

Sammy Baugh Retires

From 1937, when he joined the Washington Redskins, until his retirement in 1952, Hall of Fame quarterback Sammy Baugh was among the most proficient and colorful players in the history of the NFL. Povich covered nearly all his games.

The first time I saw Sammy Baugh, his feet were hurting and he was softly cussing his new boss, George Marshall. Baugh was deplaning from a tin crate that had flown him in from Sweetwater, Tex., for his contract-signing ceremonies with the Redskins, in 1937, dressed according to the Marshall plan.

In his zeal to introduce Baugh as a rootin', tootin' son of the Wild West, Marshall decreed the 1937 version of the Hopalong Cassidy outfit for him. The fact that Baugh was a citified Texan who didn't know which side of a horse to mount was brushed aside. Sammy went for the fancy shirt, the flaring Stetson, the whipcord pants and, worse luck, those high-heeled boots.

Those narrow Texas boots were his undoing. He literally limped into the Occidental Hotel dining room for his welcome-to-Washington luncheon. In confidential asides, he admitted he was the phony-est cowboy ever to hit Washington, but Marshall was paying his expenses both ways and giving him a $500 bonus for signing, and "Ah guess Ah gotta dress to suit him, not me."

The prettier story is, and a true one, that Tenderfoot Baugh of the literally tender feet, who started out to go cowboy as a gag, in later years became as genuine a cow-poke as any wild-riding sonofagun on the range. He wound up with his own ranch, thanks to his pro football earnings, a passion for horses and enough ability with a rope to get him into some rodeo acts.

Sammy Baugh wasn't the Redskins' quarterback in those early days. He didn't know enough about running a pro football team. Sammy was a halfback in the single-wing generalled by Riley Smith. The other halfback was Cliff Battles and the fullback, mostly, was Don Irwin. Sammy was supposed to do the team's passing, but he was not above running that ball, either, and he did with a funny jack-rabbit stride that got him over the ground.

Unforgettable was that dressing room speech by Coach Ray Flaherty the night the Redskins were making their debut in 1937 as Washington's own against the Giants in Griffith Stadium. Flaherty got right down to realism in his pregame oration, and it went something like this, as he addressed his Redskins:

"Virtually every passing record fell to his skill," said Povich of Sammy Baugh. (1942)

"You're in a new town," he said. "Marshall is paying us good money. You're getting paid for 60 minutes of football a week, so start giving it. Up in Boston, you kept moaning that we didn't have any guy who could pass for us. Now we've brought you Sammy Baugh, the greatest passer in the world. I want you guys to give Sammy plenty of protection. The Giants will be out to get him, we know that. Don't let them do it. Get them first."

The Redskins beat the Giants that night, and the most fabulous career in pro football, Sammy Baugh's, was launched. His passes became the most destructive weapon in the history of the game. Virtually every passing record in the book fell to his skill. As he comes up to his farewell game on Sunday against the Eagles, he still owns 16 all-time records to show for his 16 seasons in the league, including one for longevity.

Coach Ray Flaherty himself used to like to tell the story of his first briefing of Baugh when he was attempting to indoctrinate the slim Texan into the more rugged tactics of pro football. "And these receivers in the pro league expect their passers to be good," he told Sammy. "None of those wild heaves you see the college boys throw.

"When they go down field, our eligible pass receivers want that ball where they can catch it," he told Sammy. "They like to be hit right in the eye, understand?"

To which Baugh, after hearing Flaherty out, was supposed to have replied, "Which eye, coach?"

Baugh was a 60-minute football player in those early years with the Redskins. He played safety man on defense, and was the team's most valuable man on pass defense, not too surprising a skill on Sammy's part. After all, he had been All-Texas in basketball at TCU.

I was Sammy's ghost writer in those early days, batting out three articles a week under his byline. He gave me a blank check. "You write it, I'll read it after it gets in the paper," he said. Unwittingly, I put him in the grease with one article that acclaimed Tommy Thompson of Tulsa U. as "the finest forward passer now in college ranks."

From Texas, where the Baugh articles were printed, Baugh was overwhelmed by telephone, telegrams and letters with complaints about the Thompson article under his signature. He called me, frantic. "I'm in trouble," he said. "You didn't mention Davey O'Brien of TCU, and all those Texans think I'm jealous because he's threatening my record down there."

So, the next day, we collaborated on a piece amending our esteem of Tommy Thompson. "Thompson is the greatest college passer in the United States," we wrote, "and almost as good as Davey O'Brien of TCU, who is out of this world." The Texans were appeased.

Along with the passing records Sammy put into the books he leaves also one immortal quote. That was following the disastrous 73–0 game with the Bears in 1940. The outcome might have been different, fans were saying, if Charlie Malone had held onto a Baugh pass in the end zone that would have made it 7–7 at that point and stopped the Bear stampede. "Yeah," said Baugh, refusing to blame Malone. "It would have been different. It wouldn't have ended 73–0. It would have been 73–7."

DECEMBER 10, 1952

Writing for Justice

Povich spent a lifetime writing in favor of equal opportunity for athletes of all races and religions. His crusade to integrate Major League Baseball culminated in this 13-part series in 1953 called "No More Shutouts," which won the prestigious National Headliners Award. Here are three of the pieces:

Negro Has Found Real Democracy in Baseball

Four hundred and fifty-five years after Columbus eagerly discovered America, major league baseball reluctantly discovered the American Negro; discovered that he could play ball as well, sometimes better, than the white boys and men to whom the national game supposedly belonged by right of pigmentation.

The Negro ball player, in turn, made a discovery of his own once the Color Curtain was lifted in the enlightened year of 1947 when Jackie Robinson became a member of the Brooklyn Dodgers. The Negro player found that there is more democracy in the locker room than in baseball's front offices or even in the street.

In what can be described perhaps as uneasy stages, the club owners learned that Jim Crow-ism was not a necessary safeguard to their thriving business and that profits would not come tumbling down because an American citizen of colored blood was playing alongside a white American

Two kinds of club owners had kept the Negro out of organized baseball: (1.) the outré bigots among them and (2) those owners who had built up an edifice of false fear that the fans would be outraged by the sight of a Negro in a big league lineup and would stay away from the park; that valuable players of Southern origin would refuse to take the field with, and against, Negroes; and that no Negro player was skillful enough to make a big league club.

All the while there were pious protestations by the game's most important figures, including the late Commissioner Kenesaw Landis, that no rule in the structure of organized baseball was keeping the Negroes out. No written rule, they meant. The rules that were unwritten, they knew well.

In 1938, Commissioner Landis agreed to permit a delegation of Negroes to address the major leagues' joint meeting of club owners with an appeal for racial equality in baseball. The leader made a sincere and moving presentation of the Negroes' case and the wounds from the big league policy that was dooming them to second-class baseball citizenship.

"Is that all, gentlemen?" Landis asked, when the speaker had finished.

"Yes it is, Commissioner. Thank you for hearing us," he said.

"Thank you for coming," purred Landis.

The delegation filed out, and Landis turned to the secretary, asking, "What's next on the agenda?"

"Wait a moment," said one club owner. "Aren't we going to discuss this Negro question?"

Said Landis, "What is there to discuss? The gentlemen asked us for an opportunity to address this joint meeting. They were given the opportunity. What's next on the agenda?"

For Negroes in baseball, it was one more shutout, typical of the cold brush-off they encountered in every attempt to lift the color barrier. Landis didn't originate organized baseball's Negro Exclusion Act, but he didn't disturb it, either.

Branch Rickey, who brought Robinson into the majors in defiance of the grim precedent, is rightfully hailed as the emancipator of the Negro in baseball but only because Bill Veeck couldn't get clearance for a plan to bring Negroes into the National League in 1942, four years before Rickey signed Robinson from Montreal.

"Landis stopped me, I think," Veeck recently told this reporter. "It was after Gerry Nugent had tossed in the towel with the Philadelphia Phillies and the franchise was back in the lap of the league. Abe Saperstein, an owner in the National League, and I had plans.

"We went to Landis, telling him we would buy the Phillies franchise from the National League and field a team comprised wholly of stars from the Negro National League. An all-Negro team would solve some of the racial restrictions, we pointed out. Landis didn't commit himself. He referred us to Ford Frick, president of the National League.

"I will always believe Landis leaked our plans to Frick. Frick wouldn't talk business with us. Instead he sold the Phillies to William Cox, whom Landis later had the pleasure of kicking out of baseball on charges of betting on games."

Veeck, later to sponsor more colored players than any other owner, revealed that he would have put into Philadelphia the cream of the colored league crop. "We'd have had Satchel Paige pitching for us and winning 30 games a year and both Josh Gibson and Roy Campanella catching. Monte Irvin and Oscar Charleston would have been in our outfield and Buck Leonard at first base. I don't blame the other club owners. We'd have walked away with the pennant."

Actually, a Negro was signed to a major league contract in 1901, but he never broke into a major league boxscore. John McGraw, then managing the Baltimore Orioles in the American League and desperate for a second baseman, signed a light-skinned Negro from Cincinnati named Charley Grant. He attempted to pass Grant off as an Indian and indeed, the Cincinnati Enquirer of March 11, 1901, announced, "McGraw has signed a Cherokee Indian named Tokohoma."

McGraw's subterfuge collapsed, however, when the team reached Chicago for a preseason game with the White Sox. So many of Grant's Negro friends recognized him there that they marched into the team's hotel bearing floral tributes and staged a parade in his honor.

The White Sox, then managed by Clark Griffith and owned by Charlie Comiskey, wouldn't take the field against McGraw's team, on Comiskey's orders. He told the Chicago Tribune, "If McGraw really keeps this 'Indian' I will put a Chinaman on third base. This Cherokee is really Grant fixed up with war paint and feathers. His father is a well-known Negro in Cincinnati where he trains horses."

Not until 45 years later did another baseball man, Rickey, come up with the gumption to face the question head on and announce he was signing a colored ball player—college-bred Jackie Robinson—with no questions asked of his fellow magnates.

After Robinson, they came in a flood as rival club owners, taking heart, began to tap the lode that Rickey had opened up—Doby, Irvin, Easter, Paige, Campanella, Jethroe, Thompson, Minoso, Newcombe, Mays, Black, Gilliam and Bruton. All they needed to be big leaguers, they demonstrated, was the chance.

But the true equality wasn't reached, perhaps, until a few weeks ago. The Western International League signed a new umpire:

Emmett Ashford, Negro. A fair deal for white and colored alike, and violating no American decency.

MAY 10, 1953

South Protests Entrance of Negro into Majors

So hushed were Branch Rickey's preliminary arrangements for bringing a Negro player into organized baseball that the actual signing of Jackie Robinson by the Montreal team broke like a thunderclap over the baseball world on October 23, 1945.

From the South, as expected, came the roars of protest at Rickey's demolition of the racial barriers. One of the first to raise his voice was the late William G. Bramham, president of the nation's minor leagues, with offices in Durham, N.C.

Bramham went into an old-fashioned breast-beating harangue. "Father Divine will have to look at his laurels, for you can expect Rickey Temple to be in the course of construction in Harlem soon," he said. Then he reached back for some of the rancor of reconstruction days.

"It is those of the carpetbagger stripe of the white race, under the guise of helping, but in truth using the Negro for their own selfish interests, who retard the race... And whenever I hear a white man, whether he be from the North, South, East or West, broadcasting what a Moses he is to the Negro race, then I know the Negro needs a bodyguard."

Baseball officials otherwise maintained a virtually complete calm, however. Almost unanimously, the Nation's press applauded Rickey's action. But The Sporting News, the game's well-respected trade journal, assembled some biting quotes from Southern players.

Dixie Walker, Birmingham, Ala. citizen and former National

League batting champion, said of Robinson's signing: "As long as he's not with the Dodgers, I'm not worried." That philosophy was echoed by Virgil (Spud) Davis, Pittsburgh catcher and coach, also an Alabaman, who said: "As long as the Pittsburgh club hasn't signed a Negro, there's no need for me to worry now."

At Columbus, Ga., Elmer Riddle, star pitcher of the Cincinnati Reds, voiced the same line. "I've been looking for such an action as the signing of Negroes, and I guess it's all right as long as they are on some other team," he said.

Rogers Hornsby, former batting king of the majors and a manager in both big leagues but temporarily unemployed in 1945, had more blunt comment. "It won't work out," he said.

Ironically, the most strenuous protest came from J.L. Wilkinson, co-owner of the Kansas City Monarchs, the Negro team from which Rickey took Robinson. Wilkinson accused Rickey of stealing the player, declaring, "We had money invested in Jackie. They got a

Brooklyn Dodgers star Jackie Robinson, the first African-American in the major leagues, steals home under catcher Yogi Berra in the 1955 World Series against the Yankees.

$100,000 player from us for nothing." However, Kansas City could not produce a contract bearing Robinson's name.

Clark Griffith, Washington's owner, publicly deplored what he called the "raids" on the Negro teams by Rickey and drew the sharp retort that "Mr. Griffith initiated the practice of bringing Negroes into baseball under the guise of Cubans." Rickey added, "I investigated the Negro organizations and have found out they are not leagues, not even organizations. Negro baseball is in the zone of a racket, and Mr. Griffith knows this very well."

Perhaps the most unfortunate statement of the times was that of Branch Rickey Jr., who had presided over the contract-signing ceremonies at Montreal in the absence of his father. Asked what would happen if Southern players refused to play in the same league with a Negro, young Rickey said:

"They'll be back after a year or two in the cotton mills."

That comment set off a new wave of protest, most directed at the younger Rickey. It was typified best, perhaps, by a letter to Rickey Sr., sent by Bill Werber of Washington D.C., Duke University graduate and former star third baseman with the Red Sox, Athletics and Indians. Werber, prosperous business man, wrote:

> A large segment of the ball players who have in the past and who are presently contributing to the continued success of major league baseball are of Southern ancestry or actually live in the South. Your effort to force them to accept socially and to play with a Negro, or Negroes, is highly distasteful.
>
> You are, in fact, for some unaccountable reasons, discriminating against the majority. The attitude that your son has assumed is certainly not conducive to the morale of your own organization or baseball in general. His reference to ball players from the South is a definite insult to every Southern boy.

Both Robinson and Rickey had reason to wonder, in the spring of 1946, whether they had not undertaken too large a mission for themselves. On the way from California to report to the Brooklyn farm system's training camp in Sanford, Fla., Robinson and his bride of a few weeks learned about Jim Crow. They were bumped off a plane at Pensacola, denied hotel accommodations and shooed away from the food bars in the airport waiting room.

They rode the bus from Jacksonville to Sanford, forced to stand in the over-crowded Negro section while seats were empty toward the front. Because Jackie couldn't stay with the white boys in the player's hotel, the club's rule against wives in training camp was waived to permit Mrs. Robinson to be with him.

To provide companionship for Jackie on the field and on trips, Rickey forehandedly signed another Negro, Johnny Wright, a pitcher, to the Montreal roster. He also invited Wendell Smith, sports writer of the Pittsburgh Courier, and a photographer, to be members of the group.

Jackie and his bride, too proud to seek service at the back door of restaurants which otherwise refused to serve them, often went hungry. Later the Sanford city authorities descended on the camp and told the team officials to "get your Negroes out of town." Robinson and the others were moved to Daytona Beach, headquarters of the Brooklyn and Montreal squads, and quartered with colored families there.

When the Montreal team went back to Sanford for an exhibition game, the sheriff forced manager Clay Hopper to keep his Negro players out of the lineup and even off the bench. Later when the team went to De Land, Fla., for another game, it found the park padlocked. A team with Negro players wasn't welcome. All the while, Rickey's men were coaching Robinson to play second base and keep his mouth shut.

May 14, 1953

Satch Paige a Very Special Case in Baseball

The most implausible player in Negro baseball was Leroy Robert (Satchel) Paige, who viewed the admission of Negroes into organized baseball with suspicion and personally courted no offer to play in the big leagues, supposedly the Utopian dream of the colored player. Paige, a very practical man, didn't want to take a salary cut.

Paige was a very special case. Baseball men like Joe DiMaggio who batted against him described Paige as "the greatest," and men like Dizzy Dean and Lefty Gomez who pitched against him agreed that Paige would be a big winner in the majors. There was skepticism about other Negroes, but none about Paige's skill as a pitcher.

When it was apparent in 1946 that Branch Rickey had cracked the color line in baseball with his introduction of Jackie Robinson, Paige joined operators of colored teams in deploring the move. It would wreck colored baseball, they declared. The mass of Negroes was rejoicing at the time, and Paige was unpopular for a spell.

Paige, no less than the men who operated the colored teams, was a capitalist of Negro baseball. As the most famed Negro pitcher in history, he commanded personal appearance fees that ran his yearly income to nearly $50,000. The majors couldn't pay him as much. Colored baseball was good to him even if the others played for meager wages.

There wasn't much dispute about Paige's pitching talents, however. Satch, or Satchmo, or Satchelfoot, as he was called by those sticklers for formality, was the colored player most in demand when big league teams sought opposition in their post–World Series barnstorming tours. He was the guarantee there would be big crowds.

Off and on, Paige was a member of the Negro League teams, but more often he was touring with his own outfits. Whenever the league teams needed a stimulant for the gate, they'd send for Satch. Fans of both races, white and colored, flocked to watch him. They saw an angular, six-foot-four right hander with the biggest feet in baseball who was part clown and all pitcher. In his bush-town appearances, he'd guarantee that he would strike out the first nine men to face him, and most of the time he did. It's documentary that he out-pitched Dizzy Dean four straight times on barnstorming tours, and on one occasion when he was in a scoreless tie with Dean for 10 innings, he told Dean:

"Hey, Diz, iffen you don't give us a run, I'se gonna keep you out here all night."

The hitters used to complain that Satchel's out-sized feet made him double tough. He'd go into an intricate windup, described as a one-man melee, and the last thing the batter saw was Satch's No. 14 shoe looking down his throat, concealing the ball until it was midway to the plate.

Major leaguers who faced Paige a decade ago declared his fast ball was faster than Feller's. "When he cuts loose with his hard one," said Jeff Heath, "you think you're swinging at an aspirin tablet; better make that a young aspirin."

When, in July 1948, Paige accepted a contract from the Cleveland Indians for $15,000 for the remainder of the season, he was 43 years

When he signed with the Cleveland Indians in 1948, Leroy "Satchel" Paige was considered the greatest pitcher in the history of the Negro Leagues. (1956)

old, according to the best-authenticated records. Bill Veeck was accused of injecting circus stuff into the majors in an attempt to stimulate the gate receipts. On the gate receipts count he was certainly guilty. Paige in his first three starts averaged 67,000 fans. He won all three, the last a 1–0 shutout over Chicago, and without him the Indians would not have won the pennant.

Without Larry Doby, they wouldn't have won the pennant in '48 either. Doby, the flop of 1947 as a second baseman, was a potent .301 hitter the next season as an outfielder. And he was the Indians' leading hitter in the World Series against the Braves. Doby was something different among Negro players who had reached the majors. He was only 22 when he broke in.

As the first Negro to break into the American League, Doby had it rough here and there. He couldn't stay in the Indians hotels in Chicago, St. Louis and Philadelphia. If there was any coolness toward Doby in the Cleveland dressing room in 1947, it soon vanished the next season. The guy who can help you win those games and get that World Series check is always welcome. Doby, with his big bat and speed in the outfield and on the bases, and with those big 14 home runs, was doing that.

It was Joe Gordon, the veteran ex-Yankee on the Cleveland club, who set the example of comradeship with the first Negro to enter the American league. That was passing strange because such was not the reputation of Gordon. "He's a griper. He doesn't get friendly with anybody," they used to say of Gordon when he was with the Yankees. But Joe was nice to Doby.

On the day Doby made his first appearance in the Cleveland lineup and struck out as a pinch hitter, Gordon was next at bat. He patted the dejected Doby friendly-like on the rump and said, "We all do that. Watch me."

The Gordon-Doby friendship eased the tensions, if any, in the Indians clubhouse. When Doby pointed to a bruise on his leg after being hit by a pitched ball, he said, "Hey Joe, look at this red spot." Gordon looked and then mock-sneered. "Whaddyamean, red spot?

You're still chocolate brown all over." From Gordon, Doby could take the rib.

Nevertheless, Doby was a bust in his first half season with Cleveland. Used chiefly as a pinch hitter, he went to bat 32 times, and struck out 16 times. The pressures were obvious. He was aching to make good with such fervor that he was swinging at everything. He batted only .156.

In his second year up, though, Doby gained the relaxation that Jackie Robinson had brought into the majors with him. He batted only .250 for half the season, but he was getting extra base hits and after June, he caught fire, winding up with a .301 average in the Indians' winning pennant drive.

It was during that drive that Doby set history in Griffith Stadium. Against Sid Hudson he banged a home run that landed in the loud speakers atop the center field fence, where no ball had ever been hit before. Actually, he was saving his job that day. The Indians were ready to send him back to the minors before he hit the historic homer.

There were pitches thrown at Doby's head, probably more than at the heads of white hitters, but he was philosophical about that. I pointed out to him one day that following his big homer in Washington, Hudson promptly knocked him down the next time he came to bat.

"That's right," he said, "and I don't blame him. I'd knock myself down if I was pitching at me, and I had just hit a homer last time up. That's part of the game."

MAY 18, 1953

Bill Tilden

Even though tennis ranked with basketball and hockey as the least favored sports in Povich's world, he admired greatness when he saw it. That is displayed in this obituary of one of the pillars of the "Golden Era" of sports, Bill Tilden. Notice Povich's description of Tilden's off-

court activities. Today's sports writers would not be as gentle in allowing the reader the truth.

Because it was late in the night when Bill Tilden died and the presses were already rolling, the obituaries were necessarily short, hardly befitting the man who had been the greatest figure in American tennis. There is one certainty though—if he'd had a racket in his hand, Tilden would have been guilty of no such poor timing.

He had the famed cannonball service that could have enabled him to blast most of his opposition off the courts, but Tilden rarely chose that method of victory. "I like to let them beat their brains out against my defense and then attack against their state of exhaustion," he once said.

Inevitably, the obits noted that William Tatem Tilden II was the last active member of the great athletes of the Golden Era of sports. In that torrid decade from 1920–30 the others were, of course, Jack Dempsey, Bobby Jones, Babe Ruth, Helen Wills, Walter Hagen and Earl Sande.

Tilden towered above his field no whit less than did Ruth, Jones and Dempsey and his fame has withstood the challenges of later-day greats perhaps better than theirs. Joe Louis came along to crowd Dempsey for top ranking; Ben Hogan to threaten the pre-eminence of Jones and Hagen; Eddie Arcaro may be even a better rider than Sande and Ruth's home run records are constantly in danger.

But no tennist has ever come close to matching Tilden's record of six national titles, and at the age of 60 he could still be seen with racket in hand ready to show his pupils how the world's best tennis should be played, even if he wasn't up to it himself at that point.

For all his face, Tilden was not a happy man. He was in and out of jails on morals charges that would have carried more severe sentences except for judges who were moved more to sympathy than censure and viewed his deviationism as a sickness. At the time of his death, he was on probation, a marked man.

Yet two generations of U.S. tennis fans and players can remember him with gratitude for the kind of tennis he could display. One of the finer accolades to Tilden was delivered by Author-Critic-Professor William Lyons Phelps 20 years ago when he wrote: "It is something to say to your grandchildren, 'I saw Tilden play,' just as I'm proud to say 'I saw Salvini on the stage.' It is a beautiful sight to see anything done perfectly."

Tilden never had to be told that he was the best. He knew it, and sort of wondered why there was such furor over so clearly an established fact as his superiority over all contemporaries. When, in 1950, the Associated Press informed him that he had been voted the greatest tennis player of the first 50 years of the century, Tilden wanted to argue.

He would not argue, of course about his own deserved ranking, but he did take issue with the poll that ranked others among the first five. They were Jack Kramer, Don Budge, Helen Wills Moody and Suzanne Lenglen. Tilden's first-five nominees included Henri Chochet and Rene LaCoste, Bill Johnson and Don Budge. There was no question in his mind but that the best players of his day could beat the modern greats.

"Today we have attack, attack," he said. "Before, we had attack and finesse. I believe our attack, or power, when applied was just as powerful as today's power. In addition, we had finesse. We had defense. That I believe, would have spelled the difference." That was the extra Tilden used to bring onto the court, the "finesse" that left the galleries worshipful whether he was bewildering the man across the court or playing possum on his own side until he was ready to cut loose.

Unlike most of the others of the Golden Era, Tilden was no youthful prodigy at his chosen game. Bobby Jones was a boy wonder while still in his teens, and so was Jockey Sande. Helen Wills was the pig-tailed prodigy of the courts and Babe Ruth was the schoolboy toast of Baltimore. In his youth, Tilden almost had to be dragged onto the tennis courts, and he didn't win his first national singles title until he was 27.

He was an unruly kid in fashionable Germantown, Pa., and his wealthy family was viewing him as a problem. An old brother, Herbert, decried pampering the boy and took him to the courts of the Germantown Cricket Club. Bill Tilden got interested in tennis only after he discovered he could beat the other sons of members who were ball boys at the club.

He played in the national singles for five years before he won the title, in the finals with Little Bill Johnson. Until then, Tilden was something of a historic flop in the national singles. Rarely did he last beyond the first round of play, and he earned the nickname "One Round Tilden." It was to become the biggest misnomer in the history of tennis.

JUNE 8, 1953

Throwing Out the First Pitch

The happiest day of the year for Shirley Povich was Opening Day of the baseball season in Washington, where the President often threw out the first ball. Povich watched Coolidge, Hoover, Roosevelt, Truman, Eisenhower, Kennedy, Johnson, and Nixon all make their ceremonial pitches in Washington, until the Senators left for Texas in 1972. After that, Povich never attended nor covered another Opening Day in baseball.

President Eisenhower's decision to make himself available for the opening pitch at Griffith Stadium on Tuesday could be a manifestation of his new political savvy. A year ago, he announced he would forego the opener in favor of playing some golf. The Republicans almost lost control of Congress.

The opening game in Washington is a must for the President. He is supposed to check in, unless there is a war on. Mr. Eisenhower's brush-off of the opener last year produced something of a public pout. A one-man sample of public opinion fetched the comment, "Who needs him?"

The President was able to make a partial recovery when last year's original opener was rained out and he presented himself for a warmed-over inaugural a couple of days later. Whether he achieved a full pardon is doubtful however.

Mr. Eisenhower made no mistakes this time. At the first asking, he told Clark Griffith he'd be there. A few hours later, when he made a chummy talk to the people on a national hook-up stressing vigilance as against fear in this atomic age, it was acclaimed as one of his finest speeches. He had a friendly audience.

Paradoxically, Mr. Eisenhower is the most-fan among all the Presidents who have tossed out the opening ball. Before the golf bug bit him so deeply, he was so baseball-minded his friends were of the belief he stepped up the war's mop-up in Europe so he could get to see another ball game. He beat it from the victory parade to the ball yard.

In the gallery of Presidents who have thrown out the first ball since 1912 when Taft inaugurated the custom, Mr. Eisenhower is a standout. He goes into his wind-up like a pro, as if he knows the feel of a baseball, which he does. He played the outfield for West Point, and one story identifies him as the center fielder in C League under an assumed name.

He's Clark Griffith's favorite president, "because we can talk a lot of baseball with each other." Typical was Mr. Eisenhower's first question the other day, "What's the matter with Mickey McDermott?" The fact that the left hander had a sore arm had not escaped the President, even under the mounting pressures of the H-Bomb atmosphere and other affairs of state.

The fans' favorite president, however, was a Democrat. Franklin Roosevelt used to send 'em with his happy-warrior entrances into the park and the fighter's handshake of greeting, with both hands clasped high over his head. His four terms helped him to set the new record for most appearances by a President at the opener.

The pixie among the Presidential pitchers was Harry Truman, who confounded the cameraman and the crowd by making the first pitch left-handed, after previously establishing himself as a right-handed thrower. It developed that Mr. Truman, in preparation for his prank, had pre-empted the White House lawn for secret workouts throwing southpaw.

The least White House fan was Mr. Coolidge. He had to be prodded to stand up in the home team's seventh and once walked out on a World Series game. The Coolidges wind up with a high family rating, however. Mrs. Coolidge saw more ball games than all of the Presidents combined, and rarely missed a World Series, a fact which the American League noted when it implemented her lifetime pass with the choice seats to the series wherever it was played.

The White House used to be Clark Griffith's private preserve until a few years back. He was the only sports figure with ready entry to 1600 Pennsylvania Avenue on his annual treks to present the Chief Executive and the First Lady with their gold passes. Of late, however, other sports figures have horned into the act. The President receives the nabobs from football and golf.

The participation of the President in the opening-game ceremonies has helped to label baseball as the national game, and so importantly is it viewed that the American League in alternate years gives the Washington club an advanced opening. That is to insure the President's presence and the White House blessings on the game at the start of the season, rather than later in the week after the Nats have opened on the road.

Baseball is the only industry to command such Presidential blessings annually. It's a command performance, in reverse. The White House lends its dignity to no other private enterprise. The President, for instance, may send a word of greeting to the annual convention of the Master Plumbers, but he has yet to throw out the first plumber.

APRIL 7, 1954

He's Willie "The Wonderful" Mays to Giants

New York, June 26—In May of 1952 when the United States Army tapped Willie Mays for a two-year hitch as a draftee, Willie waved good-by to his teammates on the New York Giants and yelled, "Hold 'em, fellers, 'til I get back."

Willie's back, and he's the hottest article in a major league uniform. The Giants are leading the National, and Willie Mays is the most exciting ball player in either league. He belted six home runs this week, and New Yorkers are in a stampede to join the growing cult of Willie Mays fans.

Their new hero is a brown-skinned, burr-head Negro lad who likes to come back to the Giants' bench after his home runs and inquire happily, "How'm I doin'?"

That Willie Mays is doing all right is obvious. He has 24 homers to date, a pace exactly equalling Babe Ruth's record year of 60 homers, and a fat .330 average to prove he is getting other hits as well.

That the Giants are doing all right, with Willie's help, is obvious, too. Their attendance is up 130,000 over a comparative stage of the 1953 season. Willie is knocking the ball out of the park and putting the fans into it, in increasing numbers.

Willie was always a favorite with the Giants' fans, but this season he has captivated them completely with his heroics with his bat, on the bases and in center field. Willie's fans are home-run-conscious these days, and he has obliged them quickly. His last five homers were hit on his first appearances at bat in the ball games.

The man most worshipful of Mays is Horace Stoneham, owner of the Giants. Until Willie came along, he was waging a losing battle with the Yankees and Dodgers for New York patronage and was bemoaning the lack of a big name on his ball club.

After only one full year in a Giants uniform, Willie was raised from the $6,000 minimum salary to a $15,000 figure by the grateful Stoneham who added today, "He's still underpaid."

There's gloating at the Polo Grounds, thanks to Willie. One of the Giants spokesmen poked fun at the Yankees effort to build Mickey Mantle up to a box-office attraction.

"They run out there with tape measures on Mantle's long homers," he said, "and try to make him a big shot personality. They're trying to build him up as the greatest center fielder since Speaker, and what happens?

"Mantle isn't even the best center fielder in town. He runs a bad third to Mays and Duke Snider."

The Giants' fans were wary of Willie, remembered being fooled by another young phenom, Clint Hartung, a few years back. They adopted a policy of watchful waiting and then took Willie completely to their hearts.

Owner Stoneham is guarding Willie more carefully than he ever handled any other valuable chattel of the Giants. He has put on his payroll a special mentor for 23-year-old bachelor Willie, who invites mash notes not only with his ball playing but with his snazzy new robins-egg blue Chrysler convertible that is a sure-fire attraction on the Harlem streets.

Harry Forbes, a community leader in Harlem, and a licensed referee of the New York Boxing Commission, is the man who tells Willie where to go on the off-hours, who to go with and what time to get to bed.

The folks who are getting the biggest belt out of Willie's belts are his Giant teammates. They cheer loud for Willie, whose ball playing they admire and whose team spirit is always flaming. He leads the cheers for them when they wallop their own homers.

Willie plays baseball as if it were a game and the money he gets were unimportant. With Willie, the game doesn't end with the last out. He wants to talk baseball until the start of the next day's game. Monte Irvin, his roommate on the road, complains that Willie has awakened him as early as 6:30 in the morning to discuss a play the Giants might have made better.

Irvin was a certified star in the majors when Willie came along as a rookie in 1951, but currently he is in a woeful hitting slump that has dragged his average to .248, eighty points less than Willie's. When Irvin ribbed Mays the other day for striking out, Willie feigned anger. "I'm tired," he said. "I'm tired of doing the hitting for the room, you lightweight."

There are clubs in the league which have charged Willie is a showboat. He lends himself to that accusation by the Fancy-Dan whirl he gives it in the outfield. Every play Willie makes, hard or easy, is a production. If he isn't charging a routine hit through the infield with express speed, he's making outfield catches with his hands cupped at his waist as if making the play were a trifling matter to him.

But Birdie Tebbetts, manager of the Cincinnati Reds, put it best when he said of Willie, "Sure, he makes the easy plays look hard, but he makes all the hard plays, too. How can you fault him?"

Hoot Evers, a new addition to the Giants from the Red Sox, testifies that Willie as an outfielder is incredible. "I never thought they'd ever come better than Jim Piersall," said Evers, "but Willie could give Piersall two jumps on every ball and outfield him."

Warren Spahn, ace pitcher of the Milwaukee Brewers, had a special tribute for Willie this year. The first time he faced Mays, Spahn's pitch was socked for a home run by Willie. After the game Spahn was moaning.

"I know the Army has taught a lot of fellows how to do a lot of things," he said, "but Willie's the only man the Army ever taught how to hit a curve ball. He used to be a push-over for the curve before he went into the service."

It was routine for the National League pitchers to throw at Willie's head and brush him back when he started to become too dangerous a hitter, and they still do. "I don't mind it," said Willie, "because when them pitches are too close I go 'way from there. But how 'bout that Vern Law the other day? He knocked my cap off. I don't mind the others throwing at me, but Law was my buddy in the Army and I thought he was my friend."

Manager Leo Durocher set Willie straight quickly on what sort of friendship he could expect in the National League. "Remember this, Willie," he said, "the only friends you got in this league are us fellows on the Giants."

Willie has not only been getting a lot of hits for the Giants, but he has been getting the big hits. The other day, he drove in a run that put

the Giants ahead of the Reds, 4–3, and four innings later that score
became final. He makes his feats stick on the scoreboard. He hit a
two-run homer in the first inning to wipe out the Braves' one-run lead
the other day, and the score that stuck on the board for the rest of the
day was 2–1, Giants.

"If Willie gets only one hit, that's the one that puts us over," said
one of the Giants happy official family. "Look at the difference
between him and Ted Williams. This season when Williams broke in,
he made nine hits in ten times at bat, and the Red Sox lose both
games in a doubleheader."

Willie weighs 184 now, a trim six-footer who is 10 pounds heavier
than when he came up to the Giants in 1951. They bought him for
$15,000 from the Birmingham Black Barons, who at the time were in
a bit of financial distress because their bus caught fire and went up in
flames in the Holland Tunnel.

He made the Barons, one of the better colored teams, when he was
a mere 16-year-old, playing both infield and outfield. The Giants
stumbled on him by a happy accident. They sent Eddie Montague to
look at the Barons for a report on Alonzo Perry, a first baseman the
Giants wanted to install in their Sioux City farm club.

Montague lost interest in Perry when he saw young Mays perform.
"First he caught my eye with those throws," said Montague. "Then I
watched him bat. He doubled off the right field wall first time up,
then sent the left fielder back to the wall his second time up, and then
he doubled to center.

"He made short, fast moves like Joe Louis. I clocked him at four
seconds getting down to first base. Only the fast left-handed hitters do
that. Willie's a righthander."

The Giants put Willie at Trenton in 1950 and he hit .353. They
moved him up to Minneapolis and he was batting .477 when
Durocher no longer could resist and demanded he be brought up to
the Giants. Minneapolis was unhappy at losing the colored Willie, and
one sports editor grumbled, "Now what will we have to talk about?"

Willie hit an estimable .274 for the Giants in 1951 and Durocher credited him with sparking the team to the pennant. But he was overeager, and a bust in the World Series, hitting only .182. He was hitting only .236 when the Army grabbed him in May of '52.

Stealing home one day for the Eustis team, Willie fractured a toe, but the doctors declared no cast was required. "Put his foot in a cast," Durocher ordered, "or he'll be playing ball again in a week. We don't want that. The cast will protect him for six weeks."

Durocher is the chief tub-thumper for Willie. "I don't know if I ever saw a better ball player," he says. "He has all the instincts and all the weapons. He could be the perfect ball player."

"I rate the perfect player as one who has five points — (1) hitting, (2) power hitting, (3) running, (4) throwing and (5) defensive ability. Willie has everything but the proof that he can consistently hit for a good average."

Willie likes the idea of leading the league in homers, but he says he isn't going to worry about breaking Ruth's record. With a homely bit of philosophy, he said, "If you worry about one thing, pretty soon you start worrying about others. So I don't worry about nothing."

JUNE 27, 1954

Granny Rice

Grantland Rice will be laid to rest in New York today in what the announcements said would be the last rites for the Tennessee gentleman who suffered a fatal heart attack at his work last Tuesday.

But the last rites for Granny Rice will not be conducted in fact until that day in the very distant future when they hold a wake over the last sports writer who strived for even a pale semblance of the lyrical prose Granny brought to the profession.

No writer ever brought such impact to his field as Rice brought sports writing. He was the first to prove, I think, that sport writers could write; at least one of them. Until he came along in the early years of the century to give art to the work, our profession was the despised stepchild of journalism.

Those were the days when the sports departments were the catch-all for the incompetents dumped into them by editors eager to rid their own staffs of their flops; otherwise the sports pages were the products mostly of the unschooled dese-and-dem guys from the prize rings and the race tracks, which was then considered a sufficient background for sports journalism.

Like a fumigating breeze Grantland Rice burst on the scene, circa 1905, to demonstrate that sports could be written with a talent for writing and that even in the sports pages a writer could dominate the language. If he didn't exactly introduce syntax to the sports sections he lifted it to a new extreme with compositions that bordered on the literary.

He was a giant in his profession even while steadfastly holding to the gee-whiz school of sports journalism and all but deifying his special heroes like Jack Dempsey and Babe Ruth and Ty Cobb and Bobby Jones and Man o' War. He resisted the provocative tone and the groping for cynicism that was to mark the efforts of latter-day syndicate writers who grew up in his shadow and sought by controversy a compensation for their own lack of his talent.

He could write poetry, too, not the doggerel that sometimes reaches print in the sports sections, but subscribing to the best accepted definition of that art, which as I recall from English Lit I at Georgetown, went something like: "...the imaginative representation, through the medium of language, for the expression of the noble emotions." Two of his volumes of verse found eager publishers.

Granny lost none of the force in his articles despite an addiction to the imaginative, as when he likened Notre Dame's all conquering backfield of 1924 to the Four Horsemen of the Apocalypse. Latter-day sports writing is still clogged with the Rice-isms he gave to it and he is still the most quotable man who ever graced our profession.

Georgetowners are continuously proud that it was their team which the Great Man once singled out as figuring in "the greatest football game I ever saw"—the Georgetown–Boston College game of 1940. But I got a bigger belt out of a line of Granny's after that contest that I treasure as perhaps the most descriptive ever written about a football game.

We all were impressed with the ferocity of that battle, as the two teams moved against each other, and the crunching line play between Frank Leahy's BC Eagles and Jack Haggerty's Georgetown Hoyas so evident all afternoon. But it remained for Rice to capture in capsule the entire spirit of the contest when he wrote: "I not only saw football played today; I could hear it."

One of Granny's steadfast heroes was old Bill Alexander, Georgia Tech coach, and thus it is remembered that on only one occasion did Rice have a cutting word to say to any assembly. That was when during the war a Naval Academy football team sallied down to Atlanta for the first time to take on a Georgia Tech team comprised mainly of civilian 4-F's.

Navy was a heavy favorite. The night before the game Navy braid and brass assembled for a previctory banquet. Granny was the toastmaster. He praised the Navy team. Then they asked him the big question: "What would the score be on the morrow?" Rice retreated not at all from his esteemed and old friend Alex.

"Well, gentlemen," he said, "it is like this. Navy's football team is 16 points better than Georgia Tech's. But Georgia Tech's coaching is 24 points better than Navy." Next day Tech won the game.

It was as I say, the only record of any Grantland Rice act bordering at all on unkindness. The men in the press boxes who knew him were in near-adoration of the man. There sprouted, in fact, a Grantland Rice cult of worshippers. Once there was actually a fight between two sportswriters. What had been their argument? That was simple. They had argued merely over who loved Granny the most.

JULY 16, 1954

Eddie Arcaro

Eddie Arcaro was a dominant jockey for the better part of two decades, riding for the best stables, winning Triple Crown races, and earning as much as $200,000 a year. But he also was a man about town. He loved being part of the sports scene and was a frequent patron of Toots Shor's restaurant in New York, where he and Povich dined together occasionally. It was a unique time for horse racing and sports, when the scene was often as colorful as the main event.

New York, July 27—Eddie Arcaro, the riding man, had only one mount at Arlington on Saturday, but he brought home three winners, a neat trick. He got down in front with Royal Note in the rich Arlington Futurity, and in Texas, two of his oil-well ventures hit. Arcaro will not soon become a public charge.

In Shor's last night, though, he was saying he was not a total success, however. "I come back to New York and open my mail and find out that the Arlington stewards have set me down for 10 days," he said. "I don't know what they didn't like about my ride. I thought it was pretty good. I won by more than two lengths."

He conceded that the stewards had looked at the films of the $149,000 race and "there might have been something in the running they didn't like. Them movies are like fingerprints and they got you dead to right. I'm catching a quick plane back to New York, and I don't get a look at the films."

Could have been, he said, that he pinched somebody off in the early running. "I'm trying to get to the front," he said, "like I usually do with Royal Note but he acts a bit sore and it takes longer. But who am I to squawk? They don't disqualify me, and my 10 percent of the purse is $9300 and I'll be getting the check for it pretty soon."

It's better for everybody, these days, when they film all the races and nail the miscreants who try to rough the field up. "They don't do this thing like a star chamber," said Arcaro. "They bring the films back to the jocks' room and show 'em to all the riders, and the boy who is to blame don't get any sympathy from the other jocks. They know somebody could get killed in this business."

Ten days, he said, could cost him as much as $20,000 in riding fees. "I had three stakes lined up on a Wednesday and a couple of Saturdays and if I got lucky I could win 'em all. But it isn't a total loss," he added philosophically. "I got 10 days to sharpen up my short game and take some of those guys who have been winning my money at golf."

The colt he won with at Arlington, Royal Note, could wind up as the 2-year-old of the year, he said. "Nobody beats him in the only six starts he's had, and he's by Spy Song, who's a hot sire now. He pulls up sore in the Futurity, but a chronic soreness ain't too important, and could be he'll come up to the Derby next year unbeaten, and could be I'll be trying with him for my sixth Derby winner."

Arcaro isn't sure, though, that Royal Note will go through the 2-year-old season undefeated. "We'll know more about that in the Belmont Futurity, I figure," he said. "That's when the Note hooks up with Nashua, another good one. Maybe I'll be riding Nashua in that one."

He liked everything about Nashua, he said. "He's by Nasrullah, the good sire the syndicate has down at the Hancock Farm in Kentucky. Most everything by Nasrullah is running smart the last two-three weeks. I was on Nashua at Garden State in the Cherry Hill Stakes a few weeks ago, and we hooked up with Royal Note. I was beaten only a neck on Nashua, and I'm thinking if they hook up again Nashua could reverse it. It probably won't happen 'til the Belmont, though."

He said racing is always interesting to him and that class pays off in breeding as well as in riding. "Seems like the good sires come in cycles. A couple of years ago the things by Bull Lea were mopping up. Now Spy Song's get are getting fashionable. He's had Tidewater, Trysong and Duc De Fer, all good stakes winners this year. But if you have to name the top sire now you'd have to say Nasrullah with all the good ones he's sending to the races."

They'll never have to throw any benefits for Arcaro, as I was saying.

In addition to riding fees that sometimes hit 200 grand a year, he has those oil wells, and business interests in his native Kentucky, and last week he invested in a syndicate that staked 30 uranium claims in Utah and Colorado, two of which have already been productive.

With his pretty wife, Ruth, Arcaro is a figure on the Broadway scene. He dines out every night, makes most of the clubs and is no tee-totaler. Between riding engagements he is something of a bon vivant, but was saying, "I keep in pretty good shape, because I'm a fool if I don't. When I can't bring those winners home, the money stops coming in from the trade I know best."

He said, though, "that if I were a ball player or a golfer, I couldn't live it up so much. Most of the things those fellows have to do is physical. I can think a pretty good race when I'm on a colt's back. I'm not knocking conditioning, because that's for everybody. But the riders get something of a break. There's a better than good chance that the colt we're riding has had a good night's sleep and the best kind of rest, so the riders are not on their own. They get some help when they're at work."

JULY 28, 1954

Babe Didrikson Zaharias

Povich rarely wrote about women and sports, even after they began to gain widespread acceptance as professional athletes in the 1970s. But he did admire Babe Didrikson Zaharias, the most dominant female athlete of the first half of the century. She won Olympic gold medals in the javelin and hurdles, was a teenage basketball star and became a professional golf champion with many titles and a 17-tournament winning streak to her credit. She also was one of the founders of the Ladies Professional Golf Association (LPGA).

The Babe, Mildred Didrikson Zaharias, didn't quite make it 83 winning tournaments. She lost her three-year bout with cancer in a

Galveston hospital yesterday, leaving the world to mourn the greatest girl athlete of them all.

The opponent that licked her, it must be noted, was the same deliverer of the sneak body-attack that also cut down those other champions, Jim Thorpe and Babe Ruth. It was not a stand-up foe to be out-gamed or out-performed, else Babe Zaharias would have won this one, too, her admirers are sure.

Never was there such virtuosity in athletics as the one-time skinny tomboy from Port Arthur, Tex., daughter of a Norwegian carpenter, brought to our times. Her mind that was bent on excelling gave few commands that her remarkable body couldn't keep. The two Olympic titles she won at 18 were only the beginning of a fame that transcended her world of sports. Greatest woman athlete of the half century, she was voted in the Associated Press poll of 1960. It certified her as the female counter-part of Jim Thorpe. But she was more versatile even than Thorpe, she proved, when at an age considered late for big-time golf she flung herself into that game, too, and shattered even more records.

The Babe's triumphs ranged from the javelin throw, the high hurdles, baseball pitching, basketball, golf and the harmonica. Of her skill with the harmonica she once said, characteristically, "just picked one up when I was seven years old and been blowing it ever since."

She won her fans with her frolic as well as with her skills. It was on the stage of the Statler Hotel's Embassy room during the week of a National Celebrities Tournament here that Hildegarde invited the Babe into her act and asked the usual question: How does a girl hit the ball that far? That's when the uninhibited Babe gave the tip that became the most-quoted in women's golf: "Just take off your girdle and swing."

The day in 1947 when, in Scotland, she won her 19th straight golf tournament—a record unapproachable—cameramen asked her to pose with Jean Donald, the Scotch lassie who had also been in the finals of the British Open.

"A Highland Fling, please," they asked of the Norwegian girl from Texas.

The Scotch girl put her arm around Babe, showed her how to raise her knee and start the dance. The Babe obliged, but then called a halt. "Wait until I can get my toe pointed right," she said. That was Didrikson, the perfectionist.

The Babe shattered one record that doesn't show in the books. In 1947, she became the first girl ever to invade the precincts of the Washington Touchdown Club as an honored-guest speaker. The toastmaster that day introduced her with some remarkable truths.

"Here's the girl," he said, "who can run, jump, hurdle, toss a javelin, a baseball and a football farther than any other. She can swim, ride, shoot, box and beat them all at golf. She broke two Olympic records in one day, and just kidding around in a swimming pool she came within one second of the world record for the 100-yard free style (women's)."

"And cook, too," Babe added as she went to the lectern.

The next day in the Celebrities Tournament at Columbia, she declined Bob Considine's bit of gallantry in offering her the privilege of driving off first. "Thanks," she said, "but I guess you'd better tee off first, because I suspect it's the last time you'll have the honor." She was the imp, and nobody ever got mad at the Babe.

She was winning so many tournaments in 1947–48, twenty-one in a row, that she threw a severe fright into the staid United States Golf Association when she filed her entry in the National Open. They could find no rules to bar her and avoid what might be the embarrassment of having a gal golfer knock off some of their pets, so they muttered something about "intent" of the rules to limit the Open to men.

Then they hastily re-wrote their own rules to insert the important word "male" in spelling out eligibility.

The Babe had no greater admirers on the golf course than the men champions she often played with. Snead, Demaret, Hogan, Harrison played with her and marveled at her flawless "action" with the clubs. Never did she pretend that she could beat them, but sometimes, here and there, she would.

Characteristic of her willingness to shoulder the pressure of a match was her exhibition in the two-ball International at Orlando where her partner was George Bolesta, the Tampa pro. They came to the 18th needing a win to close the match out. They surveyed their respective drives and the gallery assumed Bolesta would play Didrikson's drive when the Babe cut in with "let me rap that little old thing up on the green, George." Thus she took her partner off the spot, boomed a two-iron next to the pin and asked everybody, "How'd I do?" She was so wonderful.

SEPTEMBER 28, 1956

The Perfect Game

One of the great thrills of all time for me or any other baseball fan occurred on October 8, 1956, the perfect game by Don Larsen in the World Series. Like any classic achievement, its very excitement represents an instant challenge to the writer being paid to describe it for tomorrow's reader. For me, Larsen had just posed the biggest challenge ever, as I sat there and watched him become the only man in history to pitch a perfect game in the World Series.

When it was over, my frightening task began: How to handle this aurora borealis? I sat, among four hundred other writers transfixed, my eyes staring at the Yankee Stadium turf, my mind trying to absorb and ponder the magnitude of the achievement, all the while knowing the clock is moving and the deadline is mocking.

I shifted my stare to the empty white sheet of paper in my typewriter until snow-blindness threatened to set in. Then my fingers began moving across the keyboard of my portable and I was writing scared as the words began to come out:

—Shirley Povich, from his memoir, *All These Mornings* (1969)

Larsen Pitches 1st Perfect Game in Series History

New York, Oct. 8, 1956—The million-to-one shot came in. Hell froze over. A month of Sundays hit the calendar. Don Larsen today pitched a no-hit, no-run, no-man-reach-first game in a World Series.

On the mound at Yankee Stadium, the same guy who was knocked out in two innings by the Dodgers on Friday came up today with one for the record books, posting it there in solo grandeur as the only Perfect Game in World Series history.

With it, the Yankee righthander shattered the Dodgers, 2–0, and beat Sal Maglie, while taking 64,519 suspense-limp fans into his act.

First there was mild speculation, then there was hope, then breaths were held in slackened jaws in the late innings as the big mob wondered if the big Yankee righthander could bring off for them the most fabulous of all World Series games.

He did it, and the Yanks took the Series lead three games to two, to leave the Dodgers as thunderstruck as Larsen himself appeared to be at the finish of his feat.

Larsen whizzed a third strike past pinch-hitter Dale Mitchell in the ninth. That was all. It was over. Automatically, the massive 226-pounder from San Diego started walking from the mound toward the dugout, as pitchers are supposed to do at the finish.

But this time there was a woodenness in his steps and his stride was that of a man in a daze. The spell was broken for Larsen when Yogi Berra stormed on to the infield to embrace him.

It was not Larsen jumping for joy. It was the more demonstrative Berra. His battery-mate leaped full tilt at the big guy. In self defense, Larsen caught Berra in mid-air as one would catch a frolicking child, and that's how they made their way toward the Yankee bench, Larsen carrying Berra.

There wasn't a Brooklyn partisan left among the 64,519, it seemed, at the finish. Loyalties to the Dodgers evaporated in sheer enthrallment at the show big Larsen was giving them, for this was a day when the fans could boast that they were there.

When New York Yankee pitcher Don Larsen, hugged here by catcher Yogi Berra, pitched a "no-hit, no-run, no-man-reach-first" game in the 1956 World Series against the Brooklyn Dodgers—still the only perfect game in World Series history—it inspired one of Povich's finest leads.

So at the finish, Larsen had brought it off, and erected for himself a special throne in baseball's Hall of Fame, with the first Perfect Game pitched in major league baseball since Charlie Robertson of the White Sox against Detroit 34 years ago.

Maglie Just Watches

But this was one more special. This one was in a World Series. Three times, pitchers had almost come through with no-hitters, and there were three one-hitters in the World Series books, but never a no-man-reach-base classic.

The tragic victim of it all, sitting on the Dodger bench, was sad Sal Maglie, himself a five-hit pitcher today in his bid for a second Series victory over the Yankees. He was out of the game, technically, but he was staying to see it out and it must have been in disbelief that he saw himself beaten by another guy's World Series no-hitter.

Mickey Mantle hit a home run today in the fourth inning and that was all the impetus the Yankees needed, but no game-winning home run ever wound up with such emphatic second-billing as Mantle's this afternoon.

It was an exciting wallop but in the fourth inning only, because after that Larsen was the story today, and the dumb-founded Dodgers could wonder how this same guy who couldn't last out two innings in the second game could master them so thoroughly today.

He did it with a tremendous assortment of pitches that seemed to have five forward speeds, including a slow one that ought to have been equipped with back-up lights.

Larsen had them in hand all day. He used only 97 pitches, not an abnormally low number because 11 pitches an inning is about normal for a good day's work. But he was the boss from the outset. Only against Pee Wee Reese in the first inning did he lapse to a three-ball count, and then he struck Reese out. No other Dodger was ever favored with more than two called balls by Umpire Babe Pinelli.

Behind him, his Yankee teammates made three spectacular fielding plays to put Larsen in the Hall of Fame. There was one in the second inning that calls for special description. In the fifth, Mickey Mantle ranged far back into left center to haul in Gil Hodges' long drive with a back-hand shoetop grab that was a beaut. In the eighth, the same Hodges made another bid to break it up, but Third Baseman Andy Carey speared his line drive.

Little did Larsen, the Yankees, the Dodgers or anybody among the 64,519 in the stands suspect that when Jackie Robinson was robbed of a line drive hit in the second inning, the stage was being set for a Perfect Game.

McDougal Saves It

Robinson murdered the ball so hard that Third Baseman Andy Carey barely had time to fling his glove upward in a desperate attempt to get the ball. He could only deflect it. But, luckily, Shortstop Gil Mc-Dougal was backing up and able to grab the ball on one bounce. By a half step, McDougal got Robinson at first base, and Larsen tonight can be grateful that is was not the younger, fleeter Robinson of a few years back but a heavy-legged, 40-year-old Jackie.

As the game wore on, Larsen lost the edge that gave him five strike-outs in the first four innings and added only two in the last five. He had opened up by slipping called third strikes past both Gilliam and Reese in the first inning.

Came the sixth, and he got Furillo and Campanella on pops, fanned Maglie. Gilliam, Reese and Snider were easy in the seventh. Robinson tapped out, Hodges lined out and Amoros flied out in the eighth. And now it was the ninth, and the big Scandinavian-American was going for the works with a calm that was exclusive with him.

Furillo gave him a bit of a battle, fouled off four pitches, then flied mildly to Bauer. He got two quick strikes on Campanella, got him on a slow roller to Martin.

Now it was the left-handed Dale Mitchell, pinch-hitting for Maglie.

Ball one came in high. Larsen got a called strike.

On the next pitch, Mitchell swung for strike two.

Then the last pitch of the game: Mitchell started to swing, but didn't go through with it.

But it made no difference because Umpire Pinelli was calling it Strike Number Three, and baseball history was being made.

Magile's Brilliance Forgotten

Maglie himself was a magnificent figure out there all day, pitching hitless ball and leaving the Yankees a perplexed gang, until suddenly with two out in the fourth, Mickey Mantle, with two strikes called against him, lashed the next pitch on a line into the right field seats to give the Yanks a 1–0 lead.

There was doubt about that Mantle homer because the ball was curving and would it stay fair? It did. In their own half of the inning, the Dodgers had no such luck. Duke Snider's drive into the same seats had curved foul by a few feet. The disgusted Snider eventually took a third strike.

The Dodgers were a luckless gang and Larsen a fortunate fellow in the fifth. Like Mantle, Sandy Amoros lined one into the seats in right, and that one was a near-thing for the Yankees. By what seemed only inches, it curved foul, the umpires ruled.

Going into the sixth, Maglie was pitching a one-hitter—Mantle's homer—and being out-pitched. The old guy lost some of his stuff in the sixth, though, and the Yankees came up with their other run.

Extra Run Unnecessary

Carey led off with a single to center, and Larsen sacrificed him to second on a daring third-strike bunt. Hank Bauer got the run in with a single to left. There might have been a close play at the plate had Amoros come up with the ball cleanly, but he didn't and Carey scored unmolested.

Now there were Yanks still on first and third with only one out, but they could get no more. Hodges made a scintillating pickup of Mantle's smash, stepped on first and threw to home for a double play on Bauer who was trying to score. Bauer was trapped in a run-down and caught despite a low throw by Campanella that caused Robinson to fall into the dirt.

But the Yankees weren't needing any more runs for Larsen today. They didn't even need their second one, because they were getting a pitching job for the books this memorable day in baseball.

OCTOBER 9, 1956

High School Rivalry

For years Povich used the Landon–St. Albans game, a private high school rivalry in Washington, to underscore that football was still a game, even when the big colleges and professionals were moving beyond. Although his two sons played football for Landon for several years, they never received a mention in his annual column on The Game. It was never about him. Never about the family. It's the contest.

An awfully important football game which is, well, just the most important in the world to some young men will be played tomorrow on the field of the Landon School for Boys in nearby Maryland. It will determine, among other things, a title and also the mood of the annual football dances that are a fixture at the rival schools.

This is a crisis. It is St. Albans versus Landon again and beginning with the 3 o'clock kickoff, the hopes, dreams and fears that have been taking form for weeks in a thousand Washington households will crystallize into rugged combat.

It is Washington's most ivy-hung football game, because St. Albans and Landon have been meeting every year for 26 years, now. It is for the Interstate Academic Conference championship and St. Albans is the favorite mostly because of Porter Shreve, who is viewed by many young admirers as simply the most wonderful football player in the world perhaps.

According to the student publications, it is well-coached, power-packed St. Albans versus well-coached, power-packed Landon, with both teams confident, but not overconfident, and St. Albans has some tricks up its sleeves, and Landon will not be caught napping. Landon will shoot the works and St. Albans will also shoot the works. Neither team will be outgamed.

Coach Bob Graham of St. Albans has been telling his team all week that "this is just another ball game," and at Landon, Coach Ed Barton has been telling his team "this is just another ball game." Even the third-graders at both schools know that this is not just another ball game, but the end of the world.

One of the reasons St. Albans is the favorite is because nobody in the IAC has beaten St. Albans, which has won six straight this year after losing a 23–0 contest to Bethesda–Chevy Chase, which is not in the league. Another reason St. Albans is the favorite is because they have beaten two of the teams that licked Landon, Sidwell Friends and Georgetown Prep, although Georgetown is not in the league.

It is true that the Sidwell team which beat Landon, 26–7, was beaten by St. Albans, 25–0, but in those scores there may be more than meets the eye, because Landon played Sidwell first and may have softened them up for St. Albans, although it must be admitted that the games were a month apart. Anyway, Landon has beaten St. Albans twice in the last three years and is suffering from no complex at all, according to the reliable Landon News, which comes out once a month.

St. Albans has intact its entire backfield of last year's 14–6 victory over Landon, which means that Billy Gray, the quarterback, Johnny Warren, the wingback, and Ernie Edmunson, the fullback, will be helping Porter Shreve again, in case, as they are saying at St. Albans, Shreve needs help. Tailback Shreve, who is a very large schoolboy at 190 pounds and 6–2, kicks, passes and runs for touchdowns.

In contrast to St. Albans' backfield veterans, Landon is ready to unleash a set of eager young backs who have been improving each week. Landon suspects that the best back on the field will not be Porter Shreve but Bobby Zuckert, who directs their T-formation and handles the ball in a manner resembling Johnny Lujack with one notable exception. Unlike Lujack, Zuckert passes left-handed.

Zuckert will have some accomplished colleagues in his back field who can double as ball-toters and pass catchers. They are Wally Atwood, Dick Shaw and Danny Austin, and everybody at Landon knows that Zuckert can outpass Shreve and Pete Sendroy can outkick him. Everybody at Landon knows, too, that in the first half last year, they made a big bum out of Shreve, holding him to the three yards net in the first half, although in the second half he was very hard to arrest and scored the big touchdown by taking the ball eight straight times from 35 yards out.

St. Albans generates most of its power from a single-wing but they are really a multiple-offense team, swinging into such formations as a double-wing and unbalanced T. Landon sticks to the straight T and

Coach Barton can platoon his quarterbacks because he has Buzz Bastable to spell Zuckert, and Bastable is awfully good sometimes, whether he's working the belly series or pitching the ball. Like Zuckert, and unlike Lujack, he is a left-handed thrower, and he likes to throw far downfield to Johnny Hayden, the end.

At Landon, they suspect that Johnny Hayden will give St. Albans lots of trouble because he is almost as big and fast as Bones Taylor, who used to catch those passes for the Redskins, and he is very sticky-fingered like Bones Taylor was, and most of the time Bobby Zuckert just lays that ball right in Hayden's hands like Sammy Baugh used to do with Bones Taylor.

Landon is definitely upset-minded this year with its upset by St. Albans last year clearly in mind. That was when Landon had a 20-game winning streak, before St. Albans spoiled it. There is precedent for a Landon victory. Carnegie Tech upset Notre Dame, 19–0, in 1926, it is well-remembered by some of the Landon lads' grandfathers. Tomorrow, it should be very grim.

NOVEMBER 15, 1956

[St Albans won 14–0. Povich's son, Maury, Landon's co-captain, suffered broken ribs trying to block a punt.]

Mickey Mantle

Mickey Mantle's modesty is unquestionably one of his charms and a reason why even the most rabid Ruthophiles might not be disturbed if Mantle were to bust the Babe's home run record of 60 in a single season. If there is to be a successor to Ruth, the crown would rest becomingly on the brow of the Commerce, Okla., Strong Boy.

It could be that Mantle's fans, however, are viewing him as entirely too unassuming this week. He said the other day that Ruth's record would probably be broken in four or five years, "but not by me." His failure to assume that he is one of the players with a chance to surpass Ruth's mark could be an outbreak of over-modesty.

Mickey said he thought "there are four or five players capable of reaching or topping the 60-homer record," and the fellow he mentioned as having the best chance is Duke Snider of the Dodgers. Mantle fans could accuse him of down-rating Mickey Mantle.

Mantle's readiness to count himself out of the challenge for Ruth's record is at least premature. Mickey at the age of 25 reached the 52-mark in homers last season. When Ruth in 1927 belted his 60, he was a ripening 32 after 12 seasons as a hard-living big leaguer. Time has far from run out for a young, muscular Mickey.

It was a decent thing that Mantle did when he suggested that his rival for distinction among center fielders, Snider, would be the man most likely to break the Babe's record. During Mickey's first three seasons in New York, he was in the shadow of the skillful Snider of the Dodgers and the amazing Willie Mays of the Giants.

It was possible a few years back to make the observation that Mantle, who came into the majors hailed as perhaps the best-hitting center fielder of all time, had wound up merely as the third-best center fielder in New York. Surely, both Mays and Snider rated ahead of him and were having great years while Mantle was unable to untrack himself. His present-type modesty would have been more becoming then than now.

For whatever the omission may be worth, Mantle didn't mention Mays when he suggested that Snider had the best chance to hit or pass the 60 mark. Obviously he preferred to string along with the sweet-swinging Snider whose stroke is built for home runs rather than the wild-swinging Mays. Mantle was unpersuaded by the fact that Mays' 51 homers of a couple of seasons ago were more than Snider has ever hit in any year.

The factor that could tumble Snider is his slumps. He is the streakiest kind of home-run hitter, connecting during certain periods for clusters of homers. He can distress his fans, though, with his sieges of doldrums. Those who aren't Snider fans have an urge to shoot him dead from the stands when he swings from the spikes on every pitch at a time when it's a mere single or any kind of safe hit that the Dodgers need, not necessarily a home run that would boost the Duke's homer total.

Another fellow who isn't a bad home-run hitter is Mantle. His 52 of last season were more than Snider or Mays or any of the "four or five players" Mickey says might break Ruth's record have ever hit. He has to be counted among those with a bright chance to lift the record for a season's homers to a new high, and his seems to be the brightest chance.

It is pretty well established now that Mantle is a good hitter. He became the major league's first Triple Crown winner since the forties with his heroics last season and actually led in five departments of hitting. He is the master of the tape-measure home run, the one that calls for ooh's and ah's and wonderment from the customers who doubt that anybody ever hit a home run any farther.

Snider has that classic swing and that nice Brooklyn park in which to hit his homers, and Mays has the Polo Grounds and Ted Kluszewski has the fences in Cincinnati but Mantle needs none of those conveniences. Most of the homers he hits are homers all over the world, and there is none to contest the sheer power and distance of the Mantle swats.

Going for Mantle is a special asset that neither Snider nor Mays is fortunate enough to boast and Ruth didn't have. That is his switch-hitting skill, carefully developed for Mickey by his ball-playing Daddy on the back lots of Commerce, Okla. There have been days when it appeared that Snider would have preferred to sprint somewhere and hide when a left hander was facing the Dodgers. When Mantle is up there with a bat in his hand, the situation becomes the problem for the pitcher of any persuasion.

At 25, the future for Mantle must be counted as very bright. Whatever doubts may have been riding with his swing in previous years were nicely liquidated in his favor last season when he hit those 52 homers and led the league's hitters in everything except old sweat-shirts. High on everybody's list of those who could break Ruth's record, you'd have to put Mantle's name, no matter what the boy himself says.

DECEMBER 26, 1956

Basketball: A Famous Dissent

Povich often wrote freelance pieces to help send his children to private schools. This article for Sports Illustrated, *for which Povich received $1,000, supplemented his son David's first year at Columbia Law School. As the magazine said in a sidebar, "This article will probably create some unrest in the family of Shirley Povich. . . . Two of his off-spring, David, 23, and Maury, 19, were ardent basketball players in school and remain loyal fans. Their father changed from fan to ex-fan in that period: 'It got so I was rooting as hard against the referees as I was for the boys,' he says."*

Povich's irreverent description of basketball noted how the game is for "carnival freaks" with "runaway pituitary glands" who "stuff baskets like taxidermists." The story resulted in thousands of letters of protest to the magazine and was also included in a college writing guide as an example of "making effective sentences."

Basketball is for the Birds

The late H.L. Mencken some years ago warned that the language was changing and wrote a book about it. A newly recognized entry in the American lexicon at that time was the word goon. Mencken's goons were simple, workaday strikebreakers who might have to bash in a few skulls to get the job done. America's latter-day goons are the biological blowups with runaway pituitary glands who play at basketball.

Basketball is for the birds—the gooney birds. The game lost this particular patron years back when it went vertical and put the accent on carnival freaks who achieved upper space by growing into it. They don't shoot baskets any more, they stuff them, like taxidermists.

In a single generation, there has been a revved-up degeneration of basketball from a game to a mess. It now offers a mad confection of absurdities, with ladder-size groundlings stretching their gristle in aerial dogfights amid the whistle screeches of apoplectic referees trying to enforce ridiculous rules that empty the game of interest.

Dr. James Naismith, an earnest man, could be justifiably spinning in his mausoleum in a schizophrenia of rage and despair at what they've done to the game he invented in 1891. When he inspired basketball by placing two peach baskets at opposite ends of a YMCA hall in Springfield, Mass., the sincere doctor could hardly foretell the degree to which his creation would become all fuzzed up by the senseless tinkerers who have grabbed hold of it. And if the native pride of peach trees is remembered, it is obvious that the tint of their fruit now is less the glow of ripeness than the blush of shame for their part in helping to bring basketball into the world.

The towering 6-footers who were the giants of the basketball court only a couple of decades ago and were eagerly sought for the important center jump need not apply any more unless they are content to be the game's runts. If the mere 6-footer is permitted to suit up at all by coaches, whose ruling passion is collecting two-legged giraffes with an eye-level approach to the basket, he is reduced to rooting around in the undergrowth of the forests of bone and marrow that rear above him. It is time for him to curse the utter normality of his glands which stunted his growth.

This basketball apostate makes confession that he is a onetime aficionado who couldn't wait to get up in the morning to play the game or watch it. That was in the era when it was a game, not a bewildering whistle-fest with the referees eager to bring to book the naughty-naughties who are so bold or so careless as to commit something of a firm nature, like laying a hand on the hem of an opponent's garment.

It used to be a game that could be comfortably won by a team total of 26 points, in the not-so-distant days when a slightly malevolent glance at an opponent with the ball was simply a frame of mind, not a personal foul. I read incredulously that the New York Knickerbockers averaged 112 points a game last season and finished last in their division of the pro league.

They've weighted the rules so heavily in favor of the team with the ball that the missed basket is now more incredible than the shot that is made. Referees not content with enforcing the letter of the rules impose no-no, mustn't touch injunctions that leave the defense in a constant state of fright lest their tactics be adjudged too manly.

The way they have it rigged and the way the coaches have wheeled in all available altitude, basketball and basket shooting now offer a close substitute interest for those doughty sportsmen who dream of shooting fish in a barrel. They've made the basketball court a virtual shooting gallery with the bull's-eye affixed to the rifle barrel, just to encourage success.

It has all served to simplify coaching skills. An eye for the basket isn't necessary as long as the coach can corral enough tall hands to plumb it. Then it becomes a game of can-you-top-this against rival coaches who counter with their own altitudinous tribes of basket shrinkers.

From time to time apologists for the game have made attempts to define the motivations that impel the buffs to attend these encounters, but their conclusions are almost invariably desultory and pathetic. The best that this observer, who has also delved into the matter, can say is that there is no accounting for people's tastes, because it is well known that some even like fried baby bees, kidney stew, Garroway and yodeling, and some root for the Washington Senators.

This discouraged spectator, who has tried intermittently to warm toward the game in efforts to relive it up, finds nothing left to cheer for a basketball contest. Who can applaud Wilt the Stilt or his ilk when they outflank the basket from above and pelt it like an open city? These fellows are biological accidents who ought to be more usefully employed, like hiring out as rainmakers and going to sow a few clouds.

Even that last precious motivation of healthy partisanship, the pleasure of rooting for somebody, evaporates at a basketball game in common outrage against the referee who is usually wronging both teams, as well as the spectators.

Basketball is always attended by a shrieking dissent from this character, who is trying to enforce fine-line rules that defy sensible interpretation. It is thus inevitable that the referee must wind up as the enemy of all cheering sections. King Solomon would have wisely disqualified himself as incompetent had he been asked to deliver a fair ruling on blocking vs. charging on the basketball court of today.

Nothing in the prospectus ever suggested that anybody should pay admission to watch a basketball referee perform, but their actions would seem to imply that they believe this to be the case. Most of them consider the basketball court as their public stage, having taken the cue from the late great Pat Kennedy, an extraordinary dramatist who invented the role of the domineering, infallible, showboat referee. The first indication of a rules infraction would set Actor Kennedy aquiver and his whistle to shrieking. His eyes bulged from their sockets, the veins showed purple in his neck as he tracked down the miscreant who had violated something about Kennedy's game. He would put the positive finger on the culprit with an outward show of anger that others usually reserve for a rapist.

Cornball and Keystone Cops

Kennedy's antics were at least diverting, but peopling the referee ranks now are only the lesser hams who have no reason to fancy themselves in his image. The result is pure cornball as, playing screech-owl tunes on their tin whistles, these Keystone cops blow the action to a stop apparently on a whim.

The game, in fact, is crawling with would-be scene stealers. In that department the referees are hard pressed by the coaches on the players' benches. Modern coaches are a breed better born for the revival tents. They play to the crowd by kicking up a public fuss at every grievance real or fancied, and communicate by their gestures that the referees are utter no-goodniks.

The coaches warm up to their phony sympathy pitch with suitable and audible sighs and groans. Then come the head-in-hands gestures of utter despair, the falling to the knees in posture of prayer for greater justice, and then the arms flung wide in "Please, Almighty," supplication for deliverance from the fiends blowing whistles. For the most part it adds up to incitement to riot.

Among the pro teams, all this has filtered up from the colleges where the coaches first discovered that they, too, could be characters. As usual, the pros have improved on it, as they have done with most everything else from the colleges, so that in basketball you now have, in addition to the goons, the flip-top coach.

The basketball rules, in themselves, are enough to baffle anybody with an orderly mind. The game launched its popularity with simple restrictives like five players to a side and don't step outside the marked lines. Now it is a confounding jumble of personal fouls, traveling fouls, dribbling fouls, whistles, buzzers and bonuses for injured innocence.

It was not much overdrawn when somebody once said that the basketball people scribble new rules with a pen in each hand for fear of being caught up with. What was permitted last year is this year's foul. In the pro league, even last night's rule book is apt to be outmoded, with President Maurice Podoloff ordering revisions at any hour he can get his referees on the telephone.

The pros' mania for changing the rules cropped up again in October when two new rules governing foul shots were adopted. There is actually the stipulation that one of the new rules would be considered official only during an allotted one-month tryout—a sort of rookie rule, as it were.

The other new rule of the pros deals with double fouls and now provides for a jump ball between the centers of the two teams. But wait. Identifying the centers apparently is not so simple in this modern age of basketball, because the rule takes care to spell out, "If a dispute arises as to who is center of a team, it shall be resolved by the referees."

The once-respected place tags have gone from the game. Every position is now so freewheeling that the centers, guards and forwards can be positively identified as such only by lip tattoo. It amounts to basketball's for-real version of the "Who's on First?" vaudeville routine of Abbott and Costello.

To add to the confusion, the colleges a few years back introduced a queer something called the "one-and-one" foul. The bright minds who thought that one up should be cited for deportation as saboteurs of the American way of life.

It is flabbergasting to know that the one-and-one foul, which is awarded victims of aggression, is sometimes two shots, sometimes one, depending on the inaccuracy of the man on the free-throw line. If he sinks his first free shot, he is deemed to have exacted the offender's debt to basketball society and the referee says that's all.

But if the fouled citizen misses his first free throw, he is now entitled to take another, honest. Failure is rewarded, success is penalized. It is George Orwell's 1984 in action. Black is white, Truth is false. Love is hate, and Big Brother Referee is always present.

The pros have gimmicked it up even more. Now there is a something extra called a bonus free throw. That goes to the aggrieved team if the fouls by the other side total as many as seven in any period. The spectator without a Comptometer is lost, and only certified public accountants can follow the scoring, except when the board lights up like a jackpot-hit machine.

In what exact year basketball began to go sour as a game cannot be precisely determined here, but there had to be alarm on a certain night in 1949. That was when one man, Paul Arizin, of Villanova, scored 85 points in one game. To the basketball fundamentalists, that was as disgraceful as it was remarkable.

Later on a whirlybird named Bevo Francis of Rio Grande College made numerous descents on the basket and ladled in 113 points in one night against Ashland College. They've got some kind of a game all right, but it isn't basketball. What is happening reawakens for this disenchanted fellow a gratitude for one of America's most little-mentioned freedoms—the freedom to stay away from it.

Sports Illustrated, September 8, 1958

The Colts–Giants Game

Baltimore's 23–17 overtime victory over the New York Giants in the 1958 championship game at Yankee Stadium put the now-dominant National Football League on the same playing field as Major League Baseball. Hall of Fame quarterback Johnny Unitas led the Colts on a late-fourth-quarter drive resulting in a field goal that tied the score. Alan Ameche's short touchdown plunge in overtime won the game. Povich understood the importance of the game and often said it was one of the greatest pro-football games he'd ever seen.

Here 'tis two days later and the Colts-Giants game is hard to let go of. It is being replayed wherever as many as two football fans assemble. Like a precious experience before it is yielded up to the torrent of workaday affairs, the inclination is to fondle this one for a while.

Yankee Stadium with all its World Series epics and heavyweight championships never rocked with the excitement provided by Sunday's pro football gladiators. The Giants and Colts served up one to quicken the breath of a cast-iron gargoyle and make him emote. As art form, it had an aspect of Greek tragedy with sudden death the inexorable ticket of one of the antagonists. And it launched a million debates.

Were the Giants too faint-hearted in the late minutes when they twice elected to punt instead of going for the big first down that was less than a yard away? Was Johnny Unitas of the Colts gambling recklessly with the fate of all Baltimore when in the sudden-death period he scorned the close-up field goal in favor of three more tries for a touchdown?

The better team for 57 1/2 minutes lost the football game. The Giants were the magnificent fellows who held the Colts for downs on the 1-foot line, then slashed away at their 14–3 lead and went in front with two touchdowns in 5 minutes. And then, with 150 remaining seconds showing on the clock, the Giants were to learn that for them the 1958 season was 150 seconds too long.

Unfairly, the Giants at the finish became victims of the massive second-guess. They had their 17–14 lead with 2 1/2 minutes to play when they gambled that they could punt and restrain the Colts thereafter instead of going for 2 feet on fourth down. Against the dissent with that strategy of the Giants is the argument that the greater gamble would have been a running play. This was a day when ball-carriers weren't always getting back to the scrimmage line, so fierce was the combat.

It came up again in the sudden-death prologue when the Giants chose the punt instead of the try for a yard on fourth down at their own 29. From their own 21, the Colts drove to the winning touchdown but if the Giants were over-sure of their own defense, that was pardonable. All season, the Giants' defense had been winning football games for them, not losing them. A Giants' line that had stopped the Colts on four downs from the 1-yard line earlier seemed to have excellent credentials.

If there was one play that turned the game, it was Johnny Unitas' maneuver with his fellow conspirator, Ray Berry, the Colts' superb pass-catching end. The Colts were needing 8 yards on third down near midfield with time running out before the Regulation game ended when Unitas rolled out to pass. He had time, and he was blessed because the Giant's defender nearest Berry had slipped to the ground. Unitas calmly withheld the throw the play called for, motioned Berry farther down field like a cop directing traffic, and then threw the big one that helped the Colts within field-goal kicking distance.

The field goal that reprieved the Colts with 10 seconds left and gave them a 17–17 tie was a splendid contribution by Steve Myhra from the 20-yard line. At that late hour, he was the only man who could do the Colts any good. He was talking about it later, in the dressing room.

"I tried to shut the noise out of my ears and the crowd out of my view," Myhra said. "I tried to think this was just another practice kick like a thousand others. It was useless. I heard all that noise and I saw every one of those 64,000 people. I prayed for a good snap, and a good hold by George Shaw, and when both of those things happened, I prayed for a good kick."

They were asking Unitas about the fancy stuff he tried in the extra period after scrounging a place kick that would get the game over when the Colts had first down on the Giants' 10. He was taking a chance on fumbles or interceptions with his passes to Ray Berry and Jim Mutscheller down near the goalline, they said. "I don't expect my passes to be intercepted," Unitas said, simply.

For the Giants, there was nothing merciful about the sudden-death episode. It was a cruel thing. They were losing to a team they had licked once before. They had put miracles back to back by beating Cleveland twice. They scored first on Sunday and had reason to dream they had the Colts licked when only an 85-yard scoring drive crowded into the last 2 1/2 minutes could get the Colts out of the trap.

The Giants were acting out their reputation as the team of destiny. They threw the Colts back from first down on the Giants' one. They moved in front after trailing the Colts, 14–3, and the threat of a rout confronting them. They were proving to be the opportunist team.

The Giants got their big break when Kyle Rote's fumble was converted into an additional 25-yard gain that took the Giants to the Colts' one-yard line and paved the way for a big touchdown. At that point, the Colts could curse their own luck. But if the Giants were guilty of exploiting the Colts' miseries, the Colts might have patiently remembered Sophocles' warning that time catches up with guilt; justice is never out of breath.

DECEMBER 30, 1958

Who's She?

In 1959, the Marquis Company in Chicago, who assembled the respected Who's Who in America, *decided to publish its first edition of* Who's Who of American Women. *They sent a letter to Miss Shirley Povich of* The Washington Post, *inviting Povich to submit a biography for the book. He flipped the letter into the waste basket. But despite the fact that his daily column ran with a clear photo of the author, Povich was included in the new edition. Papers all over the country picked up the AP story on the embarrassing error. The* Los Angeles Times *splashed it across the page showing pictures of Mamie Eisenhower, Liz Taylor, Eleanor Roosevelt, Clare Booth Luce, and Povich—with a cigar. Walter Cronkite sent a telegram asking, "Miss Povich, will you marry me?" The Marquis Company quickly sent an apology to Povich, hoping he wasn't embarrassed by the incident. Typically, Povich responded saying, "For years I have been hearing this is no longer a man's world and I am glad to be listed officially on the winning side."*

Who's Who of U.S. Women?

18,999 Shes and One He

By Millicent Adams

The Washington Post

The first edition of "Who's Who of American Women," hot off the presses, includes among the names of some 19,000 prominent U.S. women, The Washington Post's award-winning sports columnist Shirley Povich—who happens to be the proud father of three children.

But, Povich is not complaining. "I now belong to the most exclusive club in America," said the ace writer whose accounts of bruising ring bouts and tense baseball and gridiron games are page one sports news.

And, he's so right. The company he's keeping in the 1400-plus page tome includes First Lady Mamie Eisenhower, Eleanor Roosevelt and screen siren Marilyn Monroe.

While these celebrities received the nod from the publishers, such personages as former U.S. Minister to Luxemburg Perle Mesta, the widow of former President Woodrow Wilson, and Mrs. J. Borden Harriman, former Minister to Norway, were cold shouldered.

Being mistaken for a member of the opposite sex is not new for Povich who at one time was invited to join the League of American Pen Women.

They were a little more "alert," he remembers. When filling out an application for membership with the group he was called upon to answer some ticklish questions.

One of them read: "Has your sex been a handicap in your profession?" Povich's reply was, "I can honestly say none whatsoever."

Another query wanted to know: "How do you get along with the men in your profession?" Povich replied truthfully, "I simply try to be one of the boys."

During World War II days, war correspondent Povich innocently shattered the dreams of some battle weary GIs on the tiny Pacific Island of Anguar who had been eagerly awaiting the arrival of a girl correspondent.

The Who's Who mix-up started last July when Povich received a letter (addressed to Miss Shirley L. Povich) containing his listing as it would appear in "Who's Who of American Women."

Povich dismissed it assuming they would discover their own error, "especially when it clearly stated that I am married to a girl named Ethyl."

Months went by ("maybe my silence was dishonest") and it was a forgotten matter until a coworker notified a "surprised" Povich of his conspicuous presence in the book.

To his great amusement, and that of his family and friends, Shirley Povich was mistak-enly listed in the first edition of Who's Who of American Women. *(1959)*

"I guess you call that winning by default," said Povich. "But, if it's all right with them, it's all right with me."

The book has been compiled by the publishers of the highly-esteemed "Who's Who in America," the Marquis Co. of Chicago.

The professions mentioned included artists, actresses, dancers, civic leaders, church women, social workers, educators, editors, jour-nalists, music patrons, philanthropists, doctors, nurses, nuns, lawyers and stamp collectors—just to name a few!

In the case of Mrs. Eisenhower, however, any reference to a career is omitted altogether.

Former First Lady Bess Truman's name is among the missing, but daughter Margaret is present and accounted for as Margaret Truman Daniel, "concert singer."

Former American Ambassador to Italy Clare Boothe Luce is listed simply as Clare Boothe, playwright, ex congresswomen, ex ambassa-dor, in that order.

Among others listed are contralto Marian Anderson, Ivy Baker Priest, Mrs. Oswald Lord, Barbara Gunderson and Elizabeth Taylor.

Along with the new editions the editors have conceded on an enclosed slip of paper that "... it is our feeling that any errors made were of inclusion rather than exlusion..."

JANUARY 14, 1959

THE SIXTIES

THE 1960S WAS A DECADE OF SWEEPING CHANGE IN THE U.S. The civil rights movement was in full swing; John F. Kennedy, Martin Luther King, and Robert Kennedy were assassinated; riots charred the cities, including Washington; and Vietnam war protestors filled the streets of the nation's capital.

Sports also changed. Shirley Povich, in his fifth decade at the *Post*, pushed hard for integration of teams and leagues. His sharp pen was often evident, as in a 1961 column on the Jim Brown–led Cleveland Browns' defeat of the all-white Washington Redskins:

> From 25 yards out, Brown was served the football by Milt Plum on a pitch-out and he integrated the Redskins' goal line with more than deliberate speed, perhaps exceeding the famous Supreme Court decree. Brown fled the 25 yards like a man in an uncommon hurry and the Redskins' goal line, at least, became interracial.

"The thing about Shirley," recalls former Executive Editor Ben Bradlee, "is that when he wrote a critical column it was a sculpted blow. It wasn't head-on. You weren't colliding with a truck. After he was through with you, you probably wouldn't have many scars but you probably couldn't move your head or couldn't walk."

Povich continued to pound George Marshall and his all-white Redskins. He even enlisted the help of John Kennedy's Secretary of the Interior, Stuart Udall, when it was announced that since the government was going to help build RFK Stadium, it would not house the Redskins unless integrated. That would change, too.

The decade of civil rights in sports was perhaps never more embodied than in the person of Muhammad Ali. Povich was there at the start, covering a young Cassius Clay in the Rome Olympics. And he was there when the World Boxing Association tried to strip Ali of his title in 1964. He was also there four years later in Mexico City when black stars Tommy Smith and John Carlos shook the track world and millions of viewers by raising their gloved fists in racial defiance during the playing of "The Star-Spangled Banner." He approved.

It was also the decade that produced match-ups that made their lasting imprint on the sports world, and he was there in the press box, painfully finding the right note to capture the rivalry—the classic Mickey Mantle–Roger Maris battle to see who would break Babe Ruth's record, the young upstart Jack Nicklaus catching and passing golf's everyman hero Arnold Palmer, and, of course, the two famous fights between Muhammad Ali and Sonny Liston.

For Washington, it was also a decade that saw two great sports heroes come to town and give Povich a real story to write. Ted Williams, having retired in 1960, returned as the manager of the Washington Senators in 1969, and legendary Green Bay Packers coach Vince Lombardi, who had moved to the front office in 1968, came to town to coach the Redskins in 1969. Washington's luck: a year later, Lombardi died of cancer.

In 1969, Povich wrote a memoir called *All These Mornings. Sporting News* writer Dave Kindred who worked at *The Washington Post* in those days, still keeps the book in his desk and refers to it often. "One morning the book fell open to page 35 and I started reading. Before long, I took notes of words on that page and the next. The words were 'honesty,' 'modesty,' 'joy,' 'kindness,' 'affection,' 'happy,' 'helping,' 'high moral sense,' and 'revered.' Shirley's choice of words is telling. If what we say of others is a measure of ourselves, and it is, then readers soon learned what to expect in a Shirley Povich column. He worked with a columnist's greatest assets: respect for his subjects, respect for his readers.

"He wrote simple declarative sentences that gained power with each word. And he did it, as he said of others, with joy, kindness, and a high moral sense. He even did it with as much modesty as is possible in a job that calls for public displays of ego.

"One day in the 1980s Shirley made his estimated 613th comeback from retirement with a rhapsody on something or other; at the risk of devaluing the work across half a century that had identified him as a great man, I said, 'You're writing better than ever.'

"'David, David,' he said. 'Do this long enough, you learn to eliminate your mistakes.'"

Sugar Ray Robinson

Povich loved covering boxing. That meant he wrote a lot about comebacks. Joe Louis, Sugar Ray Robinson, Sugar Ray Leonard, and Muhammad Ali all climbed back in the ring after they had retired — and the results usually were not pretty.

The Boy named Walker Smith who used to dance for pennies on the sidewalks of Harlem now at 39 is presiding over a shrinking empire as Sugar Ray Robinson, the middleweight champion. The bounce is still in those feet and much of it is synchronized with those fists, but only two of the 48 states recognize him as champion.

These are New York and Massachusetts, which gave a loud bazzoo to the National Boxing Association edict that stripped Robinson of his title for defending it too infrequently. So on Friday night at Boston, Robinson will strike a blow, or as many as needed, to re-emphasize for his admirers that he is still invincible.

He will wedge his fists into the regulation gloves for the 152nd time in his career and throw confusion at Challenger Paul Pender, barring the upset of the ages. It is scheduled for the championship distance of 15 rounds but Robinson is expected to resolve it at his convenience.

Pender is fighting Robinson mostly because he is local box-office as a one-time sensation who won 20 bouts in a row before he chucked the whole business to take steadier employment with the nearby Brookline, Mass., fire department. He is 10 years younger than Sugar Ray and has a creditable record of 35 victories in his 42 fights, but along the line he was knocked out by fellows named Gene Hairston and Jimmy Beau.

Suger Ray antagonized the NBA by laying off 22 months and was stripped of his title. His defense was that proper financial arrangements for a return bout with Carmen Basilio couldn't be made. Meanwhile, the NBA recognized the winner of a Gene Fullmer–Basilio bout as the champion, and it proved to be Fullmer.

But the elevation of Fullmer or Basilio or anybody atop Robinson in the rankings finds little popular support for two wonderful reasons. The last time Fullmer had business with Robinson, he was knocked out at Chicago in the fifth round by a Robinson left hook of such classic beauty it deserved hanging in the Louvre. He didn't knock out Basilio last time, but it would have been more merciful if he had.

Pender could be a lucky fellow for the fact that it is his first time around against Robinson. Of the five men who have beaten Robinson in his 152 fights—Jake La Motta, Randy Turpin, Basilio, Fullmer and Joey Maxim—only Maxim escaped a brutal beating in the return match, and that could have been because there was no return bout between Maxim and Sugar Ray.

Robinson fought in Boston last month, taking a warm-up bout with an obscure middleweight named Bob Young who upset his timetable. Sugar Ray, who said he needed the fight, said he would permit Young to stay around for six-seven rounds, but when Young shook him up with a left hook in the first round, he panicked and knocked Young out in the next.

Sugar Ray never lost a professional fight until his 41st bout when he was outpointed by Jake La Motta in 1950. He came back to knock out La Motta and started a new winning streak of 91 straight. Then, fat and saucy on a European tour, he was astonished to learn he couldn't lick Randy Turpin in a London fight. In the New York rematch, he clobbered Turpin to regain the title.

He dominated the middleweights by so much that he abandoned that title to go for Maxim's light heavyweight crown in 1952. He was beating Maxim for 13 rounds and then, for the first time in his life, was unable to answer a bell. Unmarked and unhurt, he collapsed in his corner from heat exhaustion on a night that was so fiercely hot the original referee couldn't go the distance, either, and had to be replaced.

After that, Sugar Ray kicked off his boxing shoes in favor of his dancing pumps and set out to make his name on the night club and ballroom circuit with his own band. He could dance and he could play the drums, but he was no champion in those professions, and the crowds didn't come and Robinson missed the big paydays of his fighting career.

After nearly three years out of the ring, he tried a comeback in 1955. He was slow, fat and a target for third-raters who couldn't carry his mouth-piece in his glory days. He was so arm-weary and helpless against Tiger Jones in a Detroit bout that Robinson fans turned their heads from their television sets and prayed that he would give up the whole idea of a comeback.

But a few months later, he was the old destroyer again in a match with Bobo Olson, then the middleweight titleholder. He belted Olson out in two rounds, held the title for two more years, lost it on a decision to Gene Fullmer in 1957 and was again consigned to the scrapheap as a fellow who had hung around too long. Six months later, he knocked out Fullmer and had the title back. Watch him on television Friday night.

JANUARY 20, 1960

[Pender won in a decision and won again in a split decision in June.]

Redskin Colors

The Redskins were the last NFL team to add Negro players to its roster. In column after column, Povich used his rapier wit to hound Redskins owner George Marshall to integrate the team, which Marshall finally did in 1962. Here are excerpts from some of those pieces:

For 18 minutes the Redskins were enjoying equal rights with the Cleveland Browns yesterday, in the sense that there was no score in the contest. Then it suddenly became unequal in favor of the Browns, who brought along Jim Brown, their rugged colored fullback from Syracuse.

From 25 yards out, Brown was served the football by Milt Plum on a pitch-out and he integrated the Redskins' goal line with more than deliberate speed, perhaps exceeding the famous Supreme Court decree. Brown fled the 25 yards like a man in an uncommon hurry and the Redskins' goal line, at least, became interracial . . .

OCTOBER 31, 1960

. . . In recent years, Marshall has been doing a disservice to all of his coaches and putting them in an unfair posture against the other coaches in the league. This is his adamant position against drafting or trading for Negro football players, thereby cutting his coaches off from a flow of talent that every other team finds valuable.

On this basis, the Redskins'coaches have need to be super coaches. The Cleveland Browns on Sunday got four touchdowns from their colored backs, Jim Brown and Bobby Mitchell. There are Negroes in the lineups of both division champions, the Eagles and Packers. The likes of the great interior linemen of the league, Daddy Lipscomb, Roosevelt Grier and Roosevelt Brown, are not for the Redskins who hold the color line better than they hold the scrimmage line. . . .

The Washington fans are losers in Marshall's refusal to hire colored players. His passion for identifying the Redskins as the South's team, even to rewriting the lyrics of the team's song to make them read "Fight for Old Dixie" instead of the original "Fight for old D.C." is bewildering. . . .

DECEMBER 20, 1960

There was this fellow named Bob Gaiters playing halfback for undefeated New Mexico State University the past season and he was very good. He outgained every college back in the country and averaged 6.8 yards per carry. He scored 23 touchdowns and no other collegian could match that production either.

The New York Giants admired many things about Gaiters, including the statistics that say he weighs 205 pounds and can run the 100-yard dash in 9.8 seconds. So on Tuesday, at Philadelphia, the Giants claimed Gaiters as their first draft choice form the pool of graduating college players.

The Redskins, who play in the same league with the Giants and are the worst-scoring team in it except for Dallas, didn't draft Gaiters. They couldn't on account of George Marshall's eligibility rules. The New Mexico boy was born ineligible for the Redskins, whose colors are inflexibly burgundy, gold and Caucasian. Gaiters is a Negro....

DECEMBER 29, 1960

... The Redskins have suffered, competitively, from their racial policies. "We try a little harder when we play the Washington team," said Ollie Matson, then with the Chicago Cardinals. He said he was speaking for all the Negro players in the league. Bobby Mitchell and Jim Brown, the Negro aces of the Cleveland Browns' backfield, have had some of their finest days in Washington.

The Washington fans have been victim, too, of the Redskins' disposition to nurture their profitable Southern TV-radio network. Marshall has been passing up competent Negro players in what is a too-important concern for his non-paying Southern fans who watch the games from their parlor hassocks. There is no certainty, either, that they would resent a Negro player on the Redskins, particularly if he could score touchdowns, in living color....

APRIL 27, 1961

Ty Cobb

This week's obituaries must fall short. A year before Ty Cobb died, it remained for Yogi Berra perhaps to say it best, when Cobb's place in baseball history again was being debated. The question put to Mr. Berra: "How much would Cobb hit against today's pitchers?"

Berra gave it reflection and then said: "Against today's pitchers, he'd be lucky to hit .250." Surely, Yogi wasn't serious. Had not Cobb compiled a lifetime batting average of .367 for 24 seasons in the majors? "Yeah," said Yogi, "I know. But remember Cobb is at least 70 years old."

Despite his feats that wrote more records into the book than any other man, Cobb was denied the era of the lively ball that was to come, and he might have had the justifiable complaint he was born ahead of his time. This happily was not the complaint of two generations of baseball fans born into Cobb's era and treated to the high excitement he gave a ball park.

Invevitably, there were the comparisons: Cobb or Ruth. These were unnecessary. The two were far apart, each the master of a domain. Ruth's was the home run. Cobb's was the whole sweep of other baseball skills, his dominance in his sphere as unchallenged as Ruth's kingship of the batted ball for distance.

On fan impact, if not skills, the comparison need not be ruled out. Both could tense up a whole ball park, in their special ways. With Ruth it was the build-up to climax, with his fans awaiting the Ruthian homer from the moment the large man threw away the extra bat and stepped up to the plate. In effect, they were awaiting release of their own gasps at Ruth hitting one more.

The Cobb man gave them a different show. He was electric, both at the plate and on the bases. He conned both pitchers and fielders. As an individual, he could destroy a whole ball team. To Ruth, a single was only a single. For Cobb, it was merely the start of a progressive tour around the bases with excitement at each point, whether he was stealing or scrambling for an extra base on somebody's hit, often his own.

Of Hemingway, it was said he revolutionized writing with his limpid prose. It might be said that Cobb revolutionized baseball with his daring, aggressive style that brought him more hits, more stolen bases, more of so many things than any other player living or dead. But in the sense that he stood alone, unmatched in his skills, he was not bringing revolution to the game, merely new excitement. There have been no followers in his image.

Cobb's approach to baseball was that of a clinicist. He probed and examined the opposition for weaknesses, knew the pitchers who were vulnerable to the bunt, the outfielders against whom he could take an extra base, the catchers he could trust to make the wrong play. Thus it was that he once exploited the rookie catcher of the Athletics, Wally Schang, with the complaint, "Get back a step, you're bothering my swing." When Schang complied, Cobb laid down a bunt in front of the plate and beat it out with the extra step he had gained on Schang.

It was the late Harry Heilmann who always contended that his Detroit teammate, Cobb, "would have been a great banker, a famous general, a successful industrialist—outstanding in any field he chose. No other man ever had his frenzy for excellence. Cobb's passion was to finish first in everything."

Cobb was managing the Tigers in spring training in New Orleans when he noted a cluster of his players around the sliding pit. Del Gainor, a rookie first baseman out of college who had been some of kind of broad jump champion, was putting on an exhibition. Cobb joined in, outjumped everybody but Gainor. Two weeks later, he ordered the rookie back to the sliding pit. Then he outjumped Gainor and was content. Only later was it learned that Cobb had been taking instructions in secret from the track coach at nearby Loyola University.

The 12 American League batting championships Cobb won, nine of them in a row, from 1907–15, permit little debate that he was the greatest hitter than ever lived, even though his home run total is pale alongside Ruth's. But his nine home runs were enough to tie him for the league lead in 1909 and he was recognized as a power man at least in his era. But with his choked grip and his crouch stance, he was more dedicated to managing his bat than swinging for the fence.

In a magazine article written in 1952, Cobb had scorn for the modern ball player. "They Don't Play Baseball" was the title. He singled out Stan Musial and Phil Rizzuto as the only moderns who would have been outstanding in his era, omitting Ted Williams, Rogers Hornsby and Joe DiMaggio. He said they don't give out their best efforts. Cobb, who often stole second, third and home on one tour of the bases, pointed out that the four highest-salaried players of 1951, DiMaggio, Musial, Williams and Kiner, could steal only a total of seven bases that season.

For that Cobb was criticized. Rogers Hornsby, in a counter-article, described Cobb as a selfish ball player more interested in his own accomplishments than the team's. Hornsby said Cobb did not belong in an all-time great outfield of Joe Jackson, Tris Speaker and Ruth. How to pitch to Hornsby in the Cobb controversy? That was easy. Just throw the book at him. Of Cobb, it can always be said, there he stands, high against the baseball sky, perhaps as the longest-enduring baseball figure.

JULY 19, 1961

Chasing Ruth

In 1961, New York Yankee sluggers Roger Maris and Mickey Mantle had a memorable summer chasing Babe Ruth's record of 60 home runs in one season. Maris ended up setting the record with 61 home runs, which would last until 1998, when Mark McGwire of the St. Louis Cardinals hit 70. Povich's last column would compare McGwire with the Babe, but first Maris and Mantle:

In Griffith Stadium that day in 1953 when Mickey Mantle boggled the eyes of the fans with a home run that cleared everything, there was immediate incredulity. For the first time in history a ball had been knocked over the leftfield bleacher wall, over the expanse of seats and completely out of the park.

It was then that the gasps gave way to invented reason. Why not? He had the wind with him. It was blowing a young gale in Mantle's favor. He was the beneficiary of circumstances. Complete credit was withheld from Mantle.

But not by 83-year-old Clark Griffith against whose team Mantle had struck the devastating blow. Griffith, with one short comment, expended complete applause to Mantle. "That wind has been blowing for 80 years and nobody else ever hit one that far," said Griffith. "They all had a shot at it."

All of which is by way of comment on those who may be withholding applause for Roger Maris, the fellow who is making the biggest run at Babe Ruth's record of 60 homers. Maris, less muscular than most of the previous challengers and far from the popular conception of the home-run hitter, is nevertheless playing the fiercest brinkmanship with Ruth's sacred mark.

They've all had their shot at it, the big men like Foxx and Greenberg and Kiner and Hack Wilson and Mantle, and now Maris is getting his. He is already closer on games played than they ever were. He hasn't wished any of those home runs over the fences, but has been driving them there. Under the pressures he hasn't slackened.

It was presumed in mid-season, even when Maris was five homers ahead of Mickey Mantle, that if any man were to break Ruth's record in the flood of homers being hit this season, Mantle would be that

New York Yankees' slugger Mickey Mantle, shown here at spring training in 1964, was "the biggest hitter . . . and also the fastest man on his team," said Povich.

man. But here it is nearing mid-September and Mantle's own pacer is a remarkable one, but out ahead of him is Maris.

The threat to Ruth's record was noted to be so serious early in the season that commissioner Ford Frick was impelled to prescribe the special rule that it had to be achieved within the framework of the 154-game schedule of Ruth's era, not the 162 games of the modern schedule. The new champ could not be synthetic. Perhaps this was unfair, but Mantle and Maris raised no howl to point out that a season is a season, irrespective of schedules.

It wasn't presumed that a .269 hitter would ever make a serious charge at Ruth's record, and that could be the reason for the prevalence of anti-Maris feeling. Mantle would fit more nearly the picture of the man who, in at least one big year, could surpass Ruth and, besides, Mantle is carrying a respectable .320 average.

But even Ruth was not subject to the pressures that Maris has been meeting in these final critical days of the test. When Ruth was going for his 60 in 1927, it wasn't actually important to him or anybody else. Failure to reach that mark would only mean that Ruth was unable to excel Ruth. After all, he was the only man who had hit 59.

Certainly Maris has done nothing to alienate support for himself. His behavior has been excellent, heavily marked by modesty at a time when he is figuring in the Nation's biggest conversational topic, not excluding the Berlin crisis. His deportment has been that of a guy indicating simply I'm-trying-to-do-my-best.

There was a seven-day home run famine for Maris a couple of weeks ago when it appeared that he was doomed in his race against the record. In the Yankees' dressing room they asked him about his last out, the one he had popped up. "No, it wasn't a bad pitch," he said. "It was a good pitch. I took a lousy swing."

Maris and Mantle are the most covered personalities of the year by the journalists, if Caroline Kennedy isn't. They have had to fend off more than their share of silly questions by the brigade of sports writers who descend on them after each home run game. When Maris hit his 56th, the questioning began with, "How did it feel, Roger?" Maris could only sigh, look at the ceiling and finally say profoundly, "It felt good."

For Maris the next four home runs will be the hardest earned, if he gets them. His bat will be weighted by more pressures than any man ever took to the plate with him. It calls for fairness even among those devout sentimentalists who reject the home run image in any shape except that of the rotund Babe.

September 11, 1961

Segregation at Spring Training

The Washington baseball team inevitably was going to hear criticism of the racial segregation in its Florida training camp because the fact of it is undeniable. To most persons, it is also reprehensible. The complaint as registered by Congressman Herbert Zelenko of New York was justifiable, but the threat that accompanied it wasn't.

Zelenko's attempt to equate the practices of the baseball team with what have been those of the Washington Redskins is a specious one. In demanding that Secretary of Interior Udall expel the Senators from the Federally-owned D.C. Stadium under his control, exactly as Udall threatened to exclude the Redskins, Zelenko has failed to touch first base.

Udall threatened to banish the Redskins for their clear pattern of racial bias in their refusal to hire Negro athletes. On that point, the Senators are not to be criticized and deserve only applause. Gen. Elwood R. Quesada not only points to the three colored ballplayers on his team but said he is eager to sign more.

Quesada himself deplores the local condition in Pompano Beach that has forced him to house Bennie Daniels, Chuck Hinton and Willie Tasby, his three Negro players, in quarters other than the hotel that houses the rest of the squad. "We don't condone this segregation, we have strongly protested against it, before Congressman Zelenko protested," Quesada said.

As evidence of his good faith, Quesada produces correspondence with the Pompano Beach hotel asking equal treatment of all of his ballplayers. "It is the hotel that has discriminated against the team," Quesada said. "We do not like it and we do not want it in our future at Pompano Beach."

There will be efforts, Quesada said, to obtain housing for all the players under one roof. "The problem of the Washington team has to be understood," he said. "When we bought the Washington franchise a little more than a year ago we had to act quickly to find a training site in Florida and Pompano Beach was one the very few readily available. None will be happier than I when that day comes when our players will be in one group."

That the barriers against housing for Negro ballplayers have been steadily falling in Florida is apparent. The majority of teams have solved their problems by leasing or buying entire hotels or motels. "I want the day to come when the Washington team can manage it on that basis," Quesada said. "It is unfair to say we condone segregation."

The inequities of conditions in the South have long been unhappily apparent to the white players as well as to the Negro colleagues. Teammates who share the same hotels and dining quarters once the season opens in the North also share resentment of the first and second class citizenship imposed in the Florida camps.

The feelings of the Negro ballplayers were especially understandable. For years in the White Sox camp, Minnie Minoso, a Negro and established star, was forced to tie himself to the Negro settlement on the fringe of Tampa's shantytown to bed down at night. The rawest rookie who happened to be white retired to the plush hotel headquarters in town.

Negro stars like Jackie Robinson also accepted this kind of discrimination in the early years when colored players were sort of on trial for behaviorism, but the freedoms from injustices in baseball began to come quickly. Even before there were demands by the players themselves, enlightened club owners took the first steps to erase the bias in housing.

The first Negro didn't come into baseball until 1947 and since that date the game has desegregated faster than the labor unions and those public school systems that needed to be prodded by Supreme Court dictum. On a population basis, the Negro ballplayers are proportionately more numerous than whites in the major leagues.

In the 15 seasons since the racial barriers came down in the majors, the strides of the Negroes have been immense. Not only did they demonstrate that they are sometimes better ballplayers than the whites, but the acceptability they have won has been reflected in the cheers for them. More importantly, the Negro ballplayer is eagerly sought by scouts, who ask only the question: "How good is he?"

The last injustices will not be erased, however, until the brotherhood of baseball extends to housing equality in the South, and not in the sense of separate but equal. Congressman Zelenko's complaint is useful as a prod, but in the nature of a threat it was at least premature.

February 16, 1962

Palmer and Nicklaus

Povich loved to speculate on mano a mano rivalries, and no game lent itself to such opinion more than golf. In his earliest years, it was Jones and Hagen. Later, Hogan and Snead. As the golf enthusiasts grew by millions in the early 1960s, thanks to television, another major rivalry emerged, this time Palmer and Nicklaus.

It is still reasonable to call Arnold Palmer the finest golfer in the world but the small doubts are now intriguing. Big Jack Nicklaus did outdrive and outputt him to win the U.S. Open playoff and a couple of other young pros are also charging on Palmer in a manner to raise the question whether his dominance can continue.

For a period of two years, Palmer was the unchallenged stick-out with two victories in the Masters, then a U.S. Open title in 1960, and then a third Masters' triumph. He destroyed both the golf courses and the opposition. As an added filip to the sound game he plays was his talent for winning gallery applause for the tough shots that earned him repute as the gambling fool.

Who could beat Palmer? It seemed that nobody could. Like Man O' War and Babe Ruth he appeared to be one of a generation. Not since Ben Hogan outlasted his fiery rivals, Byron Nelson and Sam Snead, had any golfer been so prevailing. Palmer's kind appeared to be one of an era. But now is it?

Certainly Nicklaus is now around to keep Palmer honest. He can outhit Palmer off most any tee and like Palmer he has every shot in his bag. But more interestingly, there are a couple of others as well. They, too, can police a tournament against any romp by Palmer. These are Phil Rodgers and Bobby Nichols, other young pros who also have all the shots.

Rodgers and Nichols, it is remembered, finished only two strokes shy of getting in the playoff with Nicklaus and Palmer in the Open. Rodgers turned pro only six months before Nicklaus. He is just as blond and if not quite as big he is nevertheless a rugged 180-pounder who can unload the big hit. Nichols gets most of his leverage from his six feet, two inches.

Recapitulating, Rodgers would have been the winner of the Open save for one misadventure on the 17th hole in the opening round when he took four strokes in a pine tree. Or he can trace his defeat to a four-putt 10th hole in the third round. "It was a four-putt hole, but none of Rodgers' putts was a bad one," Maury Fitzgerald reports. "A turtleback green with a bad, tricky rise threw him."

It was at the $50,000 Doral Open in Florida last March that Jimmy Demaret was asked the question and said, "Phil Rodgers is the finest young golfer around, after Nicklaus." Demaret's ideas of March appear to be sound ones. He was forecasting the Open finish one-three, not an unnotable prediction.

Nicklaus, like Palmer, appears to be the complete golfer, if lacking some of Palmer's derring-do on the hazardous shots. No amateur leaving the pro ranks has cut as wide a swathe so quickly among the pros as the husky young man from Ohio State. Nor has an amateur gotten such speedy acceptance by the circuit pros who affectionately call Nicklaus "Ohio Fats."

The Nicklaus swing is a bit more classic than Palmer's, which runs to a duffer-type finish in his eagerness to get extra distance. Nicklaus' distance is built into his 205 pounds, 35 more than Palmer, but he does make a concession to his ample midriff by adopting an open stance for more freedom of arms. This is the style, too, of paunchy Bob Rosburg and Billy Casper.

There must be a reluctance, though, to consider any of his challengers the absolute equal, as yet, of Palmer. On the point of competitive fire, Palmer still stands alone as his many late-round triumphs attest. At Oakmont, he was battling more than Nicklaus and the others. He was cast as do-it-for-us-Arnold hope of the huge, stampeding galleries of his native Pennsylvania.

The conditions were a special pressure for Palmer whose feat of getting into the playoff was alone a magnificent one. In his third-round twosome with Bob Rosburg, Arnold gallantly permitted Rosburg to putt out first on every hole lest his opponent be disturbed by the gallery which had been taking off in a noisy herd for the next hole after Palmer putted, leaving Rosburg to putt out in a hub-bub.

Only once did Palmer display any annoyance, and that was when he walked away from a tricky putt on No. 17 to glare at a television commentator who wouldn't stay hushed. In the press tent afterward they asked him about that, and Palmer said, "It wasn't how loud he was talking, but what he was saying. He was analyzing my putt for me as I stood over the ball."

Tom Gallery, the NBC man, put on a great show of the Open for television except for an unfortunate choice in announcers. I'm thinking particularly of the fellow who grabbed Palmer at the finish of the last hole and had us all wincing when he said, "Did you choke, Arnold?"

JUNE 20, 1962

Facing Kofax

New York, Oct.2—At the finish, the Yankees were left to ponder not alone at the fact that more of them had just struck out in a World Series game than any other team's hitters in the 61 years of Series history. Sandy Koufax had just sent 15 Yankees back to the bench with their bats as miserable companions of their thoughts.

Into the World Series opening, Koufax had taken his glittering 24–5 pitching record in the National League, and, at game's end, this was the item that caused one Yankee to give tongue to the Yankees reaction in the clubhouse. "I wonder," he said, "how come he lost five games this year."

This was the supreme Yankee tribute to Koufax and the Yankees could be left as well to wonder about their future in this World Series. There is a Koufax in their future for perhaps two more World Series starts, and this could not be pleasant for the Yankees.

Seldom has one pitcher ever put a new face on the World Series estimate to the degree that Koufax has done after one start. Now the odds must be revised to favor not the Yankees, but the Dodgers, simply because of this one magnificent presence.

The important Series question was: Could Koufax beat Whitey Ford, the Yankees' reliable old pro? The answer was there today for 69,000 stadium fans and millions on television. And the carry-forward conclusion is that Koufax cannot only beat Ford again, but any other pitcher the Yankees toss at him.

Koufax not only made believers of the Yankees with the 15 strikeouts he notched, but by the manner of them. He had good hitters groping for his stuff, a baffling admixture of curve-ball speed spiced with an occasional hard one that came out of the same delivery.

In the press box, statisticians were making furious notations about the experience of Yankee hitters against Koufax. When he struck out little Bobby Richardson the first two times he faced him, this was notable, because it is not done with frequence. Richardson is not interested in homers and likes to slap, and the figures show that he strikes out only twice every 28 times up. Koufax fanned him not twice, but three times today.

For all the good stuff it did them, the Yankees went in forewarned of the skills of Koufax. "Simply the best," was the report of Yankee scout Mayo Smith brought back to Ralph Houk after weeks of Yankee espionage when it was clear the Dodgers would be their World Series foes. The only Yankee who looked good today was Yankee Spy Smith.

Yankee Manager Houk was one of the non-believers when there were attempts to point out that the Dodgers are a frightfully weak-hitting team that got into the World Series only on its pitching and its base running. "No bad team gets into a World Series," Houk said. "There must be something more to the Dodgers than pitching and running."

Indeed, there was today, and it could not be obscured by the brilliance of Koufax's pitching. The Yankees learned, too, about Tommy Davis and why he led the National League in hitting, because he thumped out three lovely singles in his four times up against Yankee pitching.

The first by Davis was an opposite-field single to right when Ford attempted to pitch him wide, and the next time up he showed his speed to leg out a hit. He raked Stan Williams for another right-field single for his third straight hit, and, with two out, there was wonder if Davis would test Elston Howard's throwing arm. Davis was willing, and he stole, but blessed mostly by the jump he got on the pitcher.

Koufax and his strikeout pitching left managers Alston and Houk with little opportunity to exercise any strategic brain-waves, so much did he dominate the game. Nor did either manager distinguish himself with a post-game comment. Of John Roseboro's three-run homer, which accounted for sixty per cent of the Dodgers runs, Houk was moved to remark, "I'd call it the big hit of the game."

Alston was free with his praise for Koufax, but one of his statements, taken a bit out of context, sounded like the nadir of praise for a pitcher who had just set a World Series strikeout record. "I'd say," said Alston, "that it was one of Sandy's better games."

This was remindful of the eager young baseball writer who sought out Casey Stengel in 1956, after Don Larsen's feat against the Dodgers. That was the day Larsen pitched the first perfect game in Worlds Series history, not a hitter reaching base, and Stengel was asked: "Did you ever see Larsen pitch a better game?" Stengel, for the first time in his life, was rendered speechless.

[The Dodgers swept the Yankees in four games.]

OCTOBER 3, 1963

JFK Assassination: To Play or Not?

Pete Rozelle said it was his biggest mistake in his three decades as commissioner of the National Football League. Two days after John F. Kennedy was assassinated in Dallas on November 22, 1963, Rozelle ordered NFL teams to play their scheduled Sunday games. It was a decision criticized by Povich and many others.

It is known that among thinkers there has been scorn for the claims of the three year-old American Football League that it plays football of major league calibre. This reaction has been manifested mostly in the 14 cities where the long-entrenched National League operates every Sunday.

The view has been taken that the AFL does not play the same basic football as the NFL, and that touchdowns are cheaper in that league. Indeed, AFL football may be more helter-skelter but its own fans do not complain on that score and neither do television viewers left a-tingle by the gambling type of AFL game.

Pete Rozelle, commissioner of the National Football League, has been steadfast in his deafness to AFL pleas for a title game show-down between the two leagues. Thus far he has dictated that never the twain shall meet, and this is the continuing prospect.

But the two football leagues did come up to a common test on Friday afternoon. It was unrelated to their respective prowess, but it did relate to the philosophies of their respective commissioners. President Kennedy was assassinated and a stunned Nation was desolate in tragedy. For the two pro leagues it was a bit of a poser.

To play or not to play the league games that were scheduled for Sunday? What would be the measure of pro football respect for the late President? By his lights, Rozelle ruled it meet and proper that the NFL schedule be played without interuption, and with no disrespect to the President. Certainly none was to be intended.

That was the day when new growth came to the American Football League. Immediate was the decision of its commissioner, Joe Foss, that the AFL would suspend its schedule. In its executive office, at least, the AFL was big league. Foss was saying, in effect, that pro football was not sacred, and in that action the AFL seems to have come off best.

The AFL action could be the more applauded because here was a league in financial trouble, still grubbing desperately for the weekly gate receipts that would enable at least some of its eight teams to attain the break-even point on the season In contrast, the NFL had been bragging about its new attendance records and the bloated coffers in so many of its cities.

To the credit of some of the NFL club owners there was distress at Rozelle's decision to go on with the show. The Washington and Philadelphia teams openly dissented, spoke their preference for not playing. In other cities, there was no zest for the games at least among club owners, although big crowds did show. Individual players said Sunday's were the games they did not care to play.

Rozelle was saved from an even more embarrassing decision by the NFL luck in the scheduling. Suppose the Redskins were scheduled to play in Washington that day, instead of Philadelphia, and only 20 blocks from the Capitol rotunda where, at the game hour, the Nation's leaders were in public bereavement before the coffin of the late President, with millions glued to television? How unseemly would have been a pro football game with its sounds echoing from nearby.

Rozelle, in his decision to go on with the shows, said he was taking comfort in tradition. "The tradition in sports for all is to perform in times of great personal tragedy."

He said there has been indeed a precedent for that, but mostly it has been in cases of grieving individuals, not as a league practice.

Harvard and Yale, with a tradition that makes a mockery of the tender roots of Rozelle's league, refuted him bluntly, if not by design. For the first time in 88 years they suspended Harvard vs. Yale, unaffected by any feeling that the show must go on. That Harvard was the alma mater of President Kennedy may not have been a deciding factor in this tribute to him. Almost all of the other major games of the Nation were also canceled or postponed.

True, there were no telecasts of the NFL games on Sunday, no raucous invasion of a Nation's sadness at home. But this was the decision of the networks, not of the league. Theirs was the taste to proclaim that this was no day for football carnival.

Even in Las Vegas, the new bastion of show business, there was no official sentiment that the show must go on. On Monday's day of national mourning, all productions and gambling casinos were ordered closed. Unlike business as usual in the NFL.

NOVEMBER 26, 1963

Muhammad Ali

Muhammad Ali pulled off one of the greatest upsets in boxing history when he defeated Sonny Liston on February, 26, 1964, and began a decade of dominating the heavyweight division. Ali also created headlines by becoming a Black Muslim, changing his name from Cassius Clay, and refusing to be drafted into the army. The Champ eventually prevailed in court and returned to the ring in 1970, meeting Joe Frazier in the first of three epic bouts, winning two of them. Almost a month after the 1964 Liston fight, the World Boxing Association tried to strip

Ali of his title, which outraged Povich. Although Povich had trouble coming to grips with the politics and religion swirling around Ali, as well as his name change, he came to admire him as a person of conviction and ideas. He also thought Ali to be one of the greatest boxers of all time.

Miami Beach, Fla., Feb. 26—It was surprise on surprise that Cassius Clay was pulling. Here he was the next morning, his first as heavyweight champion of the world, and now in a performance no less stunning than his conquest of Sonny Liston the night before when he left Liston a bloodied and beaten hulk on his ring stool at the end of six rounds.

This was his first press conference as champion and it was five minutes along when it was interrupted by one request considered the least likely ever to be made of Clay. "Cassius, talk louder," was the plea from the floor. Indeed, this was necessary, if incredible.

Cassius, who had loud-mouthed his way to the title match in the first place and then licked Liston, now had the working stiffs of the press off balance. He was the mannerly, subdued young man now talking about himself and his victory in controlled tones that bordered on whispers. He was almost shy, respectful to everybody.

Not a mark did he bare from his battle with Liston: "I am through talking," Cassius said, almost sotto voice, "I don't have to talk anymore. All I have to do now is be a nice clean gentleman." This was an upset to equal his feat of the night before.

His new modesty was accompanied by confession. "I wanted to quit in the fifth round when that stuff got in my eyes. I couldn't see, it smotted so much. I told my trainer Angelo (Dundee), 'Cut the gloves off me,' and he pushed me out of the corner and said, 'Go out and fight. This is for the title. You're gonna be the new champion.' Whatever was hurting my eyes cleared up."

Trainer Dundee said he blamed it on the carbolated Vaseline blended with perspiration that came off Liston's glove from his own cut. "It wasn't from the sponge I was using on Cassius' face in our corner. I sponged my eyes with it and there was no hurt. Same thing with the towel they were using. It had to come from Liston's corner."

Had Cassius' hysterical harangue at the weigh-in been an act? "Yes, it was one of my best shows." Was he acting now with his new quiet attitude? "No. I want to be nice to people. Rocky Marciano is retired and when they introduce him anywhere they give him a big hand. I want a big hand when they introduce me after I retire."

He said he felt sorry for Liston, but didn't think much of him as a fighter. "He's strong but he's got no balance. Balance is the name of fighting. He was just a Patterson killer, and that's all." Some of the new modesty began to wear off. "If Liston is great I must be double great. You experts put a big load on that old man. You made me fight harder. But I ain't mad at you. You just let my mouth overshadow my ability."

About Liston's damaged left shoulder, Clay said, "I don't know anything about that. He said he hurt it in the first round but he was punching pretty good with both hands in the fifth. Look at the pictures. I had him slowed up in the first and second round. He was numb. He was tired. I knew I'd get him."

First understanding that the fight was over, and that Liston wasn't answering the bell for the seventh, came from Cassius himself Tuesday night in Convention Hall. When he went into his victory dance, how did he know the fight was finished? "I got a habit of counting to myself and the 10-second warning bell. I go 'buzz-one, buzz-two, buzz-three,' like that. When I counted to seven and Liston wasn't getting up to fight, I knew I had the title."

An hour later though there was strong evidence that Clay had beaten a one-arm fighter, that he had licked only one side of Sonny Liston. After the exit of Cassius, Liston moved on stage to meet the press. His left arm was in a sling. Dark glasses hid the bruises. He brought with him an official report of eight examining physicians that he had suffered a torn bicep muscle near his left shoulder. At the hospital, it left him unable to raise his left arm, the doctors said.

Otherwise, the fallen champion appeared strangely unconcerned by the loss of his title. He said he hoped Clay would give him a rematch. "He's the boss now." Sonny said he had respected Cassius. "I don't hold no fighter cheap."

The doctor said the injury could follow a sudden thrust by a fighter, not necessarily from a punch. Sonny said it happened in the first round. He said he asked his handlers to let the fight go on but they would not. He denied he quit. He said he would have nailed Cassius except for the bad arm. About those wide misses with his good one, his right, he said, "You don't miss with your right if you got a good left working."

How did he rate Clay? "Not as good as Machen or Patterson or Folley. They come to fight. He runs like a thief; like he stole something."

FEBRUARY 27, 1964

A Preposterous Punishment

Miami, Fla. March 23 — The World Boxing Association is a confederation of state boxing commissions claiming some vague connection with foreign countries. Its rulings are not always respected within its loose membership, and now there is some evidence that the WBA has also gone slightly loose in the head.

The WBA's announced attempt to strip Cassius Clay of his heavyweight title is a behavior more preposterous than anything in its charges against Cassius X. The blanket indictment of Clay is that his general conduct has been detrimental to the best interests of boxing "in provoking world-wide criticism and setting a poor example for the youth of the nation."

Three notable things have happened to Clay in the nine months since the WBA itself announced he was the thoroughly acceptable No. 1 challenger for Sonny Liston's heavyweight title. (1) He licked

Liston, (2) He joined the Black Muslims and (3) He flunked the arithmetic test of his Army draft board.

It is still very doubtful if any of these episodes is a crime against the state, the people or the World Boxing Association. Actually, Cassius' defeat of Liston could be acclaimed as a public service which removed that twice-convicted felon from the heavyweight throne.

The WBA did not mention Cassius' declaration in favor of the Black Muslims but this was tacit in its criticism of him. Membership in the Black Muslims does not increase Clay's popularity, but it is not yet a crime, according to the constitution of the World Boxing Association.

Clay has implemented his Black Muslim membership by assuming his new name of Muhammad Ali. Neither is this any kind of a sin. Mostly it is amusing. Also, Cassius makes the valid point that he chooses in these enlightened times of emancipation to discard the slave name of Cassius Marcellus Clay to which he was born of plantation serfs.

It was not quite terrible, either, when Clay flunked the Army draft board test. Something like 24 per cent of the incipient inductees do, the Army reports. It may not be nice to have as the reigning heavyweight champion a youth who never learned his multiplication tables, but the WBA never raised its voice against Sonny Liston with his record of 16 arrests and two jail terms until last week.

There is no indication that Cassius, unlike Liston, ever assaulted anybody, outside of a prize ring, where he was expected to. And he has never carried a gun or associated with hoodlums. His sponsors have been 11 respected Louisville businessmen. Until the Black Muslims are legally outlawed, the laws of the WBA can hardly supersede the law of the United States.

Mostly, Clay is a crashing bore with his repetitious "I am the greatest" and "I am too pretty to lose." These, though, are innocent boasts. He has already stripped himself of much of his popularity, if not most of it, with his Muslim-ism and his ludicrous efforts to set himself up now as an inspirational world figure who has a devoted following.

The WBA has brought up Clay's action in signing a kind of return-bout contract with Liston's people in the event he won the title. This, indeed is against WBA rules and the oft-stated sentiment of the Senate Anti-Monopoly Subcommittee and there was a secrecy about it that was not exposed until Liston's group lost the title.

But even this misconduct was more Liston's than Clay's. The $50,000 extra payment of Clay for the return bout rights was a bludgeon of the promoters against him before he could get a shot of the title. And where were the 11 respected Louisville businessmen who called the shots for Clay and were as much party to it as he?

The WBA was aware of the secret contract instantly at the end of the Liston–Clay fight on Feb. 27, but not until Cassius flunked the Army tests and declared openly for the Muslims did they get outraged. Their mills grind slowly, indeed, without the virtue of grinding exceedingly fine.

It can be conceded that Cassius' conduct has not been a good example for the youth of the nation, as is charged, but he would seem nevertheless to have a wonderful defense for any threat of punitive action by the WBA. Prizefighting has never been the domicile of altar boys and he is guilty of no statutory offense against its good name, which is suspicious, anyway. His behavior since winning the title may not have been popular, but he isn't quite a public official to be removed from office for misconduct.

[The World Boxing Association took the title from Ali in 1967.]

MARCH 24, 1964

The 1964 Open

Golf's 1964 U.S. Open in Washington, D.C., dropped nicely into Povich's lap. Ken Venturi was the least likely winner, barely upright at the end in the scorching heat. Three decades later, Povich remembered that dramatic day.

THE 1964 U.S. OPEN; Victory in the Heat of Battle;

Venturi's Main Opponents at Congressional Were Exhaustion and Dehydration

This was 33 years ago, and in the baking heat that climbed to around 100 degrees the unthinkable was happening—maybe—on the links of the Congressional Country Club.

A sick man, playing the last rounds under a doctor's care by special permission of the United States Golf Association and wracked by the tortures of heat exhaustion and dehydration, was struggling to hold his lead in the U.S. Open—and confronted with the longest course ever selected in the 69 years of Open play.

Ken Venturi was playing with an entourage: one accompanying doctor who was administering salt tablets and ice packs; a marshal with an umbrella to shield him from more of the sun's heat; another marshal equipped with a first-aid walkie-talkie; the executive director of the USGA; a police officer in uniform; and his playing partner, a kid named Ray Floyd.

Venturi had given startling evidence of his deteriorating health on the last two holes of the morning 18. A magnificent putter all morning with his smart round of 66 that included a 30 on the first nine, he nevertheless blew an 18-inch putt on No. 17 and a 30-incher on No. 18.

So the round went from miraculous to merely magnificent. The field averaged more than 75 strokes; Venturi had 66, with those two missed easy putts he would have had a 64. Among the rest, only Billy Casper, with a 69, could manage better than 70.

On the No. 17 tee, Floyd would later testify that the haggard and unsteady Venturi had told him, "I don't think I'll make it, Ray."

"I didn't want to agree with him," Floyd said. An old friend Jay Hebert, who also visited Venturi as he drove off on No. 17, said, "I stood there and worried that he was about to fall."

But now there would be another 18 to play because the USGA, wit-

less copycat of everything British, for years had ordered a 36-hole finish on the last day. (This experience would result in ending that non-
sense.)

In the locker room between rounds Dr. John E. Everett, a Congressional member, counseled Venturi to quit, saying, "To continue
might be fatal." But he agreed to accompany Venturi if provided with
salt tablets and ice packs. Between rounds, Everett advised rest as a
priority over lunch for Venturi, who ate nothing. The USGA granted
Venturi a 30-minute extension before the final 18.

"You know, dehydration can be fatal," Everett told him.

"I'm already dying," Venturi responded. "I have no place else to go."

Venturi stretched himself prone on the first tee of the final round to
catch an extra few minutes of rest. On the 13th hole he asked the USGA
official if he could, because of his condition, avoid the two-stroke
penalty usually meted out for slow play, and reprieve was granted.

Starting that final 18, Venturi was two strokes off the lead and being
asked to beat a golfer, Tommy Jacobs, who had just set an Open
record of 206 for 54 holes, bettering Ben Hogan's 207 set in 1948.
Could this wavering, enfeebled man bring that off? Could he survive
the day? Yes. Yes.

The upshot would be that Venturi would win that Open by four
strokes with an astonishing last-round 70 while second-place finisher
Jacobs ballooned to 76.

Venturi had come from six back of Jacobs and five behind Arnie
Palmer at the halfway mark.

By the 63rd hole, Venturi—plodding slowly down each fairway—
had caught and passed them both. Despite his condition, Venturi was
not playing it cagily. Twice he boldly exploded out of bunkers, "when
the best thing would have been to chip out and avoid the ponds," he
recalled. "But the wedges settled nicely on the greens."

The last bunker shot left him a 10-foot putt on No. 18, and when it
went in Venturi's eyes widened, and he flung his arms high in the air.
"My God, I've won the Open," he could be heard to exclaim.

Venturi, a religious man, considered himself close to the Deity and had arranged with a priest to say his prayers at a local Catholic church the night before the final rounds. He later explained, "I was asking God to help me believe in myself."

His triumph at Congressional netted Venturi a $17,500 check, a reflection of those times. This year, the same amount could be won by finishing in a tie for 35th place at The Masters.

That Venturi would even be a figure in the 1964 U.S. Open would have commanded the longest of odds. He had not won a tournament in four years. He was less than mediocre on the PGA Tour, reduced to asking old friends for sponsor exemptions so he could compete for some of the needed purse money. He dropped from No. 14 on the money list in 1961 to 94th in 1963, winning a $3,800 pittance that year.

The handsome 32-year-old out of San Francisco, where his father was a pro at a driving range, had once caused Jimmy Demaret to tab him "the sweetest swinger among the amateurs."

So sweet, in fact, that Venturi would make a big threat in 1956 to win The Masters as an amateur only to waste his lead in the last round when he stumbled to a miserable 80 and lost by a stroke to Jackie Burke Jr.

He won money consistently on the tour, but he was plagued by injuries to his back and wrist and his game went so sour that he even talked about giving up golf nine months before the Open at Congressional, said his then-wife, Conni. He had not been invited to play in The Masters in 1964 and was considering himself an outcast, unwanted on the tour as evidenced by his failure to get an invitation to play in the $100,000 Thunderbird tournament a month before the Open. That was because he did not finish in the top 50 at the Indianapolis Speedway tournament.

In desperation, Venturi telephoned Bill Jennings, the Thunderbird tournament director, pleading, "Hey, Bill, can you let me in?" Happily, Jennings had one of five sponsor invitations left and was touched, saying, "Come on up, Ken." Venturi virtually galloped to the Westchester Country Club in Harrison, N.Y., and won a $6,400 check by finishing third, a four-year high, and evidence that his game had perhaps come back.

But he still had to qualify for the Open, like so many other also-rans and rabbits. Neither had he been invited to the PGA Championship after the Open (same thing: he didn't belong). But that was taken care of when Venturi got his nose-thumbing revenge.

For most of his career Venturi was haunted by his collapse that cheated him of a victory in the '56 Masters and then two more losses there as a pro.

But then came 1964 and, out of nowhere, Venturi. There he was, standing on the 18th green at Congressional, nearly too delirious to embrace his own accomplishment, too weak even to bend down and take the winning ball from the cup. All that work was done by his partner. Floyd reached down and lifted the ball out, and when he looked up to give it to Venturi, the young man was weeping.

It was not the tightest finish in the U.S. Open that Venturi won, but unequaled was the drama of it. And even as Patrick Henry was not the first to declaim, "Give me liberty or give me death," he was remembered for it because he said it best. And by the same lights, Ken Venturi had given golf one to remember, an epic.

JUNE 11, 1997

Who Was the Greatest?

The picture of the three of them in the newspapers said they were, left to right, Willie Mays, Joe DiMaggio and Mickey Mantle. Although it was DiMaggio's 50th birthday party, it was an unspoken invitation to pick your own hero. Mays, DiMaggio or Mantle? It was an almost blunder-proof situation. Any choice could be an excellent one.

The fact that they all are, or were, center fielders does not negate the fact that this was the dream outfield of the major leagues, or at least the best since the legendary composite of Ruth-Speaker-Cobb.

The group picture also offered a new game at which any number can play, separating the skills of Mays, DiMaggio and Mantle, and who was the greatest?

Mays has been the most exciting. Mantle hit the most home runs. DiMaggio, it occurs, was probably the best ballplayer. But this is a debate that will belong to the ages. Each had their own fan-cults. Mays's admirers may be the loudest. Mantle, and the things he can do, have won the pragmatists. The student of the game could mostly favor DiMag.

There is little dispute that Mays does things more flamboyantly and wins ball games in more different ways. He excelled on the base-lines, made catches that only DiMaggio could have made, and made them more sensationally. He had the special virtue of both of the others in that he could carry a whole team.

Mays may have had the best arm. In any event, he exploited it more than DiMag or Mantle by the fast-charging ground balls hit to the outfield. On the bases, he was the biggest threat, could discombobulate the pitcher and a whole infield. Mays has been the very model of a winning ball player, and he, too, can hit home runs. A bat in Mays's hands was a reversible rapier or bludgeon.

Yet the greatest of them all could have been Mantle. His home runs were not only the more frequent, but the longest. None since Ruth could match Mantle's power, and there has been debate about that. The tragedy of Mantle has been his one frailty, his legs. What heights he may have achieved could have been limitless had he been unplagued by those dratted and recurrent leg injuries.

Mantle has been the paradox, the longest hitter and best bunter in the majors. His arm may not have compared too favorably with Mays's and DiMag's but it was strong and good. And he, too, could go and get a fly ball, perhaps as far as they, if it called for sheer speed. When his legs permitted, Mantle has been the fastest man in the majors.

For those who like the quiet hero, DiMaggio is their man. A tribute to DiMaggio is that his greatest admirers were the players on those Yankees teams he led. With them, there was always the silent under-

Povich between Joe DiMaggio (left) and Yogi Berra in the Yankee dugout (1963)

standing that DiMaggio would get the big hit or make the big play when the Yankees needed it most.

For the scholars of the game, DiMaggio was the picture ballplayer. He had the grace that has escaped both Mays and Mantle. What Mays achieved was usually in some kind of sprawl. Whether he was making a tough catch, or winging into a base or plate, he gave the impression of being a walking power plant.

But DiMaggio at the plate looked like the sculptured ballplayer, his bat held high and rigid, his stride only infinitesimal as he laid into a pitch, and his whole presence in the batter's box was a kind of dare to the pitcher to throw one past him. The DiMaggio base hit was, typically, a thing of beauty.

DiMaggio could catch anything Mays ever caught, but the illusion was different. DiMag made few catches the hard way. He surrounded the ball, thanks to his own speed, which was deceptive. And until his arm went bad, it struck as much terror as Mays's and was fully as strong and accurate. It was his mere reputation for a good arm that kept base runners honest in his later years.

DiMaggio didn't bunt, but his manager, Bucky Harris, explained that when he said simply, "DiMag is too valuable a hitter to bunt." It is true that DiMag rarely stole a base but he was advised against this injury risk. The fact is that he was the best base runner on the Yankees, exploiting to the hilt not only his own hits but those of his mates when he was on base.

More than any other ball player, DiMaggio probably exemplified the pride of the Yankees. His own was wounded on that latter day when a Yankee batting order posted by Casey Stengel said DiMaggio was hitting in the fifth place instead of the fourth. With three hits that day, he batted his way back to cleanup. Somehow, the feeling is they don't make ballplayers like DiMaggio anymore.

NOVEMBER 20, 1964

Super Bowl I

At the time, it wasn't that big a deal. But Vince Lombardi's Green Bay Packers defeat of the Kansas City Chiefs, 35–10, before a less-than-capacity crowd at the Los Angeles Coliseum, was the beginning of a new tradition. Like the Colts victory over the Giants in 1958, Povich understood the impact of the game. But even he could not have predicted that the Super Bowl would become the closest single U.S. sports event to a national holiday.

Los Angeles, Jan. 15—This was just before the opening kickoff, and there was a ceremony. National Football League Commissioner Pete Rozelle, with a signal to the prop men on the sideline, sent hundreds of uncaged doves fluttering into the Coliseum's skies. There was no mistaking Rozelle's message. This was symbolic of the new peace that had come to the newly merged pro football leagues.

Rozelle must have been joking. His NFL champions, the Green Bay Packers, gave the Kansas City Chiefs virtually no peace at all thereafter. They scored a touchdown against the American Football League representatives the second time they got the ball and poured it on mercilessly in the second half. It was the NFL telling the AFL that if you hang around with the Packers too long you get hurt, badly.

The final score of 35–10 in the Super Bowl was a fair commentary on the flow of battle and also where the greater skills lay. For a half, the Chiefs kept it respectable and even tossed a scare into Green Bay partisans. Also, there were some aggressive individuals among the AFL personnel who were putting a big rush on Bart Starr.

But the Packers blew the game open almost immediately in the third quarter and it was one of their defensemen, Willie Wood, who did it. Len Dawson aimed a long pass down field to his tight end, Fred Abranas, and Wood snagged it. He also raced it 50 yards upfield to the Kansas City five-yard line and pretty soon the Packers had the touchdown that made it 21–10, Green Bay, and if that wasn't the ball game there would be great surprise.

For the AFL, this contest was a rude admittance to the company of the NFL, especially after being snared into visions of an upset victory. Quickly, Len Dawson got the Chiefs' tying touchdown in the second quarter and at the half it was only 14–10, Green Bay, and the Packers were looking not at all as if they were invincible.

And then the Packers caved them in. Wood stole that Dawson pass to set up the 21–10 gap. The Green Bay rush line that had been baffled a bit by Dawon's moveable pocket in the first half began to read his movements and put him under pressure. Bart Starr, who had a creditable 8-for–13 passing record in the first half, began exploiting the Kansas City defenses anew and connected with eight of his ten second-half pitches.

In the Super Bowl, Starr made Willie Mitchell and Fred Williamson of the K.C. defense his super-dupes. His first touchdown pitch, for 37 yards to Max McGee, found defender Mitchell in the wrong place. Starr later lost a 64-yard touchdown when his pass to Carroll Dale was called back because of offside, but on that play Mitchell and Williamson were lucky, both having goofed on the coverage of Dale.

The same blocking on his passes that Dawson was getting in the first half didn't hold up in the second when the Packers had a better book on his movements. It was quickly established that the Chief's running game, even with Mike Garrett sometimes able to dazzle, wasn't going to be a great problem for the Packers, and the second-half statistics tell of the Chiefs' futility against Green Bay's defenses.

In that second half, Kansas City had the ball for only four plays in Packer territory and never could move it beyond the Green Bay 45-yard-line. This was the Chiefs getting an understanding of Packer defenses that had allowed NFL clubs an average of only 12.6 points a game. On this day, each of the Packers had that potential $15,000 paycheck in mind and by their lights it was a sight better than the $7500 fee for the losers.

Vince Lombardi, the Packer coach, said he didn't make any special adjustments in the second half, but obviously his athletes did. Ron Kostelnik, Henry Jordan and Bob Brown put the smear on Dawson a total of six times for losses. Dawson had not been getting this kind of pressure in the AFL and his record of 16 completions in 27 pitches was an excellent one.

If Lombardi was under any anxiety in the first half when the Chiefs were refusing to submit to the Packers' reputations, he did not betray it in his postgame statement. The Packers' coach was even a little bit caustic when he was asked, "How does Kansas City compare to the National League clubs?" Said Lombardi, "They don't." He added later on that he didn't want to get into such comparisons, but it was already on the record.

The Chiefs for most of the first half were indistinguishable from a good NFL team, and indeed the best lineman on the field was their Buck Buchanan, a 6–7, 285-pound tiger at tackle who was belting through the Packers' blocking. Kansas City got its touchdown to tie it at 7–7 on an elegant maneuver by Dawson, whose fake handoff to Bert Coan drew defender Willie Wood out of the path of Curtis McClinton, the eventual receiver of a wafted toss into the end zone.

There could be admiration for this sort of thing, even on the Packers' side of the field. The Packers as well as the Chiefs were under some tension, betraying it with a pair of costly off-side penalties. They had made much of the over-anxiety by Dallas a couple of weeks before which resulted in an offside that perhaps cost the Cowboys the tying touchdown in the NFL playoff, but here were the old pro Packers making the same kind of mistake.

But there are always two halves to a football game, and it was in the second half that the AFL learned more about the Packers. Not only did Green Bay put Dawson under the rush that set up the 50-yard interception by Wood, but down on the five-yard line where the going is supposed to be the stickiest, Elijah Pitts went all the way through the left-tackle passage carved out by Bob Skoronski.

That made it 21–10, Packers, and to get them their next touchdown Starr beat the third-down situations consistently, Packer depth showed through when Max McGee grabbed a pass for 16 on third and 11 and later snatched a 13-yard bullet pitch into the end zone. McGee got into the game as backup man for Boyd Dowler, who was hurt in the first quarter. Tax Packer's No. 2 flanker tried so hard he caught seven passes from Starr, two for touchdowns.

In the fourth quarter, it wasn't quite fair. The Chiefs were reduced to playing catch-up and their attack was sheer desperation. They couldn't afford a single run, and all of their 15 offensive plays were easily read passes that produced mostly gift yardage. It was not a good day for the AFL.

JANUARY 15, 1967

Olympic Protest

Sports has always been a lightning rod for social change in the country. But when track stars John Carlos and Tommie Smith stood on the viewing stand in Mexico City in 1968 to accept their Olympic medals—and raised their black-gloved fists while lowering their heads in protest over treatment of blacks in the U.S. — their actions took the debate to a new level. Povich, like many of his contemporaries, was very patriotic. But he respected Carlos and Smith for the cause they were protesting and understood their grievances. He also felt the U.S. Olympic Committee leaders were reactionary to a fault and never forgave them, particularly its leader, Avery Brundage, for excluding Jewish athletes from the U.S. team at Berlin in 1936.

Mexico City, Oct. 18 — U.S. Olympic officials conveniently might have chosen to cast a blind eye at two black gloves encasing the upraised fists of two Negro medal winners. It seemed, in fact, that was their intention until the International Olympic Committee brought strong pressure. So they kicked the two sprinters, Tommie Smith and John Carlos, out of the Olympic Village and off the American team.

Whether this strong action by the IOC was necessary is highly debatable. Smith and Carlos, who ran one-three in the 200-meter finals, did not disrupt any Olympic event by their actions on the cere-monial stand. Their sin was the technical one of violating the U.S. Olympic manual which prescribes the official U.S. uniform on the winners' stand. Without added adornments.

In their protest of the Negro's racial position in America, Smith and Carlos showed up in black-power symbols. They wore knee-length black socks that were conspicuously a new thought. Smith wore a black scarf. And each wore a black glove on one hand.

One American Olympic official said he was willing to overlook these appurtenances, but that he was outraged by the failure of Smith and Car-los to respect the American Flag and the National Anthem that was being played in salute to their capture of gold and bronze medals. Throughout the Star Spangled Banner, the two athletes cast their faces to the ground. In contrast, the silver-medal winner, Australia's Peter Nor-man, on the stand with them, was at erect attention during the anthem.

When Smith and Carlos marched down from the stands and across the track toward their quarters in the stadium it was with their black-gloved fists still held high and resolute in protest. If it was unpatriotic in the view of most observers, the courage and dignity of their revolt-gesture was inescapable. The mild revolutionists are rare.

By finishing first and third they had won their chance to exploit their protest. Worldwide television cameras and news services do not tune in on losers. Even those who would deplore the time and the place of their demonstration will concede that a right of protest was theirs. Passage of the Civil Rights Acts by the American Congress affirmed the Negroes' complaint of 300 years of injustice.

This, then, was the chance of Smith and Carlos to tell the world of their militancy and protest with an impact never before offered a Negro, athlete or otherwise. They took that chance, took the consequences, took their medals and were going home. It was not nice that

In an act of "courage and dignity," wrote Povich, track star medalists Tommie Smith (center) and John Carlos (right) protested the treatment of blacks in the U.S. at the 1968 Olympics in Mexico.

they did not give full attention to the American flag but their sin otherwise was less than horrible.

There is a reason for thinking the Olympic panjandrums blundered in dealing out the ultimate punishment to Smith and Carlos. They thus trebled the impact of the entire episode and also the martyrdom of those two militants, who now are better able to carry their cause to more places.

Actually, there was reason to believe the U.S. committee was prepared to ignore the incident until the International Olympic Committee stuck in its oar with a statement processed through Avery Brundage, protesting the U.S. athletes' "deliberate violation of the accepted principle by using the occasion to advertise domestic political views." The statement deliberately put the U.S. committee on responsibility to the other Olympic nations.

The U.S. committee did not react late Wednesday when the black-power revolt occurred. Not until the IOC made the suggestion did the U.S. committee take action. The expulsion of the pair had quick effects in the American compound in Olympic Village, splitting the colony into factions. From one window on the eighth floor, a hung bedsheet proclaimed, "Down with Brundage." This proved to be the room occupied by Carlos and Lee Evans.

Signs on a third-story window told of support for the U.S. Olympic Committee, plus racial implications: "Wallace for President. Win the War in Vietnam." Interestingly enough, a probe proved that these third-story rooms were occupied by members of the U.S. Olympic rifle team, members of the National Rifle Association, which is not famous for advocacy of the Negroes' progress in America.

Carlos, the most militant of the Negroes on the U.S. team, has not been a popular figure in the village. Somebody snuck into his room and smashed his record player after complaining for days at the repetitious loud soul music he likes in the dining room. Japanese and Canadian athletes complained officially that Carlos was bringing his record player with him and annoying them with his loud records.

Tom McKibbon, an oarsman from San Diego in the single sculls, expressed the point of view of the moderates in Olympic Village after the expulsion was announced. "I've got mixed emotions,'" he said. "It was a strong action to take, throwing them off the team. But they had a strong reason to protest, and this is the right place for it. No nation is free of race problems." The Harvard crew said the same sort of thing.

OCTOBER 19, 1968

Williams Voted Manager of Year

Naturally Ted Williams was voted the American League's Manager of the Year. And under what monumental delusions did the Twins' Billy Martin and the Orioles' Earl Weaver ever presume the award could be theirs? There had to be a complete unawareness of the Ted Williams mystique as an achiever.

Reasons, all of them specious, could be advanced by Martin and Weaver to show they were more deserving of selection than Williams. But in their own simple honesty they were ensnared by the belief that winning division titles in the American League was the ultimate and clear upmanship over Williams' fourth-place finish with his Washington Senators, 23 games back in the ruck and never a pennant threat.

But on perspective, Williams' job was the surpassing one, the 286 sports writers and broadcasters concluded with their ballots. When Williams created, from the ninth-place seaweed he inherited here, a team that won 10 more games than it lost and produced the Senators' first plus-.500 finish in 17 seasons, it was the masterful managerial feat in his league.

The sweep of Williams' success was the greater because he was not only a rookie manager, untutored in the leadership of men, but as a baseball figure he was covered with the rust of nine years away from the game.

Everything appeared to be against Williams as a successful man-

Povich celebrating his memoir with legends Vince Lombardi (left) and Ted Williams (right), who came to town in 1969 to lead the Redskins and Senators, respectively.

ager, including his own initial reluctance to take the job. Against him also was his reputation as a loner and a brooder who had stood apart from his own Red Sox teammates during those many years, and how could a guy like that be a unifying agent as manager with tender understanding of the diverse problems of a 25-man roster?

But now, in retrospect, it is remembered that there never was any ceiling on the potential of Ted Williams in any pursuit he chose for himself. He determined, at about the age of 8, that he would be the finest hitter in the major leagues, and he was, and the records prove it.

In Marine flying school during World War II, Williams' college-bred classmates were flunking the navigational tests and washing out, while he managed splendidly with his high-school arithmetic to become a daring and decorated pilot.

When he quit baseball as the American League's only .400 hitter of the past 47 years, he traded his bat for a fishing rod and became perhaps the nation's best finest flycaster, commanding $10,000 for each appearance at a sports show. And at the art of fly tying, supposedly requiring only the most nimble of fingers, his hands turned out exhibits acclaimed as the finest.

Williams' feat of taking the Senators to an 88–76 record, a 21-game improvement with the same cast that was a joke team in 1968, was testimony to his sheer genius, leadership and his practice of the black art of the sorcerer. Ten of the 12 "regulars" under Williams had better batting averages than the previous season, and the manager who could make a dangerous .266 hitter out of Eddie Brinkman was to be admired.

Williams' adjustment to the role of manager from his life as a loner in baseball was a remarkable one. His was a steep switch to a camaraderie he had never practiced as a player, and never was it considered that he could ever be an outgoing cheerleader for his team.

Neither of the two expansion clubs, Seattle and Kansas City, was interested in drafting names on the Senators' roster after the close of the 1968 season. They preferred to take eight players from the Washington farm teams. Anybody offering $400 for Hank Allen, a .219-hitting infielder or outfielder, could have had him. Under Williams' tutelage last season Allen was a valuable .278 performer.

It was evident that Williams liked Allen in spring training and was taken with the physical lines and batting stance remindful of his famous brother, Richie. Soon, under Williams' coaching, Allen was hitting only line drives in Florida. When it was remarked to Williams that "You like Hank Allen," his answer, accompanied by a wink, was, "More important, he likes me." It was the new Williams as a practicing psychologist.

By persuading Williams to return to baseball as the manager of the Senators, Robert E. Short virtually qualified as the Owner of the Year. In his long career, Williams has been associated with two losing causes. He didn't hit well in Boston's losing 1946 World Series, and in the Israeli–Arab six-day war in June, 1967, among the loot the Israelis captured from the Arabs in the desert were 8,000 Ted Williams tents, marketed by Sears Roebuck.

October 21, 1969

THE SEVENTIES

THE 1970S HAD THEIR SPORTS MOMENTS—ALI–FRAZIER, Curt Flood's epic court battle for baseball's free agency, Secretariat's Triple Crown, the Redskins' first Super Bowl appearance, and Henry Aaron's eclipse of Babe Ruth's home run record.

But for Povich there were two gut-wrenching events—the Senators' desertion from Washington and the terror of the Munich Olympics.

In 1972, already in his late sixties, Povich was there in Munich, up close and personal, when the terrorists struck. He conned his way into the compound, donning the uniform of a Puerto Rican team trainer and becoming one of the few journalists inside the fence. His reporting went beyond the sports page. He was the *Post*'s front-page reporter.

Of course, Povich never got over the Senators deserting Washington for Texas after the 1971 season, ending 71 years of major league baseball in the nation's capital. He spent the next three decades in an unsuccessful crusade to regain a ball club for his city.

On Sept. 30, 1971, the final night of big league baseball in Washington, his words written from the press box at RFK stadium were haunting:

> To those among the crowd who had come in sorrow, the Star Spangled Banner never before sounded so much like a dirge. Francis Scott Key, if he had taken another peek at the dawn's early light, would have seen that the flag ain't still there, and lyricized accordingly. It was captured and in transit to Arlington, Tex., which, to embittered Washington fans, is some jerk town with the single boast it is equidistant from Dallas and Fort Worth.

He simply could not understand why Major League Baseball executives and club owners would not want a team in the nation's capital with the president throwing out the first ball of every season. He held this against every commissioner, except Bowie Kuhn, a Washington native who grew up reading Povich and working the scoreboard at Griffith Stadium. It took 33 years after the Senators left town—six year's after Povich's death—before Washington would be awarded another major league franchise in 2004.

Povich's passion for the American pastime was never more eloquent than in his April 1975 piece, "Baseball is Dull Only to the Dull Mind." Describing the one-on-one dynamics of what some see as merely boring interludes, he captured the "pure sport" of the game:

> The batter is not merely knocking the dirt out of his spikes. It's probably imaginary dirt anyway. He's just a little bit reluctant to get into the batter's box against that old pro 60 feet, six inches away. And when he does he'll be wondering whether the bum is gonna curve him again or try to blow him down with that good fast ball. It's High Noon on almost every pitched ball.

The Washington Post columnist Tom Boswell was a copyboy at the Post in the early 1970s when he decided to become a sportswriter—but he had some doubts. "What I didn't know was whether it was a life that was worth living," he recalls. "At fifty, sixty or seventy, do you seem bitter? My profession has its share of burnouts, fact-twisters, grudge-holders, careerists. I wanted to see just One Exception—one person who proved that you could age with dignity, have a face still capable of a sincere smile and, in general, have a full life and family while still keeping your integrity as a journalist.

"Voila, Shirley!

"There he was, day after day, in what seemed to me an elegant suit, treating everyone in a gentle, friendly manner. I could hear him interviewing on his back-office phone by the hour. He laughed. He still enjoyed the people he talked to. He'd get serious and you could tell he was grilling somebody. Even in his grunts and little exclamations you could tell whether he was buying the tale he was being told.

"Though he was in his sixties at the time, he was clearly having a ball. He didn't think the games were dumb or monotonous. He thought they fit into a continuum of decades of games that he, and very few others, could place in their proper perspective. He liked his colleagues and they liked him. He had a wonderful family—though how that could happen, with six or seven columns a week, I still don't know. I'm guessing that Ethyl Povich was the key concept here."

The 1970s were supposed to be the beginning of leisure for Shirley Povich, who was 68 when he officially retired from the *Post* in 1974. But as he would later write of retirement, "I've found my own unique way to deal with retirement—I retired it." He began his "retirement" by covering Muhammad Ali regaining the heavyweight

A celebration of Povich's 50 years with The Washington Post *in 1974 hosted by publisher Katharine Graham, brought together Ethyl and Shirley, from left, with Graham, Hearst columnist Bob Considine, and* New York Times *sportswriter Red Smith.*

championship from George Foreman in Zaire in 1974, the famous "Rumble in the Jungle." Over the next 24 years, readers of the *Post* would be the beneficiaries of more than a thousand Povich columns. Some retirement.

Flood Changes Baseball

In 1970, St. Louis outfielder Curt Flood filed suit against Major League Baseball, challenging its reserve clause that tied a ball player to one team and gave that team the right to trade the player. Though Flood did not win, his legal action was the beginning of free agency in base-ball. A traditionalist, Povich nevertheless respected Flood for giving up his $90,000 a year salary when many of his fellow players were content with the status quo. Povich also believed the game would survive when change came, as it always had. He was right.

Curt Flood is an agitator, a boat rocker and some kind of nut. He is ill-advised and a tool of money-grubbing lawyers. He wants to throw out of work the 959 other ball players who were perfectly content to sign major-league contracts under the reserve clause and bring the whole game of organized baseball crashing down on their heads.

Goodness knows how much he could hurt all those club owners who have the best interests of the game at heart and have put their faith in it, also those millions of investment dollars. Flood is opposed to the American League way of life and also the National League's. He's an anarchist.

On the other hand, Curt Flood is a very good center fielder who makes $90,000 a year and would probably make more if he just went along like a good boy and signed that contract with the Philadelphia Phillies, who got him by trade from St. Louis. He is a committed man who is battling for a principle and is willing to take all the abuse he knew would come his way.

Flood is defying baseball's reserve clause. He is asking the courts to rule illegal the instrument by which, for nearly 100 years, the players have found themselves indentured for their playing life to the major-league team that signs them. Under the reserve clause they can be sold or traded at will, or even on whim, but always the team owners', never their own.

Ultimately Flood wants to get his case into the Supreme Court of the United States and have that highest tribunal take another look at its previous decisions upholding the reserve clause. There has been an upgrading of human rights as against property rights in the nation's courts since baseball benefited from earlier decisions exempting club owners from the antitrust laws.

Meanwhile, not all of his fellow athletes are making common cause with Flood. They don't want to be befriended by him and in fact all of them recently quoted on the subject, Carl Yastrzemski, Ted Williams, Harmon Killebrew and Frank Howard, say they prefer to go along with the club owners and the reserve clause, and some of them suggest Flood is being used.

The intimation is that Flood is merely lending his name to a grand gesture by Marvin Miller, the $50,000-a-year players' consultant, to scare the owners into more concessions. Wrong, according to Miller, who would hardly dare to vow, as he does, that Flood came to him as a volunteer, out of the blue sky, and asked him for help in the courts.

The yelp of the club owners is that their whole game would come tumbling down if there were no reserve clause binding players to teams until they were sold or traded. This has been their popular defense for years. No reserve clause, and the richer teams would get the best players, athletes would be unhappy with the poor teams and would start negotiating with a rich club while playing with a poor one. The game couldn't survive.

None questions the fact that it is better for the club owners this way, the reserve-clause way. And their athletes have not been disposed against it all these years. Flood is the first to raise a cry and it is natural that those long uncomplaining natives of the system would wonder what kind of a radical they have in their midst.

Baseball could probably operate without the reserve clause despite all nightmares of the club owners. Pro football found a way after it was denied immunity from the nation's antitrust laws, adopting a longer-term contract with an option clause that at least gives the athletes an appearance of freedom to move to another club or be declared a free agent.

To this point, the baseball owners have been very resourceful in meeting most of the game's exigencies. When the players asked for greater pensions, the owners sold more of their games to television. When player salaries and operational costs went up, so did ticket prices. When there was a demand for more franchises, the entrenched major-league club owners generously complied, each one of them getting about $3 million for letting four new teams into each league.

So the club owners, if defeated on the reserve-clause issue, will probably work that one out, too. Actually Flood has said that he would be content with a modification of the reserve clause, to get rid of its demeaning, for-life aspects, something that the athletes and the owners can live with. He doesn't want to put anybody out of business.

In previous tests of the reserve clause in the Supreme Court, the petitioners are 0-for-3. But the sentiment of the bulk of the players in favor of existing practices will matter little if the court finds the reserve clause repugnant in the next go-round. The biggest gamble in the case is being taken by Flood, who is willing to write off his $90,000 salary for perhaps two years. He makes it sound like a rebel with a cause.

JANUARY 26, 1970

[The Supreme Court ruled in favor of organized baseball in the Flood case, but within five years the reserve clause was gone.]

Arthur Ashe

Tennis, anyone? Arthur Ashe, America's third-ranked tennis player, is desperately in need of playmates. As an individual, he cannot obtain a visa to play in South Africa, but that country's sports minister declared it would be perfectly all right, or anyway less indecent, if Ashe came with a group like, say, the American Davis Cup.

Still a bit unclear is the reasoning by which Ashe is unacceptable as an individual entry in the South African open tennis championship, yet worthy of a visa were he on a team. One possibility is the belief that Ashe would be less conspicuous if accompanied by all the non-playing captains and managers and the players of a Davis Cup team, who form a small crowd, and that Ashe would get lost in it.

The trouble with an Arthur Ashe wanting to play tennis in South Africa is that he lacked a choice of colors at birth. Ashe was born a Negro, and in South Africa black ain't beautiful, and for this kind of thinking, and its segregationist policy, South Africa also was kicked out of the last Olympic Games, in 1968.

In all truth it must be noted that South Africa is not discriminating against Ashe as a person. South Africa discriminates against all Negroes. But its latest example of bigotry could get that country thrown out of international tennis competition as well as the Olympic Games. The Davis Cup nations will meet in London March 23 and will have something to say on the subject.

Ashe has been too active in the past voicing strong anti-South African sentiments, that country says, and can't be trusted to keep his promise to keep his mouth shut. Ashe had said he would make no statements on South Africa's apartheid or anything except tennis until three or four weeks after the tournament was completed.

The whole business has boiled up to a state where the South African Embassy in Washington has decided to get into the act. From somewhere, the embassy has come up with a whole file of anti–South African utterances charged to Ashe and recounts some of them. "South Africa is a very bigoted country, the most bigoted in the world," and "I just want to take an H-bomb and drop it on Johannesburg," and "put a crack in the racist wall down there."

These are Ashe's alleged utterances, but Ashe in turn says he's been forbearing toward South Africa. "I've bent over backwards to be nice to them—to the extent that some of the black militants back home think I'm nuts," he said.

The embassy in Washington also has come up with a new charge against Ashe, which possibly will surprise him. The embassy statement says he impeded the progress of his own race and helped exclude Negroes and other nonwhites from participating, for the first time in history, on a South African Olympic team.

This came about, it is pointed out, because the South African team was expelled from the 1968 Olympics just when it had promised to integrate, for the first time, its Olympic squad. A majority of the nations on the International Olympic Committee nevertheless cast the vote against South Africa because of its general racist policies.

Ashe could be confounded by this charge against him. He is a tennis player, and tennis isn't even on the Olympic program, and Avery Brundage would swoon if Arthur Ashe tried to muscle in on an International Olympic Committee vote. But the embassy statement says, "Mr. Ashe associated himself with a movement to prevent South Africa's participation in the Olympic Games ... [and] must therefore bear a share of the responsibility of depriving South African nonwhites."

The president of the United Sates Lawn Tennis Association has been quick to go to Ashe's defense. Alastair B. Martin denies South Africa's allegation that Ashe intended to visit the country as an agitator, and "the only criticism ever expressed by Ashe is that South Africa excluded athletes based solely on their color. The denial of his visa proves his criticism was correct and justified."

A South African native, a golfer named Sewsunker Papwa Sewgolum, can give testimony that some citizens are more equal than others in his country. He is not a Negro, he is an off-white, an Indian from the Natal province. He won the 1963 South African Open in the Orange Free State province with special help from the government.

For golfer Sewgolum, the government waived an old ordinance which prohibits Indians from staying in the Orange Free State for more than 20 hours. At the same time the government warned him that if he played in the Orange Free State again he might be forced to leave the territory every night to sleep at Kimberely, 150 miles away, where the race laws are more liberal. When he won the Natal Open, he had to collect his prize in the rain. Indians are not allowed in the clubhouse.

January 30, 1970

Lombardi: A Legend Passes

The Vince Lombardi story has ended too soon, his allotted years too few. A dreaded sickness cut down a man who exceeded his renown as professional football's most distinguished and successful coach. Vince Lombardi transcended the game which made him famous and which he, in turn, honored with the genius he brought to it.

To football he gave more than the withering Green Bay sweep and the wonders of the five NFL and two world championships he won in nine years of coaching the Packers. No man has had more impact on the game, and the great legacy left to football by the son of an immigrant Italian butcher was the gift of the Vince Lombardi years.

Football was his power base but beyond his coaching skills he could qualify as one of the remarkable men of his time. The thickset figure of the latter-day Lombardi may have bespoken the rugged product of the football field, but there was vastly more. He was football coach, lecturer, philosopher, tough guy, moralist and practicing patriot who without blush put his voice atop that of the crowd in singing The Star-Spangled Banner.

Football writers, in noting the scope of Lombardi's coaching triumphs and his complete command of his players' loyalties, dwelled often on the Lombardi mystique. At this he scoffed, ascribing all spiritual powers only to the divine, in which his own belief was complete. But others persisted in the belief in his special powers of accomplishment.

In his first and only year as the Redskins' coach, Lombardi walked into a situation that seethed more than once with sub-surface racial strife. Almost mysteriously, it dissolved in a team of brotherhood. Redskin players learned, as the Packers had, that on the practice field Lombardi was a rare mix of harsh and quick disciplinarian and sensitive softie when he learned of a player's limitations.

A less-than-best effort by his good football players infuriated him. But he could easily rationalize an inadequate effort by his inferior players. He made something of a morality game out of pro football, with all its violence, by his steadfast devotion to the rectitudes. With Lombardi, the old-fashioned virtues of hard work and deep faith and team loyalties never went out of style. In the roughest game of them all, these forces were his preachment to his athletes.

In Green Bay, there were individual Packers who loved him and hated him, yet won for him the three straight titles never equaled before or since. "To this day, I don't know whether Lombardi liked me or not," former all-pro tackle Henry Jordan told Milwaukee writer Ken Hartnett, "but we'd go through fire for him."

During the Green Bay years Lombardi was a contradiction to his players. "He was close to us and aloof at the same time," one of them wrote in a book. Yet even those Packers who were not certain they liked their coach said he motivated them to their very best. Thus did the Lombardi mystique thrive. Bill Austin, the Redskin coach Lombardi hand-picked as his successor, relates that several years ago Lombardi sat up until 3 A.M. devising plays that would lick the Cleveland Browns at the strongest point of their defense just for the satisfaction of doing so. The Packers won that game, 47–14.

If Lombardi was plagued by any by-product of his strong dedication to victory it was the prevailing image of him as the curmudgeon autocrat of the practice field, quick to chew out the unfortunate wight, or any group of them, who messed up a pattern. That picture of Lombardi as an insensitive slave driver was a wildly inaccurate one. An instant after his quick angers, the kindly emotions ran deep with him.

The loyalties that Lombardi demanded from his players and his assistants were seated in his own values. Army coach Earl Blaik told of the day West Point had Northwestern beaten until the final seconds, when a 50-yard pass through an errant Army defense beat the Cadets. "I still remember the tears rolling down Lombardi's face," said Blaik. As Blaik's assistant for offense, Lombardi could be absolved of that defensive lapse, but out of team loyalty he could cry at a team defeat.

At Green Bay, as the most famous football coach of his time, Lombardi could find other interests. Concerned citizen Lombardi headed up the Wisconsin Mental Health Association, and also that state's Cancer Fund drive. His transfer to Washington forced a slight change. Lombardi found a vacancy on the board of the District of Columbia Cancer Society.

For his masterful speeches to commercial organizations, Lombardi on his lecture tours could name his own fees. But there were never any for his vastly more frequent public appearances for the numerous do-good causes to which he was dedicated. When his acceptance of a check for a commercial endorsement of AstroTurf was questioned, it was disclosed he had endorsed it over to the D.C. Cancer Society.

Years ago, his own fame had become secure. But although he was intent on victory, Lombardi neither spoke of fame nor thought in terms of it. Always, he was a deeply religious man, eager to serve a greatness that was not his own.

SEPTEMBER 4, 1970

Ali–Frazier

New York, March 8 — In round 11 he wouldn't go down. There was a definite sag to his knees, and there was hurt on Muhammad Ali's face, but he wouldn't go down from that murderous left hook to his jaw. His pride was propping him and it was his defiance against Joe Frazier in this moment of his trouble and he lasted the round out.

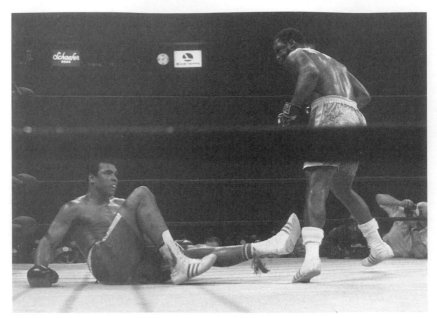

In the fight of the decade, Joe Frazier stands over Muhammad Ali in the 15th round of their heavyweight championship battle at Madison Square Garden. (1971)

But in the first minute of round 15, there was no time for Muhammad Ali to summon his pride to avert a knockdown because he was already on the flat of his back, deposited there by another of Frazier's thunderbolt lefts. He was up at the count of three, but he had to take the mandatory count of eight, and now he knew he was a beaten fighter for the first time in his professional life.

The decision in favor of Joe Frazier would be a formality as soon as Johnny Addie collected the slips from the judges and the referee at 11:40 P.M. this night. Muhammad Ali could no longer boast he was the greatest; the slow, chunky fellow he had scorned as clumsy and flat-footed was his conqueror in perhaps the fastest-paced heavyweight battle ever fought.

Each fighter received a record purse of $2.5 million and gave a performance that, for viewers, was worth every cent of it.

It was Muhammad Ali who finally buckled under the ferocity of the battling that began with the opening bell and continued almost without lull. At the finish, the whole drama was crying for instant rematch, because Ali had his own big moments in the contest and it was Frazier who was the first man in trouble, surviving a stagger in the ninth round, induced by an Ali uppercut and two hard rights.

Frazier, unbeaten now in all 27 of his pro fights and the undisputed heavyweight champion of the world, handed Ali his first setback of the night merely by answering the bell for round seven. In a bit of theater, with the hamming-up that he likes, Ali revealed his secret prediction of the outcome for closed-circuit television fans five minutes before the fight by opening an envelope in his dressing room. In a the-winner-is tableau, Ali held up his own, written vote: "Frazier to Fall in Six."

It was shorter, smaller, younger Joe Frazier bossing the fight almost all the way, mauling Ali in a manner that no other man could bring off and virtually taking away from him the classic left jab with which Ali liked to stick and cut and set up his previous 31 victims. Frazier negated Ali's jabs for the most part with his lateral action and head bobbing that had Ali missing awkwardly, and he moved in on the taller man almost at will to begin the flailing that finally brought the old champion to hook.

Ali did not play his usual waiting game and this was a switch. After weeks of scorn of Frazier's plan to "come out smoking," it was Ali who rushed to the battle and won the first two rounds. He pelted Frazier from long range with more rights than he normally throws in a whole bout, and the first two rounds were Ali's by a clear margin.

But already there were signs that this would not be one of Ali's easy nights. He wasn't finding Frazier with those stiff, textbook jabs because Frazier's bent head was not staying put. And already Frazier was showing what was for the former Cassius Clay a distressing habit of being able to bull him into a corner and slug away.

Ali was playing games in those early rounds, nodding to the crowd when backed against the ropes to signal to his fans that he wasn't hurt. And he was first up off his stool as if in scorn of needing the whole minute rest between rounds and shouting to Frazier from across the ring. But a fact was beginning to show. Ali, who never did want much truck with close-order fighting and never liked to be backed against the ropes, was being bulled back there more often than he liked, and he was soaking up more of Frazier's left hooks than he liked.

Also, by the middle rounds, in this kind of fighting, Ali usually had his opponent cut and ready to bleed badly, but the rhino-hided young bull in front of him wouldn't cut. Oh, Frazier's eyes were puffing a bit, but they were from Ali's own left hooks and occasional rights, not from those jabs that stab and cut and call the attention of referees to a fighter in trouble.

By the fifth round, Ali wasn't getting up from the corner stool before the bell was signaling "seconds out." Now he was taking the full 60 seconds of sit-down rest, because there was new understanding he had a job to do, and it was getting to be a tough one.

Frazier was doing well over all, but suddenly in round five he did not appear to be fighting a bright fight. He actually dropped his hands at mid-ring and dared Ali to find his bobbing head with any kind of a punch. Ali did pelt him with two beauts, and the stupid exhibition by Frazier was asking for the Sucker of the Year award. But he survived his stunt and at the round's end was actually laughing at Ali, and nobody had ever done this before to Muhammad Ali.

But Ali had never fought anybody like Joe Frazier who was all over him whenever he chose, banging Ali with enough left hooks that didn't miss to pile up points in the middle rounds. For a bit it appeared it was the strategy of Ali to let Frazier punch himself out, but if so he was taking too many hard left hooks during the waiting period.

In round 9, Frazier's face began to puff and perhaps there was a trace of blood around the nose, and then suddenly Ali tried to win the fight all at once. He whacked Frazier with a hard left and quickly brought up a hard right uppercut and Frazier appeared in trouble from this flurry. But the bell was not far away and Ali won only the round.

Ali was indicating now that he had come on again and would yet nail his man with one punch, giving him the Oscar Bonavena treatment. But the one big punch that happened next was Frazier's big left hook midway in round 11, the one that stopped all guessing whether Ali was playing possum on the ropes, because now Ali was in an honest stagger, wounded in flesh and pride and barely able to stay erect. He was succored in part by Frazier's own overeagerness to finish him off.

They called a doctor in to take a look at Ali at the end of the round and this was an indignity he had never before known. He passed muster but his face was puffy, especially the left side of his jaw, which was actually misshapen and getting a bit grotesque.

Ali threw all that he had into the 12th, and after resting through the 13th he revved up again for round 14, but all that he had was now feeble, and there were boos from Frazier's partisans when Ali was reduced to holding on in those dratted corners where Frazier was always the boss. Inside, Frazier's short arms were now no curse. They were an advantage.

Frazier was as advertised, an energy machine, tirelessly fueled by those sinews piled on sinews and a heart always eager for battle. Ali's face told the story of the decisive 15th round. He had the look of surprise followed by panic as he struggled up from his knockdown. It was as if he were asking how this could happen to the greatest, and knowing now he no longer was.

MARCH 9, 1971

A Masters for Whom?

There was an Associated Press story out of Augusta, Ga., the other day, under the eye catching headline, "Masters Changes Format, Opening Doors for Blacks." It gave the impression that Massa Cliff Roberts was now making a sweeping bow to Negro golf pros in a new readiness to usher them at once into the new comradeship of the Masters tournament held each year on the 18-hole plantation of the Augusta National Club.

Henceforth, tournament chairman Roberts announced, any winner of any of the 40 tournaments on the pro golf tour would be invited to play in the following year's Masters. Now, nobody ever again could impute that the Masters people were arbitrarily barring Negroes or accuse the tournament of being snob-racist.

There had been such suspicions in the past, based on circumstantial evidence, including the fact that in the 37 years of Masters tournaments no Negroes were ever invited or involved, except those attired in waiters' breeches or caddy coveralls.

Ever since Roberts helped to think up the first Masters, in 1934, the Augusta people have liked to soak their tournament in the fragrance of ante-bellum magnolia. They were pleased also with their plantation-style clubhouse and other touches suggestive of the Old South. The official brochure emphasizes that "The Masters is strictly an invitation tournament sponsored by a private organization."

Even those golfers considered automatically eligible under the Masters tournament regulations, including former Masters champions and current or former U.S. and British Open and Amateur champs, and those who finished high in major tournaments could not be certain they would be welcomed to Augusta. The Masters people have spelled out the warning that "eligibility under these regulations does not oblige the Tournament Committee to issue an invitation." What the Masters people can give, they can take away.

The so-called new format that is supposed to open the doors to the Masters for the Negro golfers could be more of a disservice than an opportunity. It also gets the Masters people off the hook in one sense because they have now eliminated one group of candidates, the eight golfers not otherwise eligible, who last year were selected on the basis of good tour performances. The Masters people can thus escape criticism they ignored qualified blacks in that group.

But in asking the Negro golfers to win a tournament on the tour before they can get an invitation to the Masters, they are doing the blacks no favor. It all may sound decently fair—win just one of the 40 tour tournaments and you're in—but the black pros will hardly be deluded by the seeming generosity of the offer.

Winning a tournament on the tour is no easy matter for any of the pros, especially a Negro pro who is instantly a victim of the arithmetic of the tour. Of the 150 golfers now on the pro circuit, only four or five are Negroes, and only two of these, Pete Brown and Lee Elder, are regarded as potential winners and they are so out-numbered by whites they must be regarded as long shots.

In all the history of the pro tour, only four tournaments have been won by Negroes. Brown won at WACO in 1964 and in the 1970 Andy Williams tournament. Charley Sifford, after 14 years on the tour, finally won the Greater Hartford Open in 1967 and the Los Angeles Open two years later. But at 48, the amiable, baggy-panted, cigar-smoking Sifford is hardly in his prime.

The record books are thick with the evidence of how tough it is to win a tournament on the tour. Arnold Palmer himself, despite the fact that in 1970 he earned $128, 853 as the fifth-leading money winner on the tour, failed to win a single tournament.

That the Masters is comparatively safe from an immediate invasion by one or more Negro golfers may be assumed. Tommy Aaron, one of the most respected pros on the tour, made something of a break-through when he won the 1970 Atlanta Open. It was Aaron's first victory after 10 years on the tour.

Frank Beard led all of the money winners on the tour with his $175,224 in earnings in 1969, but even so he won only two tournaments. This was a great improvement, however, over 1968 when this skilled golfer was unable to win a single event. Gay Brewer once won a Masters, but hasn't won a tournament since 1968. His best finish last year was sixth place in the Bahama Open.

Even super pro Jack Nicklaus could win only one tournament on the tour last year. Such criteria promotes the feeling that the Masters people, with their new win-a-tournament format for getting an invitation, have not left the door very ajar for the few black pros.

[In 1975, Lee Elder became the first black man to play in the Masters.]

JUNE 29, 1971

The Senators Leave—Again

They won't hear it in Washington next spring when the cry through-out the rest of the land is the joy sound of "Play Ball," the command that remobilizes a million dreams of pennant, however fanciful. After 71 years, the vacuum and the stillness. The Washington Senators are no more.

Seldom has a raped community been offered so wide a choice of villains. The focus centers first on Bob Short, the baseball carpetbag-ger from Minneapolis who schemed for most of two years to abduct the Washington franchise to Texas as a hedge against any failure to bulldoze the Armory Board into the virtual free rental he demanded.

The counts are many against Short who dropped just enough hints of his plans so as to escape charges of duplicity. But the major accusa-tions can be directed against the 10 unconscionable and money-grub-bing American League club owners who inflicted the debt-ridden Short on the Washington scene in the first place and then gave him the votes to move to Dallas because he was too short of funds to oper-ate in Washington.

Nor is the Armory Board itself without guilt in the city's loss of its team. Its stubborn, shortsighted refusal to grant most of the stadium concessions Short asked two years earlier sharpened his plans to get to Texas. When he did get a better stadium deal, he gave warning with his comment of "It's a little late in the game." The city, in its now-fran-tic efforts to get a new team for its empty stadium, will find itself spending many more dollars than the cost of the full concessions to Short.

His fellow club owners let go unrecognized Short's continual mis-takes that got him into the mess that, he says, threatened to bankrupt him. They opted instead to bankrupt Washington of its major-league status. Instead of holding Short to account for his outrageous opera-tions in Washington, they rewarded him for those mistakes by letting him skip town.

They paid scant heed to the fact that Short foolishly overborrowed to buy the team and then pleaded poverty, and to the stubborn refusal of this novice club owner to hire a general manager, and his record of wrecking the club with his absurd deals.

They didn't call him to book about all his extravagant expenditures when, pleading lack of revenue, he brought a spray hitter, Curt Flood, out of retirement at $100,000 salary. Nor in a money crisis like Short's could the Senators afford an untried, $100,000-a-year manager, expenses included, like Ted Williams. And the impoverished Senators were the only team in the league billed for the owner's private jet, with copilots. The owners had ears only for his complaint that he couldn't operate profitably in Washington.

They showed utterly no concern for the Washington fans, who were asked to support last-place teams by paying the highest prices in the league, a little matter Short arranged by trading away his infield and boosting the ticket prices far beyond those of the Baltimore Orioles, who were playing the best baseball in the league only 40 miles away. It took Short only one year of ownership to get a ticket up to $6 while the Orioles were charging $4 tops. Reserved grandstand tickets went from $1.50 to $3.50 within Short's first two years, with no other team in baseball making such spectacular progress in that department.

Organized baseball also thumbed its nose at Congress, which had been sending up warnings that the game was trifling with its antitrust exemptions in its continual shifting of franchises. This latest one happened directly under the noses of the senators and congressmen who were readying new legislation against the game.

President Nixon didn't exactly help Washington in its baseball crisis when he said it would be "heartbreaking" if the Senators were moved, but added that he didn't want to get into a scrap with Dallas over the thing.

This may have been practical politics by the President, who can count and is aware of Texas' 28 electoral votes compared to the District of Columbia's mere three. But it was also pussyfooting, and entirely unlike the pronouncement in 1958 by then Vice President

Nixon that a Washington without major-league baseball would be "unthinkable."

The heroes of the sad Boston tea party in which Washington lost its franchise were baseball commissioner Bowie Kuhn, who fought a stubborn holding action against Texas but who, unfortunately, does not own a vote; and Joseph B. Danzansky, who with his associates, went their full limit in their bid to buy the team.

For Washington, the wound is deep. If the Baltimore Orioles are persuaded to play a few games in Kennedy Stadium, it would amount to little more than a bone tossed to Washington fans, who still would not have a team to call their own. And those optimists who indulge in the hope of a National League franchise for Washington in the immediate future years are only encouraging a cruel misbelief it will happen.

SEPTEMBER 23, 1971

The Last Waltz

Everybody in Kennedy Stadium stood up at 7:30 P.M. because the voice on the loudspeaker said, "We ask you to join Robert Merrill in singing the National Anthem." The voice did not bother to explain that Merrill was on wax, and that Robert, baby, was not deserting the Metropolitan Opera stage for this occasion. It was merely one more of management's deceptions Senators' fans had long been taught to live with.

To those among the crowd who had come in sorrow, the Star Spangled Banner never before sounded so much like a dirge. Francis Scott Key, if he had taken another peek by the dawn's early light, would have seen that the flag ain't still there and lyricized accordingly. It was captured and in transit to Arlington, Tex., which, to embittered Washington fans, is some jerk town with the single boast it is equidistant from Dallas and Fort Worth.

But the jocularity of so many among the 14,460 fans who were present challenged any belief that they had come to a death-bed scene. The Washington Senators, at the end of this game, would be no more after 71 years on earth. The deceased, actually, was a pretty good draw, pulling those who had come to give a last cheer for remembered heroes, or, perforce, to wipe away some tears in public.

But for every mourner who made it to the ball park, there were multiple empty seats to testify that 30,000 others had averted their eyes from the scene, shunning it either in indifference to the whole business or in reluctance to give chortling Bob Short one last handout at the highest admission prices in the league.

Those who were savoring this last, fond look at the Senators let it be known by their cheers that they absolved the athletes of all blame in the messy machinations that rooked the city of its major-league status. Even the .190 hitters heard the hearty farewells, and in the case of big Frank Howard it was thunderous when he came to the plate.

If there was no general wet-eyed melancholia in the stadium, there were still unmistakable pockets of bitterness. From the upper stands hung banners spelling out four-letter words in large design, all of them reviling club owner Bob Short for shanghaiing the team to Texas.

Special police dispatched by management to remove the hanging vulgarities in the second inning drew the boos of the crowd, which was making no secret that its sentiments were pro-banners and anti-police. And then in the third inning, the six-letter word made its appearance in the left-field upper stands in a new, vertical banner that read "Short Stinks." There were new cheers for that little number, which had a life of approximately 10 minutes before police took it by storm.

In the stands, neighbor nudged neighbor in glee while pointing to the sprouting number of anti-Short graffiti in the stadium. But in the sixth inning, with one swipe of his bat, Frank Howard redirected all attention, back to the ball game. He did it with No. 26, one of his super jobs.

It brought on a crowd delirium that for the next many minutes effaced any sadness the people had brought to the stadium on this supposedly sorrowful night. Howard responded with emotion of his own, tipping his hat to a cheering crowd for the first time in his seven years with the Washington club. After whirling his batting helmet in the air as he rounded the bases, he flipped his soft playing cap into the stands as a gift symbol of his gladness.

It was a four-run inning that tied the score for the Senators at 5–5, and in the eighth they went in front, 7–5, but now, oddly, the temper of the crowd was changing. As if in sudden awareness that the end of major-league baseball in Washington was only one inning away, the mood hardened. "We want Bob Short!" was the cry that picked up in loud and angry chorus, and it was the baying-fury sound of a lynch mob.

Then a swarm of young kids, squirts who wouldn't know what it had meant to have a big-league team all these years, or what it would mean to lose one, flooded onto the field from all points of the stands. A public-address announcement warned that the home team could forfeit the game unless the field was cleared, and pretty soon the game resumed.

It got as far as two out in the ninth, the Senators' 7–5 lead intact, no Yankee on base, when one young rebel from the stands set off again. He grabbed first base and ran off with it. Some unbelievers, undaunted by the warning of forfeit, cheered, and from out of the stands poured hundreds, maybe a couple of thousand fans. They took over the infield, the outfield, grabbed off every base as a souvenir, tried to get the numbers and lights from the scoreboard or anything else removable, and by their numbers left police and the four umpires helpless to intervene.

The mad scene on the field, with the athletes of both teams taking refuge in their dugouts, brought official announcement of Yankees 9, Senators 0, baseball's traditional forfeit count almost since Abner Doubleday notched the first baseball score on the handiest twig at Cooperstown. But by then the crowd-mood was a philosophical "So what?" Or more accurately, "So whatha hell?" The Senators were finished, even if the ball game wasn't.

OCTOBER 1, 1971

ABC Monday Nightcap Is One for the Week

A certified phenomenon of the times is Monday-night football on network television, and how it grew. Quite unfounded was the original fear that Mom and the others of the distaff side would have to be carried kicking and screaming from their TV sets before the putative master of the household could make a move toward dialing in another game, so soon after Sunday's pro football orgy.

Monday Night Football has worked so well for ABC that all other programs on the other two major networks, with ratings ambitions, have been forced to skedaddle to other time slots or take an unholy beating in the polls. ABC has discovered that Sunday's pro football fan is eager to come back for more on Monday night, especially when the matchups are so selective.

The whole, wonderful idea was conceived for ABC by Roone Arledge, an imaginative chap who has made ABC the leading sports network. ABC, after five years on the outside looking in while CBS and NBC hogged the pro football ratings, last year gambled $8 1/2 million to buy the brand new Monday-night package.

For ABC, whose Monday-night ratings went up 55 per cent with the purchase of its football show, the games are proving a better bargain than what CBS and NBC bought at higher prices. ABC is paying the National Football League $8 1/2 million for the Monday-night games. CBS for its $20 million and NBC for its $15 million are showing more games but without the single high focus of interest.

ABC's Monday Night Football is sometimes called the Howard

Cosell Show, and that is not always a misnomer. On it, Cosell is irrepressible for much of the time as television's greatest apostle of an anti-background role. He is, in the jocular sense, a charming rogue, who hasn't brought to the role of third man on the telecast nearly as much as he promised. But perhaps nobody could.

In the beginning, Cosell traipsed the country late in the summer of 1970, ballyhooing this new idea ABC had about pro football on Monday nights and how, with his help, it would be a different kind of football show: "We'll bring a new dimension to football telecasting ... we'll tell it like it is."

In emphasizing his determination to tell it like it is, Cosell's own rhetoric sometimes wallowed between his twin passions for the florid and the orotund. At one point he was caught saying, "Times have changed, and the constant reiteration of clichés provides a litany of fatigue..." This, perhaps, was assurance he wouldn't say the same thing the same way twice.

There have been too many times when the only new dimension Cosell has brought to the Monday-night games has been more of himself and his vapid generalities that tell little about the contest. Cosell's banter with Don Meredith is pleasant fun, and he is properly respectful of play-by-play man Frank Gifford. But when he attempts his football expertise the new dimension he brings to the game is wading-pool depth.

Nor is Cosell quite the master of the language, despite his fondness for preening himself in that department. He has scoffed at the networks' custom of hiring semiliterate jocks as sports commentators while paying them handsome sums for their on-the-job training in the language. In this, Cosell could be properly resentful, but he need also look to his own malapropisms, including his recent discovery that a good move by one of the Monday-night players was "instinctual."

Cosell is not unamusing. With his continual groping for the polysyllable, like a dedicated elf chasing moonbeams, he titillates. The trouble with Baltimore against the Rams in the first half the other night, he said, "has been an absence of opportunism." And as for those highlights of the NFL action he would show between the halves, Cosell denied he had made the choice of the games. "They were selected," he explained, "by the producers of this show in their (what else) infinite knowledgability."

The new format which Cosell promised would get rid of the "constant reiteration of clichés that provide a litany of fatigue" has somehow been misfiring with Cosell himself the culprit.

It may be a bit indecent to keep book on Howard, but the fact is that he sometimes gets trapped, and needs his own recognition course in clichés. Like that rainy night in Milwaukee when Cosell assured everybody it was "an incessant downpour," and also that the field was, whaddayaknow, "a virtual quagmire." Just as inevitably came from the bright phrasemaker a reference to Milwaukee's "inclement weather."

That same night, when Paul Hornung delivered the comment that Green Bay rookie quarterback Scott Hunter is "two-three years away," Cosell had a rejoinder. "That's forthrightly stated," he said, a profundity that nobody can deny.

NOVEMBER 11, 1971

The Munich Olympics

The 1972 Munich Olympics witnessed the most heinous crimes in sporting history. Arab terrorists crept into the Olympic Village in early morning and murdered two Israeli teammates, taking the others hostage. In a botched rescue attempt by the German police at the Munich airfield, nine other Israeli athletes and four Arab terrorists were killed; three of the Arab gunmen were captured.

Povich was in a taxi to the Olympic Village that morning when he first heard about the Arab terrorists. Here, he recalls in 1992 how he managed to talk his way into the Village and hide with the Puerto Rican team—40 yards from the Israeli compound—to report on the massacre. His on-scene columns that follow are chilling—and unforgiving of International Olympics President Avery Brundage.

That morning of the 10th day of the Games began for me with the usual long taxi ride from Munich's Hilton hotel to the Olympic Village. My driver was a high school teacher, one of the many types drafted to serve the thousands from all over the world who convened for the Games.

Halfway to the Village, the cab's radio music gave way to an excited babble. My driver turned to me with half-shouted words that seemed to be saying, "Arabi! ... Israeli! ... Olympischeni! ... Arabi ..." In his agitated German he was saying more.

He was unaware that my understanding of his fast German bordered on the futile. But on earlier visits to Germany I had made do, linguistically, by applying my decadent and remnant Yiddish to the German tongue.

Now my driver was saying, "Arabi schiessen Israeli!"

Ah, "schiessen" could mean the Yiddish "shissen," or a shooting. I cocked my thumb and forefinger at him in the universal language of the pistol and said, "Shissen," and he said, "Ja."

"My God, faster to the Olympischen," I said. "Mach schnell."

The scene at the Village gates bespoke a military operation. German soldiers, their light machine guns at the ready, ringed the premises, telling me this wasn't your ordinary peacetime Olympic Village entrance. Nobody was getting in except the army and the police.

Backed by his ABC camera crew, Howard Cosell was vainly trying to tell the German army whom he worked for. They didn't care who he was.

While Cosell was haranguing and occupying the German Army, Jim Murray of the *Los Angeles Times* and I somehow executed a small end run and, surprisingly, found ourselves safely inside the Village.

It was a bit later that the German military crumbled before Cosell's frontal assault and we all raced to Building 31 on Connolly Strasse that we knew was the Israeli compound.

When Arab commandos seized members of the Israeli team at the Munich Olympics in 1972, Povich was one of the few journalists to report from inside the Village compound.

At Building 31 the scene had the smell of war. Grim. Gun-toting terrorists were seen patrolling the upstairs porches. Below on the street the Germans had brought up ambulances but they were not as innocent as they appeared. They stood for more than do-good medics and stretchers. White jacketed German doctors, some with stethoscopes, were milling about, but with suspicious bulges in the pocket areas. It was camouflage. The terrorists themselves were under siege.

The terrorists, to show the Germans that they meant business, already had flung the dead body of Moshe Weinberg, a 33-year-old wrestling coach, onto the street for all to contemplate.

We had ringside seats to the goings-on but presently all newsmen were ordered out of that Olympic Village sector, with the German army and police beginning a determined sweep. At least two of us escaped it. This correspondent found a hiding place along with Dave Wolf, a *Newsweek* reporter who said he had a liaison with the coach of the Puerto Rican team. A friendly coach provided us with Puerto Rican sweatsuits and we looked sufficiently at ease when the police came in and were nicely duped.

We now had a box seat less than 40 yards from the war scene. I also had binoculars and a direct telephone that permitted me to dictate the situation in progress. This was a line to the *Post-Newsweek* station in Paris, thence to *The Washington Post* syndicate. I took advantage of it to ask Paris to call the Munich Hilton and tell Mrs. Povich I would not be back for dinner that night. . . .

JULY 9, 1992 (excerpt)

Over the Fences They Came, With Big Bags

Munich, Sept. 5 — The night shift workers at the Olympic Village post office merely nudged each other and pointed to the fence-climbers outside, in the dim light of early dawn.

There was no great to-do about that scene. It happened all the time in the village, those agile Olympic athletes scaling the eight-foot fence to bypass the gatekeepers and sneak back to their dorms after violating curfew.

You couldn't tell an Arab from a blond Scandinavian in the half light of 4 A.M., especially if he was dressed in those long sweatsuits favored in the Olympic Village. This time it wasn't just a couple of kids sneaking home. There were a number of them, "and they all were carrying those big Adidas or Puma bags," a postal worker said later. A common site in the village, those carry-all bags. But big enough to conceal a snub-nosed machine gun, if necessary.

As for getting over the fences, "there's never any trouble about that," said another athlete, a cyclist from Holland.

"Two nights ago my friend and I slung our bikes over the same fence before we crawled over and got back to the dorms," he said.

The first shots rang out at 4:30 A.M. in three-story Building 31.

That's where the Israeli team was living on the first two floors. The top floor was occupied by part of the East German contingent.

A knocking at the door of one of the four first-floor rooms aroused Dr. Weigel, an Israeli team physician who partially opened the door. "You're an Arab, go away," he screamed.

The leader of the Arab terrorists fired through the door, instantly killing Moshe Weinberg, 33-year old coach of the wrestling team. Then the Arabs forced their way into the building.

The Israelis on the second floor began scrambling for safety, and 15 of the contingent of 25 athletes and team officials made it, by stairway and window.

Tuvia Solofsky, the team's weightlifting coach, dove through a closed window at gunpoint and zig-zagged his way to freedom between adjacent buildings despite a hail of fire.

The second Israeli who didn't make it was Joseph Romano, another weightlifter, who was hit by the first hail of fire through the partially ajar door. In mid-morning he died from his wounds.

The Arab terrorists, their leader speaking German, gave a safe escort out of the building to the 10 East Germans occupying the top floor.

The Arabs were carrying what one of the escaped Israelis told Munich police were Russian Klashnikovs, snub-nosed high velocity machine guns.

The first shots in the early morning brought the village ambulances, whose drivers reported they, too, were met with gunfire. When the Arabs shoved the body of their first victim, Weinberg, out to the road, the ambulances returned to pick up the victim.

For the Olympic Village the predawn shooting was a macabre wake-up call. As ambulances sped through the gates and Munich police cars congregated in the vicinity of Building 31, the compounds of the 122 nations housed in the village began to stir, and heads popped from windows.

Rumor was racing the length of the village before truth got its boots on. That truth was learned quickly when the Arab leader, still dressed in a red sweatsuit, leaned out a second-story window of Building 31 and dropped papers announcing he was holding 10 Israeli hostages under the following terms:

- The Arabs wanted safe conduct along with their hostages, helicopters to the Munich airport and three airplanes in which to take off consecutively for different points in the Arab world.
- The Arabs would kill all the hostage Israelis unless more than 200 Palestinian prisoners, now held by Israel, were released.

Munich police organized quickly to combat what they now knew was a well-planned plot by the terrorists, beginning with the Arabs' disguise in typical Olympic warmup suits and their perfectly timed raid on the well-cased Israeli compound.

The Arabs' chief spokesman at one point leaned out of that second-story window and conversed with German police in near-perfect German, boasting that he had spent eight years in Germany while learning the language.

By 8 A.M. the Olympic Village was completely awake and in an uproar, with athletes watching from high-balcony vantage points as German police mobilized in an evident move to lay siege to Building 31.

Beyond the view of the Arabs, eight German tank vehicles rolled into the parkways beneath adjacent buildings. Personnel carriers also streamed into the village. Olympic Village police, unarmed during the Games, reached into the trucks for rifles and sidearms.

Meanwhile, it was reported that Hans-Dietrich Genscher, the West German Minister of Interior who had taken control of the police, had made the Arabs a ransom offer. He held out safe conduct to them if they would release the Israelis, and as to the amount of the ransom, he said, "You state it and we will pay it."

The offer was rejected by the Arabs.

Repeated movement among the German police at the scene, gathered around their trucks and the ambulance held in readiness, led to reports they were planning to storm Building 31.

The police, though, were content to lay siege. They did make

some sly moves remindful of FBI tactics in dealing with plane hijack-
ers, dressing their own police in sweatsuits matching those of the athletes, just as the Arabs had done.

Black-jacketed police appeared, with automatic rifles slung over
their shoulders, but primarily the police were wearing sidearms, concealed and otherwise. At one point men dressed as white-jacketed doctors, with stethoscopes hanging in plain sight, showed suspicious
bulges that denoted hidden guns.

On the adjoining roofs, overlooking the Israeli compound, sharp-
shooters were posted behind overhangs and other points of protection.

The terrorists could be seen peering from windows on the second
floor, and from a balcony on the third floor. Their movements
appeared furtive, but at certain points heads boldly poked from windows told of negotiations with German spokesmen on the ground.

The passing hours and the lack of movement by either Arabs or
police foreshadowed a stalemate through the night and produced a
change in Olympic Village life. Tedium set in, replacing the initial
excitement, and the rock concerts resumed at the chief intersections.

Except for the now-diminished numbers peering from their bal-
conies toward Building 31, it could have been any other of the 11 days
in the village since the Games began.

But standing their ground in continued curiosity, if not concern,
were the thousands of spectators who ringed the hills overlooking the
village. It was an eventless day in the competition for the most part,
but from downtown Munich and other areas they came in droves to
get a glimpse of a real, live Arab terror attack, if a remote one.

Laying fallow all day was the quickly improvised helicopter port
contrived in an Olympic Village square scarcely 100 yards from the
Arabs' hole-up. Whirlybirds hovering all day indicated that there would
be a decision to give the Arabs safe escort, if not to meet their terms.

When darkness fell, the Arabs were still unchallenged and their
terms unmet. The curious dispersed and, finally, hostages and guerril-
las marched through a tunnel to the helicopter pad—and their destiny.

September 6, 1972

Only Six of 123 Remember

Munich, Sept. 7—At Munich's Riem Airport, 10 coffins were lifted onto an El Al plane bound this morning for Jerusalem.

At a nearby military air base, on orders from the White House, a U.S. Air Force Starlifter was being readied to fly the body of the 11th dead Israeli Olympic team member to his parents' home in Cleveland.

These were the 11 killed in the sneak attack of Arab terrorists on the Israeli Olympic compound. The body of the first murdered Israeli was kicked out into the street to show the Arabs meant business. The second died of wounds a bit later. The other nine Israelis were bound hands-and-foot and terrorized at gunpoint for 23 hours until they were slaughtered wholesale by the Arabs' machine-gun and grenade attack in a botched getaway attempt by helicopter.

But that was Tuesday. That happened two days ago, so what else is new?

The 80,000 who always show up at the big Olympic Stadium for the track-and-field events made it again today. Big day in track and field, you know. The men's 400-meter and high-hurdles finals. Also the shot-put and hammer-throw finals. The 80,000 began making their way in at just about the same hour the planes were lifting off with the stilled Olympians of Israel.

At Olympic Stadium, on somebody's orders, all flags of the 123 nations that had been at half-mast went up to the tops of their poles. Only the still-lowered Olympic flag on the stadium floor suggested there had been horror and the death of nearly a dozen of their fellows.

The Olympic Village smelled of quiet today but it was not any pall of sentimental concern. The streets were emptier because hundreds of the athletes had already bugged out, either because they had finished their events or were homesick, and hundreds of officials with no more to do were making for the planes.

Down on Connolly Strasse, in front of Building 31, where bullet holes were showing in the walls, five wreaths lay. Later in the day, the United States team's offering made it six of the 123 nations who remembered their Israeli comrades with floral tributes. On holiday was all that chest-thumping about brotherhood in Olympic Village.

For three of the Arab nations, including Egypt, it must have been getting uncomfortable. They pulled out. There was a big swarm at the flight-booking offices in the Village. And if the crowd in the stadium appeared to be subdued at the outset of the program in the decathlon events, the old, on-their-feet excitement returned at the close finishes in the 5,000-meter trials. And then came the hurdles and the 400-meter dash that unloosed the full-throated roars of the 80,000.

The chap that Air Force plane was taking back to Cleveland was David Berger, who lived in Shaker Heights, went to Tulane, got his masters degree at Columbia and decided in 1970 to live in Israel under dual U.S.-Israel citizenship. He was a weight lifter.

He survived the Arabs' initial attack, but got it at the airport shoot-out.

The Israelis won't keep the date they had with the Munich Jewish community leaders tonight. Still taped to the door at Building 31 is a blanket invitation from Werner Nachman to join Munich's Jews in a pre–Rosh Hashanah feast in the city. And they won't be holding Jewish New Year's services they planned for Olympic Village starting Friday at sundown.

Around the Olympic complex, the Germans have given up their aim that all was to be joy, and comradeship, and non-military at their Olympics. Now the polizei were out in the open, in full uniform instead of in plain clothes, and they were wearing the sidearms that were verboten before Tuesday's shooting.

These Olympics were Germany's bid to rejoin the family of nations, to expunge the memory of the swastikas and the goose-steps and the "achtungs" of the Nazi gangs. And until the Arabs' shots rang out the Germans were well pleased with their effort.

Today, though, the uniformed police were out in force. Wearing patches that showed they came from as far away as Frankfurt, a couple of hundred miles north of Munich, they were patrolling in no-nonsense style with guns showing. Germany's Olympics has changed, all on account of what happened at 4:30 in Tuesday's dawn when the Olympic Village heard that macabre, Arab-style wake-up call.

SEPTEMBER 8, 1972

Brundage Brushes Off Eulogy in 27 Words

Munich, Sept. 6—This was the most cheerless day in Olympic history which has a natal year of 776 B.C. It began with Beethoven's funeral march. It was concluded with Avery Brundage seizing on the scene to get in more plugs for his cherished Olympics in a tasteless pep talk to his captive audience of 80,000 heavy hearts in the big Munich Olympic Stadium.

In exactly 27 words at the start of his speech, Brundage brushed off the mass murder of 11 Israeli Olympic athletes and team officials by Arab terrorists Tuesday. This was the tragedy that fetched the thousands of mourners to today's memorial services. Oh there were the standard amenities by Brundage. He did say that "every civilized person recoils in horror at the barbarous criminal intrusion of the terrorists." And he said with evident sincerity that "we mourn our Israeli friends."

Well, so much for that. Time now in Brundage's speech, which could be measured in ugly contrast with the humble searches for guilt by the dignitaries who preceded him in the program, to make a quick switch to that Rhodesia mess and also the high importance of continuing the Olympic Games that Brundage has fathered for the last 20 years as International Olympic Committee president.

Brundage, incredibly, coupled the terrible tragedy that left 11 Israelis dead at the hands of Arab terrorists with the ouster of Rhodesia against his wishes, before the Games started. He was giving the Rhodesia thing almost equal billing with the massacre when he noted, "The Games of the 20th Olympiad have been subjected to two savage attacks."

When the octogenarian Brundage said in his odd tribute at the Israeli memorial service, "We lost the Rhodesian battle against naked political blackmail," his West German hosts, showing more sensitivity, refused to permit Brundage's vindication of himself. Significantly, they deleted his reference to "political blackmail" in the French and German translations of his speech given to the press.

As usual, Brundage thundered, "The Games must go on," because of the ideal they represent. But there may be no great unanimity about that. The Olympic Games are pegged, indeed, to a wonderful ideal but they have been getting so big, so important, so political and offer such a theater for political demonstrations and shoot-ups that they may also be getting dangerous.

It's time to deflate that guff about the great brotherhood the Olympics promote. They are torn by constant bickering among team officials of all the nations and political alignments influence the judging in events like boxing, diving and gymnastics. Olympic Village was a shame to behold Tuesday afternoon, after the first shock at the news that two Israelis were dead and nine held hostage by Arab raiders. A few hours after the initial excitement subsided, you couldn't find an empty ping-pong table in the village, rock music was blaring as usual, and it was just another day in Olympic Village. There was other evidence of boredom all around, even with their Israeli comrades having all that trouble in Building 31.

As a presentation, the Olympics have been getting bigger and better every four years, due greatly to the contribution of the ABC-TV network with its booming ratings. ABC, if it participated in the opening-day parade, could field the biggest team in the Olympics, bigger than the U.S. or Russia's, with its 520 Olympic hands laboring in Munich and deserving a composite Oscar-Emmy-Pulitzer Prize for its superb work. ABC rented 190 hotel rooms here during the Games.

The impact of ABC's show from Munich has made Olympic-conscious millions of Americans who didn't know the 100-meter dash from the 100-meter butterfly. Olympic talk is "in." Only the dunces do not know what is going on in Munich, according to reports from America.

But not only America is getting the Games. The Japanese, German, French and British networks, too, are here in force. Any episode at the Olympics can claim an audience in the hundreds of millions. Bust into the Olympics and you get your message across with a thrust unmatched by any other medium. Next Olympics, the Belfast terrorists? Al Fatah? Somebody's new defense league? Who knows?

SEPTEMBER 7, 1972

Secretariat and Man o' War

Povich saw Secretariat win the Belmont by 31 lengths for the Triple Crown in June 1973. He wrote one column detailing the victory and then, a week later, another column, comparing Secretariat to the other great racing thoroughbred—Man o' War.

1 1/2-Mile Belmont: A Race For Only a Quarter Mile

Belmont, N.Y., June 9—The 150th Belmont Stakes that was advertised at 1 1/2 miles was run and concluded in the first quarter mile today. Secretariat, winning the dash to the first turn, reduced the rest of the distance to a showpiece of a Triple Crown winner in action, 24 feet to each stride.

It was Secretariat, the big horse, so far out of cry at the finish that the nearest challenger was 31 lengths behind, and up there on the board was a new American record of 2:24 flat for the 1 1/2 mile. Secretariat had saved for the Belmont, the race rated the toughest hurdle for Triple Crown aspirants, a performance that was more smashing than either of his victories in the Kentucky Derby or the Preakness.

There was a bit of a flurry at the outset when first My Gallant, from No. 3 post position, and then Sham from No. 5, tried to take the track away from Secretariat and Ron Turcotte who were breaking from the rail stall. But Turcotte was having none of that and asked for an early lick from the big copper-red son of Bold Ruler lest he be pocketed behind from runners.

Secretariat was so charged up that Turcotte had him under a bit of restraint after nailing down his spot on the rail, and Sham, the one to fear, actually stuck his nose in from midway of the turn. But Turcotte and Secretariat were keeping Sham safely on the outside and their own track open, and the next nose to poke in front was Secretariat's as the small field of five squared away for the run down the backstretch.

Sham was still lapped on Secretariat looking down most on the backstretch and the public-address announcer had scarcely noted "there they go stride for stride," when it was no longer stride for stride. Turcotte was clucking to the son of Bold Ruler who began to rip off the first six furlongs in an outstanding 1:09 4/5, and Sham was outdistanced first by two lengths, then by seven, with nothing else in the field any kind of a threat.

This was Secretariat running the race on his own terms, with Turcotte laying no demanding whip on his flanks and still riding high in the saddle. It was Secretariat giving his boy a joy ride with no openings to look for, no tight quarters anywhere. Turcotte did steal two looks at the lollygaggers far behind and liked what he saw, returning to the small job of keeping his mount in rhythm.

At that point the Belmont Stakes was no longer a horse race. It was an exhibition by Secretariat of the Bold Ruler family's thirst for running, and when they turned in on the home stretch the big horse, the one they called Big Boy as a yearling at Meadow Stud, was an incredible 20 lengths in front of the nearest horse on the track. It was no longer Sham running second. He'd had enough of Secretariat's enduring flash and was now in third place, trailing Twice A Prince,

Secretariat on his way to winning the Belmont by 31 lengths and the 1973 Triple Crown.

the longest shot in the five-horse field, that was proving the best of the others.

As they turned for home, Turcotte gave one more look over his shoulder at what might be behind, and this time he needed his distance goggles because it was 28 lengths now back to the second horse. Sham, the one that was supposed to finish second and thus rack up a Triple Crown record for running second in all three races, was now receding to fourth place on his way to finishing last. In the Belmont, Sham had blown it. He wouldn't be known as the William Jennings Bryan of second-place fame.

Secretariat had the Triple Crown safely tucked away with the race half over. But Turcotte was still urging him with a hand ride all the way. He was reading the fractions on the infield time clocks he said after the race and he wanted the world record for the horse of this age. Secretariat appeared to want it, too, as if aware that this was Triple Crown day unlike Sir Barton, the first winner on the Triple Crown in

1919 when Sir Barton, poor colt, didn't know he had won it. It was three years later that Charley Hatton, of the Racing Form, in a burst of lyrical prose, invented the term Triple Crown.

There has been no private life for Secretariat after winning the Derby and Preakness, and today in Belmont's big goldfish bowl, 69,136 fans were measuring him for greatness. It was in the jockey's lounge where the unemployed riders were watching TV that little Jorge Velasquez picked the exact point at which the race was won. Watching Secretariat drawing away from Sham heading into the backstretch, he articulated for the whole gang when he said, "Bye-bye."

JUNE 10, 1973

Man o' War Retains Rank as at Least Co-Greatest

"Man o' War is delaying the start . . . and now, they're off! . . . in the dream race! . . . and it's Secretariat breaking fast from the outside to take the rail away from Man o' War . . . if he can . . . and going into the first turn and around the bend they're head and head . . . They've hit the backstretch striding as one horse . . . and devouring the race track . . . one copper-colored colt superimposed on another, like a galloping picture of a single animal . . . At the far turn it's Turcotte wanting the lead with Secretariat and going to the whip . . . but just once . . . turning for home it's Secretariat in front by a half length but Kummer now is digging into Man 'o War . . . and now Big Red is stretching himself out, with the whiff of battle in his nostrils and his tail fanning the wind . . . But less than a sixteenth from home, Secretariat, too, is flying . . . and Man o' War still has him to catch . . . it's a photo!"

Did Man o' War, the legend, catch wonder colt Secretariat in that last sixteenth and settle all those bets his way? Until the finish line's cameras, perhaps with the help of some future Skylab discovery, are able to pan back 53 years for a measurement of horse against horse, the outcome of the dream race will never be known. Except to the mind's eye, with its built-in bias at both ends of the generation gap.

Man o' War vs. Secretariat in a hypothesized match race is a natural product of man's restless compulsion to compare. And perhaps the inconclusive Lady or the Tiger ending, even if a bit teasy, is for the best, lest libel be done to one noble animal or the other. There was such a warning in one of the ancient aphorisms that spelled out its reproof that "comparison oftimes do great grievance."

Yet it is a wholesome curiosity whether Secretariat, the first Triple Crown winner in 25 years, belongs to the ages like Man o' War or merely to an age.

Even the most honored sage of the horse-breeding industry, Humphrey Finney, a man who helped put the $6.08 million syndication tag on Secretariat, shies at picking the winner of a Secretariat–Man o' War match race in imagery. "Lord be merciful," said Finney, "I'd rather call it a dead heat. Yet if I must make a choice I'd have to go with the older horse. But only because I'm an older man."

There was no waffling by Finney when he compared Secretariat with Man o' War in other respects. "Man o' War was just a bit taller, and burlier and more rugged-looking. I'd say he had more bone and substance and held his head higher. But he didn't have as straight a back as Secretariat. There was a sag. In sum, I'd say on appearance Secretariat had a better quality and was more esthetic-looking, even if his rump did droop a bit. By that I mean Secretariat drops off at the tail. Rather something of a flat ass, you could call it. But you can also say that Secretariat had all the butt he needed to win."

By Finney's lights, Secretariat is a certified wonder colt. "Of course he is. He not only knocked off the Triple Crown but set records in the Derby and Belmont and probably beat the Preakness record, too." He noted that Secretariat with his three white stockings also beat the old superstition about the curse of "too much white." Finney reached far back to recite the old Devonshire rhyme: "One white foot/Ride him for your life;/Two white feet/give him to your wife;/Three white feet/send him far away;/Four white feet/keep him not a day."

On the race track and around the barns, Secretariat has been a more placid type than was Man o' War, which inherited all the violent personality of his sire, Fair Play. Only once in his career, when they tried to drape him with the roses at Churchill Downs, did Secretariat kick up a fuss and get across his message that he didn't like roses, at that particular hour at least. Man o' War was a career rebel, nasty of temper, and wouldn't submit to his first saddle for more than a week. He tried to throw every rider he had, delayed every start.

Despite his attempt at an even-handed stance on the question of Man o' War vis-a-vis Secretariat, Finney's memory sparkled in discussing Man o' War, betraying a respect reserved for that one alone. "He exulted in his strength and power. You can say that, too, about Secretariat. But, my heavens, Man o' War has no blot on his record like Secretariat's Wood Memorial."

In the Wood, before going to the Kentucky Derby. Secretariat had his first and only energy crisis. He could make up little ground, ran a dismal third to Angie Light and Sham. It was the second time he failed to finish first in his 14 races. In the Wood, Secretariat had no excuse—like Man o' War in his lone defeat of his 21 races, his 2-year-old upset by the appropriately named Upset in the Sanford Memorial. In that era of the walk-up start Big Red was banged around and knocked sideways at the start and left at the post when a substitute starter sent the field off too quickly. He got no help from jockey Johnny Loftus, who constantly ran him into pockets, he carried 130 pounds to Upset's 115, yet he lost the race by only a half length.

Secretariat's smashing race in the Belmont in dazzling record time not only lifted him to the eminence of the Triple Crown but nailed the canard that Bold Ruler's kids couldn't win big at a mile and a half. Even as Man o' War destroyed those that tried to run with him, Secretariat broke the heart of Sham, a colt that like himself had broken the Kentucky Derby record.

Yet Man o' War dominated his era, before he retired to stud in 1921, in even more thumping fashion that did Secretariat. So Secretariat won the Belmont by 31 lengths, compared to Man o' War's 20-

length victory in the same race. How would you like the 100 lengths by which Man o' War won the 1 5/8-mile Lawrence Realization two weeks later? Secretariat went off at 1 to 10 in his Belmont. Man o' War was a 1-to-100 shot in his Belmont, and 1 to 100 in two starts, was never as good as even-money in any of his 21 races, and for his Belmont and his Lawrence and several other of his races he scared off so much of the class of the day that he had only one horse entered against him.

Man o' War passed up the 1920 Kentucky Derby to concentrate on winning the Preakness and Belmont. His owner, Sam Riddle, saw no great importance in winning the Derby. The Triple Crown, as such, was no great shakes at that time and in fact was unknown as a series of races. They weren't named the Triple Crown until Charley Hatton of the Racing Form invented the term a year after Man o' War beat Upset five times, with no sweat.

One thing is certain, the clock would take a beating if a Secretariat–Man o' War matchup could come to pass. Man o' War needs no apologies for the times he made. Eight track records and five world records were among them, despite the fact that he finished virtually every race eased up under a choking pull. "The sod could feel the lash of his power. He's as near to a living flame as a horse could ever get," Joe Palmer wrote of Big Red.

If Man o' War did not win the Triple Crown, he could boast that he beat a Triple Crown winner. This was Sir Barton, in their famed match race that was to be Man o' War's last. Three-year-old Man o' War ran away and hid from 4-year-old Sir Barton by seven lengths, "never fully extended," the chart said.

How much of a syndication price tag would Humphrey Finney put on Man o' War were he now alive and well, and age 3 and headed for stud, like Secretariat? "The sky's the limit," Finney said. "Secretariat went for $190,000 a share. I think they'd be standing in line for a crack at Man o' War at $300,000 a share." With that, the man may have been trying to tell us something.

JUNE 17, 1973

Foreman Faked Out

Kinshasa, Zaire, Oct. 30—As early as the battling in the second round, Muhammad Ali had George Foreman looking to his corner for instructions, first out of the tail of his eye, then squarely appealing for some tactical advice.

How to deal with this opponent who was not only daring to move in on the great Foreman, but was laying it on with both jabs and right hands? Nor would Ali hold still on the ropes for the punishment that usually precedes a final clubbing and another George Foreman knockout.

It was a totally confused and arm-weary Foreman who finally gave up his title, from a horizontal position, with two seconds left in round eight. Ali had ripened him for this sort of thing, winning every round on *The Washington Post*'s scorecard.

When the end came, it was by trick. After a flailing by Foreman on the ropes, Ali slid away as he had done some 50 times previously in the fight. But this time he was sagging and appeared hurt. He was faking it. When Foreman moved in with his hands held low, on the scent of a kill, Ali sprang, bouncing the winning triple off Foreman's chin: left, right, left. Ali had back the title he first won 10 years ago.

The knockout wasn't according to his preflight plan, Ali told newsmen later today on the lawn of his training camp villa.

"I knew I could lick him, but I didn't believe I was going to stop him," Ali said. "But in those early rounds when I saw what a slow stationary target he was, and how I could handle him on the ropes, I knew he belonged to me. I knew after the sixth round that this man was going to fall."

Ali had said earlier in the week, "Foreman won't hit me with those punches he hit Joe Frazier with." Ali took Foreman's wide-swinging punches on his arms, elbows and gloves and the steam went out of Foreman's flailing by the fourth.

At times, it looked like one of Ali's defensive routines on the ropes in training camp, when he delighted in letting sparring partners pelt him without a return, content to perfect his blocking. Foreman was a study in frustration and, besides, his face was beginning to get very lumpy from the shots he was taking.

Ali changed his plans for the fight after the original date was post-poned a month ago. "Then, Foreman was fat and slow, and I was going to put on my dancing shoes and fast-move my way past him. But with him in better shape I knew I would get down off my toes and rap him with solid punches.

"Also, I wanted to show him quick who was boss. That's why I even led with some rights in the first round."

Foreman hurt him, he said, late in the second round with a long right. "But I grabbed and it cleared my head, and that's what you do when you have to, wait for your head to clear."

The harshest thing he said about Foreman was "that man probably could have got up."

What was the running chatter Ali directed at Foreman throughout the fight? "I jabbed him, then I said, 'I told you I'm the greatest. You're the champ and I'm beating you up."

On the ropes, Ali said he told Foreman, "Come on George, take your body shots."

Ali, 32, said he had trained so hard, "I could dance all night if I had to. I can fight till I'm 37. For 10 more years if I want to fight flat-footed."

A last word about Foreman: "Let me tell you writers, that man has never been no good. Didn't know how to be humble after he was champion. Wouldn't come out for press conferences. I'm glad he's gone."

OCTOBER 31, 1974

Sam Rice

Hall of Famer and Washington Senators outfielder Sam Rice would be forever remembered for a catch he claimed to have made in the eighth inning of Game 3 of the 1925 World Series between Pittsburgh and the host Senators. In a letter Rice left to be opened after his death, he still claimed to have caught Earl Smith's drive to right-center, despite Pirates manager Bill McKechnie and Pirates fans believing he dropped the ball when he fell over the fence. Povich, who championed few players in his career, campaigned for years to get Rice in the Hall of Fame. He prevailed when the late Sam Rice was voted into the Hall in 1963.

Sam Rice's Secret Is Out—He Made the Catch in '25

Sam Rice's 49-year secret has ended, with his own testimony from beyond that he did, indeed, catch that long, homer-bound drive Earl Smith hit in the 1925 World Series between the Washington Senators and Pittsburgh pirates.

The truth about the most disputed play in the 71 years of World Series history surfaced in a newly found testament written by Rice in 1965, "to be opened after my death."

The Washington outfielder died at 84 on Oct. 13, having steadfastly refused to say unqualifiedly that he had made the catch on Oct. 10, 1925, in game three of the Series. He long ago, however, had hinted he would put it in writing for the archives of the Baseball Hall of Fame.

Rice's document turned up the other day, but not at Cooperstown, N.Y., where Hall of Fame officials had combed the files for more than two weeks and were ready to dismiss reports of a Rice letter as unconfirmed rumor.

It surfaced in downtown New York City, at 30 Wall Street, where Paul S. Kerr, president of the Hall of Fame, has his office. Kerr, to whom the letter had been committed by Rice, was unaware that a search for the letter was under way.

Kerr made a ceremony of disclosing the contents of the letter left by Rice. Before witnesses, and as though ready to read a will, he slit open the envelope and recited its contents.

Rice described all the circumstances in the eighth inning of the game in which catcher Smith came to bat for Pittsburgh: "The ball was a line drive headed for the bleachers towards right center. . . . I jumped as high as I could and back handed . . . but my feet hit the barrier . . . and I toppled . . . . into the first row of the bleachers . . . at no time did I lose possession of the ball."

Such was not the view of the Pirates, who protested loudly that Washington fans in the bleachers had replaced in Rice's glove the ball he had dropped. A score of Pittsburgh supporters in the bleachers offered affidavits that Rice did not hold the ball. The Senators won the game, 4–3, but lost the Series, four games to three.

For the remainder of his life Rice helped to make mystery of the catch by refusing to make any comment except, "The umpire called him out, didn't he?" For the rest of his years, Rice's was the sardonic smile across the face of the baseball world.

It was at one of the annual, private dinners of members of the Baseball Hall of Fame at Cooperstown that Rice told fellow honorees that he had written his version of the catch, to be opened after his death.

Bill McKechnie, the Pirates' manager in 1925, was one of those whom Rice confided in 1965 that he had written down his version of the catch. In a postscript, Rice wrote, "I approached McKechnie and said, 'What do you think will be in the letter?' His answer was, 'Sam, there was never any doubt in my mind but what you caught the ball.'"

McKechnie's agreement in 1965 that Rice had made the catch off Smith did not square with his opinion of the play on that October afternoon in 1925.

According to *The Washington Post* account of the game, McKechnie was furious at the decision of umpire Cy Rigler in calling Smith out and demanded that the other umpires overrule him. Like the other Pirates, McKechnie insisted that Rice had dropped the ball when he fell over fence.

McKechnie, it was also reported in the *Post*, later took his protest to the box seat of Commissioner Kenesaw Mountain Landis, without success. Landis pointed out it was a judgment play that could not be appealed to him.

Rice's secret letter originally was supposed to go into his file at Cooperstown, but Hall of Fame officials have indicated that because of the vast public interest in it, it could have its own special display case.

The letter deposited by Rice with Kerr was actually inspired by the late Lee Allen, historian of the Hall of Fame. Allen refused to be content with Rice's evasion when questioned on the subject of the catch.

At each of Rice's visits to Cooperstown, Allen prodded Rice to make public his version of the disputed catch for the Cooperstown records.

When Rice refused to tell his secret, Allen pleaded, "You could at least leave us some kind of a document to be opened after your death." It was this suggestion that Rice accepted.

Allen's death preceded Rice's, leaving many officials at Cooperstown unaware of the existence of the letter and fouling the search for it.

Rice was inducted into the Hall of Fame in 1963 by the special Old Timers' Committee, in recognition of his .322 lifetime batting average, his fame as a base stealer and 20 years of consistent stardom in the American League.

He was more than the fielding star of the 1925 series. His 12 hits led both teams at bat.

The Testimony of Sam Rice: 'I had a Death Grip on It.'

Monday July 26, 1965
It was a cold and windy day, the right field bleachers were crowded with people in overcoats and wrapped in blankets, the ball was a line drive headed for the bleachers towards right center, I turned slightly to my right and had the ball in view all the way, going at top speed and about 15 feet from bleachers jumped as high as I could and back handed and the ball hit the center of pocket in glove (I had a death

grip on it). I hit the ground about five feet from a barrier about four feet high in front of bleachers with all my brakes on but couldn't stop so I tried to jump it to land in the crowd but my feet hit the barrier about a foot from the top and I toppled over on my stomach into the first row of bleachers. I hit my Adam's apple on something which sort of knocked me out for a few seconds but (Earl) McNeeley arrived about that time and grabbed me by the shirt and pulled me out. I remember trotting back towards the infield still carrying the ball for about halfway and then tossed it towards the pitcher's mound. (How I have wished many times I had kept it.) At no time did I lose possession of the ball.—Sam Rice

NOVEMBER 5, 1974

Baseball is Dull Only to the Dull Mind

The latest to join the dirge that baseball is in mortal trouble is James J. Kilpatrick, the glossy cherub who is, implausibly, the rugged Republican on panel shows. On Channel 9 the other night, the usually dependable Kilpatrick suddenly lost his way as the immovable traditionalist. He put in with the street rabble that has lately been given to calling baseball a dull game, dated and a drag.

"Baseball is in trouble," said Kilpatrick, who this night was doing a solo, one of those TV discourses that Eric Sevareid brought to the trade. "It's too old-fashioned and needs some rule changes to make the games more exciting." He even suggested a couple that would jazz up the scoring: credit a team with two runs on a steal of home and make it a two-run play when somebody scores on a squeeze bunt.

The originality of Kilpatrick's little gems is not to be disputed. Nobody else ever thought up anything remotely like them in all the 136 years since Abner Doubleday was reputed to have laid out the first baseball diamond. Given his changes, Kilpatrick would have some kind of a game, but it wouldn't be baseball.

It isn't baseball that is in trouble; only the people who think so. Usually, they are the people won over by such comparatively outrageous new games as pro football, hockey and basketball and are happy to have their repressions spoon-fed with double dollops of simple violence that embody only feeble skills compared to the multiple arts of the baseball player.

If Red Smith had never written more than the 11-word sentence that immortalized him for me, he would still be my hero. In what will stand forever as the classic put-down of all the idiots who qualify, Smith wrote, "Baseball is a dull game only to those with dull minds."

Those interludes in a ball game that are viewed by some as a bore are, in fact, full of dynamics. That pitcher isn't merely fiddling around with the ball in his hand; chances are he is scared to throw it to that big baboon with a bat in his hand who's ready to knock it back down his throat.

And the batter is not merely knocking the dirt out of his spikes. It's probably imaginary dirt, anyway. He's just a little bit reluctant to get into the batter's box against that old pro 60 feet, six inches away. And when he does he'll be wondering whether the bum is gonna curve him again or try to blow him down with that good fast ball. It's High Noon on almost every pitched ball.

And that first baseman who is slapping his throwing hand against his mitt may be less eager for the next play than nervous about it. Big lefthanded hitters can decapitate a first baseman, you know. If that second baseman is playing a bit close to the bag, he may be cheating a bit. He's another year older and has lost that step, maybe a step and a half. And the third baseman who has decided to play it deep against that righthanded hitter is only being discreet. Smart.

That center fielder isn't just standing there. Look at him. He's ready to break toward right where the guy usually hits.

It's the greatest one-on-one game in the world, a naked contest between man and ball, a battle against flight and bounce and no help from any teammate. In that flash when the moment of truth is apparent, he can't hand off or hope for a blocker.

To the proper baseball fan, the constant acclaim for all the skills of the football and basketball players is tiresome. Neither of those games has a single art form to compare with the ballet of baseball's double play at second base with its routine of catch, tag, pivot, relay and safe landing against 190 pounds of incoming spikes. Baseball, too, has its violence, and not only in the threat of the brush-back pitch that says it is no game for cowards.

Compared with the second baseman getting in and out of the line of fire, and executing the double play, the purveyors of basketball's fancy double-twist whatnot skyhooks and Larry Csonka's 5.5 yardage up the middle are as hulking clods in the view of the proper baseball fan. Nor is he impressed by the sideline antics of basketball's hammy, flip-flop coaches.

There is no explanation for those who prefer hockey with its over-rated violence. Hockey's athletes are padded like moon walkers, especially the goalies who get help in making saves by wearing mattresses on each arm, upholstered shin pads on each leg, gauntlet gloves pulled over everything, plus a big crooked stick. What a game, anyway. Half the time the goalie has to look behind him to see if a goal was accidentally scored, and frequently it's an unwitting scuff shot off somebody's heel, an otherwise misdirected try that got lucky.

I say it is significant, too, that of the so-called big sports only baseball has lent itself to excellent literature. Football, basketball and hockey have nothing to match Roger Kahn's "Boys of Summer" and Roger Angell's "The Summer Game" as books that will live.

The other sports have generated no such quality of writing, obviously because they could not match the deep emotions and substantive human drama in the baseball story. Dan Jenkins and Pete Gent made good tries with "Semi-Tough" and "Dallas North Forty," but at the finish they were only good, entertaining books on pro football, mere fluff compared to the moving stuff that Kahn and Angell write about the game they liked and the people in it.

Another thing. Baseball, alone of the mass-interest sports we talk about, is not governed by that gawddam clock, that miserable timepiece in the sky that reduces the final stages of football, basketball and hockey games to either (1) a meaningless bore, (2) a farcical count-down or (3) a cruel and heartless frustration for the team that is finally revved up to come from behind. In baseball, no clock, no stall, there is all day or all night in which to stage a big inning, or extra inning, in case they did not quite bring it off. No final gun until every opportunity is exhausted.

There is evidence the whole complaint about baseball is a bad rap, anyway. Where is the diminishing interest? Last season, for the second year in a row, major league attendance hit the 30 million mark. Ten years ago, they played to 20 million. A second network, ratings-crazy ABC, has just bought into the baseball business, adding up to a $92 million package for four years. The average salary of $43,000 tends to refute any claim that baseball has become a losing business, and there are more $100,000 players in baseball, 50, than in football and perhaps basketball combined.

Baseball is the only pure sport. No team gets into the playoffs unless it is a division champion. A second place team in pro football could win the playoffs and wind up as the league champion. Basket-ball, with all its gimmicks, is letting third-place teams into its playoffs, and some team could well make it with a below-500 record and even wind up as champion of the whole basketball business. For the scoffers, it is a reminder that only the grand old wonderful game of baseball is keeping the faith.

APRIL 6, 1975

THE EIGHTIES

SHIRLEY POVICH WAS IN HIS EIGHTIES DURING MUCH OF THE 1980s. He should have been winding down, but a decade of big stories kept him in front of the keyboard.

No news story was bigger than the 1989 banning from baseball of Pete Rose, the all-time major-league hits champion with 4,256 hits. Rose was given the thumb by the late commissioner, Bart Giamatti, on charges Rose bet on baseball games. (Fifteen years later, Rose would admit his guilt in his own book.) Few if any writers besides Povich had the longevity to compare Rose's transgressions with those of Shoeless Joe Jackson and his seven White Sox teammates who were banned for life as a result of fixing the 1919 World Series. Povich also would be able to recall Ty Cobb and Tris Speaker beating gambling charges in 1927.

"Shirley gracefully avoided, perhaps transcended is the better word, the tendencies of too many of his colleagues to make himself bigger than his subject, to constantly find fault or simplistic villains in the complex mirror that sport, especially baseball, offers our complicated republic," recalled *Baseball* filmmaker Ken Burns. "He is not afraid to articulate that baseball looks like the rest of America: profound, unknowable, corrupt, *and* redemptive.... To me he is a poet of the game, posterity's mole, a spy digging deeper into our psyche than all the pundits who purport to understand our national pastime and our nation."

Being able to draw from decades of experience and share these stories with readers delighted Povich, who warmed to being the historian and sage of the *Post*'s sports department, as well as its mentor. But nothing invigorated him more than the present. He might write of those he knew—Ruth, Johnson, and the rest—but he always applied them to the McGwires and the Ryans. As Tony Kornheiser says, "Shirley kept one eye on the past for the sake of perspective, but he always had both feet in the present."

While saddened by the death of close friends such as Pulitzer Prize–winning columnist Red Smith, slugger Hank Greenberg, and maverick baseball owner Bill Veeck, Povich bade them farewell with his elegant praise.

He could not convince Major League Baseball to return a team to Washington and would turn his back on preseason exhibition games at RFK Stadium, asking anyone who would listen, "Do they really think we're Chattanooga?"

But he celebrated the good fortune of his friend, Baltimore Orioles owner Edward Bennett Williams, who held the World Series trophy aloft in 1983. He also covered the career of local middleweight boxer Sugar Ray Leonard and the Joe Gibbs–coached Redskins that won two Super Bowls in the 1980s and another in 1991. He savored Jack Nicklaus winning the 1986 Masters at 46 and shared pain with friends who were Red Sox fans as the "curse" continued in the 1986 World Series—remembered for Boston first baseman Bill Buckner's error.

For Povich, excursions to Laurel Race Course were a weekly treat, as were rounds of golf at Woodmont Country Club in Rockville, Md. "I'm losing club-head speed," he complained, adding, with a gleam in his eye, "but I'm closer to the ball nowadays."

Red Smith

Povich's soul-brother in the sportswriting fraternity was Red Smith. They sat elbow-to-elbow for the better part of 40 years in the press boxes of the major sporting events. Povich endorsed Smith's view of writing—that you had to open your veins and bleed. Long after the game, with only the lights of the press box defying darkness, Smith and Povich could be

found searching, painfully, for the words to describe what they had wit-
nessed. Smith died in 1982, and Povich's feelings for his friend were
telling in this obituary.

The Death of a Friend, The Loss of an Artist

Red Smith died at noon yesterday, and there has to be a sorrow in the
land. He won't write those columns any more, and Red Smith fans are
more than saddened, they're deprived. There has been a withdrawal of
one of the steady joys of reading the artist at his work. Red wouldn't
agree, but he was like that in his persistent modesty. He preferred to
call himself a working stiff.

Those, of all persuasions, who had an appreciation of the written
word were attracted to him and his facility for using the language. He
raised the sports-writing trade to a literacy and elegance it had not
known before. Red wouldn't agree to that either, but only the most
ungrateful of sportswriters would fail to genuflect to the one-time red-
head gone white-haired on the job. He also gave their business class.

None before him had Red's wit and scope. The classical education
he got at Notre Dame erupted sometimes in his spouting of Shakespeare's lines at an evening with friends. Occasionally he might quote
from a classic in his work, but he shrank at wearing his erudition on
his sleeve, and preferred his own turn of phrase, pungent with Smith-
ism. As when he called Happy Chandler, "the greatest baseball commissioner since Judge Landis," the immediate predecessor.

To those innocents who sometimes would ask him how he had
achieved such an easy and bright writing style, Red liked to say, "I was
a good speller in school." He didn't want to appear to be a hero to
himself, this chap who won all the prizes, Pulitzer, Grantland Rice,
you name it, who while working at the job as a sportswriter, transcended it.

He was my friend and Red would be so better at writing this about a friend who died. I've been with him of a night when he had to wrench himself toward the typewriter to deliver the tribute to a friend gone from this life. He agonized over it, and it came out tender.

At his New Canaan, Conn., home, only last week, a visiting photographer was asking Red to pose for a picture for the dustjacket of a most unusual book. It was to be a collection of Red's obituaries of friends, which had appeared in his columns over the years. That any publisher would be that much interested in such stuff came as a surprise to Red, he said.

The same columns that had such easy flow didn't come easy to Red Smith. He agonized over each one, describing it as "a case of letting little drops of blood in search of the right word, the right pitch. Sometimes rolling my eyes and breaking out into cold sweats, and groaning somewhat, too." In conversation, he liked to deal in such delightful overkill.

Povich (glass in hand) lost a soul brother when Red Smith died in 1982.

Red suspected the gravity of his condition, part kidney failure, and just before being admitted to the hospital in Stamford, Conn., he said to his doctor, "I've had a good run." A bit later, he was saying to his doctor again, "I'd like to go like Granny Rice did, quietly."

Red didn't like to make a fuss about matters unless he felt somebody was getting a raw deal. He could be gentle with sinners and outraged by pompous "fiddle-bottomed" sports officials, who offended his sense of good sense. He defended some boxers and their shenanigans "because it's not a sport for altar boys."

Red always said he didn't want to write as an expert and never considered himself one. He said he wanted to write and comment as a spectator at the scene. He confessed that he liked baseball best. It was apparent that horse racing was one of his favorites, that boxing held a fascination for him, and that football was all right. He wouldn't touch basketball or winter sports, "because I don't know anything about basketball, and even less about winter things, where you could also freeze your toes off."

At the old *New York Herald Tribune*, they drafted him at political convention time to apply his wit to the goings on at those proceedings, and nobody out-wrote him. But he rejected all suggestions that he become a political or global columnist because "that's not my cup of tea. I don't know where the political stories are. But as a sportswriter needing something to write on a dull day I know where the dugouts are."

He was often at his best with his descriptive vignettes of fishermen at the streams or hunters in the woods. They were compelling reading even for those who, like Red himself, knew little about either fishing or hunting yet went along. But on a typewriter he could articulate a scene that brought a fish, or mourning dove, to life and their predators to frustration. In his glee.

Even on deadline Red was patient with autograph seekers, young sportswriters asking advice from the master and simple admiring Red Smith fans who wanted to talk. He was a study in modesty, but later at the typewriter he struggled to make up for lost time; the column that would seem later to be written so effortlessly was hard labor for the man of particular words.

This man of charm would, when necessary, take off the gloves and slug it out with any chosen adversary. Bowie Kuhn was a frequent target for letting the World Series go on in freezing weather. Red came out strongly against the U.S. Olympic Committee in urging a boycott of the 1980 Moscow Games after the Soviets invaded Afghanistan.

His syndicated anti-Olympics column was killed by the *Times* after it had gone out to a few clients, the first time a Smith column ever was embargoed by anybody. The complaint was that Red had taken up a position the *Times* had not yet fully considered and that Red appeared to be conducting a crusade.

There was a flap across the country about this, but Red finally called the whole thing "a bloody bore." He said, "Us kids should stick to fun and games, I guess, leaving things like Afghanistan invasions to more serious people than sportswriters." He couldn't resist a stinging dig at his bosses, however, adding that in the future "I guess I'll write about the infield fly rule."

Many years ago Red offered an insight into the kind of spoofing he likes when some periodical invited him to write an autobiography and he wrote: "Red Smith, christened Walter Wellesley Smith on a cold day in 1905 in Green Bay, Wis., has been bleeding out a daily sports column for the Herald Tribune for about three years. Previous conditions of servitude have included 10 years at hard labor on the *Philadelphia Record*, eight years on the *St. Louis Star-Times* and a year with the *Milwaukee Sentinel*. He admires sports for others and might have been a great athlete himself except that he is small, puny, slow, inept, uncoordinated, myopic and yellow. He is the proprietor of two small children, one large mortgage."

And the owner of a place in the hearts and the memory of so many who were his admirers, and his friends. I'd like to say thanks, old buddy, for passing through.

JANUARY 16, 1982

Washington Without Baseball

After the Senators moved to Texas in 1972, Povich was emotionally involved in a number of attempts by Washingtonians to acquire a baseball team. He rejected the Baltimore Orioles' claim that they were Washington's team, scoffed at occasional exhibition games in Washington, and lamented his town's fate when cities such as Toronto, Miami, Denver, Phoenix, and Tampa were awarded expansion franchises. He called them shtetls *in comparison to the nation's capital.*

Root, Root, Root for the What Team?

The major league baseball season opens tomorrow afternoon—and so what? For Washington, again, it is a joyless event. No team to call its own. No peanuts, no Cracker Jacks, no nothing. Eleven years now, since a city was wiped off the baseball map. Eleven Silent Springs, 11 years of melancholy. Rats!

They did it to us in September 1971, on that night of infamy in Boston where 12 scoundrelly American League club owners, destitute of feeling for an old friend of 70 years, voted Washington dead as a baseball town. Those 12 owners, high and mighty with their anti-trust exemption, and low and despicable in their greed for a greener pasture, took the word of a come-lately Robert E. Short, a baseball carpetbagger, that Arlington, Tex., was a more deserving baseball town than the capital of the United States. Arlington? Texas?

Think of it: Toronto has big league baseball. Seattle has big league baseball. Arlington, Tex., and Montreal have big league baseball. But Washington, D.C., does not have big league baseball. Certainly we think of that. Envy has no holidays. Agreed that it is also sometimes tinged with malicious grudging.

Dammit, we've been banished from the mainstream. Six weeks of

spring training has just ended. For most of the 26 cities there was exciting news of rookie phenoms who might hit .300 or even more; of kid
pitchers who would be looking for 20 wins, at least 18, and of exciting
trades in the making. But for Washington it was the 11th year of the
spring training blahs. For Washington, spring training has become an
alien rite. Nobody wears a Washington uniform.

We're out of it. No more the Yankees to hate. In our detachment
from the entire scene, the Yankees are no worse than anybody else.
The Red Sox, Tigers, Cleveland and the A's—they are mere team
names in one of those divisions of the American League. Phantoms,
who somehow appear regularly in the league standings.

For Washington fans, those teams exist only on the television tube,
playing a game that the Senators also used to play at Griffith Stadium
and Kennedy Stadium before the wipeout. Oh, there was a promise
by Bowie Kuhn that Washington would get another team as quickly as
possible, as soon as the conditions permitted. We believed him. The
chance came, in 1977, when the American League expanded. The
new franchises went to Seattle and Toronto. What endearing friends
Kuhn and the club owners proved to be. Even with beautiful Robert
F. Kennedy Stadium available at low rent, and the new Metro trains
ready to bring 54,000 fans to the very mouth of the playing field—the
best transit arrangement in any city anywhere—we got the brush.

They tell us now not to weep, and to go root for the Orioles. Some
people do, but there is an understandable reluctance by most. The
Orioles' uniforms are badly designed. They don't have W-A-S-H-I-N-
G-T-O-N written across their chests. They are Baltimore's team. They
live in Baltimore. They eat and sleep in Baltimore, and play ball in
Baltimore, and are loved in Baltimore. They are Baltimore's darlings,
not Washington's. And for Baltimore fans, the Orioles do not mean a
40-mile schlep each way.

At best, the Orioles offer an escape valve, a sneaked joint, a temporary high for Washington's most addicted baseball fans. These are said
to account for 10 percent of the Orioles' attendance. But the great
bulk of Washington fans are not embracing the Orioles as the answer
to their passion for the game, no matter how much we are told that the

Orioles also belong to our town. Baltimore has custody. Surrogate heroes are not of the true flesh.

Today, when *Take Me Out to the Ballgame* is a glorious and meaningful chant in 26 major league cities, in Washington it will be only a song, for others. Or perhaps a memory of those heady years when the Senators won three pennants, and had heroes named Walter Johnson and Bucky Harris, and Goose Goslin and Joe Judge and Ossie Bluege, and Sam Rice. And later, Earl Whitefield and Heinie Manush, and Harmon Killebrew and Mickey Vernon and Eddie Yost. And nine presidents of the United States came to the park. This didn't count when they wrote us out of the big league lineup.

In another year, those American League club owners may repent or be brought to book by the Forces of Truth. In that vein, let's hear it again from Sophocles, who once assured us: "Time will catch up with guilt. Justice is never out of breath." Stick in there, Justice, and get us a team again. Living like this is maddening.

APRIL 4, 1982

Bill Veeck, 71, Flamboyant Owner of
3 Major League Baseball Teams

Bill Veeck, owner of three major league teams and self-described baseball hustler, died of a heart attack yesterday at Illinois Masonic Medical Center in Chicago. He was hospitalized Monday after suffering from shortness of breath, and he had a malignant lung tumor removed in October 1984.

In baseball, Mr. Veeck operated as a free spirit whose light-hearted attitude toward the game's mossy traditions invited the displeasure of baseball's royalists. But they could not ignore his success as a pennant-winning owner with the 1948 Cleveland Indians and 1959 Chicago White Sox.

It was Mr. Veeck's zest for showmanship that helped him generate a 1948 season attendance of 2,620,627 at Cleveland that shattered his previous major league records. He engaged wandering minstrels to serenade the grandstands, imported orchids from Hawaii for Ladies Day fans, provided a baby-sitting service at the park, and broke out lavish firework displays to enliven the Indians' games. Crowds sometimes numbered more than 80,000.

It was written of Mr. Veeck, who was a hero to Cleveland and Chicago fans, that "he lights up a front office." At Chicago, he originated the $300,000 exploding score-board to celebrate hometeam homeruns with a burst of rockets and pinwheels. He gave the White Sox fans blaring bands and, on occasion, free beers.

Of those rival club owners who bemoaned his lack of baseball dignity and did not regard him as fit for proper baseball society, he said, "They keep pretty mum while they are taking those fat visiting team checks away from my ball yards."

He broke the American League color line in Cleveland in 1948 by signing outfielder Larry Doby as its first black player. When the mails began to fill with protests, Mr. Veeck responded by signing Satchell Paige, a black pitcher.

It was as the St. Louis Browns owner in 1951 that he most vexed his fellow baseball magnates. When Detroit pitcher Bob Cain was preparing to face the Browns' lead-off hitter in the second game of a doubleheader, he was confounded to see in the batter's box a 3-foot–7 midget, in a Browns' uniform.

This was little, 65-pound Eddie Gaedel, one of Mr. Veeck's surprises. When the Tigers appealed to umpire-in-chief Ed Hurley to halt this comedy, Mr. Veeck's manager, Zach Taylor, produced a regulation American League contract to which Mr. Veeck had signed Gaedel, and the midget was allowed to play.

Gaedel, with his tiny strike zone from armpits to kneecaps further narrowed by Mr. Veeck's orders to crouch, walked on four straight pitches and was then withdrawn from the game, his purpose served.

Also at St. Louis when Mr. Veeck fired his manager, Rogers Hornsby, he explained, "It was either fire my manager or hire 25 new ballplayers." For this act, Mr. Veeck presented himself with a loving cup in ceremonies at home plate, "In token of his valuable contribution to the team."

Mr. Veeck even made sport of the heavy blows dealt him in his lifetime. As a World War II marine he injured his right leg on Bougainville in the South Pacific in 1943 when a recoiling artillery piece crashed against him. It was amputated below the knee in 1947, and for the rest of his days he hobbled about as an amputee on an artificial limb and also was given to jesting, "The only fear I have is of termites."

Almost to the last, Mr. Veeck made mirth of his misfortunes. When he was discharged from a Chicago hospital after his second bout with lung cancer, he said, "That makes two states, Illinois and Maryland, that have now rejected my body."

A deep disappointment of his life was in 1953, when the American League club owners refused to approve Mr. Veeck's move of his foundering St. Louis Browns to Baltimore, a city prepared to welcome him. Some were settling old scores with Mr. Veeck, who had long been demanding that television revenues of all teams be shared equally.

They voted Mr. Veeck down twice on his projected move to Baltimore, but after he sold the team to a Baltimore group, a move was quickly approved. "I got the message," Mr. Veeck said.

If Mr. Veeck wasn't exactly born to baseball, his early years brought him close to it. His father, a former Chicago sportswriter, became president of the Cubs, and Mr. Veeck broke into the game as a $15-a-week office boy.

By the age of 27 he owned the Milwaukee American Association franchise, and it was there he first exhibited the band-playing and other frills that were to become his trademark. Once, to take the minds of Milwaukee fans off their poor team, he dispatched his musically minded manager Charley Grimm to home plate to play his guitar.

By the age of 32, he owned a major league team, as head of the syndicate that bought the Indians for $2.2 million. When he sold the team seven years later some of his backers were paid $20 for every $1 they invested in him. Under Mr. Veeck and his frills, the Indians took off. Two years after they drew 400,000, the Indians attendance zoomed to more than 2.6 million and they had the 1948 pennant and a World Series championship in six games over the old Boston Braves.

Mr. Veeck's personal fortune benefited little after he paid off the taxman and a generous divorce settlement to his wife, Eleanor Raymond, whom he had married in 1935. But he found operating in the big leagues to be easier and more enjoyable than in the minors.

"At Milwaukee it was a big gamble if we had to pay $10,000 for an outfielder we needed. And if he didn't pan out, it could leave us in the red," Mr. Veeck said. "Here in the majors with all that money coming in all the time, you'll pay $100,000 for a player and if he flubs you simply cover your mistake by buying another player for a hundred grand, and thus maintain fan interest."

Sartorially, as well as in his operations, he wore no man's collar, preferring tie-less, flaring sports shirts that exposed his hairy upper chest. Hats, too, were out. About neckties, he liked to quote Ted Williams: "They only get into your soup." Hatless, he was otherwise recognized by his close-cropped, tightly curled red hair, later to turn white, that was another one of his badges.

In restaurants, Mr. Veeck was a check-snatcher and a heavy tipper, a big mover in Toots Shor society. He was a three-pack-a-day cigarette smoker with beer intake to match before he gave up both on doctor's orders in 1980. As for his ubiquitous public life, he once explained, "I admit it, I'm a publicity hound."

After selling the Indians, his next venture was as owner of those renowned losers, the St. Louis Browns, which he bought for $1.5 million in 1951. In St. Louis Mr. Veeck built an apartment for his family inside the park, to be nearer his operations. His second wife was the former Mary Frances Ackerman, advance publicist for the Ice Capades, who was often called "The World's Most Beautiful Press Agent."

The Browns continued to lose games and money and by 1953 Mr. Veeck was maneuvering to get out. "I knew we were dead in St. Louis when Gussie Busch with all that money bought the Cardinals. We couldn't compete."

Mr. Veeck got a temporary financial fix by selling Sportsman's Park to Busch for $800,000 and then turned his eyes toward Baltimore, only to be slapped down by the votes of AL club owners. He sold the team to Baltimore interests.

For the next few years, he retired to his farm in Easton, Md., inappropriately named "Tranquility." In addition to Mr. Veeck and his wife, "Tranquility" was headquarters for most of his nine children from two marriages, various breeds of dogs, a chicken flock and various assorted animals. Also it was a mecca for a stream of visitors curious about Veeck's life in retirement.

At "Tranquility," Mr. Veeck also resumed his love affair with books, explaining, "I was a Kenyon College drop-out." He doted on Shakespeare and Will Durant's seven volumes on The Story of Civilization. He was a regular book reviewer for the Chicago Tribune and other newspapers, and, with writer Ed Linn, authored his biography, "Veeck as in Wreck."

He also went on the lecture circuit and took a one-year turn as commentator on Roone Arledge's Wide World of Sports for ABC. He found time too, to testify for Curt Flood in that player's defiance of baseball's reserve clause, further angering the club owners.

In 1969, he was coaxed out of retirement to operate the Suffolk Race Track in Boston by owners who valued his promotional talents.

Though new to the business, Mr. Veeck pumped up interest in Suffolk by eliminating the clubhouse and making it a one-price track, declared all pay toilets to be no-charge conveniences and otherwise won the fans' approval.

"I had to read up on racing quickly," Mr. Veeck said. So he wrote to his favorite Brentano's in his native Chicago, ordering every book it had on horses. "They sent me 20 volumes. Some of them were very helpful," Mr. Veeck said. "But I doubt I reaped any benefits from the illustrated 'Black Beauty' they sent along from their juvenile department."

He entertained Suffolk fans with a Lady Godiva Handicap for female drivers, and for male and female jockeys he concocted a Guys and Dolls Handicap. Then, he imported from Hollywood some of the props from Ben Hur and staged a bona fide chariot race on the Suffolk track.

When, in 1971, he fell out with the owners despite the track's success, Mr. Veeck noted his experience in racing by writing what he liked to call "the definitive on Suffolk." He impishly titled it "Thirty Tons a Day," an allusion to the daily output of the 1,600 horses stabled there.

He was coaxed back into baseball in 1975 by the opportunity to rebuy the White Sox, 14 years after selling the same team for what he said were "reasons of health." With his longtime friend Hank Greenberg as his chief partner, he operated the White Sox until 1980 when he sold for $20 million the franchise his group had bought five years before for $7 million.

Survivors include his wife; four daughters, Marya, Lisa, Juliana and Ellen Maggs; four sons, Michael, Gregory, Christopher and Peter; six grandchildren; and a sister, Margaret Ann Krehbiel.

JANUARY 3, 1986

Hank Greenberg

Povich admired Hank Greenberg and took pride in his being Jewish. One year, when the World Series fell on the Jewish holy day of Yom Kippur, Povich, as usual, refused to write and went to Synagogue. Greenberg also refused to play, which caused a lot of controversy on his team. As Povich recalled, "We talked, I remember, and he says, 'Shirley, I wanted to play that World Series game, I hate to let this team down.' And he says, 'Remember, too, I've been hearing all this stuff from the dugouts about Jew-Boy this and that.... You know, I think you have to pay a little more for the privilege of being a Jew.' And that was his dedication—not only to becoming the great ballplayer that he was, but his determination not to let his Jewish people down. He saw in himself a symbol."

—Interview for the documentary film
The Life and Times of Hank Greenberg

Only a few folks were aware that the big guy was out there battling an opponent that doesn't stand up and fight back. Everybody else was hearing only that Hank Greenberg now seemed to be living in California where, time to time, he was popping up in the news as a once-sought celebrity in those charity tennis tournaments that dot the landscape.

Cancer took him last week. Even at the age of 75, if he'd had a chance to swing his bat at that damnable disease he would have licked that thing, too, even as he once beat all the baseball odds to become one of the two men in his time who could seriously threaten the 60-home run season record of Babe Ruth. Jimmy Foxx also had a 58-homer season.

And in his later years in those tennis tournaments, Hank was no mere marquee name, either. In his 50s, 60s and 70s, he was winning both singles and doubles finals with fierce strokes patently adapted from his baseball swing. Compete. That's what he'd done all of his baseball years.

On a baseball field, the figure of Hank Greenberg always was easy to spot. In every park he was usually the tallest (6 feet 3 1/2) and, if arguably, the handsomest. And those loud shots hit out of ball parks did not hurt his visibility, either.

As a major league superstar, Hank Greenberg was an anomaly, anywhere. The asphalt of New York City was not supposed to be the breeding ground for big-name ball players. There hadn't been one since Lou Gehrig, and there hasn't been any since Hank Greenberg. Gehrig made it via Columbia University. Greenberg was a product of the Lower East Side's stickball games and high school ball in the Bronx.

The Yankees scouted him hard after hearing of his long ball hitting and his first base play for James Monroe High School, but young Greenberg didn't listen hard to their offers. He didn't like his future with a team that already had Lou Gehrig at first base. After going to NYU for a year, he signed a $9,000 contract with Detroit in 1930.

This was the kid who would make it so big as a big-leaguer that in time he'd be up there bracketed with Joe DiMaggio and Ted Williams as the Big Three of the American League. When the talk ran to super-stars, that was it—DiMaggio-Williams-Greenberg. Foxx would enter the discussions at times and his homers often were longer than any-body else's. But somehow, he wasn't as much of a conversation piece.

Greenberg, the first Jewish ballplayer in Cooperstown, confided to certain friends that it wasn't always easy for him. Baseball was not dis-tinguished by lofty intellects in his time, and he was a target of both subtle and flagrant anti-Semitism, an earlier version of the bigotry that later hounded Jackie Robinson with the Dodgers.

He was one of the first ball players drafted into the Army and in 1941 on a visit to the Senators' training camp in Army uniform he said, "In the early years I used to look around and see which ball players I'd have to fight some day, which bastards made one remark too many. That wouldn't bother me now. I've been hiking and sleeping on the ground for weeks, and I'm leaner and harder and stronger than I've ever been, and I'd pity any S.O.B. who gets in my way."

Greenberg's resume for his 12 years with the Tigers—there were timeouts for war service in 1941–44: four-time league leader in home runs, four-time league leader in RBIs, a .318 average for four World Series, those big 58 home runs in 1938, most valuable player in 1935 and 1940, and later, the Hall of Fame.

As with all big sluggers, there were frequent strikeouts, and Green-berg was sometimes labeled "guess hitter." He resented it. "Guess hit-ter, bull," he said. "We're all guess hitters, if everybody would only tell the truth. They're lying, those who say they aren't guessing up there."

He confessed he did get help from Del Baker, the Tigers third base coach and acknowledged genius as a sign stealer who often tipped

Hank off about the next pitch. But Greenberg begged Baker to desist one day after an experience against Joe Krakauskas, a wild left-hander with the Senators.

Krakauskas had sent one pitch zinging over Greenberg's head, another fastball that made him dance out of the way and a third pitch that almost clipped him under the chin. Greenberg told Baker, "Don't try to tell me what this guy is going to throw. He doesn't know himself."

The size of Greenberg's home runs, usually longer than those of Williams and DiMaggio, prompted discussions about how his homers compared to those of Ruth, Gehrig and Foxx. The definitive judgment was made by Walter Johnson who, when asked which man hit the longest homers, said: "Let me put it this way: Those balls the Babe hit always got smaller faster than anybody else's."

A Greenberg home run that Washington fans could take personally was the bases-loaded shot he hit that day just before the 1945 season ended. He had just come out of the Army to rejoin the Tigers, and that blow knocked the Senators and their pennant hopes back into second place. The Tigers took the title by 1 1/2 games.

In 1940, the Tigers asked first baseman Greenberg to move to the outfield, which he thought was a dirty trick because he'd be a novice out there. But they were wanting to get Rudy York's bat into the lineup everyday, and Greenberg agreed. York's home run bat compensated for his often-weak fielding.

In his early years Greenberg had been overswinging, and he received valuable advice from, of all people, an umpire. It was Bill McGowan who told him, "Hank, you don't have to hit the ball 40 rows into the seats. Home runs count just as much if they only clear the fence by this much," and McGowan held up his thumb and forefinger spaced an inch apart.

Greenberg's marriage to Carol Gimbel, of the department store millions, was a much-noted event in 1946, ending in divorce 13 years later. When his son Steve, who came out of an Ivy League college, got a tryout with the Senators at first base, Hank was not the usual enthusiastic father.

"I don't think he's good enough," Hank said frankly, and then he added something practical, with the Gimbel family investment portfolio in mind, resorting to jest: "The boy could go to bed at night and wake up in the morning having made more money than he could earn in a year in baseball."

Hank, himself, was baseball's first $100,000 player. He earned it, with that quick bat, and a first baseman's glove that covered all the territory; and he also earned his Mr. Nice Guy reputation with his 6–3 1/2 of warmth while at the top of his fame. He not only deserved Cooperstown, he's an ornament to it.

SEPTEMBER 9, 1986

Baseball's Crying Shame

New York—Americans can now register another gripe in these times of a national debt in the trillions, fruitless eyeballing with the Soviets and mishmash tax reforms: the World Series ain't quite what it used to be, and there is a growing sentiment that baseball is no longer as American as apple pie.

The 1986 World Series as played out in Boston and New York is no longer the game Americans were teethed on. Sunshine, which was present at the invention of the game, and for a hundred years after, has been ruled out. And the game is now played by 10 men to a side, with a designated hitter recruited when the American League city is the host.

The World Series is now less than the majestic, hearts-stand-still showdown between the two pennant winners. It has dissolved into an appendage to the thrill-a-minute league playoff games, 13 of which preceded this Series, compromised it and impacted on it to the extent that there is an inclination to scream "Enough already!", a symptom of that newest of maladies, World Series fatigue.

Also, never before was baseball so structured, the spontaneity of it destroyed. Play starts not when the umpire says, "Play ball," but when the TV networks say it should start. The fans are not trusted to cheer at a time of their own choosing but in New York they are instructed by the Mets' electronic scoreboard to "Let's Hear Some Noise Now." Cheer on cue.

The World Series is officially known as the Commissioner's Game. It is thus recognized by the club owners as his province, supposedly giving him supreme authority in all matters. In St. Louis years ago, when Judge Kenesaw Mountain Landis' arrival at the park was delayed 15 minutes by a traffic jam, the opening Series game was delayed 15 minutes until Landis gave the nod to the umpires that it was permissible to begin.

Now the commissioner bows to the television networks in such matters, with the result that most of the nation went sleepwalking through the final innings of Series games that edged toward midnight.

The World Series, at one time one of the proudest components in American life, has accepted a role as a TV program factored into the networks' rating game. How else to meet the $100,000 per player paychecks that go to the winning side, except to take television's money. Baseball once prided itself as "the best one-dollar entertainment value in the country." This week, box seat fans at Fenway Park and Shea Stadium were $40 per game customers.

For the fifth game, baseball dared not hew to its advertised 8:30 time. The best it could manage was 8:43, with NBC brooking no interference with the commercials following its high-rated, untouchable "Cosby Show." Baseball was being told that a situation comedy had a higher priority than the World Series, with NBC also proving that its customary and oft-boring half-hour pregame show was perhaps unnecessary. It was canceled Thursday night in favor of Cosby.

However, the networks had nothing to do with that World Series abomination called the designated hitter. That is the sad creation of AL club owners who have tampered with the very fabric of the game: should or should not the manager let the pitcher hit, or should he opt for a pinch hitter? Those situations put the fans into the dugout, made them more privy to the strategy, opened up all kinds of beautiful second-guessing opportunities.

Instead, the DH relieves the manager of a big part of what used to be demands on his decision-making, takes him off the spot, helps make it a nonstrategic plastic game, denuded of the speculation and the possibility that the pitcher could lay one down or even get a hit. The manager's decisions come free-packaged in the form of his DH. Our compliments to the National League for playing it straight.

Some pitchers can hit, you know, and in the past many a one was gleeful about it. Nobody ever hit for Wes Ferrell or Red Ruffing, and Early Wynn used to get extra pay from the Senators for his pinch-hitting duties.

No pitcher, and few ballplayers, ever hit as well as Walter Johnson, often the Senators' best pinch hitter. In 1925, in the 36 games Johnson played, he put up there the best batting average by any pitcher in baseball history, a nifty .440, including a couple of home runs. There's always euphoria when a pitcher gets a hit. These guys would scowl down a DH.

America used to look forward to a best-four-out-of-seven series to determine the best team in baseball. No more. First come the play-offs, starting 10 days in front of the Series, and newly expanded to best-of-seven, and in years like this one when the playoffs were constant drama, the World Series has to suffer.

This year, it did, and tempered as the Series has been by dull games, it has been anticlimactic. Who'd have thought it could happen, but there was a draining of interest in mid-Series. In a paraphrase of the ditty, Sam, you made the games too long. When it finally came to the World Series, in terms of high excitement there wasn't any, after the first couple of games. The Series encroached seven, eight games into the pro football season and began to resemble the interminable hockey and basketball playoffs, a most undignified state of baseball affairs.

It wasn't the same, either, with the "Star Spangled Banner" getting a Mo-Town version with its unrecognizable melody before Game 5. Used to be that Lucy Monroe belted it out so sweetly every year in the Series opener at Yankee Stadium, after a 365-day rest.

Another dismay is the disgusting, modern habit of most of the outfielders, particularly Boston's Dwight Evans, of one-handing all fly balls. Willie Mays and other great ones always seemed to find two hands necessary, considered anything else showboating. Of course, they didn't own the big fish nets that stand for modern gloves and make of modern outfielding a baseball version of jai alai.

Game 5 also found Vin Scully and Joe Garagiola, the best of all play-by-play men and commentators, at less than their best. Scully properly faulted Darryl Strawberry for his sluggish play on Jim Rice's triple to right center in the fifth, but then he belabored Strawberry and the whole subject so often thereafter that he risked sounding like an insensitive Howard Cosell at his unforgivable worst.

Garagiola chimed in that Strawberry broke late on the ball "and should have been off at the crack of the bat." Sorry, Joe. Not according to the late, great Tris Speaker, who maintained even the crack of the bat was too late. Gotta be leaning with the pitch, Speaker explained.

OCTOBER 26, 1986

Sugar Ray Leonard

The Washington area produced its share of successful professional boxers, but no one could match Sugar Ray Leonard of Palmer Park, Md., for excitement and glamour. An Olympic champion in 1976, Leonard became a welterweight champion and then middleweight title-holder, in between five retirements. His fights—particularly against Roberto Duran, Marvelous Marvin Hagler, and Thomas Hearns—attracted huge closed-circuit television audiences and increased circulation of the

Post *by about 30,000 the day after his fights. Povich wrote about a number of Leonard's most memorable fights, including this upset of Hagler in Las Vegas 1987. Leonard was a fan of Povich's and spoke at several events honoring him.*

Las Vegas—So they said it couldn't be done. So they said he was unrealistic and a giddy fool for even thinking comeback from a ring rust of nearly five years. And that he could get half-killed and even half-blinded against this brutish battler who for 11 years had been destroying natural middleweights.

So what chance did they give little Sugar Ray Leonard, a puffed-up welterweight with a once-damaged retina, against Marvelous Marvin Hagler, the monster nobody had licked in more than a decade? And without even a tuneup. More arrogance. The odds were 6 to 1 when the match was made, meaning Leonard's chances were rated minuscule at best. And when they closed at 3 to 1, it was still tantamount to saying Leonard had only a fat chance.

And so the new middleweight champion of the world is Sugar Ray Leonard. Monday night he battered Hagler good, made him look like a chump, left the champion chasing a will-o'-the-wisp who had a strong will to fight back when necessary, and when it was desirable to get out of trouble he out-punched the puncher. And never was Hagler or any other champion ever hit with so many right-hand leads, a no-no in all of boxing's textbooks. Leonard was audacious.

Sugar Ray's battle plan was a winner. He said he would frustrate Hagler and he did. In between his sudden assaults on the champion, Leonard segued out of danger on nimble dancing feet and also lured Hagler into sucker punches. Perhaps Sugar Ray didn't as much plan the victory as choreograph it.

It was a split decision with one of the three judges favoring Hagler in an egregious fit of illogic, and, of course, in the postfight interviews Hagler said he was robbed.

Hagler said he dominated the fight, a most debatable statement, and that he was never hurt, and that the bell saved Leonard three times. He said nothing about getting clouted with all those right leads or how Leonard was making him miss by ludicrous margins.

Nor did he say how Leonard was beating him to the punch all night and landing in the greatest display of eye-hand coordination since Ted Williams put away his bat.

What Hagler did say was, "I still consider myself the middleweight champion of the world," a statement that recalls the advice umpire Bill McGowan once gave an indignant base runner who said he was safe at second: "If you don't think you're out, look in the morning paper."

It was after Hagler carried on so bitterly against Leonard and the judges that Larry Merchant, the snappy HBO analyst, delivered the precious comment, "I never saw so unhappy a man who has just earned $20 million."

This reporter's scorecard shows Leonard with a clear edge in rounds, seven to four, with one even. The marginal notes say "out-punching the puncher" when Leonard was backed against the ropes and in the corners. Also, in the final two rounds, when it still may have been close, this note: "L outfinishing H." That he did in a successful show of bravura that found him willing to go toe-to-toe with the most dangerous man in the business. He piled up more important points and even won the 12th round on the card of the judge who gave the fight to Hagler.

Hagler's corner men didn't distinguish themselves either, except in a dull way when they permitted their man to take it easy in the early fighting, which later prompted Leonard to say, "I was surprised when he gave me the first few rounds." It was as if they had no study on Leonard, or the memory that he is a cutey who is not easy to catch up with late in a fight. With his style he is not easily dominated by anybody.

In Leonard's corner, Angelo Dundee had counseled Leonard to "stay smooth" on the ropes and in the corners, and after the 10th round he goaded his man with: "Give me six minutes more and you're the new champion."

Leonard gave Dundee and Hagler a ferocious six minutes in the 11th and 12th, outbanging the banger in a neutral corner where Hagler was presumed to have an advantage. It was, strangely, Leonard the boss now, stinging Hagler with a dozen piston-like shots to the head, none of them answered.

Leonard lost some rounds, too—four of them, at worst five, and there were times when he appeared in deep trouble. This was in the fifth and the ninth when his fast pace appeared to weary Leonard, who permitted Hagler to force him to the ropes, where he took fierce punishment. He was hurt, but he didn't crumble, and in the ninth he was magnificent with a counterattack that got him out of trouble, although it couldn't save the round for him.

The Leonard who answered the opening bell Monday night was the old, assured, even cocky, Sugar Ray, bearing no resemblance to the Leonard who was so tentative in his first dreary comeback three years ago against long shot Kevin Howard. Nothing apprehensive about him Monday night when he walked out and landed the first two punches against Hagler, a combination. It was a signal assuring to Leonard's friends.

And on every round he was first out of the corner at the bell.

Hagler's switch to a southpaw stance troubled Leonard in many of the middle rounds, with Hagler landing some of his best shots in long, lunging jabs. But on each occasion when he was in trouble, Leonard surprised Hagler with new, strong tactics, his willingness to go toe to toe. It worked well for him at a point when he actually appeared to be tiring.

They had been talking to each other from the middle rounds on, Hagler on the snarling side. "He called me a sissy," Leonard said. But the worst thing Hagler did was to go to sign language in the later rounds, gesturing with his gloves for Leonard to "come in and fight." It was the worst invitation he could have extended. Only his iron chin, Hagler's trademark, frustrated Leonard's hunt for a knockout.

In the final round it got to be almost comical when Hagler tried to ape Leonard, who had gone into his favorite act of urging crowd-support by waving one gloved hand over his head, in anticipation of a victory already won. Hagler tried the same thing, a posture new to him and quite unbecoming to his style. Like so many of Hagler's attempts to catch up with Leonard, this last act also was a clumsy one.

Hagler had sought a place in history by equaling Carlos Monzon's 14 successful defenses of the middleweight title. He found his place in history as the only man to lose the title to a comeback challenger who didn't even have a tune-up fight.

APRIL 8, 1987

Giamatti Bans Rose

Add the name of A. Bartlett Giamatti to the Baseball Commissioners Hall of Fame populated hitherto only by Kenesaw Mountain Landis, and even Landis's reputation for always playing hardball will not withstand intense scrutiny. It may now be said of Giamatti, while mixing more than one metaphor, that when he bit the bullet and lowered the boom on Pete Rose yesterday, banning that worthy from baseball for life, he went to the head of the class. It was a gutsy and proper decision.

It is to be recalled that Landis's reputation suffered in 1927 when he surprisingly took no action against Ty Cobb and Tris Speaker despite solid evidence that they not only bet on baseball games — Rose's alleged sin — but actually were involved in fixing a Detroit–Cleveland game in 1926, the ultimate baseball crime.

When Landis chickened out on that one it was startling because was he not the very model of the no-nonsense commissioner before whom all baseball trembled? Had he not swiftly banished for life the eight Black Sox who fixed the 1919 World Series? Was he not the stern old federal judge who once fined the Standard Oil Co. $10 million, a vast sum in 1917?

From the outset the clubowners had learned to fear Landis. On that day when a sizable delegation of owners shuffled into Landis's court to offer him the job as baseball's first commissioner, their effort to restore public confidence in the game after the fixed World Series, they ran into their first rebuke. Landis, a $10,000-a-year judge, knew of their errand, knew that they were there to offer him a $50,000 post, but he nevertheless looked at the delegation and grumped, "There will be less noise in here or this courtroom will be cleared."

In the Cobb–Speaker case there were damning letters in evidence from both Cobb and Hubert (Dutch) Leonard that told details of betting on a game, with Leonard alluding also to a conspiracy to fix one. Yet Landis, after a hearing, surprisingly let Cobb and Speaker off as "not guilty because of insufficient evidence." Therein his critics said Landis got satisfaction in what was his long and bitter feud with Ban Johnson, president of the American League, who had already declared both players guilty and banned them from the game.

Of all the other commissioners—Happy Chandler, Ford Frick, Gen. William Eckert, Bowie Kuhn and Peter Ueberroth—only Kuhn distinguished himself. Chandler took credit for bringing Jackie Robinson into the game, a bald usurpation of Branch Rickey's fame. Frick was a 200 percent owners man who functioned as their chattel. Eckert was an accident, a rank novice who when appointed commissioner was instantly acclaimed by irreverent baseball writers as "the unknown soldier." Realizing their mistake, the owners bought out his contract, and Eckert went down in history as the unknown commissioner.

Kuhn's passion for the game exceeded all the others' and it was under his regime that baseball flourished most. He showed vast courage when he forbade Charlie Finley to trade all those players off the Oakland club because it would wreck that team as a contender. It was the first time an owner's authority in that matter had been challenged by a commissioner.

Chandler won attention for suspending Leo Durocher for a year for "consorting" with suspected gambling figures and permitting them entry to the Dodgers' clubhouse. There were no charges that Durocher was betting, so the one-year penalty seemed harsh, but Chandler was determined to set him down.

If Rose is not reinstated he would be the first man to be permanently barred from baseball since 1943, when Philadelphia Phillies President William D. Cox was banished for betting on his own team. And it would appear that Rose's right to reapply with baseball is a mere formality, with no guarantees. At best it is a facesaving thing for Rose, who didn't save much face when he agreed to the life ban.

Back to Judge Landis: he banned the Black Sox Eight before they went to court and received a "not guilty" verdict. He wasn't disturbed by that and continued to ban them on the basis that Landis Law was not to be superseded. In subsequent years when friends of Joe Jackson pleaded that he was illiterate and wasn't aware of his crime when he took the money for the 1919 fixes, had had World Series statistics and a big batting figure to prove he couldn't possibly have done what was claimed, it was no dice. No commissioner was moved.

In contrast with Giamatti's news conference yesterday in which he made all points clear, Rose's conference was a lot of funny talk, a charade. No, he didn't bet on baseball, said the player who signed an agreement accepting a life ban on the commissioner's belief that he did bet on baseball.

"You can tell the fans I have too much respect for the game to bet on baseball," said the man who refused for six months to appear for a hearing on the subject. More debatable talk from Rose: "I expect to be reinstated shortly." Would he seek rehabilitation for a gambling problem? "I don't have a gambling problem." He said his deal to accept a life ban "was a compromise." Some compromise.

Conversely Giamatti's was a virtuoso performance before the press. Sometimes he was even cute. When he cocked his ear for the second part of a question he explained, "I was too enthralled by my answer to the first part to listen to the second part." He ducked no questions except the one about Rose's chances for the Hall of Fame. He gave a definitive, short-term explanation of his action: "I say he is banished for life ... He's dismissed ... He's unemployable by the Reds or by baseball ... There was absolutely no deal for reinstatement ... If he would not report for a hearing, his denials were unacceptable to me."

So there and bravo!

AUGUST 25, 1989

[In his autobiography, published in 2004, Rose admitted that he bet on baseball games.]

THE NINETIES

SHIRLEY POVICH'S LAST COLUMN FOR THE WASHINGTON POST
was written hours before he died of a heart attack on June 4, 1998. He
had been feeling weak for more than a month and a half, but kept up
with the sports scene and felt strong enough the day before to write a
column weighing in on three of baseball's hottest players of the time,
Mark McGwire, David Wells, and Barry Bonds. The day after he died,
the Post printed his obituary and his last column.

Not that Povich wanted a farewell column, or a farewell tour.
Although he died at 92, Povich never lost his hunger for news, sports,
and writing. He was writing often and well, until suffering a near fatal
heart attack in the lobby of Baltimore's Oriole Park at Camden Yards
in October 1997, an hour before the deciding game of the American
League Championship Series between Baltimore and Cleveland. Fast
and skillful work by paramedics kept Povich alive that day. An hour
after being rushed by ambulance to a nearby hospital, he was alert
and discussing the impact the late afternoon shadows would have on
the game. "Clark Griffith [owner of the Senators] would always tell
me to ignore a player's performance in September because the setting
sun late in the day made it very difficult to see the ball."

Of course, he was right. The Orioles did not see the ball very well
that day, losing 1–0 in 11 innings to the Indians.

Although Povich survived several heart attacks and hospitalizations,
his primary health concern in his last decade was his darling Ethyl,
who was losing her memory. Their's was a true love affair and he was
absolutely devoted to her. By then, Shirley had buried all of his siblings
and most of his very dear friends, but the only time he ever cried was
when a doctor finally diagnosed Ethyl with Alzheimer's in 1991. One
night he became distraught when he was in the Washington Hospital

Center and Ethyl had driven to visit him against his wishes, because she was in the early stages of the disease. After she left, he called home incessantly to make sure she had returned. When she hadn't, he called his son David and said frantically, "You must find Mother right now!" Nothing would assuage his fears or settle him. David called the hospital to make sure a doctor was with him and then went to look for her. It turned out she had turned right instead of left when she drove out of the hospital and ended up lost in Northeast Washington. Very fearful, she stopped and got directions from "a very nice man" and finally made it home. It was the worst night in Shirley's life.

In Povich's final years, he wrote some memorable pieces, including biting prose on Mike Tyson, the cancellation of the 1994 World Series because of a labor impasse, and final strokes on his canvas of Babe Ruth, Mickey Mantle, Cy Young, and Ben Hogan.

Undoubtedly, the most stirring moment of the decade for Povich was his coverage of Cal Ripken breaking Lou Gehrig's consecutive games streak of 2,130 on September 6, 1995. Povich, one of the few in the stadium that day who witnessed both events, was the subject of many interviews on the field before the game. His final paragraph on the column he wrote the day after Ripken established his own standard is worth repeating:

> The late Lou Gehrig would probably be abashed at the news that Ripken had successfully attacked his endurance record. But he probably would be more shocked to learn that a breakdown over Ripken's salary says he is paid $47,000 a game to perform for the Orioles. At the peak of his career, Gehrig drew a salary of $37,000 for the entire season. The sign of those times, and these.

It's hard to say, when someone has written for 75 years, that he is a man of his times. But having witnessed many of the most significant sporting events of the 20th century, Povich dramatized, in his impeccable prose, the great evolution of sports. And in so doing the story of sports becomes the story of America.

Graziano: He Knew the Ropes

He never bothered with the fine arts of boxing. On the mean streets of the lower East Side, the young toughs were not interested in winning on points. It was destroy or be destroyed. The tactics were whatever came to mind. In that environment Rocky Graziano was schooled, along with the other young thieves and muggers. But later, in a remarkable transition, he was to rise above it all, saying, "Somebody up there likes me."

The other day, Rocky Graziano, at 71, lost his last fight. In the other corner was that cardiopulmonary thing that put him in that New York hospital for three weeks. It brought down all his defenses. And this time, Rocky couldn't get up off the floor, like he did against a lot of guys, especially the night he won the middleweight title from Tony Zale.

For Rocky, the early years weren't pretty ones. He stole, he fought, he lied, he was twice sentenced to the reformatory, he was a sixth-grade dropout, a roughneck, well launched toward a violent, wasted life.

It is how he turned it around that is the Rocky Graziano story. Like many prizefighters, he commanded a certain fascination for the dynamite that was in his fists. But few would suspect that Rocky Graziano would emerge as a somewhat lovable public figure, a darling of the television sponsors for whom his crooked face and simple dese-and-dose charm commanded an audience for their products.

Rocky thrived on this kind of new public exposure, even though he confessed to needing a quick, remedial reading course to understand the cue cards. He took to show business. As for his illiteracy, he knew what he was, never concealed it. His whole attitude on TV, his visage was a wink. He got more famous when a young actor named Paul Newman made a hit movie of Rocky's life story.

Rocky never forgot his roots. It was after he won Zale's title on a steamy night in Chicago in 1947 that Jake LaMotta was being suggested as his next opponent and I asked him did he think he could beat LaMotta. Said Rocky, "I always did in reform school."

Rocky was a 5-foot 7-inch flailer whose style was to walk in and swat the other guy, with the hand that was handiest. It was effective. He won 67 of 83 fights, 52 by knockouts, got six draws. But it was his three championship fights with Zale that made him most remembered. When one mentioned Graziano's name, it was almost in terms of Graziano–Zale, so violent, so climactic were those battles, all of which were for the title, all of which ended in knockouts by fighters who got up off the floor.

Zale's name thus almost became an appendage to Rocky's. It is remembered that Red Smith, like myself, covered all those fights, the first in Yankee Stadium, the second one in Chicago, the third in Newark. Red would be more candid about the unpredictability. "Yeah," he would say, "I covered each of those fights and I picked each one of them wrong." We could be forgiven. Nobody could be sure how a Graziano–Zale brawl would end.

Actually, they were, to use their real names, fights between Thomas Rocco Barbella and Anthony Florian Zaleski. Rocky had simply taken the name of his sister's boyfriend. Zale is remembered for when, after being drafted, he reported to the Navy's Great Lakes boot camp. Asked his name, he said, "Anthony Zaleski." Asked his profession, he said, "Pugilist, middleweight." Whereupon the admittance officer said, "Ho, ho. I'd hate to be you. Tony Zale is checking in here later in the day."

In their first fight in 1946, it appeared Rocky was a false 8–5 favorite when Zale, who could also be violent, floored him for five in the first round. But, ha, the man who was down in the second round, the bell saving him, was Zale. The gore was awful with both streaming blood, when, in the sixth, a weary Zale made an astonishing comeback and flattened Rocky with a massive left to the middle and a finishing right.

In their second fight the outcome was just as surprising. Rocky was a badly beaten fighter, his roundhouse swings missing widely, one eye reduced to a narrow slit and a Zale right sending him to the floor in Round 3. Somehow, Rocky brought off a comeback that battered Zale into a helpless state in Round 5 and knocked him out in Round 6. In his own fashion, the new champion did pay tribute to his victim after the fight. "That Zale ain't no slob," he said.

So, there would be a third fight and this time Rocky would be a big favorite, a false one. He would be flattened by Zale in three, in the customary wild swinging brawl. A searing left hand to the midriff set up Rocky for the knockout, and he would later say of Zale: "That body punch he's got is like a red-hot poker. He hits you with it and leaves it in there." Cocky Rocky could compliment his opponents after a fight, if never before it. In later years Rocky could say, in his gratitude, "Somebody up there likes me." And so many down here liked him too.

MAY 25, 1990

No Mistaking These Guys for Cy Young

His name was Cy Young, deceased since 1955, and he comes to mind because of the continuing travesties in his memory. The Cy Young Award designed to honor pitching excellence in his image is being profaned every year by guys with seemingly little understanding that baseball is a nine-inning game.

Cy Young is a proper icon in pitching history. He won more games than anyone, 511. More even than Walter Johnson. He was the master of the complete game, once pitching 54 in succession. He would not understand the new breed of pitchers, or managers who sometimes say in their praise, "He'll give us five good innings."

That would be a recipe for back to Binghamton in Cy Young's era. As for last year's Cy Young Award winners, he could be asking what planet did these types come from? Bob Welch of the Oakland A's, in his 35 starts, pitched only two complete games. Doug Drabek of the Pirates completed nine of 33 starts.

By Young's lights, these are pitchers? The man who pitched 750 complete games, who went the limit in 40 of his 41 starts one season, could be tempted to disassociate himself from the Cy Young Award or simply accept the truth that the complete game is a lost art.

He wouldn't understand the new language of the game or the degree to which it has changed. The relief pitcher, a minor figure in most of baseball's history, usually typed as not good enough to start, has in later years surged to highest importance. And not simply as a fellow who goes in to save a lead. Managers now talk of relief men as if they were members of several species. They speak of "short relievers," and "long relievers" and "middle relievers," with some types known as "closers." What in the world is going on here?

The degree to which relief pitchers have superceded starters is best portrayed by the Yankees' staff. Their starting pitchers as of this week were guilty of a horrendous 5.01 earned-run average. Where did the Yankees' recent success come from? Their relievers, whose 2.84 ERA kept the team alive and pennant hopeful.

It was the Yankees' pitching coach, Mark Connor, who recently gave the most graphic picture of the thinking of modern managers. "The good bullpen," he told the *New York Times*, "would have two set-up guys"—whatever they are—"one left-handed, one right-handed; two middle-inning guys, one left-handed, one right-handed; and a closer. . . . And the way things have gotten today, you'd want a sixth guy to be your long man."

Whew!

But that's the way it is in modern baseball, with the complete game an artifact and something of a surprise when one is pitched. Also, because of the frequent pitching changes, the three-hour game is the norm, with the lapses leading some folks to believe baseball actually is dull. Remembered is the contrast the day the Senators' Sid Hudson shut out the Yankees on three hits and it was written here, "Sid Hudson was the man of the hour and 34 minutes."

The emphasis on relief pitching has also produced an inner breed of swaggering intimidators, the first of whom was probably Dick

Radatz of the Red Sox, 6 feet 6, 230, a glowering flame-thrower who liked to be called "The Monster."

Later came the two bearded types of the Cardinals, Al Hrabosky, known as "The Mad Hungarian," and Bruce Sutter, both with foliage, and both throwing "heat," another descriptive that has crept into the game.

The Reds' Rob Dibble, 6–4, 235, reveled in being No. 1 in their Nasty Boys bullpen.

It is the belief here that the relief specialist was originated by Bucky Harris with the Senators in 1924 by unveiling his big Texan, Fred Marberry, as a fastballing intimidator. In 1925 Marberry set the record by appearing in 55 games without starting. Miller Huggins of the Yankees copied Harris by presenting Wilcy Moore as a relief specialist in 1927, and Casey Stengel later became the master of pitcher platooning.

Those fancy ERAs of relievers are not all that they're cracked up to be and sometimes are a complete fraud. When they go in with men on base, they have all the best of it, getting the advantage of force plays, sometimes at every base. And they can't be charged when runners they inherited score, although they could have pitched a hell of a lot better in those instances.

Let me tell you of an extreme case of a relief pitcher getting more credit than he deserved. The scene is Fenway Park, bottom of the eighth, the Senators trailing by two runs, one out, two Red Sox on base. Al Crowder goes in as a reliever. On his first pitch, a double play, the inning is over. In the top of the ninth, the Senators pinch-hit for Crowder. They get three runs and win the game when the Red Sox are shut out in the bottom of the ninth. Winning pitcher: Crowder. On his one and only pitch of the game. So much for relief pitching, sometimes.

July 7, 1991

Big Chill Descends on Spring Training

Seen at a Distance, Baseball's Annual Rite Is a Far Cry From Easygoing Days of the Past

There was a tap on his shoulder the other day and a certain baseball writer was being told by a functionary in a New York Yankees cap that he had transgressed.

"Step back on the grass, sir. You know the rules."

This was behind the batting cage and the writer's sin was standing in the dirt area around the cage. Two midget steps to the rear, and now the grass was under his feet and he had complied, his location now proper and acceptable.

The printed rules are a big thing in the Yankees' spring training camp. "...No member of the media is allowed in fair or foul territory beyond first or third base." And "45 minutes before the game, clear out of the dugouts and the clubhouse."

There is more: "Still photographers and cameramen must stay in assigned areas." ... "The clubhouse is off limits when the game starts. No player may be accessed unless he has left the game."

Whew!

In baseball's earlier and less-monied days, spring training used to be more fun for the writers and everybody else. The informality of rickety old clubhouses, wooden grandstands and the heavenly absence of TV crews and pompous public relations corpsmen brought players and writers together. They stayed and ate together in the same little hotels, called each other by first names and were uninhibited by lengthy instructions from PR departments.

Today, "access" is the buzzword. Yankees players are not approached, they are "accessed." Of all the clubs, the Yankees are the most rule-crazy, but the others are not far behind.

In contrast there was the late Clark Griffith, owner of the old Washington Senators. He was team proprietor, team president and bottle washer. Griffith saw no need for a public relations staff. On many occasions he would call *The Washington Post* sports editor and other newspapers and say, "Walter Johnson is pitching tomorrow. Gimme a headline."

Modern big league teams are enjoying the bounty of eager Florida and Arizona towns whose citizens build them modified big league stadiums for free. Lavish clubhouses with shining bathrooms and Nautilus equipment are what's in style. Plus ample individual lockers for each player whose byline is affixed to his private estate.

Not so in the era of the Senators and their contemporary clubs of an earlier day. On entering the clubhouse on the first day of spring training each player searched out the hook on which he could hang his stuff and hoped to find a stool on which to sit. Nothing like the expensive lockers provided the New York Mets in their deal with the town of Port St. Lucie, Fla., which built them to specifications that provided an extra wide locker for the catchers in recognition of their heavier equipment or, mayhap, their broader backsides.

When the Senators set up camp in Orlando, Fla., in 1936, after moving from Biloxi, Miss., they quartered themselves in the downtown Angebilt Hotel, not a luxury address. However, it was on the same street as Orlando's two movie theaters and thus advertised itself on its matchboxes as "Orlando's only fireproof hotel. In heart of theater district."

This is not to say all of the Senators were quartered in the Angebilt, which Griffith considered too rich and expensive for some of the team's lesser rookies. So, shunted to Mrs. Mason's boarding house at considerably less expense to the team were the likes of Mickey Vernon, Early Wynn, Walter Masterson and George Case, who at mealtime could practice their boarding house reach. It is memorable that from that group would evolve a two-time American League batting champion (Vernon), a Hall of Fame pitcher (Wynn) and an American League-leading base stealer (Case).

This was an era when the players, on road trips, were subsisting on $6-a-day meal money. Some of the saving types would show a profit by doting on hamburgers and hot dogs.

The Senators worked out at Tinker Field, named for Joe Tinker, an Orlando native and the old Cubs second baseman of the legendary Tinker-to-Evers-to-Chance fame. Tinker Field had a wooden grand-stand, wooden dugouts and wooden clubhouse, all graying and tilting. But it was not unlike other spring training camps in Florida in the late '30s.

Joe Tinker was almost always present at Tinker Field, in a wheel-chair. So it was that one day when a visitor in the clubhouse turned out to be Heine Groh, the old National League third baseman of Tin-ker's era. Groh asked to be taken to Tinker, an old teammate whom he hadn't seen in years.

When they met near the Senators' dugout, Groh extended his hand and said, "Guess who I am?" Tinker studied his visitor a bit and then delivered his unforgettable reply. "I don't rightly know," he said, "but if you had hair, you little SOB, you'd be Heine Groh."

It was an era when ballplayers spoke for themselves, no agents to arrange their contracts.

Vernon, after winning his second batting title, finally had to settle for a $22,000 salary, a concession by owner Griffith, who often expounded that "no ballplayer should ask for $20,000."

In a later year the Senators brought up pitcher Bobo Newsom from Chattanooga, where he refused to play for Joe Engel, operator of the Senators' farm team there, because of a contract dispute. Newsom claimed that Engel had reneged on a "gentleman's agreement." Engel, on visiting the Senators' camp, rejected that charge with the simple statement: "How could there be a gentleman's agreement, when there were no gentlemen involved?"

Helping to make the living easy in Orlando was Phil Berger's Tav-ern, the home away from home for writers covering the Washington team. The gathering at Berger's was a ritual, and Berger ran an orderly saloon, guarding all doors against pre-Berger inebriates.

Thus it was one night when a chap who already had too many snifters attempted to enter, and he was politely turned away by Berger. Presently, though, he appeared at another entrance leading from the adjoining hotel and was turned away again. Somehow, he found a third entrance leading to the tavern from yet another side. When he was confronted yet again by Berger he was taken aback and blurted, "Geez, do you own every joint in town?"

St. Petersburg was the capital of Florida training camps, for both the Yankees and New York Giants quartered there in separate and plush hotels. It was in St. Pete that Lefty Gomez of the Yankees complained: "They told me to put on 15 pounds and I'd get a better fastball. I did, and now I can't break a pane of glass. I throw harder but the ball wasn't going as fast."

It was in St. Pete that Yankees great Yogi Berra, after bragging to writers how he was taking colored pictures with his new camera, grabbed a passing *New York Mirror* photographer and asked for some information. "Tell me, Joe," he said, "how does white go in color?"

Clustered on the Florida west coast along with the New York teams were the Red Sox in Sarasota, the old Philadelphia A's in Fort Meyer, the White Sox and Reds in Tampa and the Cardinals in Bradenton. It was in Bradenton with its typical old wooden ballpark and rickety wooden press box that the remembered Henry McLemore episode took place.

It was the day the Senators were in Bradenton to play the Cardinals that we encountered McLemore, the splendid baseball writer for the United Press. But now his left arm was being carried in a sling. What happened?

Whereupon McLemore, pointing to the three steps leading to the old press box, said, "That's where it happened. In my time I have fallen three miles drunk. I fall three feet sober and look at the result."

These are memories of those times when spring training was more fun, less structured, more free spirited and more "accessible."

MARCH 10, 1994

Mo Siegel, Storyteller

He walked into my office at *The Washington Post* early in 1946, a shortish, somewhat jaunty young guy who sought a handshake while saying, "Hi. I need a job." The accent was all-Southern, and the rich timbre of it was a bit familiar, but the person wasn't. He was the perfect stranger, claiming some kind of friendship.

Then he said, "I'm Mo Siegel," and that explained everything. He had sensed the confusion. I had never seen him in civilian clothes (this had been World War II time), but now I remembered him as the low-grade seaman at the Norfolk Naval Base who was the only functionary in that whole establishment who knew that we baseball writers in the press box needed somebody to run our copy to Western Union, a most necessary act.

Seaman Siegel attended to this personally, and he also wildly exceeded his authority by rounding up a couple of jeeps to take us places, and also hustled up some grub, Navy-issue. This was 1942, when the Washington Senators, like all other major league teams, were forbidden to go South for spring training under war time measures ("Is this trip necessary?"). So now there was this series of games against the Norfolk Naval Base team, which was loaded with big leaguers in the service.

Siegel, who died yesterday at the age of 78, was our guy. He had impact even then, as he would have in Washington, D.C., for the next 48 years after I hired him on the spot that day he walked into our sports department.

In that era, the hiring was easy. No resumes, no personnel departments where you could cross-check with the past places he worked. You liked the cut of him, you gave him a job. I knew he had hustled. He had worked on newspapers in his native Atlanta and later in Richmond before he enlisted. In Atlanta, on the *Constitution*, he was exposed to the splendid prose of Ralph McGill, the sports editor. Mo knew good writing from bad, or should have.

I hired Mo on faith. It was as simple as that. In later years he would become a much-sought-after speaker and toastmaster and, ever the quipster, he would sometimes say when addressing groups, "Shirley Povich hired me as a sports writer 40 years ago. He should have had a second opinion."

He was restless, but he could write. That was why Mo always found ready employers. He ricocheted from *The Washington Post* to the *Washington Daily News* to the *Washington Star* and lastly the *Washington Times*, the lead sports columnist everywhere he went after leaving the *Post*. Oh, yes, and there were a couple of TV stations thrown in and some radio programs also. For Mo, adapting to the spoken word was a piece of cake. The late Father Hartke, head of the Catholic University drama department, once said of Mo, "With that resonance of voice he was made for the stage."

Who could forget, in Washington's television infancy, Mo refusing to wear one of those clip-on microphones, preferring the bulky radio version right in front of his mouth. Or the Christmas Eve nearly 50 years ago when he went on, perhaps with too much holiday cheer to suit management, when a taped version might have saved him from his bosses. But that was Mo.

He was our man about town. He shuttled between the noted restaurants, lunch at Duke Zeibert's, dinner at the Palm, storyteller and magnate for audiences everywhere he went. For years he occupied the same front table at Duke's, and when one patron asked, icily, "You here again?" Mo's rebuke was quick: "Yeah, I don't like to eat out."

His wit was also in evidence that Super Bowl day in Houston in 1974 when Mo and Pulitzer Prize winner Red Smith were trying to make their way to the press box against the crush of fans. "Make way, please," Mo was repeating. "Between us we have won a Pulitzer."

Mo was competitive in a competitive business, and while he'd do anything for a story, he helped many a young sportswriter find his or her way. He greatly admired the new breed of sports journalists, but couldn't understand why they all had to go home three hours before closing time.

Mo Siegel was a figure not only in Washington. He was almost as well-known in Las Vegas, in New York and Los Angeles and elsewhere, a favorite character in their press boxes and habitué of their nightspots, always with a retinue that sought his happy company.

No important sports event escaped Mo's word processor. He was there for all the big fights, the World Series, the Masters, the big football games, the Super Bowl, and he could paint word pictures. His contacts were vast and useful. He was the only sportswriter who was a confidante of Redskins owner Jack Kent Cooke.

Above all, this was a nice guy. Too bad he died yesterday. More than Myra and Leah and Michael will miss him. Like myself, so many others will feel deprived.

JUNE 3, 1994

For Years, the Game Changed

Now, It Has Stopped

Now baseball's longest unbroken streak has ended. It is reckoned not in terms of hits or homers or games, but in years. It can be accurately described in baseball's jargon as 89-for-89.

For the first time since 1904, there will be no World Series in the land. It was in that distant year when President Teddy Roosevelt was trying to stop the Russo-Japanese War, eight years before the Titanic hit the iceberg, that World Series history drew a blank.

For those 89 years the continuity of the World Series was a given in the American character, rooted in the love of the game from generation to generation. But it's a wipeout now that the club owners and the athletes refused to terminate their choke hold on the game.

Baseball has been gasping for a breath for the 35 days since the players struck, walked, on August 12—their strategy to beat the specter of a salary cap by the owners in 1995. The consequence: 1994 is fated to join 1904 as a sorry landmark year for baseball, stained by the emptiness at World Series time.

For widely different reasons those two years—1904 and 1994—are devoid of a World Series. In 1904 it was obstinacy that canceled the postseason game—John Tomlinson Brush, owner of the New York Giants, did not like Ban Johnson, president of the upstart American League, and refused to play Boston in the World Series.

All of this, despite the fact that the two leagues had reached agreement in 1903 and staged a World Series that year between Boston and Pittsburgh. But Brush never forgave Ban Johnson for invading National League territory with AL franchises. He and his manager, John McGraw, who also had had his run-ins with Johnson, resisted the urging of the Giants' players, who wanted the World Series money, so 1904 was left as a blank in World Series history.

Oh, yes, the pennant-winning Boston team in 1904 was not the Boston Red Sox, as they are now known. They were the Boston Pilgrims, who operated under that name until they became the Red Stockings in 1907 and the Red Sox two years later.

Under pressure, Brush relented in 1905 and consented to let his pennant-winning team play the Philadelphia A's in the World Series, which has continued ever since. It was the year Christy Mathewson made World Series history by pitching three winning games against the A's.

For baseball, the heavy irony now is that it is presenting itself as an ugly, strife-torn business at a time when baseball, the game, is on the brink of receiving probably its greatest salute ever as America's game, its supreme tribute in the century-and-a-half of its history.

This is the upcoming Ken Burns 18 1/2–hour TV documentary "Baseball" that exalts the game as a near-religion and passion in the genealogy of America. Did you care for Ken Burns's riveting treatment of the Civil War, his documentary that has become historic? Then you'll *qvell* at his delineation of baseball as an important facet of Americana.

It is the season when baseball should be reveling in its recognition as a game that surpasses all others. But this is the year that those in baseball are beset by bitter conflict, by their own choice, mostly the owners' choice with their insistence on introducing the hated "salary cap" factor, diverting fan interest from the most exciting season in many years.

Although it is the players who struck, it is the owners who provoked the now-situation with their dratted salary cap postulation. They have also introduced other new words into baseball's lexicon like "cost certainty" and "cost containment," all of them their whining complaints about their high payrolls, which they created themselves by wildly bidding against each other for the game's talent. They weren't thinking then of "cost restraint."

It's the salary cap, though, that has enraged the players and brought about their walkout. They have noted its curse on football payrolls, which has called for lesser-paid players to give back part of their salaries to accommodate the club's signing of more costly players and still stay within the salary cap limits. In the baseball players' view, the football players were stupid to accept a salary cap and they want none of it.

Their strike was timed, strategically, while they still had more than a half year's pay in their pocket, to counter the threat of a lockout by the owners come spring training in 1995, before the players' paychecks begin and the rent comes due.

They timed their strike, too, to scare the owners into line for fear of missing their big bundle in playoff and World Series TV revenues. But it didn't work; the owners are toughing it out. This strike has been festering for seven months, marked by little if any input from Bud Selig, who distanced himself from the whole business and has earned the new title of non-acting acting commissioner. The upshot: no World Series at all. Damn it.

SEPTEMBER 15, 1994

Mantle's Critics Swing, Miss

Writers Lack Compassion, Appreciation of His Career

The stories haven't been fair to Mickey Mantle. Here the poor guy is, in deep crisis in a Dallas hospital; one of the greatest ballplayers of all time, badly diseased and with death's door ajar, and relying now on the last roll of the dice, a liver transplant that may or may not work. Often it doesn't.

And what is being said about him? That he was one of the biggest baseball drunks of all time, and yes, he was not always friendly to kids, including his own, and he did louse up his family somewhat and — draw your own conclusions — he wasn't a nice guy. In other words, what a bum, they said.

That was the drift of so much written about him. The shame here, and the regret, is that two of the many borderline to-hell-with-Mickey Mantle pieces appeared consecutively in *The Washington Post*. Why?

Why at this time dwell on the dark side of Mickey Mantle, particularly since he had denied none of this in a full confession of his career weaknesses and misbehavior in a *Sports Illustrated* article last year? He hadn't ducked it. It wasn't exactly news anymore after his own bare-all gutsy admissions.

Where was the appreciation of Mickey Mantle's exciting contributions to the game on the playing field, particularly his eminence with his bat with all those pennant-winning Yankees teams? His many spectacular deeds that made him a super performer for most of 20 years are rating no priority for those writers who denounced his drunken binges.

And now the talk shows and others have made a big deal of the preference Mantle got on the waiting list for a liver transplant; how they promoted him to the top of the list. Ye Gods, did Mickey have anything to do with that? Was this desperately sick man able to prevail on his doctors and the whole organ transplant apparatus to jump in front of the others? At this point Mickey was virtually on life support.

It was long known that country boy Mickey Mantle couldn't cope with life in the Yankees fast lane in matters not connected with his bat or his glove; he never was an intellectual giant.

Let me repeat the lead on a story I wrote for the *Saturday Evening Post* issue of Feb. 2, 1957:

On that April 1 day in 1951 when Mickey Mantle arrived in New York for the first time he was an unsmiling and suspicious 19-year-old who detrained from the South with the rest of the New York Yankees. And already he was being acclaimed as the new wonder boy of the Yankees, called up from Joplin, Mo., where he hit .383 with 26 big home runs. . . .

But the rookie was also remembering bits of a going-away advice he had from home folks in Commerce, Okla.: "The big city is full of traps for country boys," they told him. "Don't talk to strangers."

Yet one week later in a New York hotel lobby there was this man saying he could help Mantle get very rich from endorsements and personal appearances. Then Mickey bought what was a version of the Brooklyn Bridge reincarnate. He signed his name to a curious document in which he acquired 50 percent of himself. The other 50 percent of his earnings outside of his baseball salary was delegated to his personal representative.

Mickey was years getting unhooked from that one.

In a later year Mickey Mantle bought 100 shares in an Oklahoma insurance company at a cost of $3,500. But the company had one glaring weakness. It was nonexistent, and Mantle again was the chump. All of this is being noted to record that Mantle was often afflicted with an economy of good judgment that led him into so much of his *tsoris*.

I was Mickey Mantle's friend. We golfed. As a baseball beat writer I traveled with him on those Yankees trains in the years of all those pennants. I knew his weaknesses, and it often came through that he did want to be a nice person. I knew his drinking companions—among them Whitey Ford and Billy Martin.

Unlike Mantle, the country boy from small-town Oklahoma, they didn't fall into the same prolonged traps that captured Mickey. Whitey Ford and Billy Martin had the city smarts. Unlike Mickey, they were aware the drinking was not a way of life, to begin the next binge before Bacchus was back in the bottle. They could quit, he couldn't and would pay for it dearly. Mickey Mantle had given all of the writers and columnists so much to write about in his 18 years with the Yankees. Why didn't it occur to them to emphasize that for 18 years this guy who won so many games for the Yankees, who hit the ball farther than all the players of history except Babe Ruth, was baseball's rare example of physical courage.

For 18 years, he played hurt. In deep pain. Consider it.

Not a day when he took his glove to center field or his bat to the plate that Mickey Mantle was not spavined by one damaged knee or the other, or by a formerly broken foot that visited him with some old pains, or by a calf that was ripped on a high school football field back in Oklahoma. Another of his companions was the gnarled hamstring, almost ever-present. He had that arrested case of osteomyelitis that set in early in his career but kept breaking jail.

To understand how much Mantle was contorted by pain, yet kept playing, is to listen to the medical report of the Yankees' team physician, Sidney Gaynor:

"1951, right knee cartilage operation; 1952, right knee again; 1954, knee cyst removed; 1955, pulled groin muscle; 1956, left knee sprained; 1957, right shoulder injury; 1959, broken finger; 1961, hip abscess; 1962, left knee injury; 1963, broken metatarsal bone left foot; 1965, right shoulder surgery, right elbow and left knee injuries."

Also for more than the last 10 years Mickey played with elastic bandages wrapped around his right leg from mid-calf to upper thigh, and in the last few years he wrapped his left leg in the same way for support.

Gaynor was asked whether Mickey was "brittle."

"No. It was just the demands he made on himself. He wanted to play every day and he'd minimize things to get to play."

Didn't some of this deserve mention in the hour of Mantle's des-

peration to stay alive, ahead of all the carping about his longtime battle with the bottle? So many of his injuries were by invitation, his
own, so great were these surges he gave to the game while running
down fly balls, or chugging from the batter's box to first base in 3.1 seconds, a landmark clocking.

He could run. That was an anomaly. When did it ever happen,
before Mantle, that the biggest hitter on any team, the guy who hit the
farthest in the league, was also the fastest man on his team and its best
bunter? Never.

A Mantle specialty was the drag bunt that let him break from the
left side of the plate. The drag bunt is an art of the game and none
captured it like Mickey. You lay it down to a spot that gives both the
pitcher and the first baseman a fit. Who fields it? No matter. They
wouldn't get Mickey, who was already surging toward the bag.

When did Mickey Mantle bunt? Whenever he felt like it. From
Casey Stengel he had a blank check. Bunt when you feel like it. Drag
bunting on the count of 3 and 2 when a foul tip would get you out was
rejected as a tactic until Mantle made it one of his specialties. You
could do it if you had Mickey's supreme ability to do it.

Could Mantle play the outfield? When Joe DiMaggio quit and
Mickey took over in center field there was no lowering of standards.
What a compliment. Maybe he didn't quite have DiMag's arm, but he
had more than Joe's speed. He, too, could outrun a fly ball.

For many years a thought has occurred to me. I covered Willie
Mays's great catch of that steamer Vic Wertz hit in the 1954 World
Series. Mays took one look at that zinger toward deepest center in the
Polo Grounds, turned and caught up with the ball and speared it with
his back to the plate, a wondrous catch. Who else could have made it?
Mickey Mantle. Many years ago on the pro golf tour there was a
player of some prominence named Bo Wininger. Because I learned
he had played football and baseball on the same high school team
with Mantle in Oklahoma, I asked him about Mickey. "Gawd, he was
fast," said Wininger. "Mickey ran on top of the grass."

I saw an example of that in 1956 in Yankee Stadium the day hell

froze over and Don Larsen pitched a perfect game in the World
Series. There would have been no perfect 2–0 game for Larsen without what Mantle did to Gil Hodges's line drive that was headed to the
empty reaches in left-center. That ball was certain to fall in until a flying Mantle reached the scene from nowhere and speared it back-
handed. Larsen should have blown him a kiss.

What a luck-ridden club the Yankees were to have a switch hitter
such as Mantle. No way to pitch around him. He hit those 536 home
runs, but more spectacularly he hit 18 more in World Series games to
beat Babe Ruth's record.

It is not remembered that there were any miniature home runs by
Mantle. That ferocious swing from either side of the plate would not
permit the cheap homer. He was the man who came closer than anybody else to hitting a fair ball out of vast, rearing Yankee Stadium. He
missed against Kansas City's Bill Fischer in 1963 when his swat failed
by inches to clear the facade and everything else in right-center. One
scientist said that ball might have gone 620 feet. Before that he barely
missed against the Senators' Pete Ramos.

And of course there was the history-maker that day in Griffith Stadium in 1954 when Chuck Stobbs threw that pitch and Mantle swatted
it a measured 565 feet onto the street beyond the left-center bleachers.
My god, nobody before him had ever put one out of the park over
those bleachers stretching from the left field foul line to deepest center.

I asked the Senators' owner, Clark Griffith, for his comment on
that swat, suggesting also that a slight wind was blowing that day. His
answer was conclusive: "I don't care about that. That consarned wind
has been blowing for 100 years and nobody else ever hit one out of this
ballpark like that."

Why didn't they write about things like that, or about the wonderful, the distinctive feats of the boy from Oklahoma who was the seventh player in history (other than the original inductees) to make it to
the Hall of Fame on the first ballot? As a person he was not all bad. He
was shy, and comfortable only with his friends. Some years ago when
the Alexandria Grandstand Managers club invited him to appear as

an honored guest, he agreed with a stipulation. He said he would be there if I was the master of ceremonies. He wanted a friend in view. If Mantle wasn't quite as shy as DiMaggio it was nevertheless a tight fit. It could be pointed out that Mickey was less disagreeable than shy.

He hit the golf ball a ton. The power that sped all those homers to uncharted distances could be imagined on the golf course. But he bemoaned his short game. That was the day he checked into the Yankees' Fort Lauderdale clubhouse for spring training, greeting me with, "Hi ya, Shirley, how you hitting? Let's play."

Now I am talking to one of the great men of baseball, who, with 60,000 fans in the park, the bases full, bottom of the ninth, the count 3 and 2, is the calmest guy in the place.

But Mantle is saying, "I'm hitting the ball but I can't score." I asked him why he wasn't scoring and he said, "It's my putting. Hell, Shirley, I'm gutless." It was a commentary both on golf and Mantle's self-demeaning modesty.

Why didn't they write about his magnanimity toward teammate Roger Maris when in 1961 they were both trying to break Babe Ruth's record? When he fell behind Maris it was Mantle who led the cheers for his teammate, willing to stand for all those friendly poses with Maris and smiling his friendship for the man winning the race. Who could say those smiles were phony? Not from an uncalculating, uninhibited Mickey Mantle, incapable of jealousy.

Or they could have written about Mickey and his gallant, gutsy performance that day in a Fort Lauderdale hotel when after reporting for spring training he suddenly announced it was no use anymore and said he was retiring.

He made it a bare-bones announcement, leading off with "I can't play anymore and I know it." I don't have my notes of that March 1, 1969, scene in the Yankee Clipper hotel but I have those of *St. Louis Post-Dispatch* Hall of Fame writer Bob Broeg. More from Mickey: "I'm not going to play any more baseball. I was really going to try but I didn't think I could. . . . I have had three or four bad years in a row and have received my biggest disappointment by falling under .300

[.298 career average] and I was actually dreading another season."

Also: "I can't hit. . . . I can't go from first to third when I want to. I can't steal second when I want to. . . . I can't score from second when I want to . . . these things break me up and I figure it's best for the team that I stop now." With that statement Mantle showed quality. There was a temptation here to say that he showed class, but remembered is the caution of *Post* writer Myra McPherson, who rebuked those who use that bromide, saying that "those who use 'class' don't have much."

Mickey talked about steals, but he never stole with much frequency. On the Yankees in those years there were too many guys to knock you around—DiMaggio, Hank Bauer, Yogi Berra, Tommy Henrich, Roger Maris, Gil McDougald. Stealing was not a big thing with the Yankees.

But Mickey did hang up those great batting averages of .365, .353 and .321 plus a career slugging average of .557. He was a big league star before he was 21.

During the Mantle years none in baseball could match him for distance. Four times he led the league in homers. They voted him the league's MVP three times, three times he finished second.

With Mantle back in the news as a very sick man, why did they not write of his many feats and his dauntless physical courage? They also could have said something about Mickey Mantle and Lou Gehrig, who is now causing such a hoo-rah with Cal Ripken bearing down on Lou's magnificent record of playing 2,130 consecutive games.

But Lou Gehrig does not hold the record of playing more games than anybody else in Yankee pinstripes. Who does? Mickey Mantle. More than Gehrig, more than Ruth, more than any other Yankee. None can match Mantle's 2,401 games in those pinstripes.

Was this not worthy of note when Mantle bounced back in the news last week, a very sick man with his life at high risk? Whatever happened to sentiments and judgments in our business? How did we get trapped in that mentality of the checkout racks? When are they going to call off the dogs? It's time.

JUNE 19, 1995

Ripken Breaks Gehrig's Record

Povich covered many of Lou Gehrig's games, including his farewell appearance at Yankee Stadium in 1939. He also covered Cal Ripken's breaking of Gehrig's consecutive game streak of 2,132 on September 6, 1995 at Camden Yards, one of the few people—and probably the only sportswriter—to be in the park at both events. Comparing the two ball players the night before the game, Povich wrote, "In truth, when measured against Cal Ripken, Lou Gehrig was much the better ballplayer, one who had a greater impact on the game. He was more famed for his bat than is Ripken for his glove. It was recently noted that Ripken has hit more home runs than any shortstop who ever lived. Interesting. Also interesting, Gehrig hit 170 more home runs than Ripken."

Beyond the Feat, Ripken Fills Gehrig's Shoes

Four hundred twenty five miles from Baltimore, in Boston's Fenway Park, there erupted on Wednesday night a noisy, five-minute ovation for Cal Ripken. The scoreboard there had just flashed the news: Lou Gehrig's consecutive-games record was history. Long Live Cal Ripken, and the new number is 2,131.

The cheering in Boston was only a symbol of the scope of the boon to baseball generated by Ripken's heroics, 13 years in the making. With the possible exception of Babe Ruth, has any one player had more impact on the game than Ripken with his assault on Gehrig's record of 56 years? For years, any challenge of such was derided as a fool's errand. But last year, Ripken brought it into his sights and this season he drew a bead on it.

So what would have otherwise been an ordinary Sept. 6 game between the Orioles and California Angels at Camden Yards took on the dimensions of an epic. The swarm of media rivaled—and may have exceeded—the coverage of a World Series game. The presence of the president of the United States was obligatory. The networks vied for positions for their camera crews. Baseball was back in the nation's limelight. Cal Ripken was going for the record. This would be historic, and it was.

The Orioles were providing their own army of public relations staffers for this event, to caress and provide for every need of the mass media. Available within reach of everybody were carefully placed reams of Ripken and Orioles data, biographical, statistical and more.

If they can muster a shred of decency, the lords of organized baseball should bow deeply in obeisance and gratitude for the deeds of Ripken, this extraordinary man who broke the extraordinary record of Gehrig's.

Organized baseball got luckier than it deserved in the emergence of Ripken as a savior of much of the game's charms. In a year when major league baseball has few friends, when boycott is in the air and attendance is down 20 percent; when some franchises are a wreck; when fans are soured at the greed of club owners and players alike; when the players struck and walked out on the owners, with both factions united only in their public-be-damned stance, Ripken came riding in from the east as The Peace Maker who brings fans back to the game.

Not by his super play alone or by his work ethic has Ripken renewed America's interest in baseball. The nation found a new interest in the man himself, who exemplifies the family values that politicos only talk about; who dedicated himself to making friends with the fans, so important to the game, a rebuke to overpaid colleagues who had no time for such; who, when the question was put to him point blank the other day, responded modestly that "Lou Gehrig was a better ballplayer than I am."

By acclamation, Ripken has won approval as a hero and role model. In Gehrig's day there were heroes, like himself and Babe Ruth, but folks didn't talk of role models and, anyway, they would have been hard to find. So many, like Ruth, were flawed, so many like

Gehrig were nice guys but absorbed mostly in baseball with little time
for the community.

For all his fame, Cal Ripken is homespun. On the morning of the
day he would go for the record he said it was important, too, that he
take his daughter Rachel, 5, to her first day in school. When the
cheers in Camden Yards were at their loudest—"We want Cal!"—he
asked for his mom and dad to come onto the field to share them.
When he got those eight curtain calls and he took that victory lap
around the park, he tried to shake every hand offered him. He was
being more than cheered. This was adoration.

If there has been any complaint about Ripken as a ballplayer, it
has to do with his sometime propensity for hitting into double plays.
But that has been the curse of all hard hitters whose ground balls get
to the infielders so speedily. In that respect, Ripken is also the victim

Baltimore Orioles star Cal Ripken honors
Povich's 75 years at The Post. *(1997)*

of the level swing, so prized by batting coaches, and the gospel for most batsmen. In that matter, there is a center of some prominence, name of Ted Williams, highest connoisseur of bat and ball. Williams has his own theory—oft expressed in words like "[Damn] the level swing. You've got to swing a little bit up."

It was fascinating also on Wednesday night when Ripken topped off his record-breaking act by hitting that home run in the fourth inning. In that episode, he, like the complete ballplayer he is, selected the 3–0 pitch, which offered the most home run possibilities. He knows when to be an opportunist.

The late Lou Gehrig would probably be abashed at the news that Ripken had successfully attacked his endurance record. But he would probably be more shocked to learn that a breakdown over Ripken's salary says he is paid $47,000 a game to perform for the Orioles. At the peak of his career, Gehrig drew a salary of $37,000 for the entire season. The sign of those times, and these.

SEPTEMBER 8, 1995

Not All Comebacks Are Magical

The comeback has been a staple of history ever since that phoenix bird of legend rose from its own ashes to rejoin its kind. The sports pages have been saturated with stories of the comeback, in this sport or that, by individuals trying to relive it up.

Magic Johnson is merely the latest to disavow retirement and return to the wars, his being basketball. He has, as an immediate example, a return to the game by Michael Jordan, a mere two-year retiree who has meshed so well with the Chicago Bulls that they are the class of the league.

Magic was no less a dominant player and crowd hero, but four years away from the game? It speaks of basketball as distinguished from baseball, which would regard that long a retiree as a loony bird if he tried to return to the game.

Even as Jordan's successful return to basketball stands as a goal for Johnson, it also underscores the skills of the two games. Jordan, a superb athlete, quit basketball to give baseball a try and it was a disaster. He should have heeded Ted Williams's dictate that "hitting a well-pitched ball is the toughest thing in sports"—this from the player who did it better than any other of modern times.

Even in the minor leagues, Jordan's try at becoming a professional baseball player was a complete misadventure. In the field he was passable, but even minor league pitching exposed him as a feeble batsman. So, back to basketball.

There have been no notable comebacks in baseball. And none much remembered in basketball except in the case of Jordan and Magic. Football? Too rugged a game to permit a comeback. Boxing, ha! That's the game in which the comeback has been such a regularity the phrase is now mainly associated with boxing.

Baseball players know there is no return to the game for them when the tyrant of age has diminished their skills. They knew when to call it quits forever—Babe Ruth, Joe DiMaggio, Williams, Ty Cobb, Walter Johnson and all the others. They would not risk disgracing themselves by playing the game too long, and knowing that unlike basketball one misplay by a ballplayer, one insufficiency, could cost his team the game. DiMaggio won't even suit up for those old-timers games.

Pride has always been a factor with baseball players. Cobb quit, at 41, after hitting a decent .323 for the Philadelphia A's but that number was intolerable to a man who had a .367 career average. Mention of Cobb recalls the 1961 colloquy of Yogi Berra that went like this: "How much do you think Ty Cobb would hit against today's pitching?" . . . "Oh, about .250." . . . "Is that all?" . . . "Well, remember that Cobb is at least 70 years old."

However, in boxing, the comeback is almost the norm and has produced too many sorry tales, too many cruel endings. Scarcely a heavyweight champion has not attempted it. The two notable exceptions were Gene Tunney and Rocky Marciano. Tunney pocketed $990,000 for his second fight with Jack Dempsey in 1927, then married an heiress and had no more need of boxing's bounty. Marciano, unbeaten in all his 49 fights, had some wealth and saw no more fields to conquer.

Anent the Marciano retirement I was palavering with Ted Williams behind the batting cage in Fenway Park the day the newspapers announced it. "Too bad," said Williams. Why so bad? Williams, a bug on statistics who always knew how many homers or runs batted in he needed to tie a record, said, "He should have fought one more fight. Fifty for 50 would have looked better in the book."

In most of their comebacks, boxing's old champions had answered too many gongs. Dempsey and Joe Louis were reduced to fighting palookas in their comeback years before both of them went into that lowest of careers, refereeing wrestling bouts.

After losing his title to Ezzard Charles, Louis retired, then came back to fight eight times before he encountered Marciano at Madison Square Garden. There he suffered the final indignity—knocked clear out of the ring by Marciano, a humbling experience. He wound up subsisting mostly on the handouts of gamblers in the Vegas hotels, where Joe had the honorary title of "greeter."

Sad, too, was the denouement of the great Muhammad Ali. In his last comeback against former sparring partner Larry Holmes, Ali wasn't even a ghost of his former self. Ringsiders were asking the referees to stop it as an act of mercy by the fourth round. The ref finally did in the 11th. But Ali would be remembered for that cruel spectacle.

Even Sugar Ray Robinson, greatest of them all, couldn't surmount the comeback curse. He announced his retirement in 1952 and opted for a career as a song and dance man. But he missed the big paydays of boxing and put away his dancing pumps to go back to the ring. He was still fighting at the age of 44 but he was a sorry sight. The boxer who had lost only three of his first 330 fights was beaten five times in his last 10, by some tomato cans he would once have blown out of the ring.

The most illogical and at the same time most fascinating of boxing's comebacks is that of George Foreman. Out of boxing for 10 years and discredited when he did quit, he promoted himself to big money even as an oversized 270-pounder who padded around the ring like a sleep-walking elephant, knocking out a long series of palookas. He is still functioning, sometimes at $10 million a fight, a product of pay-TV.

Sugar Ray Leonard holds the record for comebacks, four or five, depending on who's counting. He did have two glorious comeback fights, beating Marvin Hagler and fighting a draw with Tommy Hearns. But his returns to the ring were not without cost. In 1984 he was dumped on his rump by a mere novice named Kevin Howard, and later another palooka, Donny Lalonde, also splattered him to the floor. A one-sided, bloody defeat against Terry Norris ended Leonard's career. Like so many others, Leonard would learn that comebacks were not easy. They had their price, so often not a pretty one.

FEBRUARY 3, 1996

Jimmy the Greek

Jimmy the Greek, gambler-turned-oddsmaker-turned-TV-football-personality, credited Povich with launching his success. That success quickly went to the Greek's head, Povich reminded his readers from time to time. But when Jimmy, who had fallen from grace, died, Povich, who could have piled on, was kind.

It was in 1970 that the late Howard Simons, the managing editor of *The Washington Post*, walked into the office of the sports editor (me) and said, "There's a syndicate salesman in my office trying to peddle [Ben] Bradlee and me a feature on the football point spreads. What's your idea about this?"

"My idea is that it's a lot of bunkeroo," I said. "They got some wise guy somewhere trying to sell us a lot of predictions that our own staff can do better. It's the kind of boilerplate stuff we don't need in this newspaper."

"Good," said Simons, "we'll brush him off, him and his Jimmy the Greek stuff."

"Hold it," I said. "Did you say Jimmy the Greek? That's different. I know the guy. He's a pro, who's been making the odds for those casinos in Vegas. Besides, if we pass on the Greek, the *Evening Star* would probably snap him up. They're making a big pitch for their sports pages. We could use Jimmy the Greek."

About 50 times since then, or maybe only 40, Jimmy the Greek said to me, "*The Washington Post* launched me. You're my friend forever." He said the *Post*'s endorsement had meant so much. Two hundred other newspapers would sign on for the Greek's point-spread column.

We didn't exactly launch the Greek. He had been a figure in Las Vegas as a high-profile public relations man for the Howard Hughes hotel enterprises. Jimmy, with his trend for the flamboyant, once said of Howard Hughes, "When he issues a check, the bank bounces."

Jimmy liked to say he was a reformed gambler, but he was not. That was his pose. He frequented every racetrack within a day's journey and awaited the result of each race with a batch of tickets he could scarcely fit into one palm. If anybody believed that the Greek didn't take a fling at a passel of those point spreads he dealt with, then he has implicit credence in the tooth fairy.

Jimmy liked to say that Bobby Kennedy drove him out of the gambling business when brother Jack, the president, appointed him attorney general. "When Bobby Kennedy got the law passed saying it was legal to tap those phones and make a felony of cross-state bets, I decided that at 43, I didn't want to go to jail for a phone call, and I quit." Oh yeah?

When Jimmy Snyder died Sunday in Las Vegas at age 77, of a heart condition, it was retold that when he came out of Steubenville, Ohio, as a Greek kid named Emetrios Synodinos, he was already a

teenaged gambler eyeing Las Vegas. In Steubenville, betting on baseball, football and horse racing was so commonplace Snyder once said,
"I was 21 years old before I realized that gambling was illegal."

This was of a piece with a remembered remark by Billy Conn the
boxer, who grew up in a tough neighborhood in Pittsburgh where, he
said, corrupt police shook down saloon owners for "protection
money." Conn would later say, "I was 20 years old before I learned the
police were paid by the city."

The Greek branched into politics with his election predictions and
his own polling staff, achieving success when columnist Jack Anderson's
syndicate put him in 700 newspapers, with Anderson's explanation: "I
prefer the Greek's predictions over the Gallup and Harris polls."

And at a time when the National Football League was bemoaning
the prevalence of the point spreads in newspapers, Snyder flew into
the face of the NFL on CBS's "The NFL Today," the Sunday pregame
show that featured his predictions on a panel with Brent Musburger
and Phyllis George.

The Greek dressed with flamboyance, reached for checks of
friends he saw at distant tables in restaurants. He clashed with both
Musburger and George, claiming he was denied proper air time, and
he took a punch at Musburger in an East Side New York restaurant,
relative to that subject.

They claimed they made up, the two of them. But there was evidence that this, too, was a pose by Snyder, inasmuch as one day when
a friend said, "I had lunch with Musburger yesterday," the Greek said.
"Did he tell you how bright he was?"

His whole world and his $200,000 a year job with CBS collapsed
that day in 1988 when confronted by a television interviewer in Washington's Duke Zeibert's restaurant, he discussed the seeming superiority of black athletes over white athletes.

During the Civil War, "the slave owner would breed his big black
with his big woman so that he would have a big black kid," Snyder
said during the interview. A black athlete was better than a white one,
according to Snyder, because "he's been bred to be that way because

of his thigh size and big size." Bigger thighs? How did this occur to Snyder? George Vecsey of the *New York Times* called it "the Jimmy the Greek School of Genetics."

Obviously, the Greek had learned nothing from Al Campanis's remarks the year before about blacks lacking the "necessities" to be major league managers, for which the Dodgers summarily fired him. Snyder could not resist his habit of pontificating.

I did learn to respect the Greek for his contacts. One week it came up in the Redskins vs. the Giants, but with Fran Tarkenton, the Giants quarterback, in the hospital from injuries, and a likely noncompetitor, I phoned Jimmy, asking, "Will Tarkenton play?"

The Greek said, "I'll call you back." He did, saying, "Tarkenton will not only play, he'll start." I asked, "How do you know this?" He said, "I just talked to him." I said. "In the hospital?" He said, "Yes, in the hospital." The Greek was correct.

He did indeed have his sources that were always factored into those Jimmy the Greek point spreads.

APRIL 23, 1996

Mike Tyson

It was on the record that Mike Tyson was a boyhood thief, a purse snatcher and reform school inmate; a street brawler, an abuser of women and convicted rapist and grown-up inmate of an Indiana prison for three years. But until last Saturday night it was unknown that he was also a cannibal, with a fondness for an opponent's ears, both of them.

In the history of boxing, there could have been no more hideous or repulsive spectacle than the scene in Round 3 in that Las Vegas ring: a hurt and confounded Evander Holyfield, his blood running red right down the length of his body, was in a stagger and a wonder at the ungodly turn the fight had taken. (My God, he bit me twice.)

It was hardly accidental, what with Tyson deliberately shedding his mouthpiece before the round, the better to chomp a chunk out of one of Holyfield's ears, or both, whenever the opportunity presented. It did, when the two of them fell into a clinch and man-eater Tyson nudged his mouth straight up Holyfield's neck to ear-biting position and bit. He got a piece off the top of the right ear and spat it out. He also got a warning from referee Mills Lane that it had cost him two points, and one more act like that would cost him the fight.

Then, in the final seconds of the round, Tyson went cannibalistic again, getting Holyfield's left ear and proving only that he could switch ears. And so, end of fight, with Holyfield headed for the hospital and Tyson headed for who knows where after this night of his infamy.

Not only was it a cruel thing that Tyson did, it was stupid. In that third round, after losing the first two, he began indicating he might turn the fight around. And then he blew it. All those weeks and months of comeback training, all those return-to-the-championship visions, sacrificed for some kind of primitive vengeance against the man who was beating him. How did he think he could get away with it? The jerk.

Tyson's limp excuse for his mangling of Holyfield's ears was that he was getting even for the head butts by Holyfield that opened a dangerous cut above Tyson's right eye. But there is no comparison. The crash of heads involves two fighters and always raises the question of who butted whom. To bite an ear needs the firm resolve of only one fighter.

Tyson could have no complaint with the referee. The man who disqualified him was Tyson's choice, Lane, who made the right call.

Tyson's attitude before the fight could have been tell-tale. In interviews, it was clear that he was feeling sorry for himself. "I've been taken advantage of all my life," he told reporters. Not quite true, perhaps. Inasmuch as he was living in a society that provided him with two mansions, a huge farm and countless Mercedes and BMWs. And his $30 million paydays could hardly be considered a disadvantage. All that self-pity, for what?

On Monday, Tyson read an apology "to the world." Said he was sorry and all that and asked for forgiveness. He said he respected Holyfield and that he "snapped." (Twice.) And that he was now asking for some mental help for himself. That he needs it is patent. But like so many others have done, he was also copping a plea, plus the old tired one of "Let's get this behind us." That's what they all say as if it could be so easily dismissed—let's get this thing behind us. Just forget it ever happened.

And of course they are now asking the question, a fatuous one: How will this affect boxing? And the answer is not at all. Boxing has survived mob control, Sonny Liston, Jake LaMotta and Don King and all the mismatches for which Tyson is famous, in which his opponents barely survived the handshake. Sure, it's a sleazy business, but it nevertheless has appeal and has had many lives.

Ferdie Pacheco, for years Muhammad Ali's doctor and a longtime observer and keen analyst of title fights, has suggested that this is not the end of Tyson's career. Pacheco took boxing's practical view of the episode, saying, "Where there is big money, there is big forgiveness."

Again, how will the ugly scene affect boxing? That should not be the prevailing question at this time. More to the point is another question: Will Tyson's next opponent be wearing earmuffs? It is recommended.

JULY 3, 1997

Ben Hogan: Obsessed with Perfection

In his own mind there was yet a need to conquer the game he dominated for so many years. Ben Hogan, golf's leading money-winner in 1942 and 1943, beseeched his friend Jimmy Demaret to "teach me your fade." As Demaret related it to me, he told Hogan, "Dammit, Ben, you're winning everything on the tour and you're never satisfied. Mine is a natural fade. You don't need it." He spent an hour teaching Hogan to master the fade. Hogan did.

That's what the game meant to Ben Hogan, who died yesterday at the age of 84: perfection, a subject for constant study. He once said, "Every year, we learn more about golf. It is like medicine and other fields of science." He dissected the golf swing. He couldn't wait for sun-up to get out on the course to test his theories. In his hotel rooms, he practiced his swing before full-length mirrors. "He had the mind of a golf scientist," Herbert Warren Wind wrote.

It earned him the appellation of golf robot, his reticent demeanor on the links mistaken for aloofness. But Demaret, an old friend from their caddie days, attempted to explode this image of Hogan as a detached "loner," saying, "He talks to me on every green. He always says, 'You're away.'"

They grew up together in the caddie yards where the pay was 65 cents for an 18-hole round. Hogan was the son of a Dublin, Tex., blacksmith and on occasion they would steal off in Demaret's jalopy to play in tournaments in other cities, where the winner could take home $100. "Sometimes we would run out of gas," Demaret said, "but that was no problem. I spotted cars that maybe could provide me with some fuel." Somewhat appalled, I said, "You mean you used a siphon?" and Demaret said, "We called it our Oklahoma credit card."

In February of 1949, the entire country was rooting for Ben Hogan, but not because of his golf game. Driving from Phoenix to their home in Fort Worth with his wife, Valerie, a skidding bus suddenly crossed into their lane. Before the crash, Hogan flung himself in front of Valerie, who suffered only minor injuries. Hogan? Double fracture of the pelvis, broken collarbone, left ankle and right rib.

Would Ben Hogan play golf again? Within six months, in an incredible comeback that aroused the admiration of the nation, Hogan came back on his faltering legs and tied Sam Snead in the Los Angeles Open. It mattered little to his fans that he lost the playoff. But five months later, there he was at Merion, Pa., for the U.S. Open, throwing a 69 at Lloyd Mangrum and George Fazio that got him into a playoff that he won with a stiff-legged round of 69.

From there on, it was noticed that Ben Hogan was back. No matter that his step was slowed and he was never free from pain. And he began carving his niche for all time, by winning the first of his Masters titles in 1953. Still owning that grooved Hogan swing, he mopped up in The Masters, the British Open and U.S. Open, leaving the golfing world to wonder if there was ever a more accomplished practitioner of the game. It was at Carnoustie, in Scotland, that the gallery noticed his absorption into every shot at hand by naming him "The Wee Ice Mon."

There is a question whether anybody contributed more to analyzing the golf swing than Hogan, who in writing "The Fundamentals of the Game," confessed that he adapted his own swing from his constant studies of the newsreels that sometimes showed the likes of Walter Hagen, Gene Sarazen, Bobby Jones and Harry Vardon. It was eons before the quick-study cassette would be available to today's ambitious golfer.

In one of his published articles on the "absolute fundamentals for a good golf swing," Hogan emphasized three keys: 1. The waggle (don't laugh); 2. The hip turn; 3. The plane of the backswing. The waggle—a flick of the club just before a golfer begins his backswing— has been the butt of golf jokes since the first Scotsman grasped the first shepherd's crook. But Hogan found a place in the game for it.

Personally, he wrote, he adopted Johnny Revolta's waggle, Revolta being a major presence in the game when Hogan launched his own career. "Revolta, a short-game genius, had different waggles for different strokes," Hogan wrote. To produce a maximum bite on a green after hitting over a bunker, Revolta would waggle, short, staccato strokes. This type of waggle would give a foretaste of the type of shot needed. "I even adopted Revolta's longer waggle for my full shots," Hogan said.

There was a period when Hogan was still on canes and following the PGA play one day in St. Louis when we were asking him some questions. Ben said, "Guys, save the questions for lunch and I'll answer all of them then."

His answer to our first question was calculated to shock golfers everywhere, those raised on "Drive for show and putt for dough." The query was, "Ben, what's the most important shot in golf?" And Hogan said, "The drive. It governs the nature of the entire hole. It tells you whether you have problems or don't."

Even as he treated every golf course as a study in progress, the late, great Ben Hogan, golf's student-professor, wasn't afraid to explode the myths of the game.

JULY 26, 1997

The Final Column

It was Wednesday, June 3, 1998. Povich had just returned to work after a number of weeks on the sideline feeling weak. Among other things, his column took exception with colleague Tom Boswell, who suggested that Mark McGwire's slugging exploits had surpassed those of Povich's friend Babe Ruth. It is a classic Povich retort—authoritative, humorous, insightful and elegant.

[Editor's Note: Shirley Povich began writing for *The Washington Post* in 1924. While he retired "officially" in 1974 he continued to write columns for the newspaper. Although he had been feeling ill the past six weeks, Povich felt well enough Wednesday to write his final column. He died Thursday evening of a heart attack.]

During my recent and enforced sabbatical, called for by the rewarded pursuit of better health, three things happened in baseball that evoked some ruminations plus the inevitable compulsive comment.

These happenings were the home run binge of Mark McGwire that catapulted him beyond Babe Ruth's record pace and aroused the chants of the King is Dead, Long Live the King; David Wells's perfectly pitched game for the Yankees, and the startling strategy of Arizona Diamondbacks Manager Buck Showalter who, with two out and the bases full, opted to intentionally walk to Barry Bonds that forced in a run and cut the Arizona lead to 8–7.

Let us treat first McGwire, the St. Louis Cardinals' big muscle

Adonis who seems to specialize in three-homer games and has won the belief of *The Washington Post*'s Tom Boswell that McGwire is the game's new image as a royal nonesuch of home run hitters, not excluding even the fabled Babe Ruth.

Nobody writes baseball better, or as well as Boswell, a student and unmatched chronicler-philosopher of that game. Not to quibble, Boswell puts it bluntly: "Was Babe Ruth really a better home run hitter than this guy? In the past four years the correct answer has been clear. No."

Whoa there. Give McGwire the last four years, and he may be cast to hit more homers in a single season than Ruth did, but don't confuse him with the guy who inspired such sobriquets as Sultan of Swat and the King of Clout and made the name Bambino the recognized property of only one man in the entire world.

McGwire weighs 245 pounds, stands 6 foot 5, and bulked up by strength coaches and Nautilus weightlifts, plus the new diet of "nutrition shakes" popular in the clubhouses, may well hit the ball farther than the 215-pound Ruth, although there are stubborn non-believers.

To judge McGwire a better home run hitter than Ruth at a moment when McGwire is exactly 300 homers short of the Babe's career output is, well, a stretch.

It is not in the mind-set of nice guy McGwire to challenge the Babe's place as the No. 1 idol and most famed personality in the game. Too many truths forbid it. Before he started hitting home runs, did McGwire pitch three consecutive World Series shutouts? The Babe did. Does McGwire in the batter's box command the high excitement Ruth did with his head cocked back, a scowl on his face, his toes turned in, and his bat poised for that pirouetting swing that engaged all parts of his body? And if the Babe did whiff, it was with such gigantic gusto that the fans could still chortle.

One of McGwire's specialties has been the exciting three-homer game he's been producing as a special treat for his fans. But halt, Ruth was no stranger to the three-homer afternoon. Take for example, the high drama of the last big league game he ever played, in Pittsburgh in 1935. His farewell salute to himself was three home runs into the seats. And remember, Babe was doing this when he was 40 years old. It was the little things that set him a long way apart from the others in the game. Twas said of the Babe, "Put a camera on him and he performs."

The gem of the 1998 baseball season thus far is Wells's perfect game against the Minnesota Twins. There can be no demeaning the perfect game. It is far more rare than the no-hit game which can sometimes be a happening against all logic. No-hitters pop up at the strangest times.

Walter Johnson got his no-hitter in 1920 in the second worst season of a 21-year career, when he won only eight games. A contrast was the feat of another Washington Senator, Bobby Burke, who all of a sudden pitched a no-hitter against Boston at Griffith Stadium in 1934. In his entire career, Burke never won eight games in a season and I recall once characterizing him as "Bobby Burke, who had a nine-year tryout with the Senators." But the most startling no-hitter of all was that by Bobo Hollomon of the Cardinals who brought it off in his first major league start. He was gone to the minors before the season ended, winning only one of his next eight decisions.

It is correct to say that Wells joins the fabled Don Larsen in perfect-game glory. But at the risk of carping, let us recall that Larsen's feat occurred during a World Series against a pennant-winning National League club, the Dodgers, who with Duke Snider, Gil Hodges, Carl Furrillo, Jackie Robinson, Roy Campanella, and Pee Wee Reese were second best in the NL in runs scored, second in home runs with Snider's 43 leading the league and second in doubles. Hardly to be confused with Wells's passive victims, the Twins. Minnesota was the 13th worst hitting club in their 14 team league, and who opted that day to bench their top hitter, Todd Walker because of left-handed pitching. It was very inviting for Wells and he performed.

This is not to rap David Wells, a helluva pitcher, and one of the enchanting personalities of the game, with his I-do-it-my-way attitude.

His passion for baseball was known when he paid $20,000 for a Babe Ruth cap and wore it on the mound for two innings before the intrusive umpires made him replace it with Yankee head gear. They couldn't give Wells the No. 3 uniform that was retired in honor of Ruth, so he compromised by demanding No. 33.

If anybody were to reawaken the fans to the glory of baseball by pitching the perfect game, the scene could have no more appropriate protagonist than David Wells, individualist.

Baseball circles were abuzz last week when Showalter flung his new strategy into the teeth of the San Francisco Giants by signaling an intentional walk to the dangerous Bonds with two out, the bases full and Arizona with a two-run win. It worked, Arizona got the last out on Brent Mayne's liner to right field and Showalter basked in his self-created heroic vale.

Wait though, and let's play Can You Top This? I think we can. My hero and longtime friend in the cause was the late Paul Richards, former catcher, and later big league manager, and one of the acknowledged dreams of the game.

One night after dinner with Richards after a Griffith Stadium game, I said, "Paul, in the last 50 years there hasn't been a new play in baseball."

And he said, "One, and I pulled it." He said this was in the minor leagues and Richards was managing Atlanta, which had a two-run lead in the bottom of the ninth at Birmingham. And Richard said, "Now up comes the only Birmingham hitter who could ruin us.

"We worked it to 3–2 on this guy and now he was fouling off pitch after pitch. I was catching and I called time. Went out to the pitcher and called in the second baseman and shortstop to explain what I wanted.

"I told our pitcher to take a long windup and walk the guy on his next pitch, but give it to me high and outside where I could wing it down to second base. What I had seen was that hotdog base runner on first base running wild on all those foul balls, always ending up between second and third before he had to go back.

"I got the pitch I wanted, the run forced in, but that hot dog on first base was caught between second and third when I threw to the shortstop who tagged him out. The rule worked for us. He was only entitled to one base on a walk and he was fair game for any more than that and sure enough we nailed him. Game over on an intentional walk. How do you like that?" The question is referred to Buck Showalter.

JUNE 5,1998

In the beginning of 1998, Povich visited his doctors at Johns Hopkins in Baltimore. He had been experiencing heart valve difficulties again. He and his children were told that an operation would produce a 30 percent chance of success, a 30 percent chance of death in the operating room, and a 40 percent chance of permanent mental impairment.

"There will be no operation," he said. "At 92 I have long ago reconciled death. But the prospect of impairment is unbearable. I'll play this hand."

After he left the room the doctors told his children there was a good chance he would have another incident and pass away quietly within six months.

On June 4th, Povich celebrated the birthdays of his son David and daughter-in-law Connie. Later, while walking to the car, he complained that, as usual, he ate too much. David drove him two blocks to his home. When David turned to say something to his father, he found him keeled over in the back seat. He rushed him to the hospital. An hour later, David called his brother and sister.

"Dad's gone," he said. "Just the way he wanted to—at peace."

Shirley Povich in his office at The Washington Post *in the 1970s.*

Shirley Povich: The Best Ever

George Solomon

The telephone conversation usually went like this: "Shirley, Tony Zale died. Can you do a column?" or "Shirley, Pete Rose was just banned for life from baseball. You knew Shoeless Joe Jackson. Can you tie these two guys together?"

Shirley Povich would never respond immediately. Rather, he would say, "Let me have a look." Because he wanted you to know that what you asked him—and what he was about to do—was not easy. And you knew he would deliver in less than two hours, after telling his wife, Ethyl, dinner might be late. He always gave his best effort—as he did for 75 years of writing and working for *The Washington Post*.

I began reading Povich in the *Miami Herald* in the fifties when I was in high school and I met him for the first time in the sixties after I graduated from the University of Florida and hooked on with the *Fort Lauderdale News*. I was covering a Washington Senators spring training game in Pompano Beach and saw him behind the batting cage, wearing his trademark fedora, blue oxford dress shirt, and black golf sweater. It was my first spring training assignment, his 40th.

"He always dressed better than the rest of us," said Edwin Pope, the longtime sports columnist of the *Miami Herald*. "He was so dignified."

He could write beautifully, with edge, wit, opinion, and knowledge from decades of covering sports. When he was writing five or six times a week, his columns were about 800 words, averaging three sentences per paragraph. "He once told me he needed 100 words to capture the reader," *Post* colleague William Gildea said. "His column rarely ran past the front sports page and he preferred the standing 'This Morning' sig on the left side of the page to a spot under a wider headline. He didn't want a headline to give away his column."

Povich "officially" retired from the *Post* in 1974, after 52 years of working full-time for the newspaper. I took over the sports department from Don Graham a year later. Graham and I agreed that one of our greatest resources was a 68-year-old man who had been on a first-name basis with Babe Ruth, Sammy Baugh, Ty Cobb, Jack Dempsey, and Walter Johnson and could still write better and knew more about sports and the newspaper business than anyone on the staff.

How to tap into such a resource? You simply needed to ask him to write. But you had to accept his almost always accurate and pointed criticism of the section, knowing it was made with sincerity, in good cheer, and for a good reason. He always cared about the paper. For several years, he tried to make clear that he was retired. But then writing columns and being part of the sports scene and our newspaper family was more fun than retirement. He liked to say he "retired retirement" and never once mentioned that I underpaid him for years.

Several times, even though we had exceptional columnists on the payroll, we'd enter Shirley Povich in national contests. We did that because he still was among the best columnists in the country, right up until the evening he died, at 92, on June 4, 1998, the day after he wrote his final column for *The Washington Post*. Several months later, I had a conversation with writer Tom Callahan, who said Shirley Povich and Red Smith were not only the greatest sports writers ever, but also the greatest men he'd ever known.

Povich ranks No. 1 on my list of people I have known. I'm proud to have been his friend since the day we met behind the batting cage in Pompano Beach. I'm equally proud of having been his editor. And I don't know how his daughter, Lynn Povich, and I, were able to narrow down more than 17,000 columns and select the best 120 for this book. I'm sure we left out some beauties.

George Solomon joined *The Washington Post* in 1972 as a sports reporter, after working at the *Fort Lauderdale News* and *Sun-Sentinel* and *Washington Daily News*. He became sports editor in 1975. He held that position until stepping down in 2003. Though he retired in 2004, he still writes a weekly sports column for the *Post* and teaches journalism at the University of Maryland.

Life with Father

Lynn Povich

Our house revolved around Dad and sports. That meant that David, Maury, and I spent a lot of time going to ballparks, playing ball, and listening to games on the radio. Every February, when we were young, we moved to Orlando, Florida, for the Senators' spring training camp and, for two months, we went to school there. On the two-day drive down to Orlando, I would sit on the tall, hard Remington typewriter case in the front seat in between my parents. My brothers were in the backseat with our housekeeper, Essie, while our dog, Peppi, slept in the back windshield. In the evening, when everyone else dozed off, I would stay up with Dad to keep him company, peppering him with all kinds of questions—about the stars, about sports, about his childhood. I also remember trying to find a motel in South Carolina or Georgia that would let Essie spend the night. It was difficult and sometimes we would have to drop her off in the black part of town and pick her up in the morning.

Spring training in Orlando was our fantasyland long before Disney arrived. Most days, we'd hang out at Tinker Field, a dusty old ball field where the players were always just a few feet away. My brothers, who were batboys for the Senators, spent their afternoons shagging balls and collecting bats. They also sat in the dugout and hung out with the players in the clubhouse. I couldn't go into the clubhouse, of course, so Dad would arrange for Mickey Vernon or Eddie Yost to play catch with me after training.

The Povich family in 1952, from left: Shirley, Lynn, David, Ethyl, and Maury

Sports dominated our life back home as well. Dinnertime was taken up talking plays, players, teams, and stats. David and Maury both played sports and were good athletes. Dad went to as many of their games as possible and every year, in their honor, wrote about the football rivalry between their school, Landon, and St. Albans—the only high school game he would deign to cover. He never mentioned the boys in his column but he had a rooting interest. He came to my games, too, and one year, when I joined a swim team, I remember him on the sidelines yelling as I touched in third. He later said he never cheered so much as he did for me because I tried the hardest. Dad was probably the reason I was popular in school—every boy I went out with wanted to meet him. Of course, he had his own view of the matter. When I would ask what he thought of a particular guy, he always responded, "Drop him."

Shirley Povich was a celebrity in Washington, bigger than any other columnist or newsman. Everyone, it seemed, read his column—seven days a week. But despite his renown, he was a modest and humble man. He personally answered his mail and his phone (he was listed in the phone book) and many people have remarked about how kind he was to talk to them, or their sons, about a game, a play, or a sports star. When we were introduced to someone, we were always asked if we were Shirley's son or daughter and we always were so proud to say "yes." But measuring up to him was another matter altogether.

David went his own way early in his life. From the time he was 12, he wanted to be a defense lawyer like Clarence Darrow and succeeded by going to Yale, Columbia Law School, and joining the firm of Edward Bennett Williams in Washington, where he is the senior partner today. David, in fact, was really Dad's counselor for years, and later on, he gracefully stepped into the role of pater familias, which Dad had long assumed with his nine—and Mother's eight—brothers and sisters.

Maury was the rebellious son, but in the end he emulated Dad the most. He was the sports announcer for the University of Pennsylvania ballgames and then went to radio as a sports assistant. When he moved to television, he moved over to news and became a successful newscaster and talk show host. While Dad exercised his parental authority and often would criticize Maury's hair or tie on TV—a medium he never understood—he and Maury shared a love of sports and talked on the phone almost every day. In many ways, Maury took on the mantle of fame nationally that Dad had in Washington.

Although I had avoided journalism in school, I ended up getting a job at *Newsweek* right out of Vassar. While I progressed through the ranks as a researcher, reporter, and writer, I found my strengths more as an editor, probably because I could never, in my own mind, live up to my father's elegant and stylish prose. He hated being an editor— and being edited—and that somehow freed me. When I was promoted to senior editor, the first woman to achieve that position at *Newsweek*, Dad was thrilled that I had succeeded as a print journalist.

You could always count on Dad to be positive and upbeat. His first response to anything we did was usually "Great!" and he genuinely took enormous pleasure in all of our achievements.

When one of his grandchildren asked him how he was able to instill in his three children the warm love they have for each other, Dad said, in his sports vernacular, "Poviches always root for each other."

Dad was in love with the English language. At dinnertime, he would often read aloud from his favorite authors, especially the work of John Ciardi in the *Saturday Review*. But if Dad talked later about how he sweated his columns, as children we never saw the agony that went into his writing. He never talked with us about what he was going to write or had just written, and he couldn't understand people who loved their own prose. "I never read the column after I've written it," he once said, "and it's a good bet I won't read it the next day, either. I instantly despise it. I write in a state of perpetual discontent knowing full well I could have written it better."

Povich at bat and son David catching at a father-son game at Landon School (1951)

What he did communicate to us was his passion for the medium—for the words, sentences, rhythms, and ideas. He was always groping for the right word. If he spied a word he didn't know, he'd quickly looked it up in the giant 1950 edition of *Webster's New International Dictionary*, which he kept on an old music stand next to his desk at home. If he found a useful word he didn't know, he would clap his hands in delight. As his friend Hearst columnist Bob Considine once wrote, "Povich has steadfastly used the 26 sharp-edged tools of the alphabet as God—who is obviously an Englishman—intended. His daily prose. . . . never fails to pin down a point, a thought, a sentiment, a belief."

Dad was a creature of habit—after all he worked on the same newspaper for 75 years and was married to the same woman for 66 years. Until the day he died, he insisted on calling in his columns on the telephone and dictating them to a staffer. For more than 30 years it was Molly Parker, and after Molly, another woman took her place. Even when he conquered the computer and could have emailed or faxed his pieces, he still phoned them in. When I asked him why he did, he simply said, "Oh, they like to take dictation." But his dear friend Sam Stavisky, who worked with Dad in the 1930s at the *Post*, explained it best: "Shirley didn't like to be edited, not because he was egotistical about his words, but because he had a certain rhythm in his writing and he didn't want anyone to change the notes." I think that's why he also called in his columns—so he could hear his words.

As good as he was at writing, Dad was a better husband and father. He had that first-generation loyalty to family. As an Orthodox Jewish boy from Bar Harbor, Maine, he grew up keeping kosher, and, until World War II, my parents kept a Kosher home. Throughout their lives, they were religious people and observed the Sabbath rituals every Friday night. (Dad once said he had written over 15,000 articles—and not one of them on Rosh Hashonah or Yom Kippur). When his father died in 1931, he postponed his wedding to Mother for a year, so he could observe the formal grieving period.

My parents met on a blind date and Dad proposed almost that first night. He was devoted to Mother—he always called her "My Girl"—and when he finally wrote his parents about her, he said, "I've got a girl. A wonderful, darling girl, whom I adore. Of course she is Jewish. Born in the old country and from a very respectable family and quite "*frum*." ... I realize this is sudden but I hope you have confidence in my judgment. I am sure you understand I wouldn't do anything rash in so important an affair." Every year on their anniversary, Dad would say that he and Mother took a vote about whether to stay together another year. With a twinkle in his eye, he would announce that the vote had ended in a tie—so they decided to stay together one more year. Whenever he was asked about the success of his marriage, he would say, "We just take it one decade at a time."

The most difficult time in my parents' marriage was probably during World War II. Like most men of his generation, Dad was eager to serve in the war. He pestered his editor to send him and, in 1944, he finally got the call to be a war correspondent for the *Post*. He was nearly 40 years old. Mother later told me she was furious that he was leaving her and three small children at home, and if it hadn't been for her four sisters, who lived nearby, it would have been even harder for her. Luckily Dad came home in less than a year—injured but safe.

With all his sense of propriety and duty, Dad also had a wild streak in him. His first assignment at the *Post* was the vice squad. He covered the pimps and prostitutes, the bootleggers and pickpockets—until they took his name off the byline when they realized he was only 18. He also liked to gamble. After a night of reporting on the cops busting the speakeasies, he would switch sides and go with his pals to Jimmy LaFontaine's, the gambling hall on the borderline between D.C. and Maryland. At Jimmy's, they would play dice and blackjack. If the D.C. cops beat in the front door, all the tables would be rolled over to the Maryland side of the room—and visa versa if the Maryland cops busted in. On more nights than one, apparently, Dad won his rent money at Jimmy's with a hot hand at the dice table. He also loved the track. Well into his eighties, he and his older brother, Abe, would go to the racetrack at least once a week. And he was a smoker. He smoked so much that, in 1966, he collapsed at a Yankee game from nicotine poisoning and never picked up a cigarette again.

When he was younger, Dad loved hanging out with the players, especially on those three-week train trips to Western ballgames and in Toots Shor's restaurant in New York. Toots was the saloonkeeper for the athletes, writers, mob bosses, politicians, and celebrities of the day—the "crumbums" as he called them. After a game or boxing match or high stakes race, everyone would pile into Toots', crowd into a banquette, and knock 'em back. They also complained bitterly about the food. A favorite story Dad told about Toots' happened one night when the lights suddenly went out. "Thank God," Jackie Gleason quickly ad-libbed, "they've electrocuted the chef!"

Throughout his life, Dad retained a New England formality in his demeanor with an overlay of *Yiddishkeit* humor (he used to describe the Maine Yankees as people with "pursed lips already pursed"). He also retained a clipped Yankee accent and still said "po-tah-to" and "to-mah-to." With us, and with all children, Dad was more of a tease

Povich and son Maury with Muhammad Ali on Maury's talk show, Panorama *(1970s)*

than anything else. He loved what he called silly grips. He pummeled us with knock-knock jokes and puns and he laughed hardest at his own jokes. When David built a four-car garage several years ago, Dad took one look at it and said, "Oy, Garage Mahal."

He was a highly moral man and, later in life, even prudish. I remember going to see *Carnal Knowledge* with him one summer, and he walked out as the opening credits were rolling, offended by its subject matter. At home, he always talked about the importance of "values" but while he set high standards for his children, he was also forgiving. He never told a dirty joke and hated "roasts."

His sense of propriety also governed his sense of fashion. He was a stickler for proper clothes and was considered a snappy dresser. He always wore a grey fedora and the same dapper outfit—a blue blazer or tweed sport coat with grey slacks, a blue oxford dress shirt, and a navy-and-red-striped rep tie. He had 14 of those striped ties hanging in his closet and ten pairs of the same grey Daks slacks. This was a man who didn't buy his first pair of blue jeans until he was 84 years old. When I asked what took him so long, he said, "Dungarees were what the men at the Bath Iron Works wore"—the Bath, Maine, shipyard where Dad worked as a riveter in his teens.

Looking back over this year of reading Dad's work, much of which was written before I was even born, I learned far more about my father than I expected. I had not realized how much he had written about racism—not only in baseball and football, which I knew about, but in all sports, including golf. He also went to bat for women. Although he didn't write about women athletes, he escorted the *Post's* first two women sportswriters to the Redskins locker room when the NFL wouldn't let them in.

I saw the high moral standards he held himself to in his life also show up in his work. He was outraged when the World Boxing Association tried to take away Muhammad Ali's title in 1964 and furious when George Preston Marshall, owner of the Redskins, skimmed $13,000 off a 1942 Army Relief benefit game for team expenses. His profound disappointment and sense of betrayal when the Washington

Povich and daughter, Lynn (1995)

baseball franchise was moved to another city is evident in the many eloquent columns he wrote on the subject. I'm only sorry he isn't around now to finally see a team back in his hometown.

I saw his personal compassion in his writing when I found his column on the Redskins' 73–0 loss to the Bears in 1941. It was the most gentle let-down I've ever read, and I can only imagine what sportswriters today would have said. And his 1975 column on people who think baseball is dull gave me new insight into his love of the sport, his favorite by far. His thrilling eyewitness comparisons of the old-timers with the new stars—be it Ruth with Mantle/Maris/McGwire, or Gehrig with Ripken, even Man o' War with Secretariat—as well as his comparisons of the stars of the day—like DiMaggio and Williams,

Graziano and Zale, Seabiscuit and War Admiral—show his deep understanding of each sport and his unparalleled judgment.

Collecting Dad's work has been a "joyride" for me—an expression Dad always used when he described his own life. We are so lucky that he has left us such a rich legacy. His words not only hold up, they seem to have ripened with age.

Lynn Povich worked for Newsweek *for 25 years and was the first female senior editor on the magazine. She was also Editor-in-Chief of* Working Woman *magazine and Managing Editor/East Coast of MSNBC.com*

ACKNOWLEDGMENTS

When Shirley Povich died in June 1998, he had been working on his memoirs. We were hoping that he had made a significant dent, but unfortunately all we found were notes, an outline, and one complete chapter on sportswriting. So we talked about simply publishing his columns, which—amazingly—had never been collected in the 75 years that Shirley had been writing for *The Washington Post*.

For Shirley's children—David, Maury, and Lynn—and for George Solomon, Shirley's cherished colleague at the *Post*, this has been a labor of love. We also had the help of many people. Most of all, we are grateful to *The Washington Post* Chairman and CEO Don Graham, who accompanied Shirley to the Rome Olympics in 1960 as his researcher. Don opened his heart to this project. He also made available the *Post* material and photos that grace these pages. At the *Post*, we also want to thank Elissa Leibowitz and former staffer Steve Argeris for their tireless research; Bridget Roeber and Alexa Hackbarth of the Information Technology Department, and Joe Elbert, Assistant Managing Editor for Photography, for their help with the pictures; Shirley's former colleagues Martie Zad and William Gildea for their memories and insight; and Chris Ma for his help with the archives.

We also have had invaluable guidance from the people at Public-Affairs. Publisher Peter Osnos, who worked at *The Washington Post* for many years and knew Shirley, was enthusiastic about the book from the beginning and brought his considerable talents to the project. Editor Kate Darnton applied her great judgment and skill to the work;

Lindsay Jones kept us organized and on track; Publicity Director Gene Taft made sure the book got into the right hands; and Art Director Nina D'Amario supervised the handsome cover.

We'd also like to thank Simon & Schuster for its permission to use passages form Shirley's 1969 memoir *All These Mornings*; Jerry Holtzman for the interview with Shirley for his 1973 book *No Cheering in the Press Box*; and Aviva Kempner for material from her documentary film, "The Life and Times of Hank Greenberg."

Finally, many family members helped us recall the life and times of Shirley Povich. In particular, we want to thank Connie Povich, Connie Chung, and Steve Shepard, who read the words and added so much to our memories of Dad; and Hazel, Kelly, and Rachel Solomon and Erica Moskowitz, who relived the many moments Shirley and George worked side by side. We also want to thank Joey and Mickey Hamer, Barbara and Les Melnicove, Janice Povich, Larry and Edna Povich, Ron and Deborah Povich, Marcia and Lenny Klompus and Shirley's good friends Sam and Bernice Stavisky, all of whom told us countless stories and reminded us of all the fun in Shirley's life.

Shirley would have gotten a kick out of this book, not because he wanted to read his columns again, but because they would have prompted enough stories for a second volume.

DAVID, MAURY, AND LYNN POVICH
AND GEORGE SOLOMON

PHOTO CREDITS

INDEX

PublicAffairs is a publishing house founded in 1997. It is a tribute to the standards, values, and flair of three persons who have served as mentors to countless reporters, writers, editors, and book people of all kinds, including me.

I. F. STONE, proprietor of *I. F. Stone's Weekly*, combined a commitment to the First Amendment with entrepreneurial zeal and reporting skill and became one of the great independent journalists in American history. At the age of eighty, Izzy published *The Trial of Socrates*, which was a national bestseller. He wrote the book after he taught himself ancient Greek.

BENJAMIN C. BRADLEE was for nearly thirty years the charismatic editorial leader of *The Washington Post*. It was Ben who gave the *Post* the range and courage to pursue such historic issues as Watergate. He supported his reporters with a tenacity that made them fearless and it is no accident that so many became authors of influential, best-selling books.

ROBERT L. BERNSTEIN, the chief executive of Random House for more than a quarter century, guided one of the nation's premier publishing houses. Bob was personally responsible for many books of political dissent and argument that challenged tyranny around the globe. He is also the founder and longtime chair of Human Rights Watch, one of the most respected human rights organizations in the world.

———

For fifty years, the banner of Public Affairs Press was carried by its owner, Morris B. Schnapper, who published Gandhi, Nasser, Toynbee, Truman, and about 1,500 other authors. In 1983, Schnapper was described by *The Washington Post* as "a redoubtable gadfly." His legacy will endure in the books to come.

Peter Osnos, *Publisher*